Dorothy Hoshaw

Gregg Dictation

THE GREGG PUBLISHING COMPANY

Simplified

Louis A. Leslie

and Charles E. Zoubek

Business Education Division, McGraw-Hill Book Company, Inc.

New York Chicago San Francisco Dallas Toronto London

GREGG DICTATION SIMPLIFIED

Shorthand Plates Written by

CHARLES RADER

PUBLISHED BY THE GREGG PUBLISHING COMPANY

Business Education Division of the McGraw-Hill Book Company, Inc.

Printed in the United States of America

PREFACE

Gregg Dictation Simplified is planned to follow either the Basic or the Functional Method *Manual* in Gregg Shorthand. It is designed to help the student accomplish three major objectives: First, to review and to strengthen his knowledge of the system; second, to build shorthand-writing speed; and third, to prepare a foundation on which to build transcription skill.

Gregg Dictation Simplified contains 516 business letters organized into 80 assignments, each assignment planned for a class period of 40 to 50 minutes. The letters, all of them short, easy, nontechnical business letters with few exceptions, were carefully chosen to carry out the objectives of the text.

Forty of the eighty assignments in this text contain a Vocabulary Builder. The drills comprising this feature consist of groups of words illustrating the principles of outline construction in Gregg Shorthand. They follow a systematic pattern throughout the text, covering every major principle of outline construction at least four times, with eight drills on the blended consonants and eight drills on word beginnings and word endings.

In building shorthand speed and accuracy it is essential that the student read and copy a great deal of well-printed shorthand. Each assignment in *Gregg Dictation Simplified* supplies the student with ample shorthand plate material for reading and copying practice.

For the purpose of preparing a foundation on which to build transcription skill, *Gregg Dictation Simplified* provides in the margins of the shorthand plates 3,052 abbreviated marginal reminders covering simple points of punctuation, typing style, and spelling. When the marginal reminder concerns punctuation, the appropriate punctuation mark is shown in a tiny circle in the accompanying shorthand material.

A systematic pattern of drills covering various important elements of shorthand-writing speed is woven into *Gregg Dictation Simplified*. These drills include:

1. Word-Family Drills. In every fifth assignment beginning with Assignment 2, are word-family drills containing eighty analogical word-family groups. The analogical word-family grouping provides a connection that facilitates learning and recall.

2. Phrasing Drills. In every fifth assignment, beginning with Assignment 3, is an analogical grouping of commonly used business-letter phrases. The selection of phrases is based on an intensive analysis of 250,000 words of business-letter material. In addition to these phrasing drills, the first letter in every fifth assignment, beginning with Assignment 5, is a special phrase letter.

3. Accuracy Drills. Every tenth assignment, beginning with Assignment 6, contains an accuracy-practice drill. The accuracy-practice drills are penmanship drills designed to improve reading, writing, and transcribing speed and accuracy.

4. Geographical Expressions. Every fifth assignment, beginning with Assignment 3, contains a small group of geographical expressions. The sixteen assignments include the names of the forty-eight states and the names of cities frequently used in business communications.

On page 440 is a system-recall chart that contains an example of every alphabetic character and joining in Gregg Shorthand, together with a recall of each word beginning, word ending, and phrasing principle. A complete Brief-Form chart appears on pages 438-439; and special brief-form review charts, with various types of derivative drills, are given in eight assignments spaced throughout the text.

Martin J. Dupraw, World's Champion Shorthand Writer, has graciously contributed to this book some suggestions that will help the young shorthand writer attain shorthand speed. These appear in the Appendix photographically reproduced from Mr. Dupraw's own shorthand notes.

CHAPTER I

ASSIGNMENT 1

1. Brief-Form Chart

A B C D E F

1. 2. 3. 4. 5. 6. 7. 8. 9.

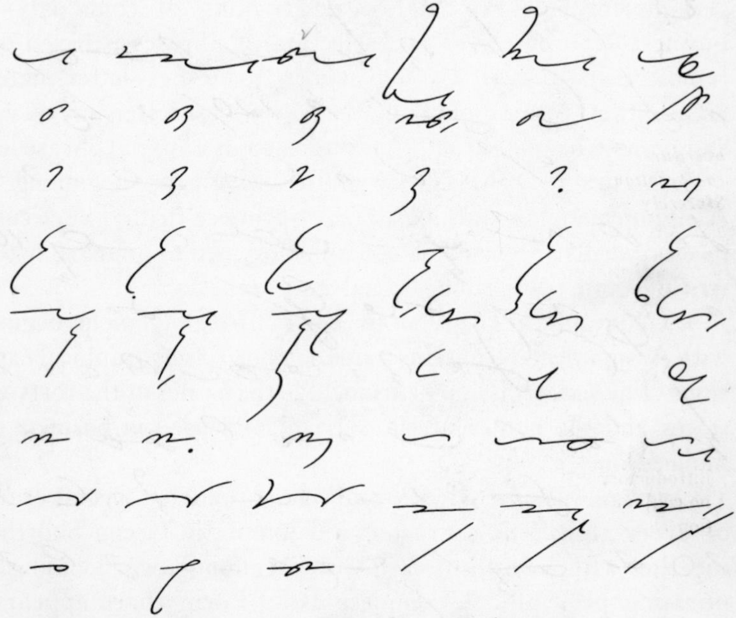

Reading and Writing Practice

2.

past-due hyphenated before noun

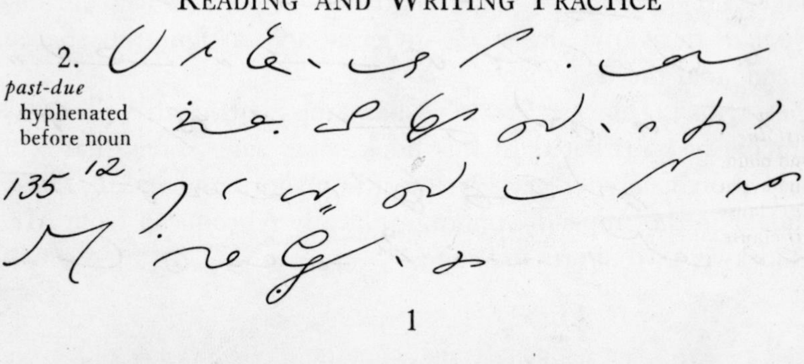

3.

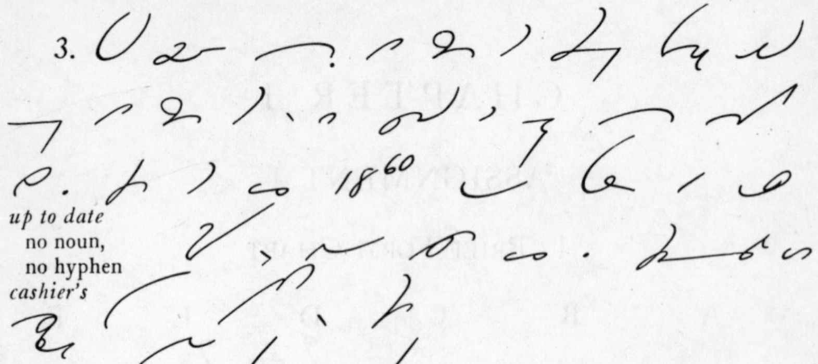

up to date
no noun,
no hyphen
cashier's

4.

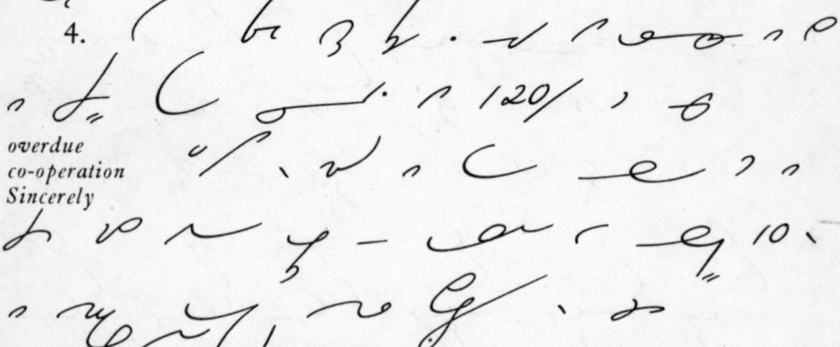

overdue
co-operation
Sincerely

5.

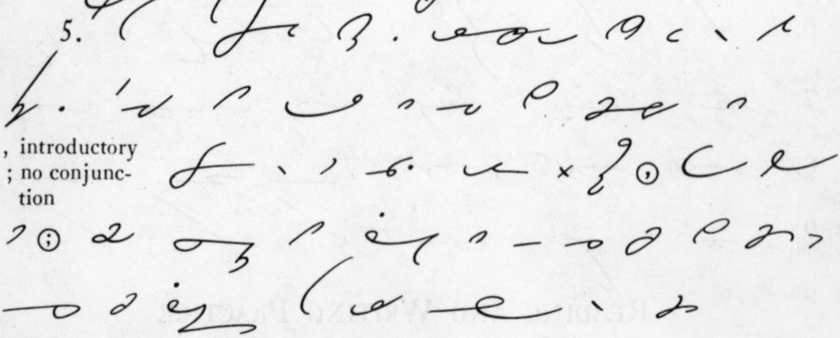

, introductory
; no conjunction

6.

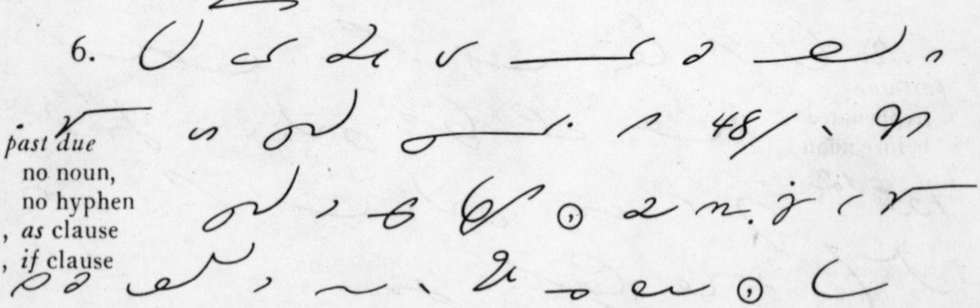

past due
no noun,
no hyphen
, *as* clause
, *if* clause

7.

today
tonight
courtesy
, *if* clause

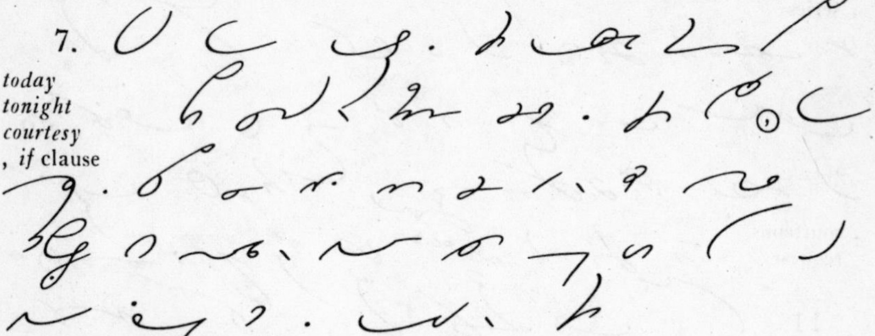

8.

Transcribe:
$25
, *if* clause
, parenthetical
; because of commas
, parenthetical

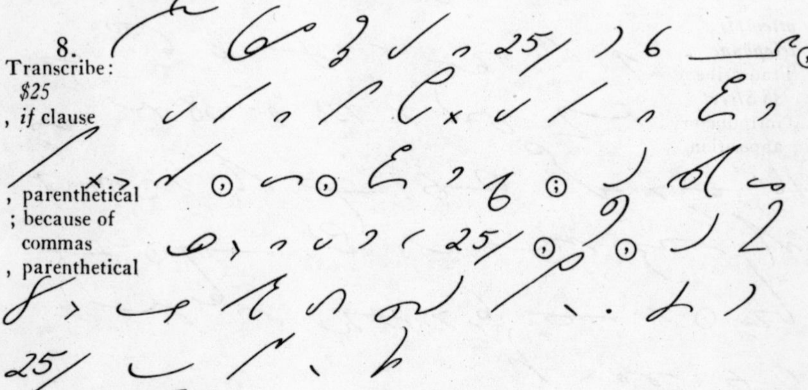

9.

one's
, series
, conjunction

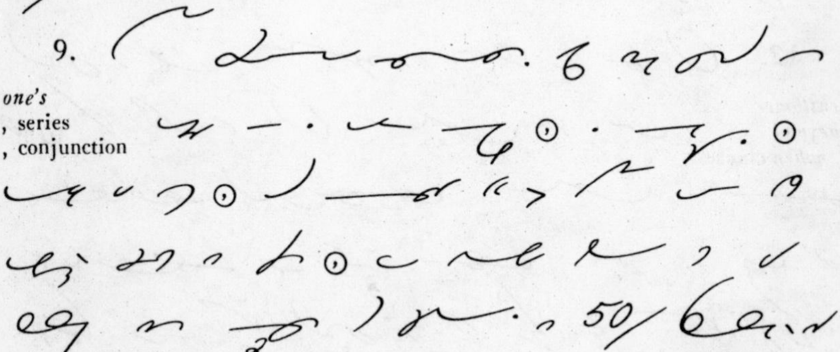

10.

, *if* clause

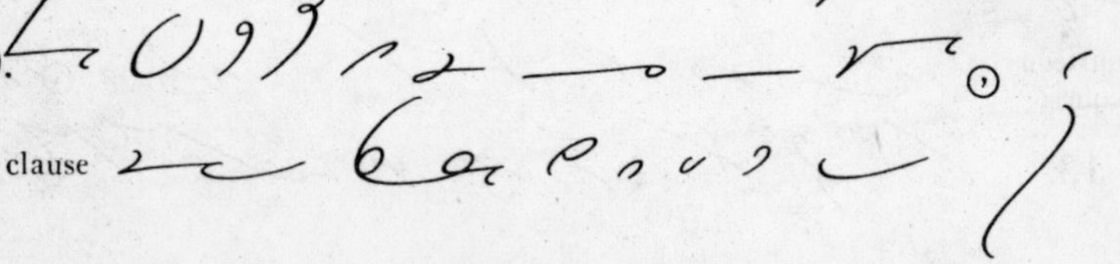

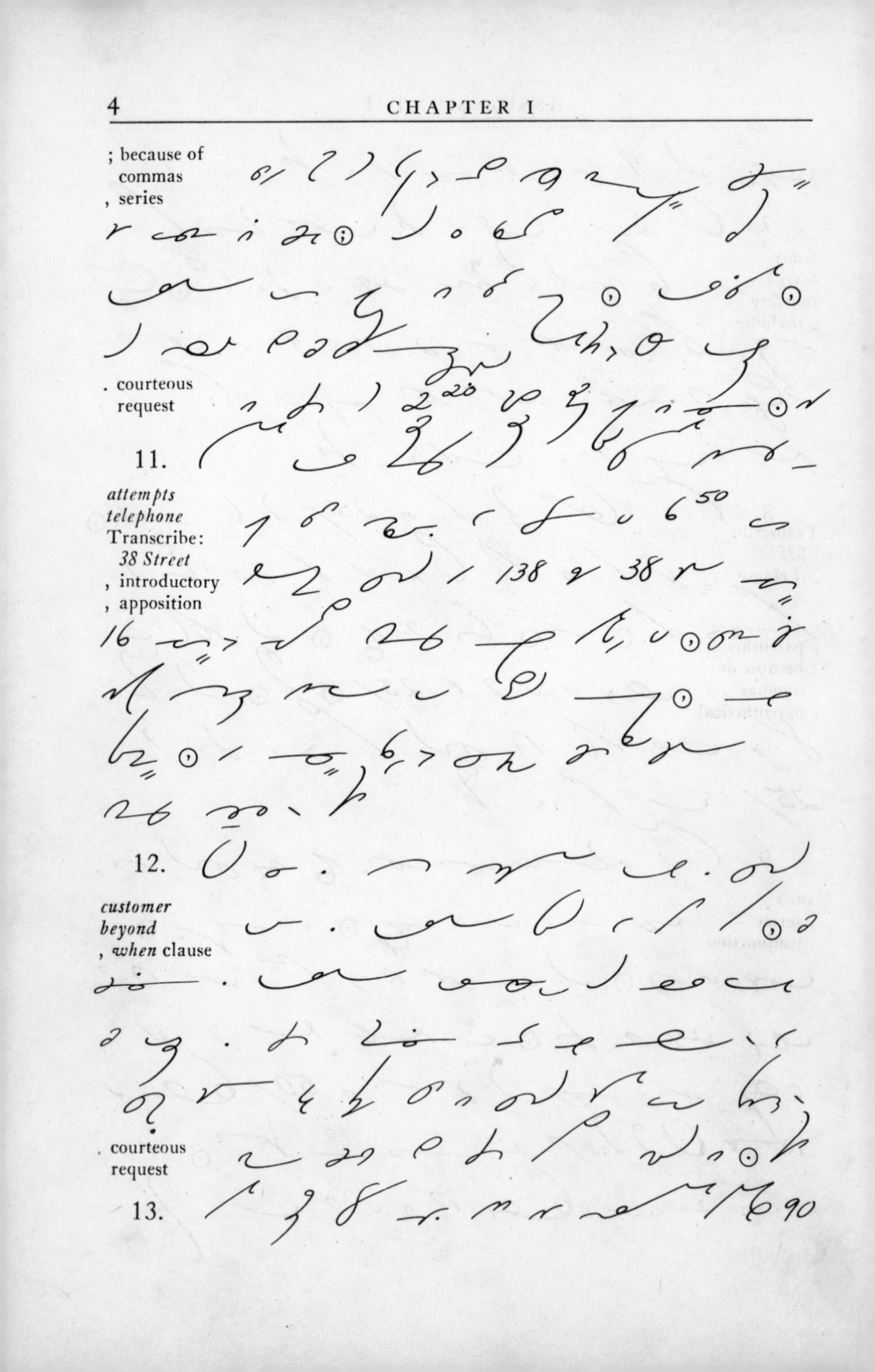

; because of
commas
, series

. courteous
request

11.

attempts
telephone
Transcribe:
38 Street
, introductory
, apposition

12.

customer
beyond
, *when* clause

. courteous
request

13.

, *if* clause

, *if* clause
, parenthetical
Cordially

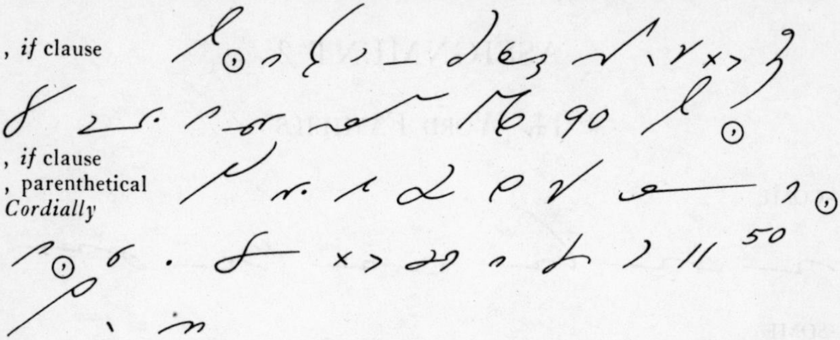

ASSIGNMENT 2

14. Word Families

-COME

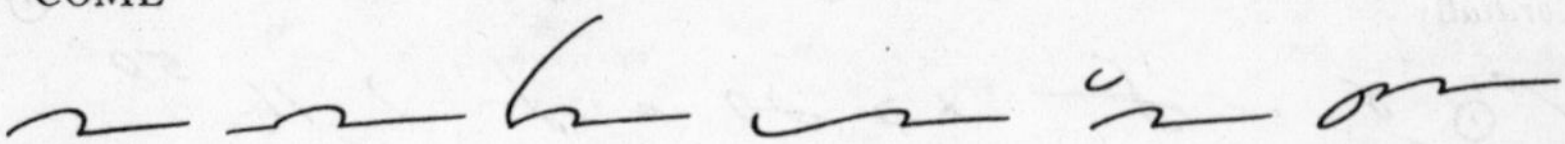

-SOME

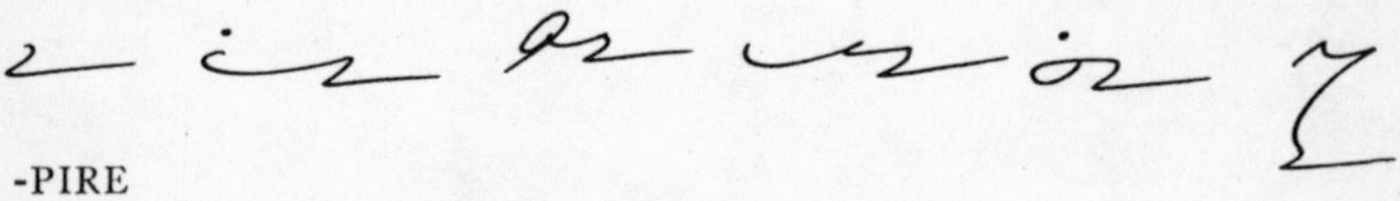

-PIRE

-IATE

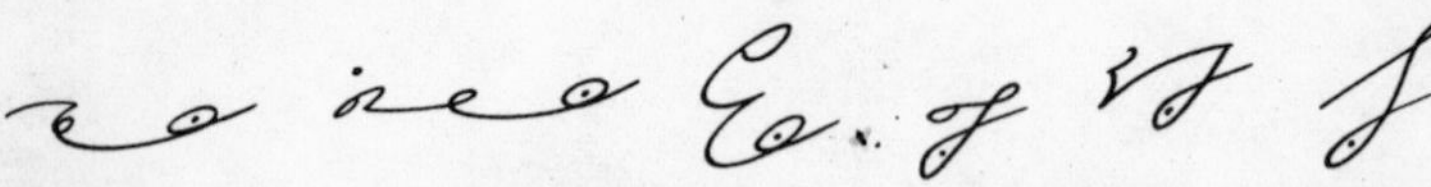

-PROVE

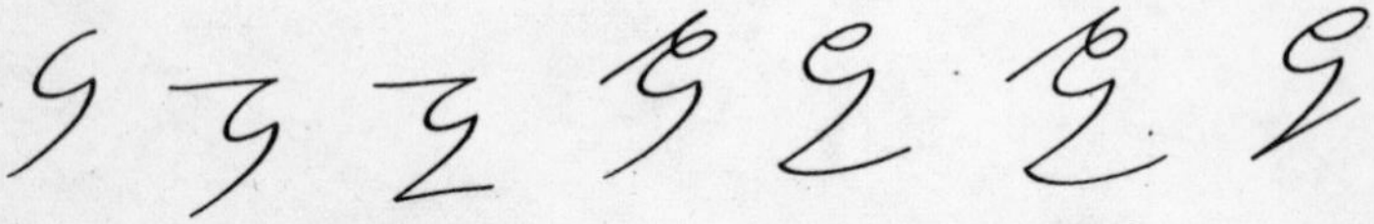

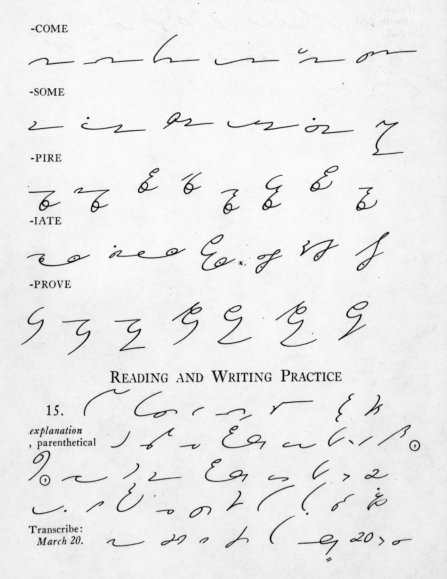

Reading and Writing Practice

15.

explanation

, parenthetical

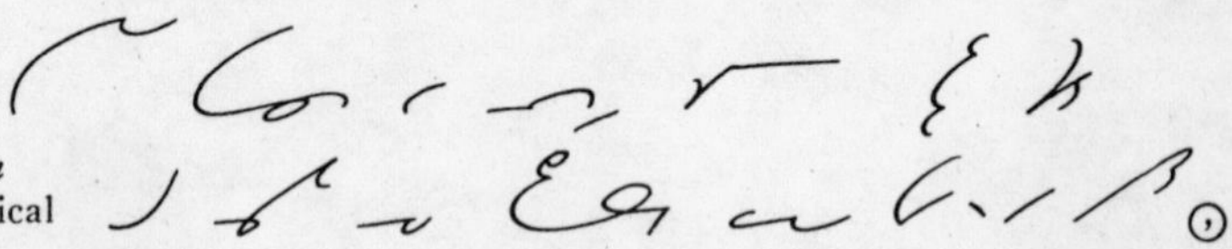

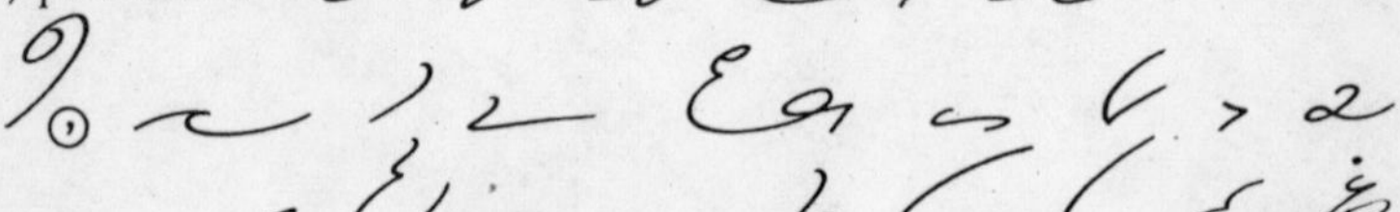

Transcribe:
March 20.

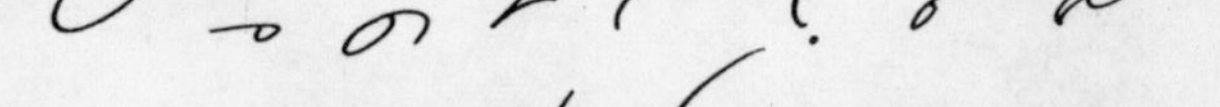

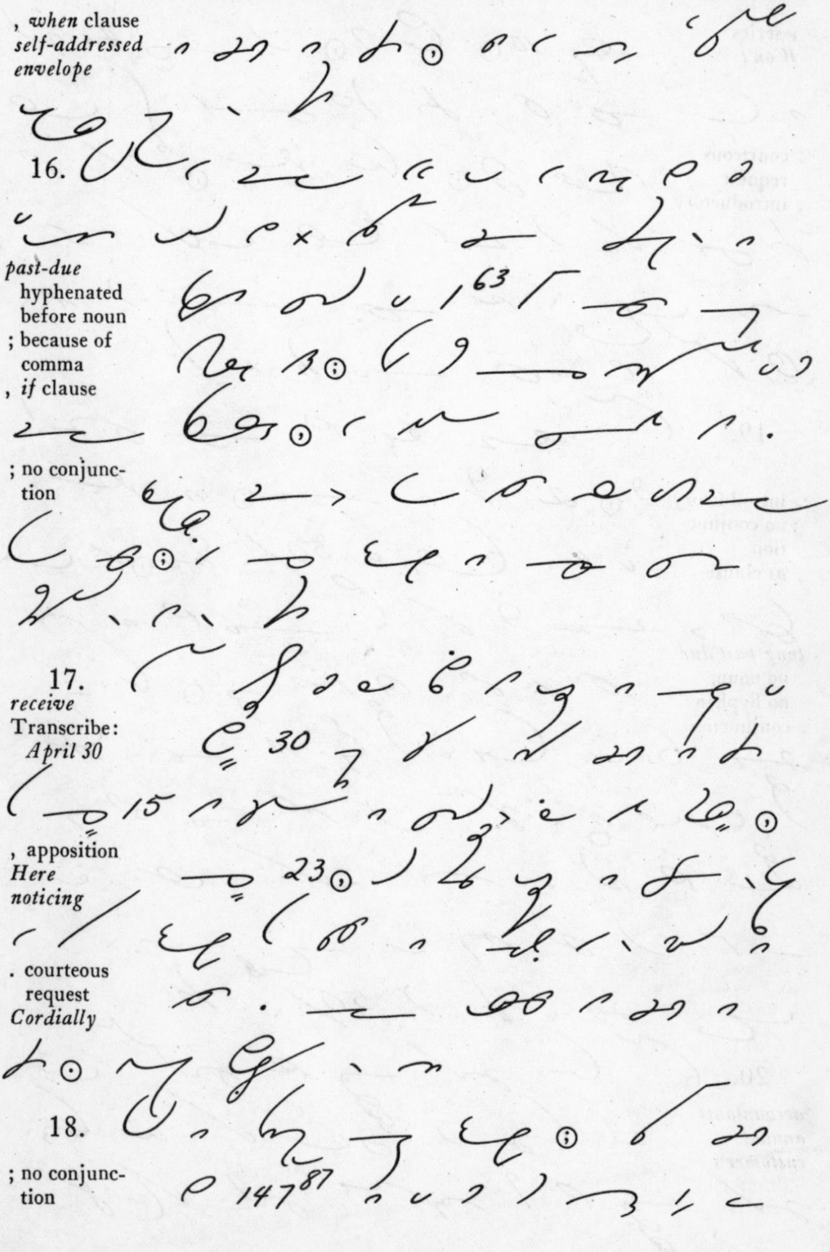

, *when* clause
self-addressed envelope

16.

past-due hyphenated before noun
; because of comma
, *if* clause

; no conjunction

17.
receive
Transcribe: *April 30*

, apposition
Here
noticing

. courteous request
Cordially

18.

; no conjunction

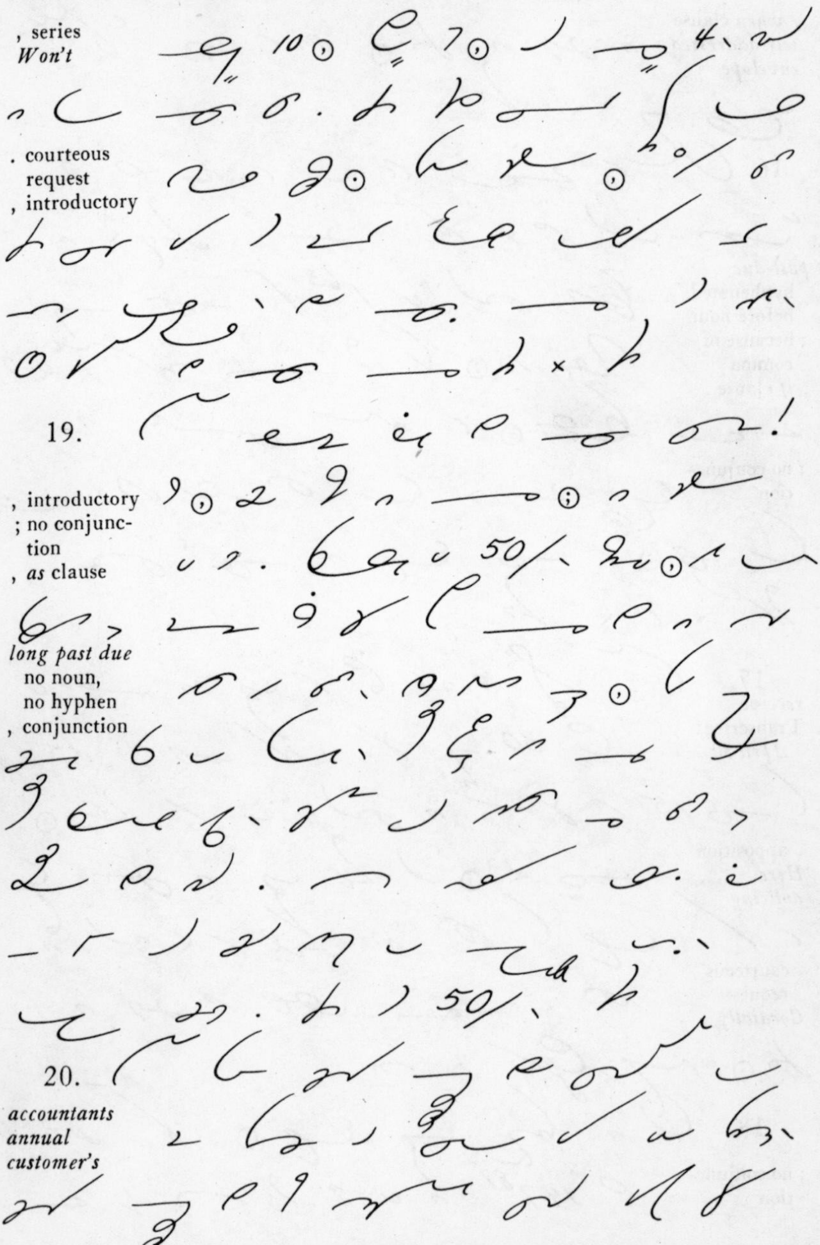
, series
Won't
. courteous request
, introductory
19.
, introductory
; no conjunction
, *as* clause
long past due
no noun, no hyphen
, conjunction
20.
accountants
annual
customer's

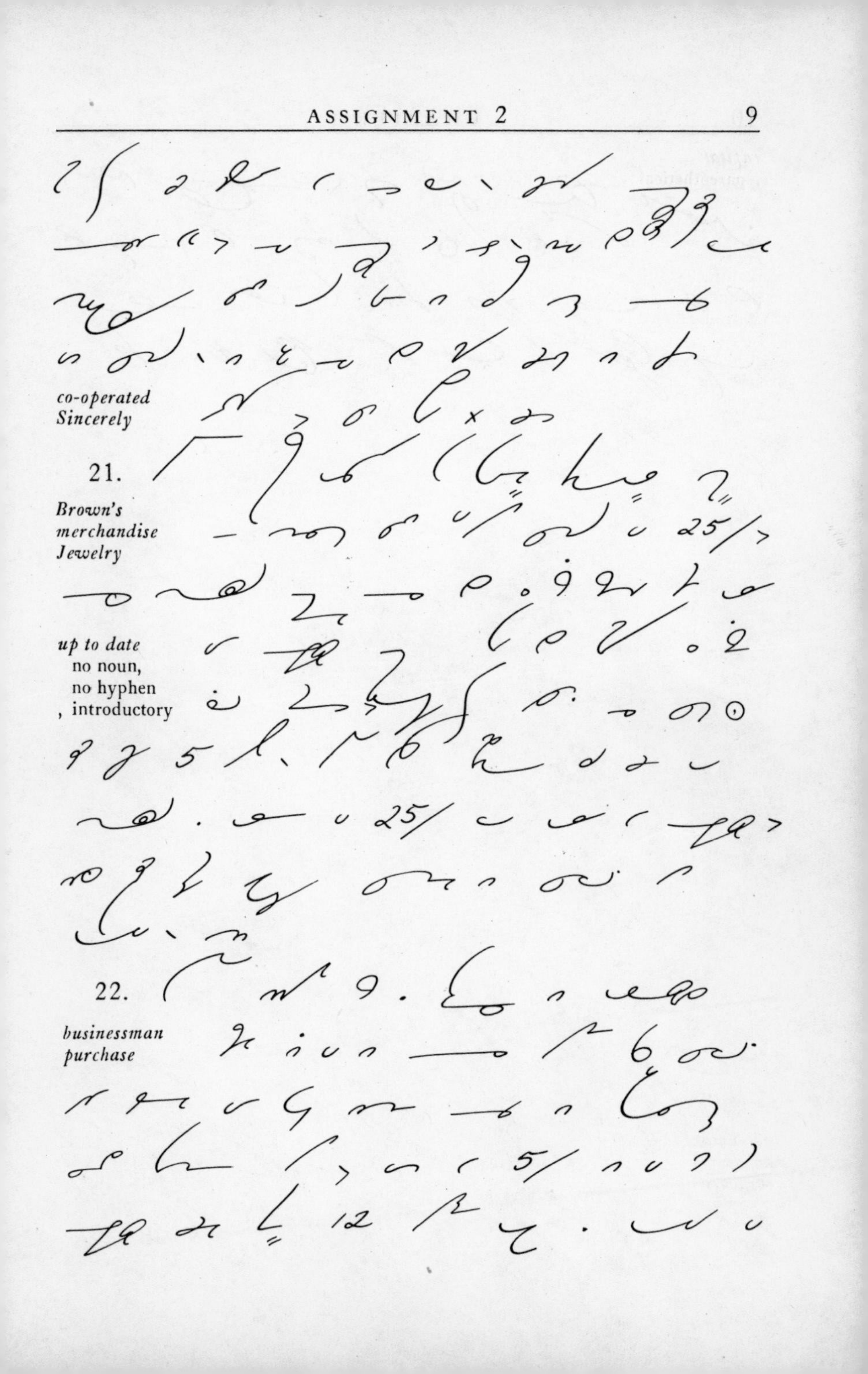

co-operated
Sincerely

21.

Brown's
merchandise
Jewelry

up to date
no noun,
no hyphen
, introductory

22.

businessman
purchase

capital
, parenthetical

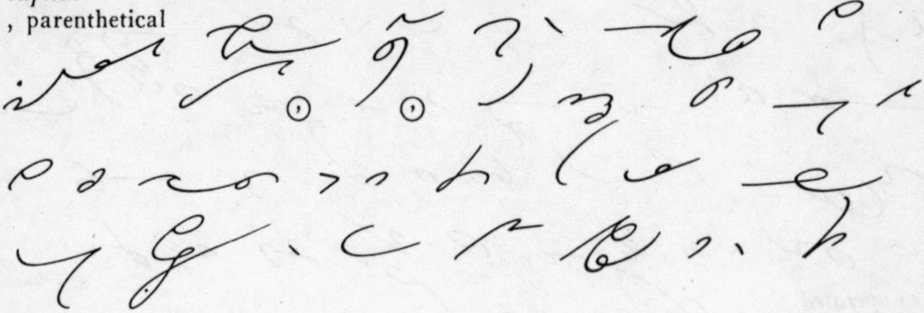

ASSIGNMENT 3

23. Most-Used Business-Letter Phrases

(The following drill contains, in the order of their frequency, the 50 phrases most frequently used in business letters.)

24. Geographical Expressions

Reading and Writing Practice

25.

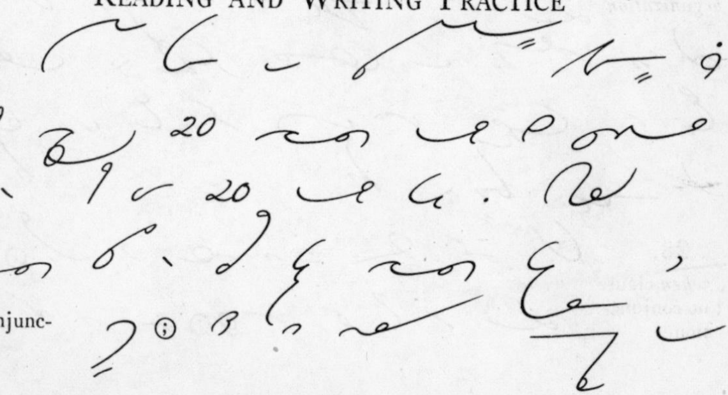

idea

; no conjunction

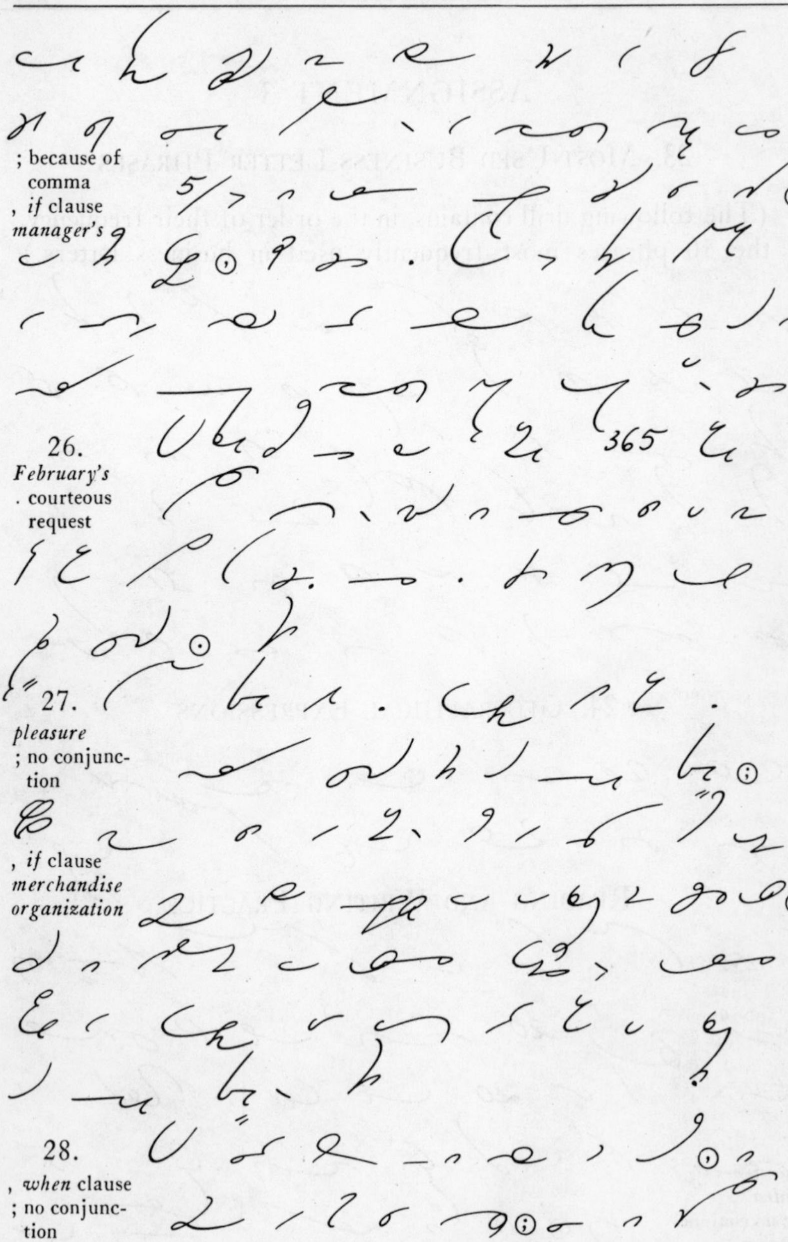

; because of
comma
, *if* clause
manager's

26.
February's
. courteous
request

27.
pleasure
; no conjunction

, *if* clause
merchandise
organization

28.
, *when* clause
; no conjunction

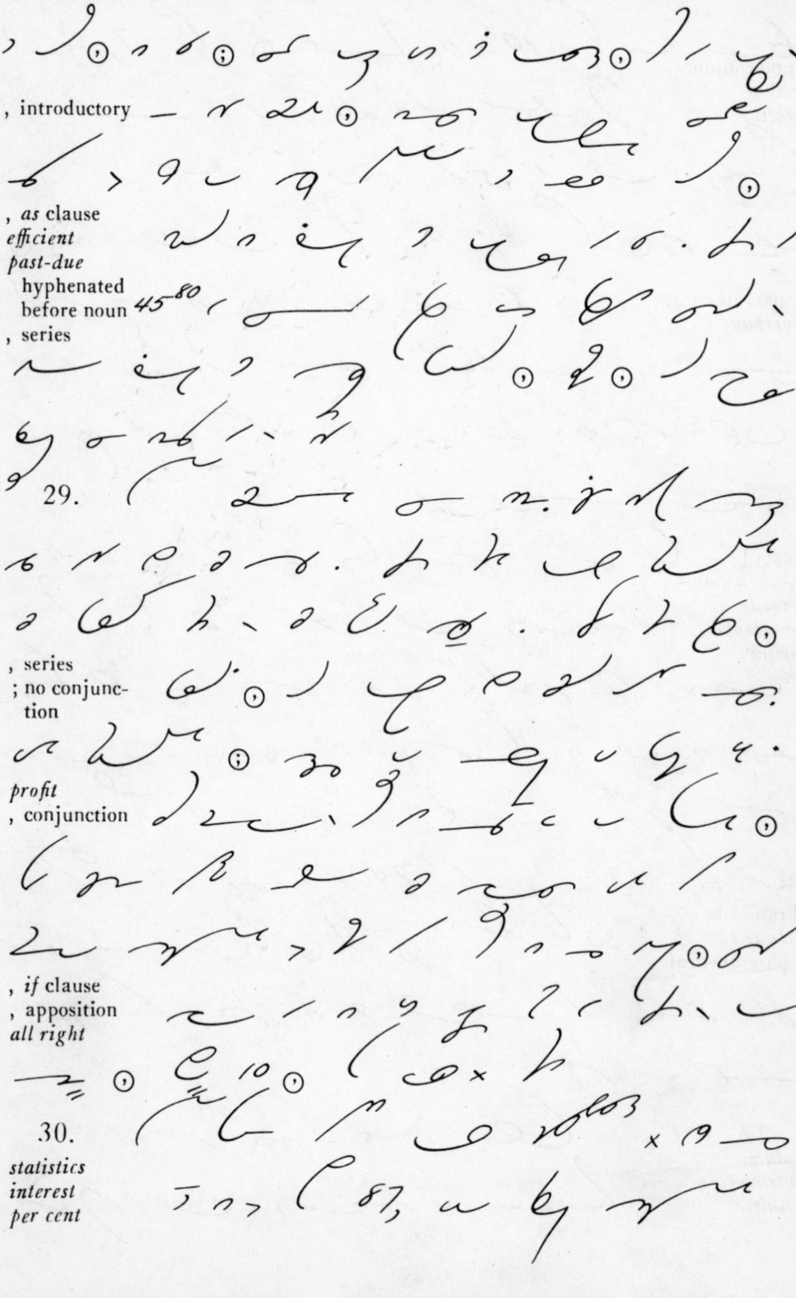
, introductory
, *as* clause
efficient
past-due
hyphenated
before noun
, series
29.
, series
; no conjunction
profit
, conjunction
, *if* clause
, apposition
all right
30.
statistics
interest
per cent

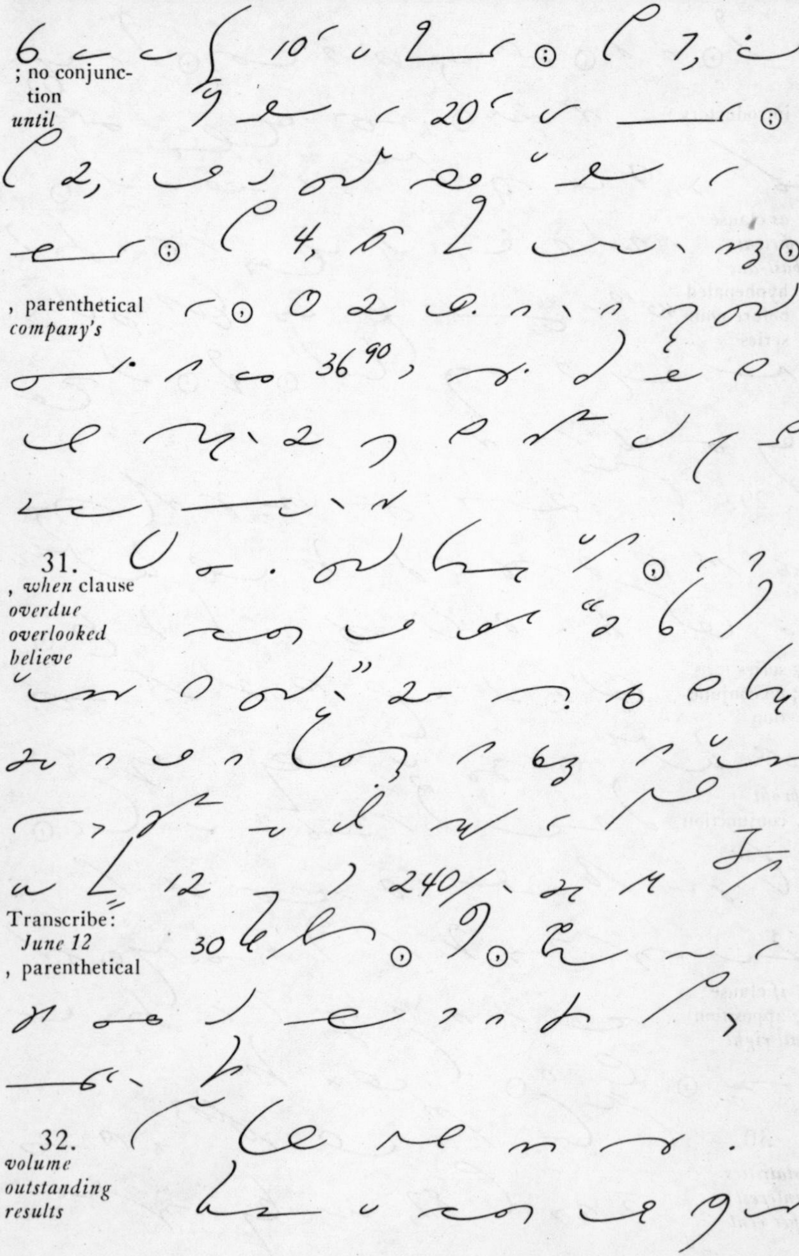

; no conjunction

until

, parenthetical

company's

31.

, *when* clause

overdue

overlooked

believe

Transcribe:

June 12

, parenthetical

32.

volume

outstanding

results

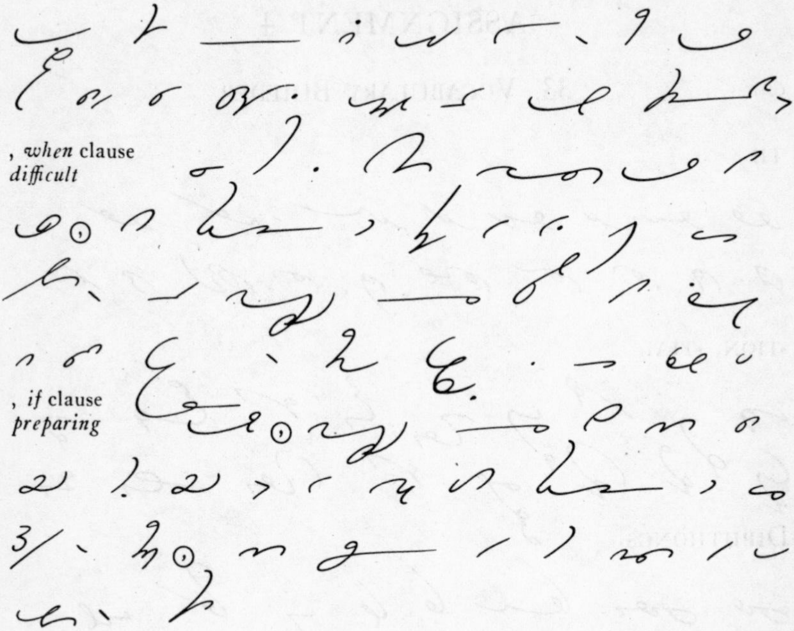

, *when* clause
difficult

, *if* clause
preparing

ASSIGNMENT 4

33. Vocabulary Builder

TH

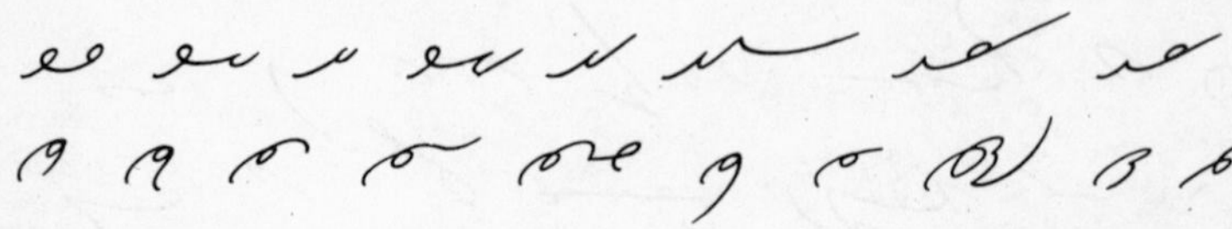

-TION, -TIAL

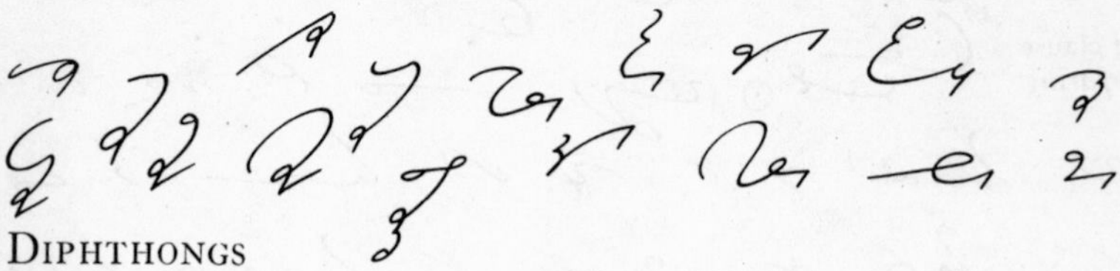

Diphthongs

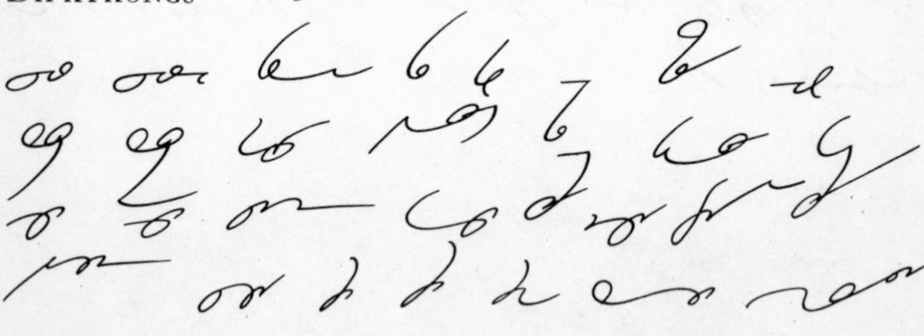

Reading and Writing Practice

34.
, *as* clause
every one
judgment
, series
–
, *when* clause

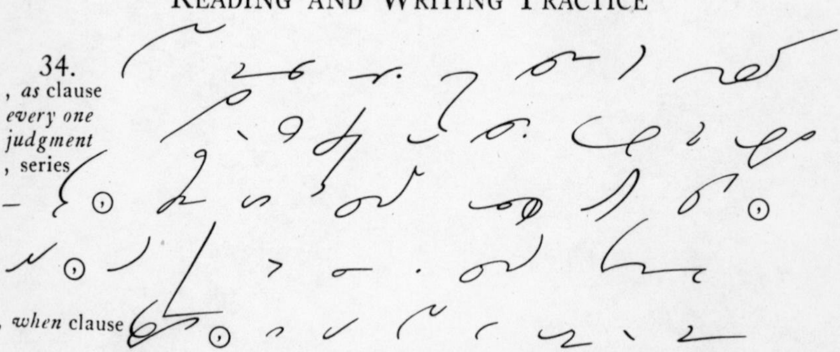

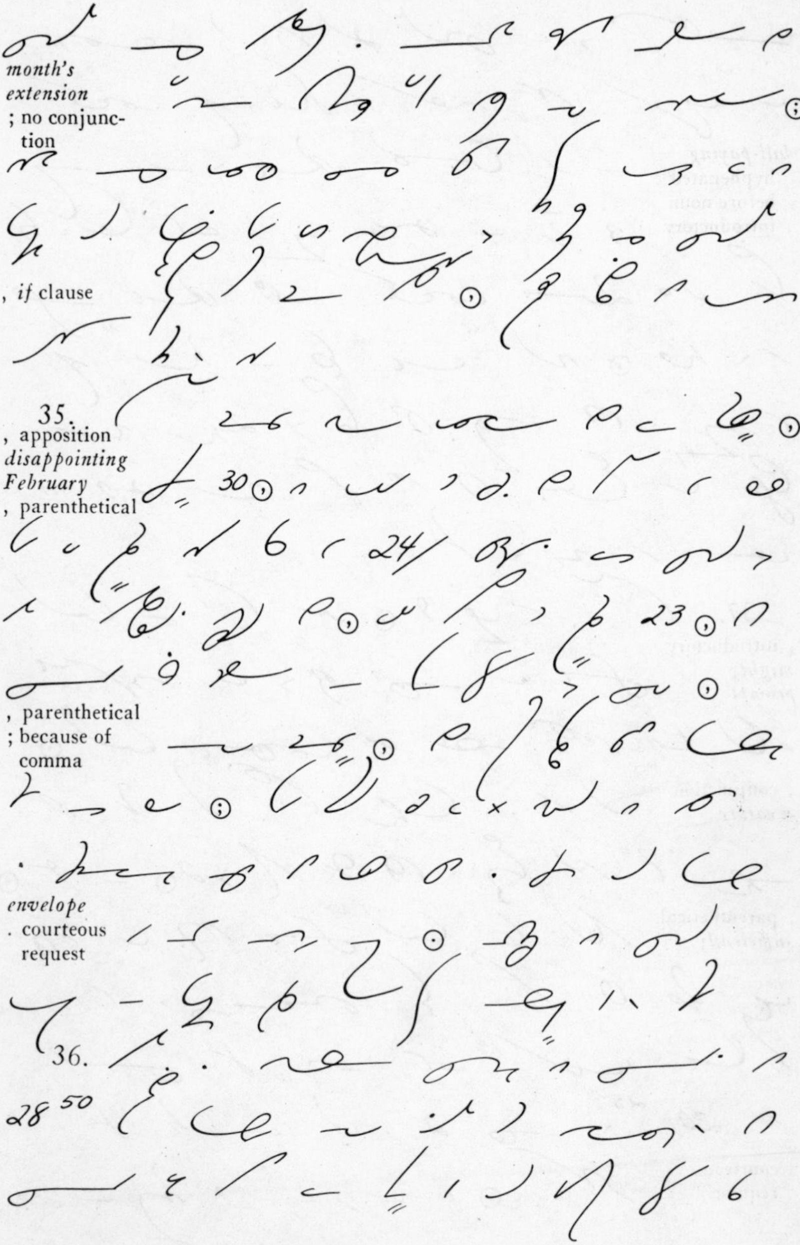

month's
extension
; no conjunction

, *if* clause

35.

, apposition
disappointing
February
, parenthetical

, parenthetical
; because of comma

envelope
. courteous request

36.

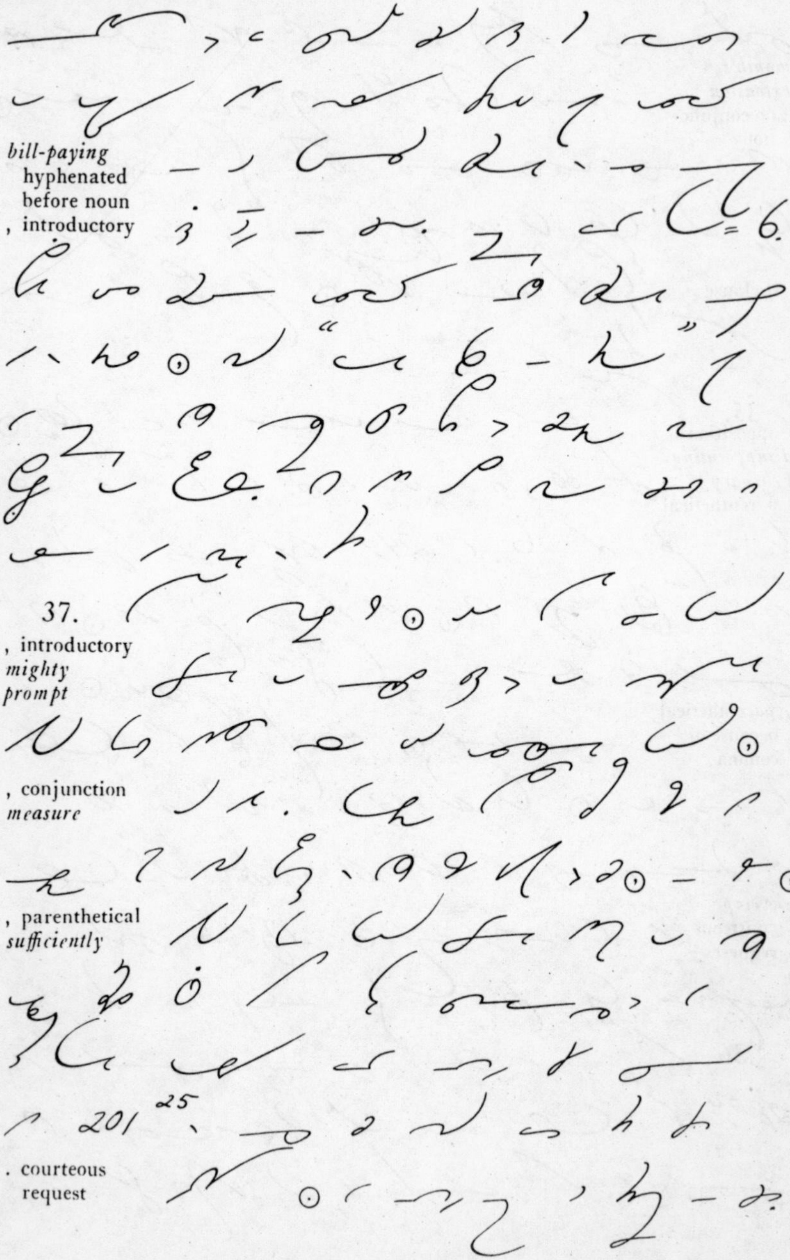

bill-paying hyphenated before noun

, introductory

37.

, introductory

mighty

prompt

, conjunction

measure

, parenthetical

sufficiently

. courteous request

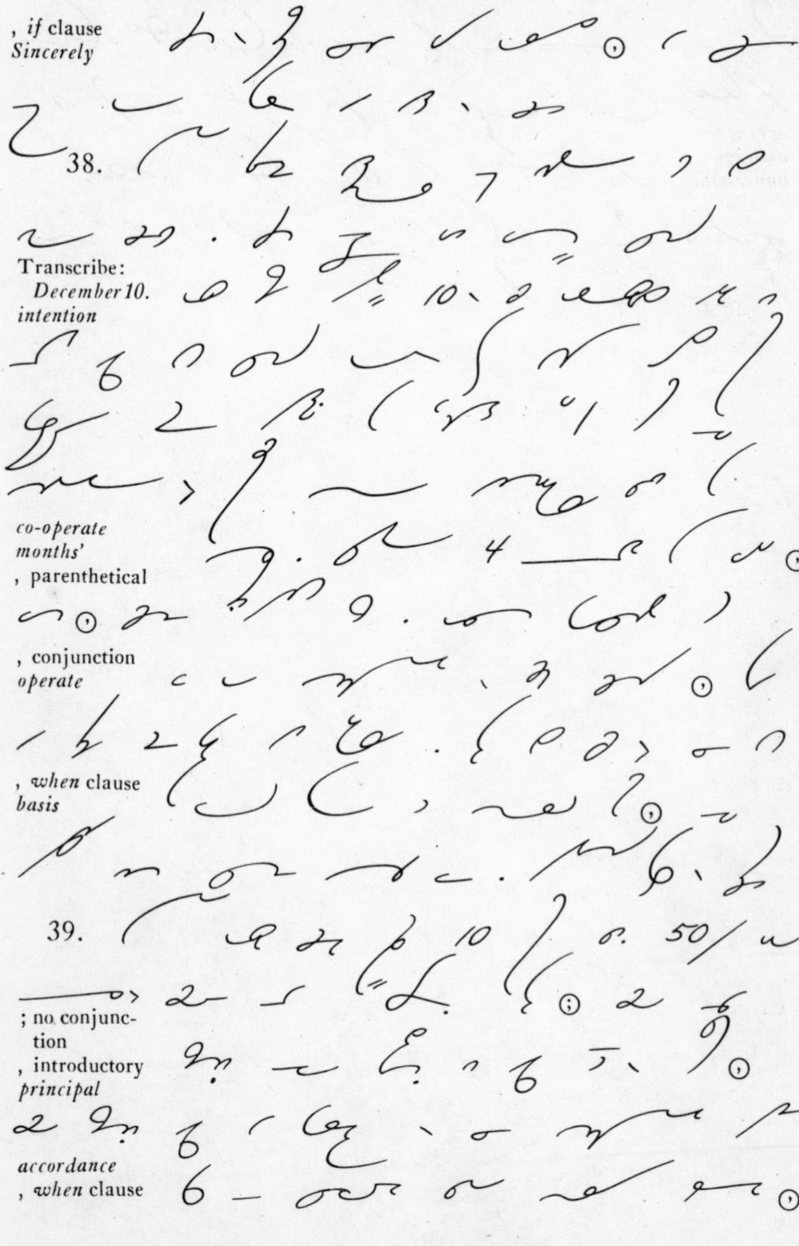

, *if* clause
Sincerely

38.

Transcribe:
December 10.
intention

co-operate
months'
, parenthetical

, conjunction
operate

, *when* clause
basis

39.

; no conjunction
, introductory
principal

accordance
, *when* clause

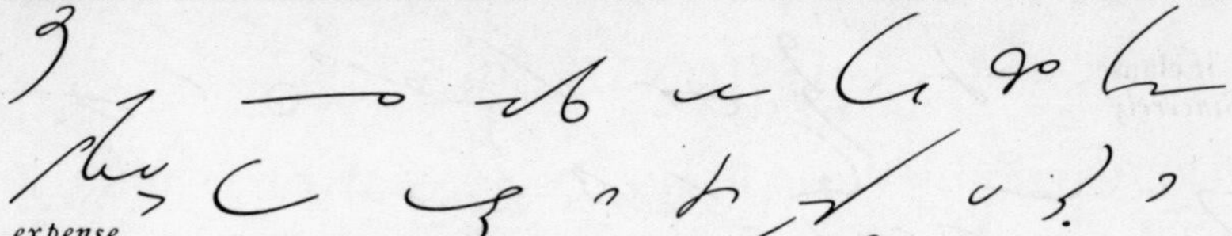

expense
undergo
unnecessary

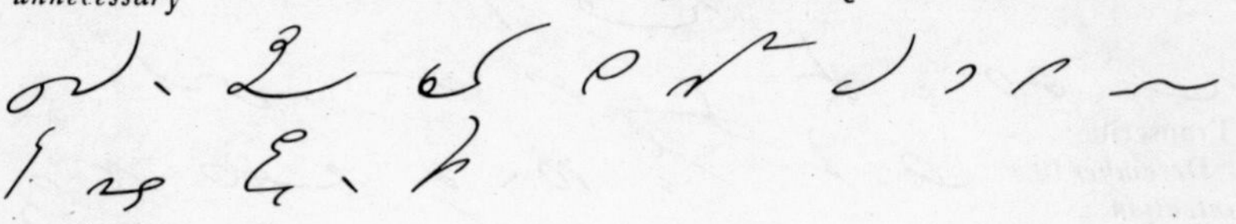

ASSIGNMENT 5

40. Chart of Word Beginnings and Word Endings

A B C D E F

1.–9.

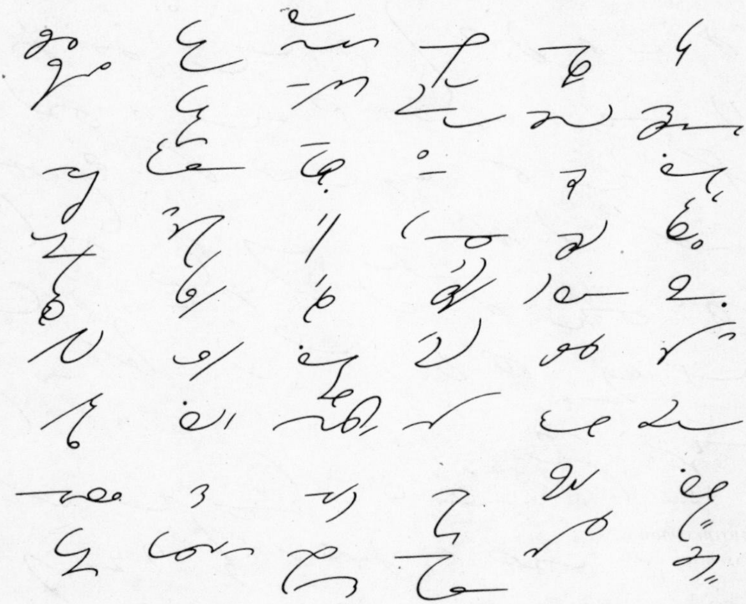

Reading and Writing Practice.

41.

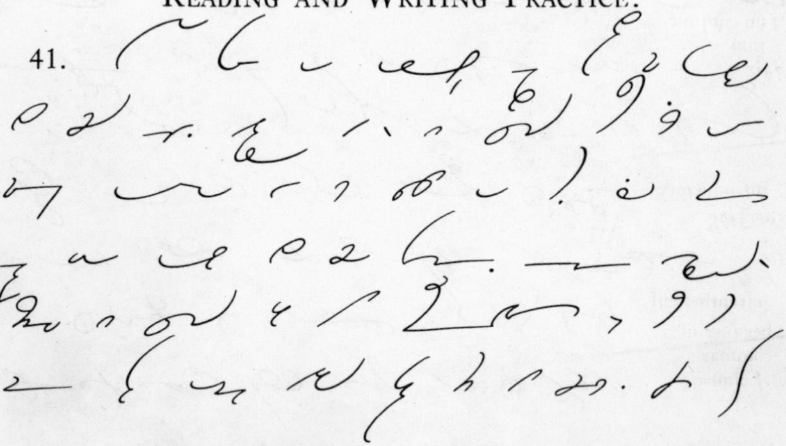

42.

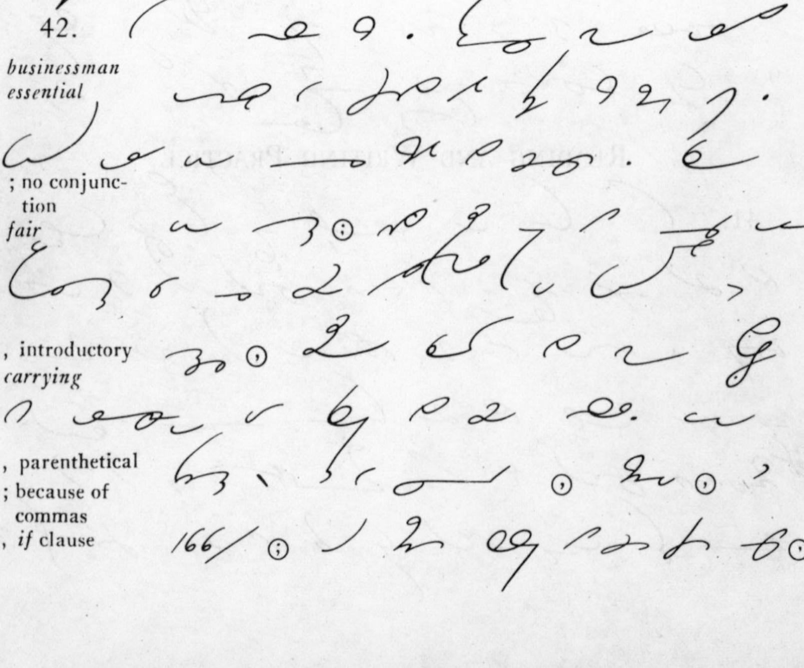

businessman
essential

; no conjunction
fair

, introductory
carrying

, parenthetical
; because of commas
, *if* clause

gratefully
received
past

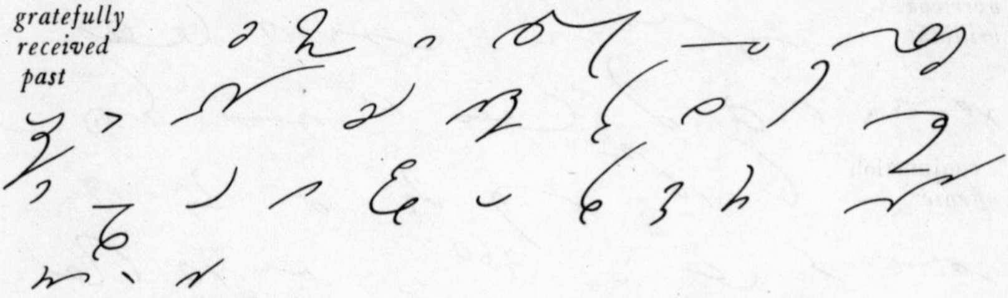

43.

valued
, parenthetical
, conjunction
, parenthetical
charge-account
hyphenated
before noun
, apposition

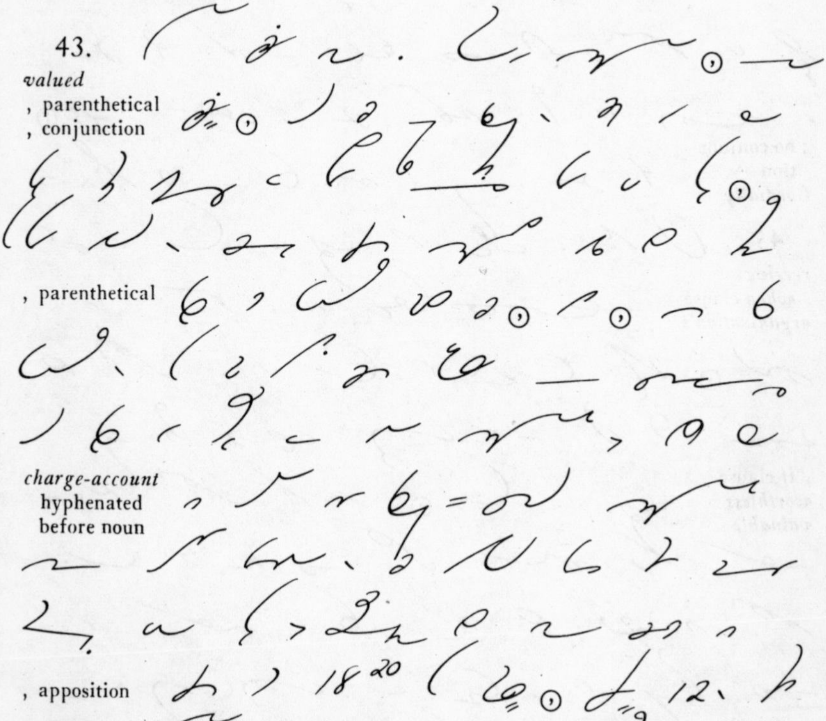

44.

, parenthetical
stickers

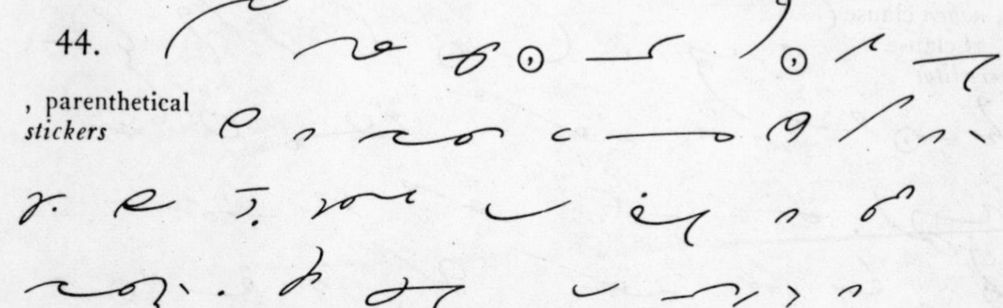

overlook
brilliant

, conjunction
offense

; no conjunction
Cordially

45.

receive
, *when* clause
organization's

, *if* clause
worthless
valuable

, *when* clause
, *if* clause
creditor

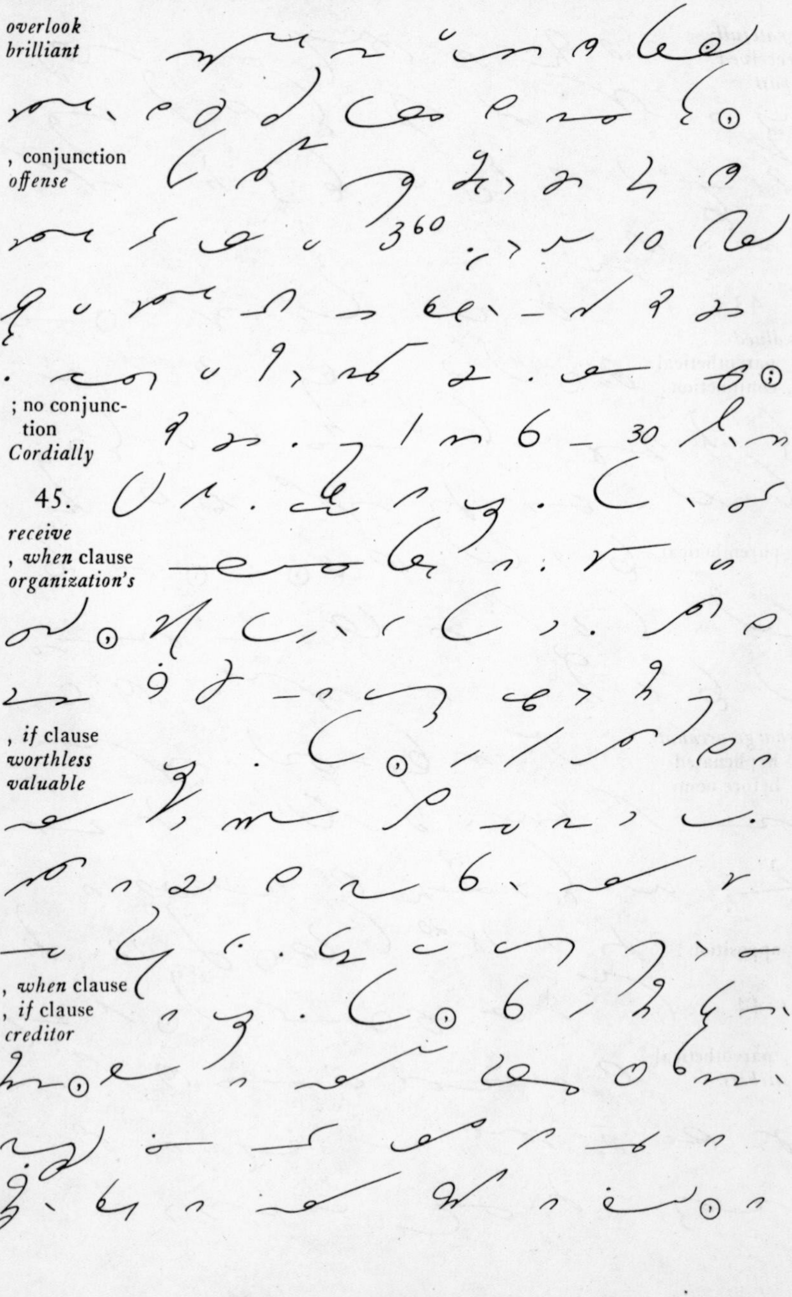

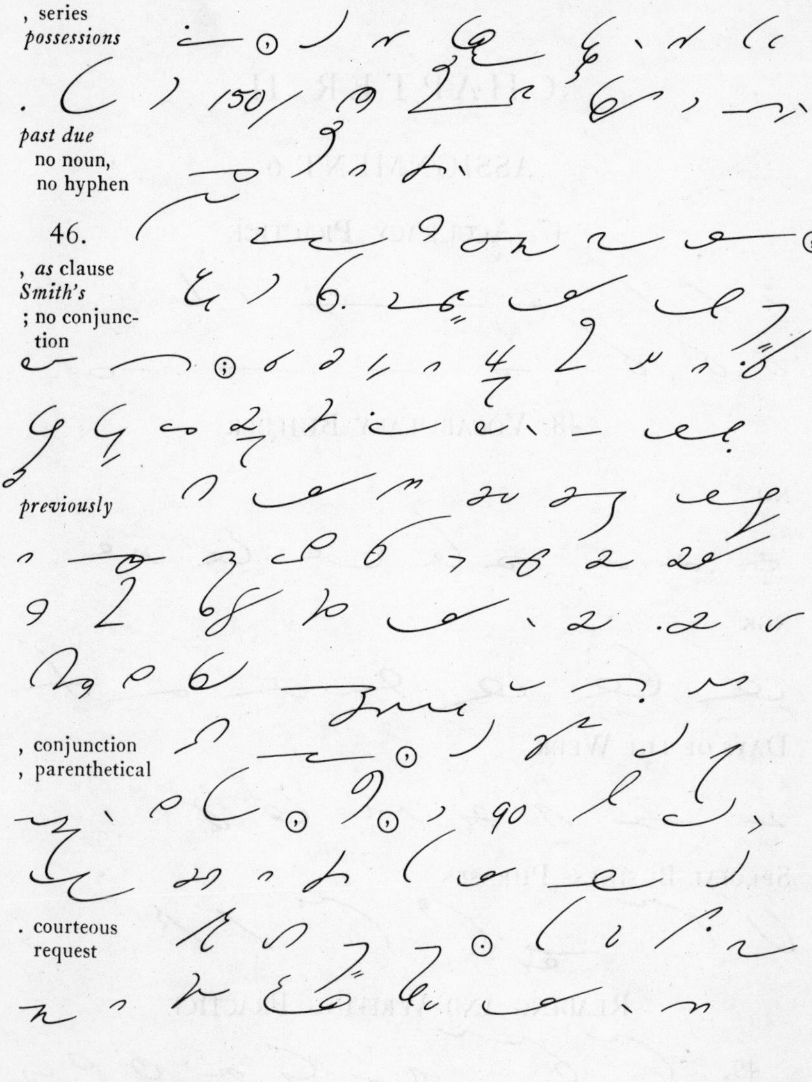
, series
possessions
past due
no noun,
no hyphen
46.
, *as* clause
Smith's
; no conjunction
previously
, conjunction
, parenthetical
. courteous
request

CHAPTER II

ASSIGNMENT 6

47. Accuracy Practice

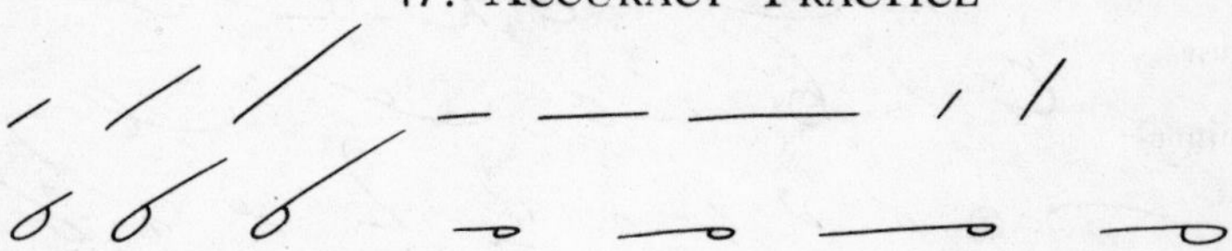

48. Vocabulary Builder

NG

NGK

Days of the Week

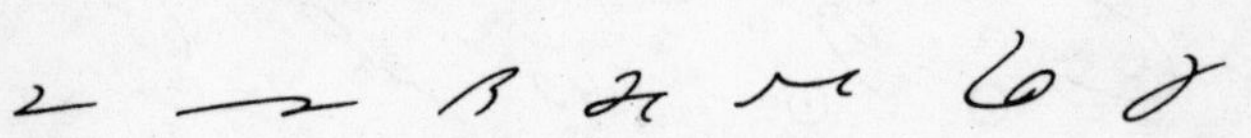

Special Business Phrases

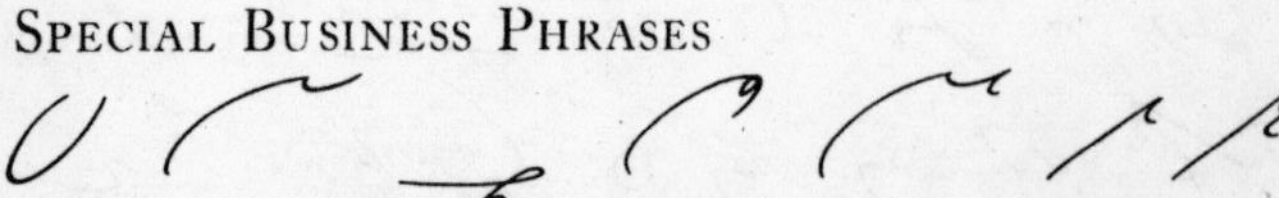

Reading and Writing Practice

49.

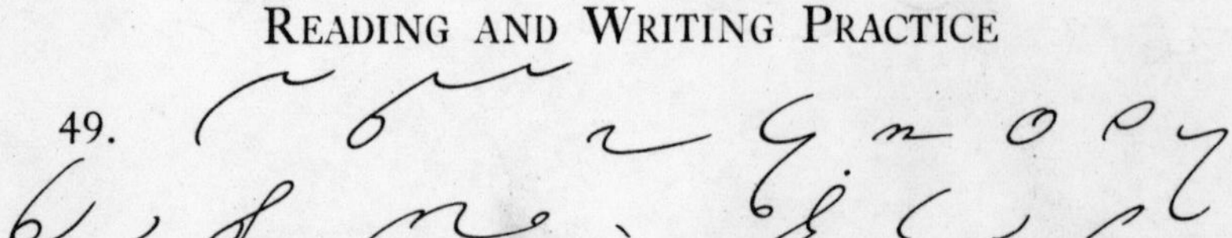

probably
principle
stretch

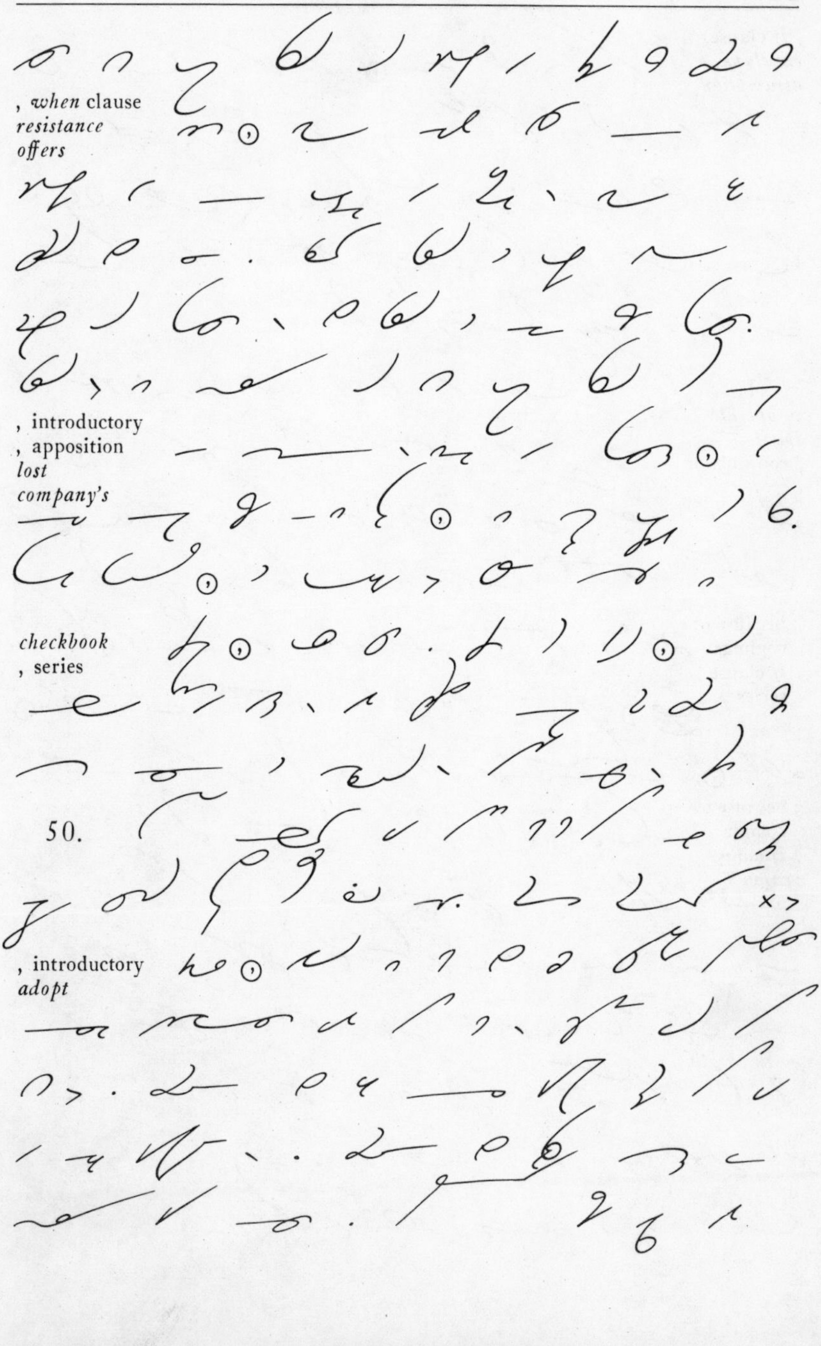
, *when* clause
resistance
offers
, introductory
, apposition
lost
company's
checkbook
, series
50.
, introductory
adopt

, *if* clause
envelope
assumption

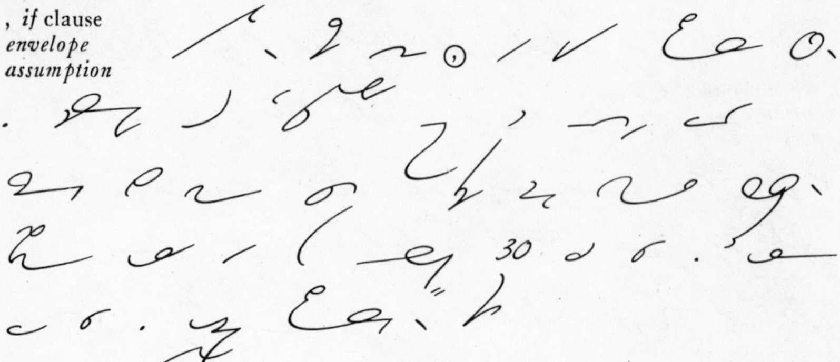

51.
co-operate
spirit
, conjunction
; because of
commas
, *if* clause
, series
; because of
comma
, *if* clause
reason

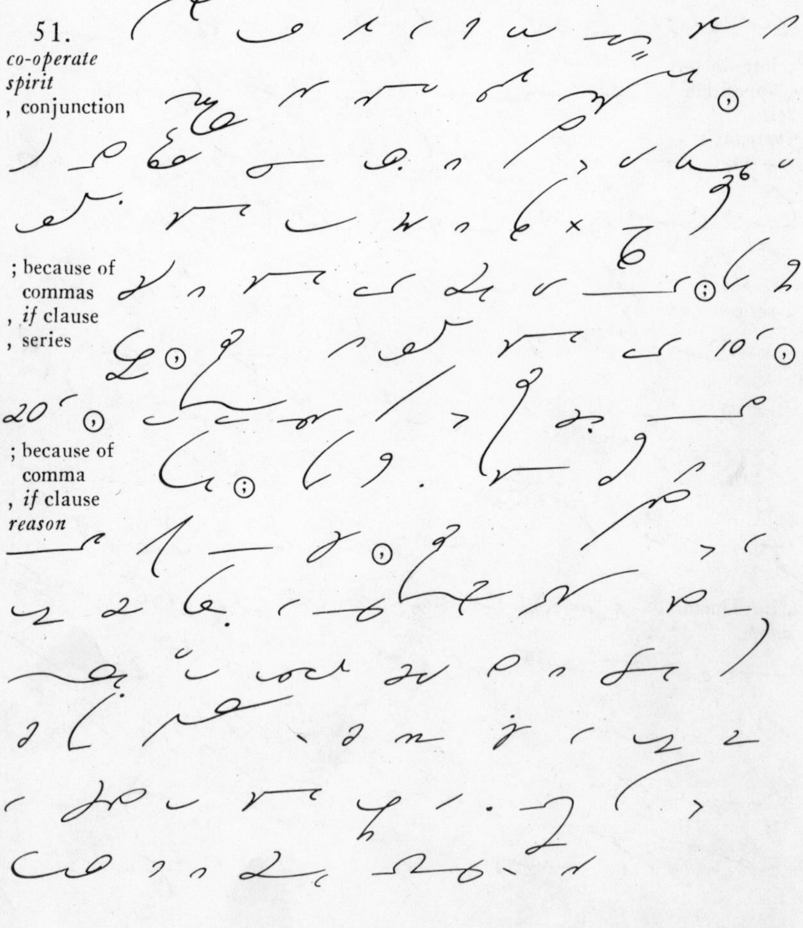

52.

, introductory
past-due
hyphenated before noun
persuade
obligation
; no conjunction
Isn't
becoming
lawsuit
, introductory
decision
Transcribe: *April 10*

53.

fourth
previous
offending
remittance
, as clause

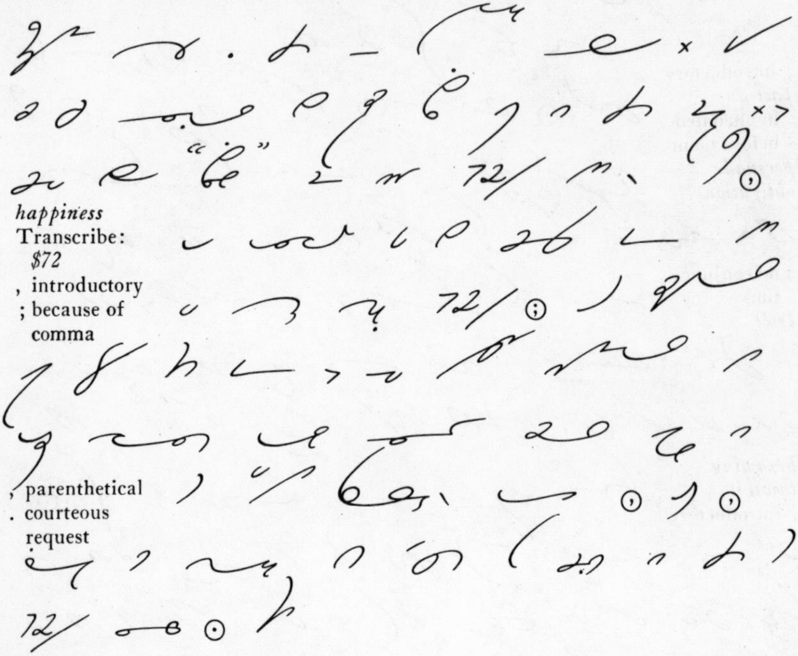

happiness
Transcribe:
$72
, introductory
; because of
comma

, parenthetical
. courteous
request

ASSIGNMENT 7

54. Word Families

IND-

UND-

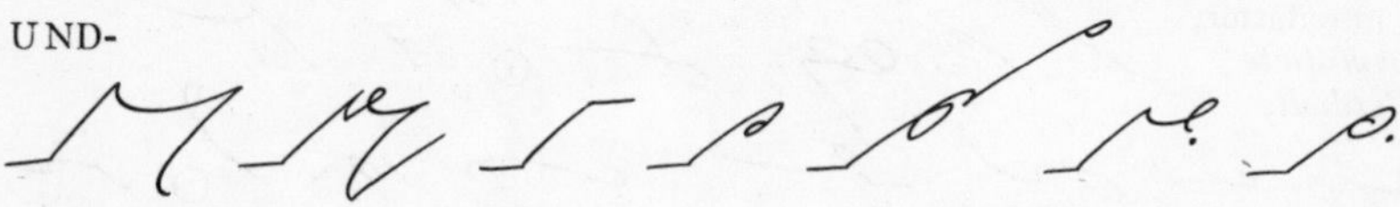

-LOGY

-LOGICAL

Reading and Writing Practice

55.

past-due hyphenated before noun

, conjunction

, *as* clause

; because of comma

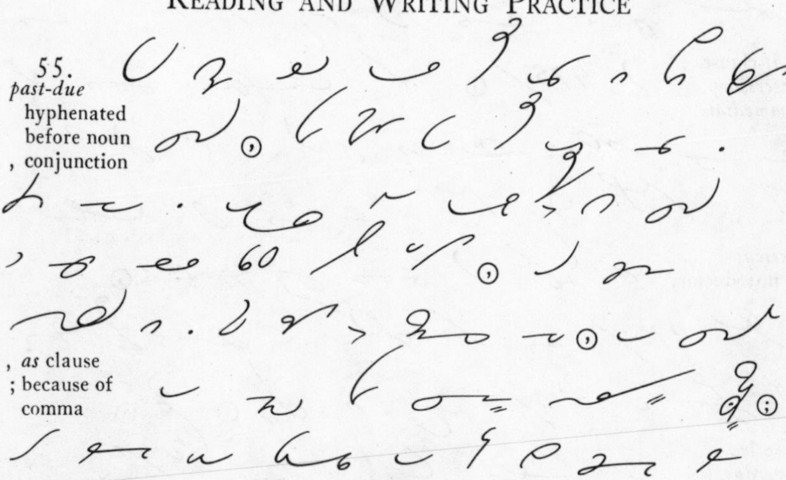

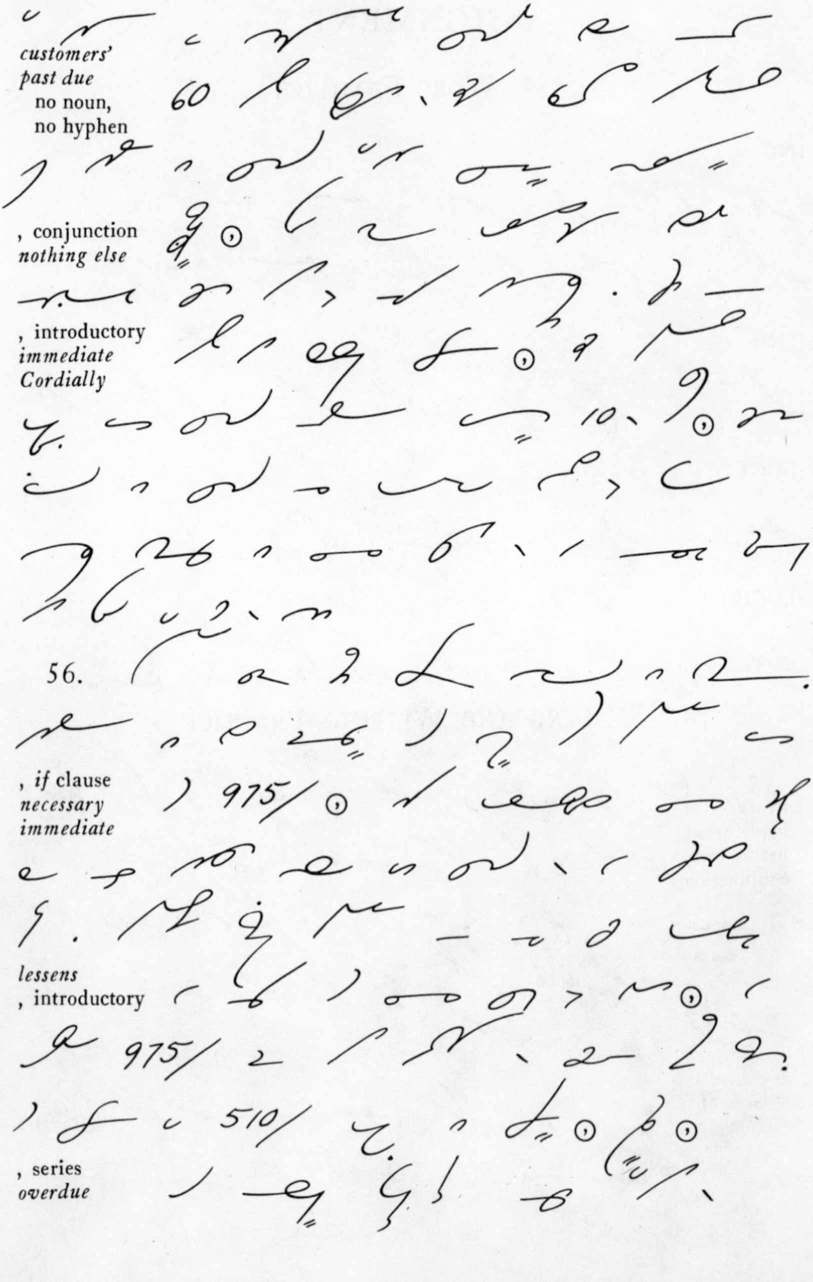

customers'
past due
no noun,
no hyphen

, conjunction
nothing else

, introductory
immediate
Cordially

56.

, *if* clause
necessary
immediate

lessens
, introductory

, series
overdue

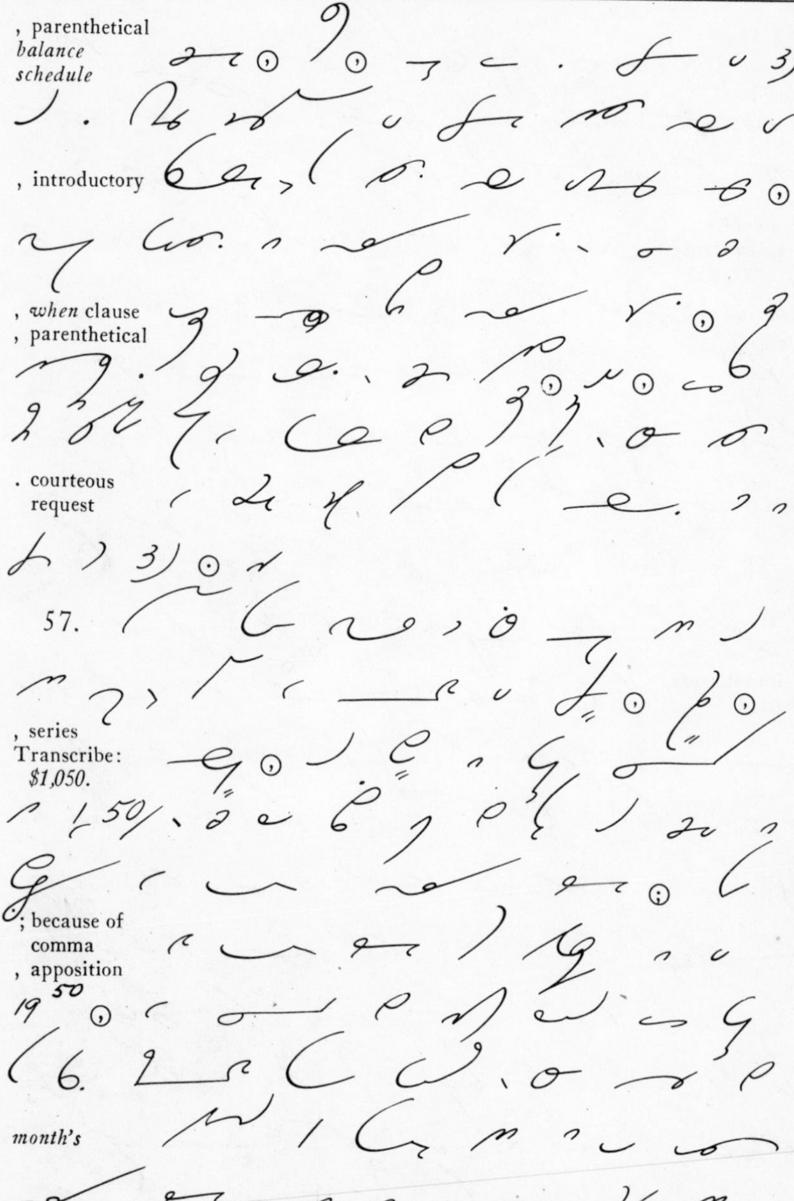
, parenthetical
balance
schedule
, introductory
, *when* clause
, parenthetical
. courteous request
57.
, series
Transcribe: *$1,050.*
; because of comma
, apposition
month's

, conjunction

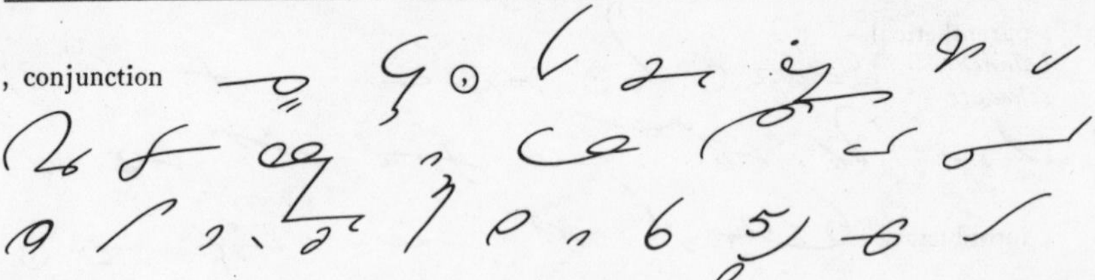

remainder
, *when* clause

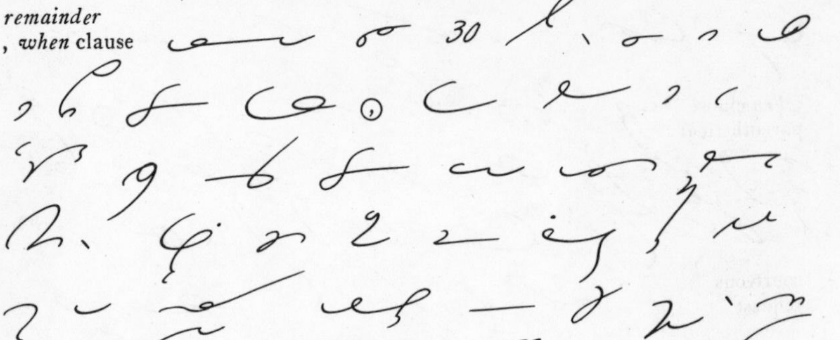

58.

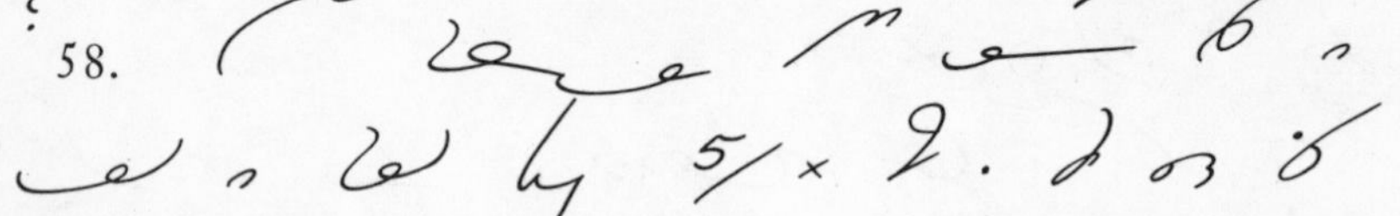

, introductory
passed

, conjunction

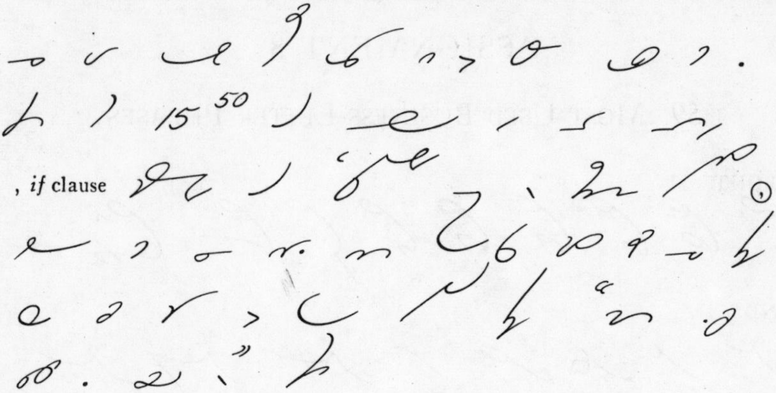
15 50
, if clause

ASSIGNMENT 8

59. Most-Used Business-Letter Phrases

ABOUT

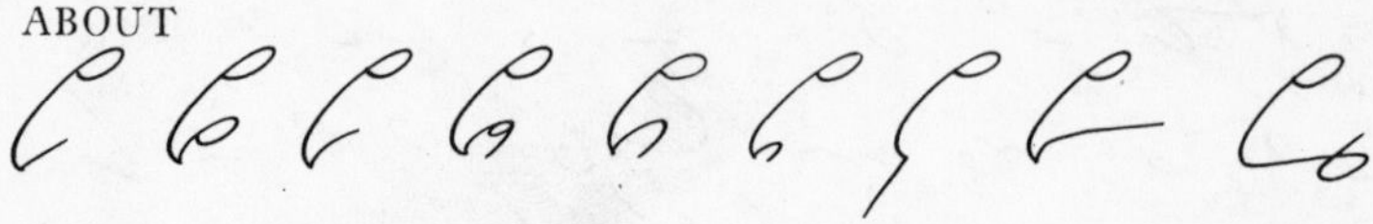

AND

ANY

AS

AT

60. Geographical Expressions

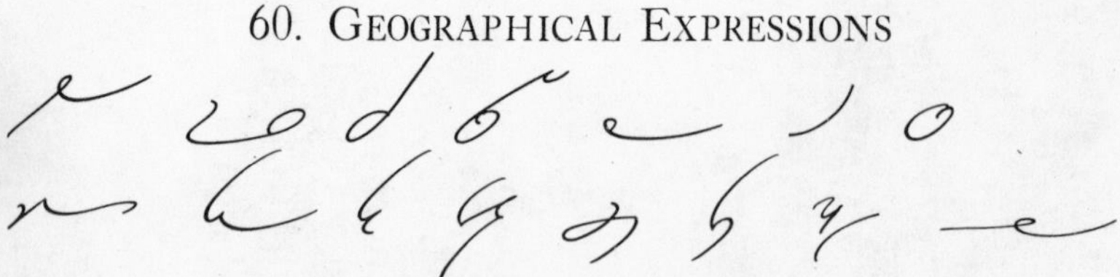

Reading and Writing Practice

61.

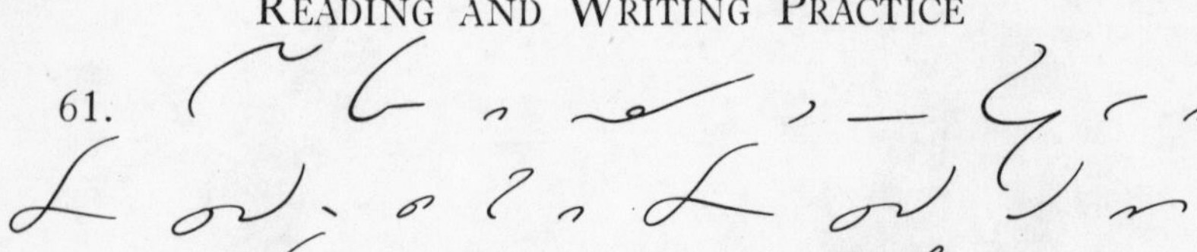

; no conjunction

forever
whether
familiar

their
, *if* clause
firm's

; because of
commas
, parenthetical

62.

; no conjunction
reputation
, introductory

; no conjunction
yours

first-class hyphenated before noun
Transcribe: *$100*

63.

, *when* clause
invoice

, conjunction
naturally

, introductory
received
explanation

, *as* clause

envelope
today
fair

64.

across
following
; no conjunction
, apposition
, introductory
past due
no noun, no hyphen

65.

exception
, *when* clause
, series
responsibilities
believe
, introductory
, parenthetical

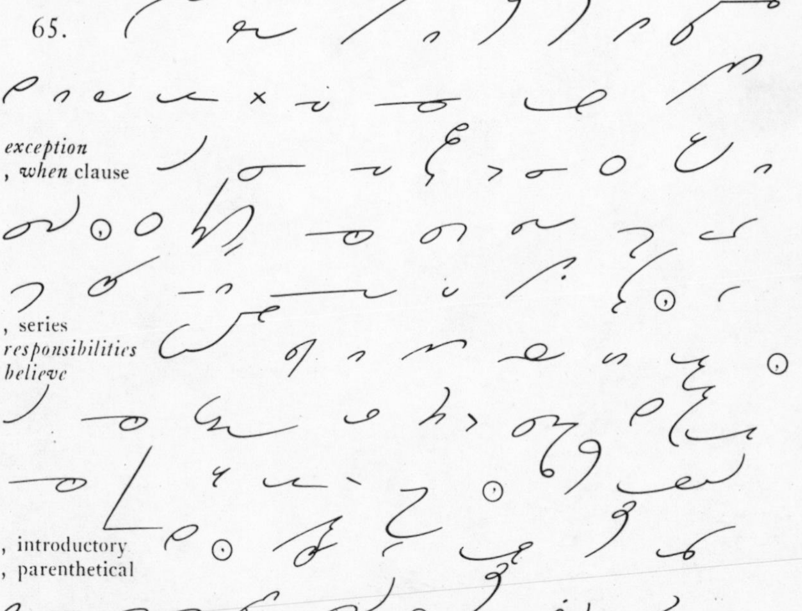

whether

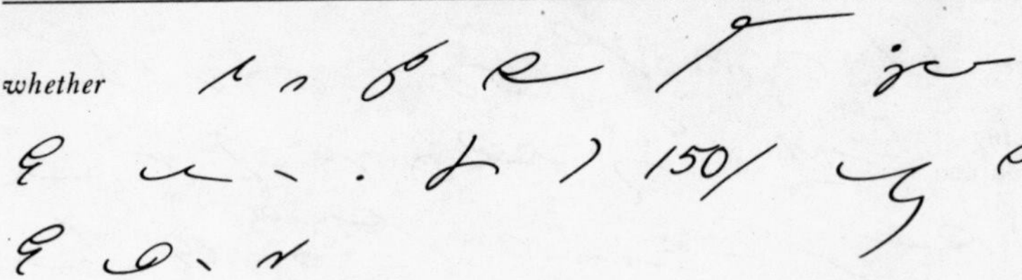

ASSIGNMENT 9

66. Vocabulary Builder

Vowel Omission

IA, EA

Y

Double Circle

Reading and Writing Practice

67.

announce
removal
First

, series

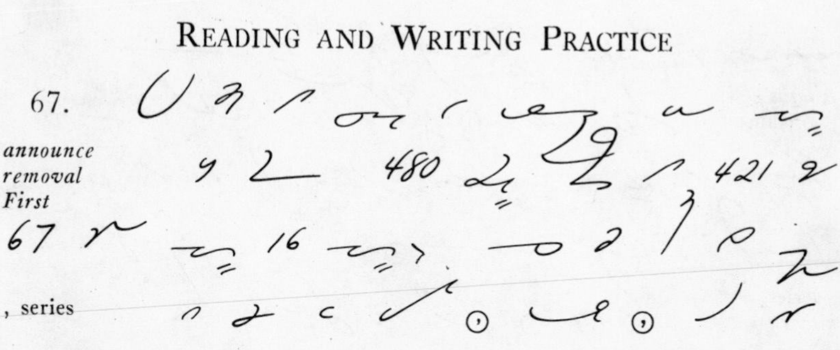

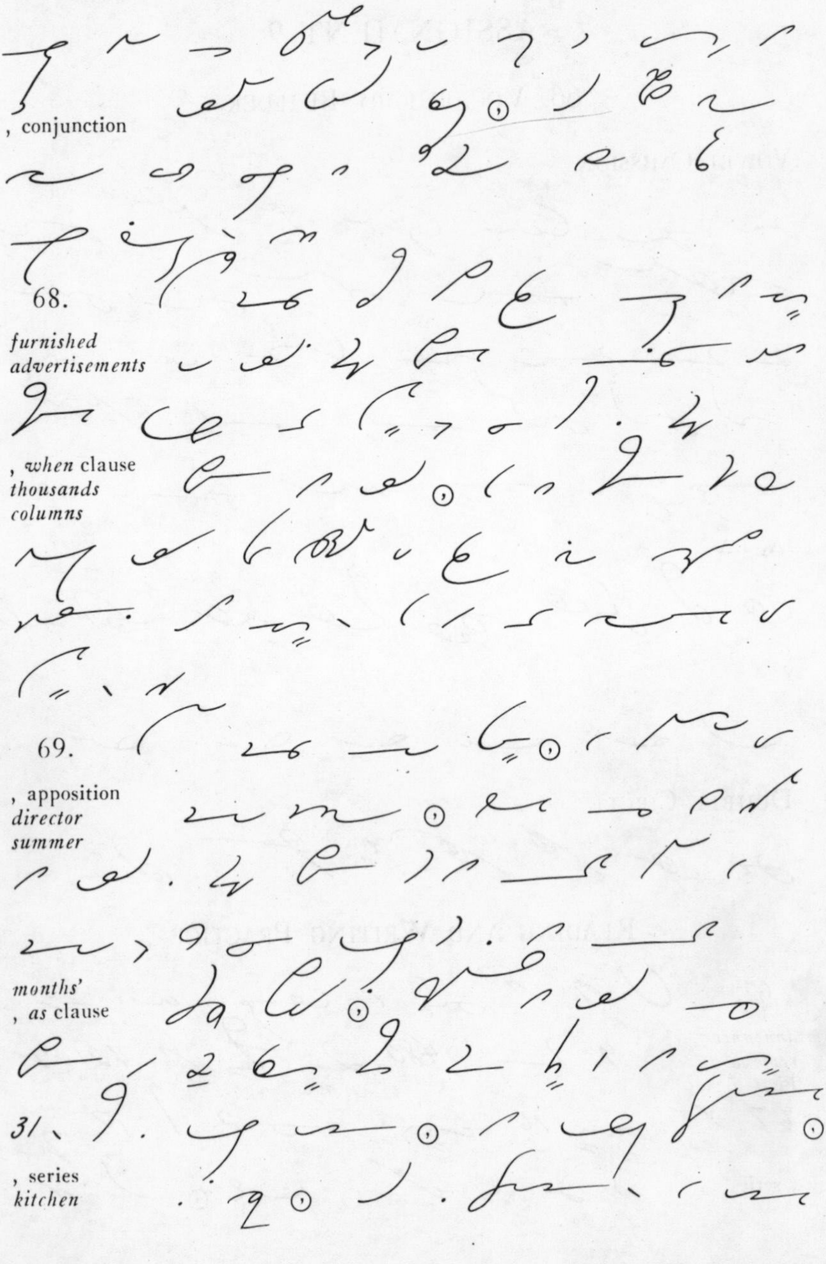

, conjunction

68.

furnished
advertisements

, *when* clause
thousands
columns

69.

, apposition
director
summer

months'
, *as* clause

31.

, series
kitchen

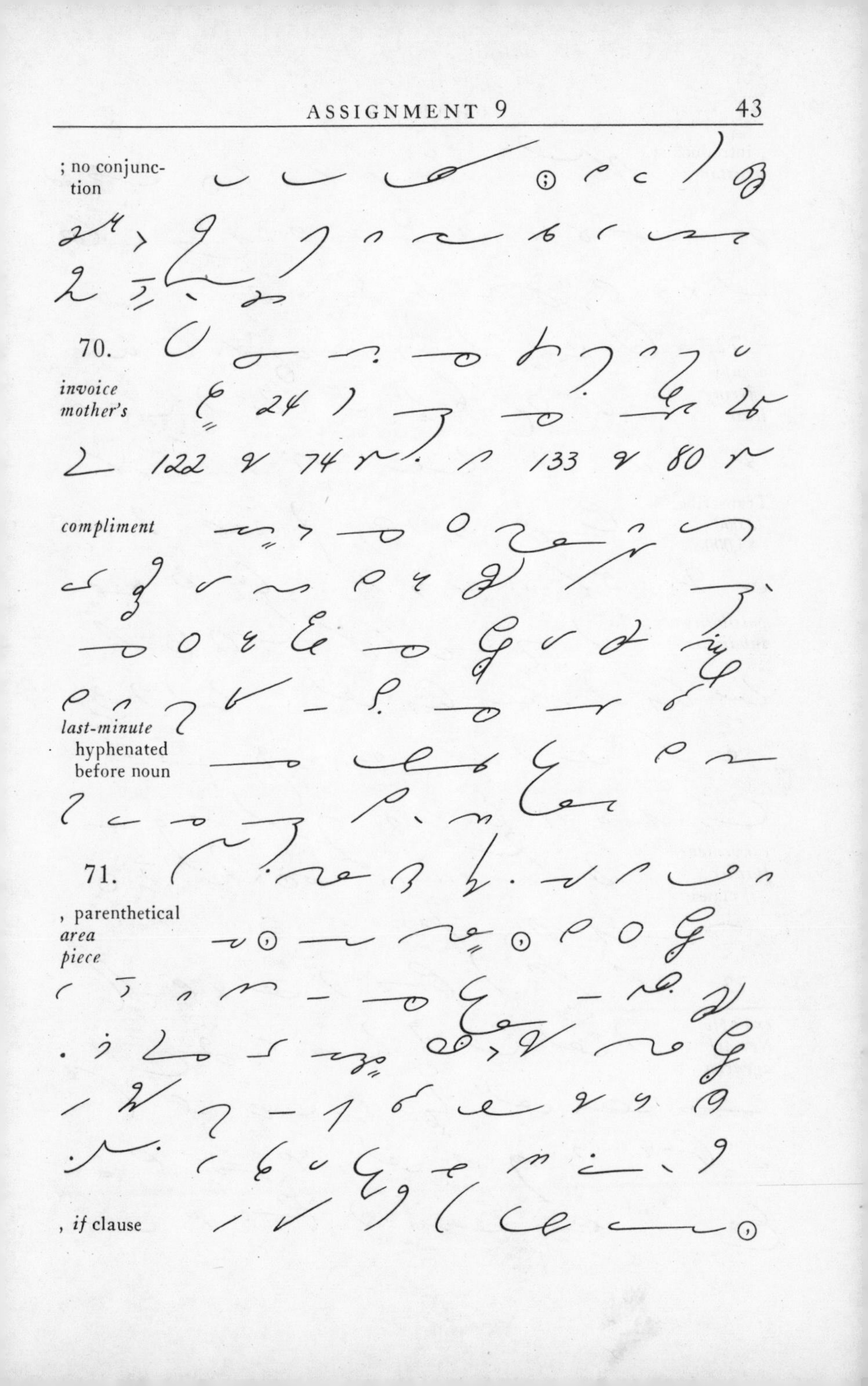

; no conjunction

70.

invoice
mother's

compliment

last-minute
hyphenated
before noun

71.

, parenthetical
area
piece

, *if* clause

, introductory
assistance

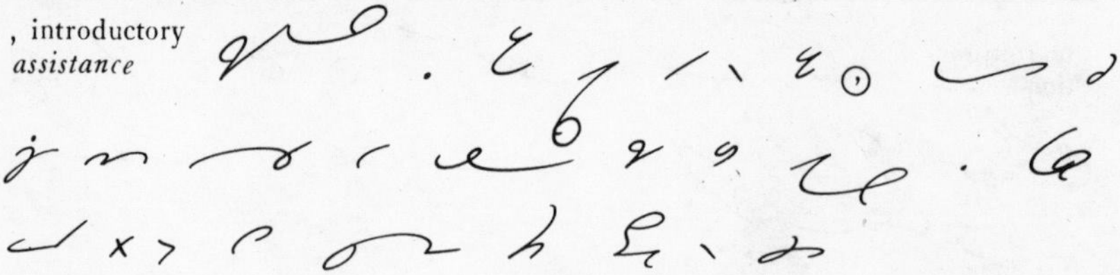

72.

occupy
offering
lease

Transcribe:
3,000
$5,000

possibility
subdivide

convenience
further
, *if clause*

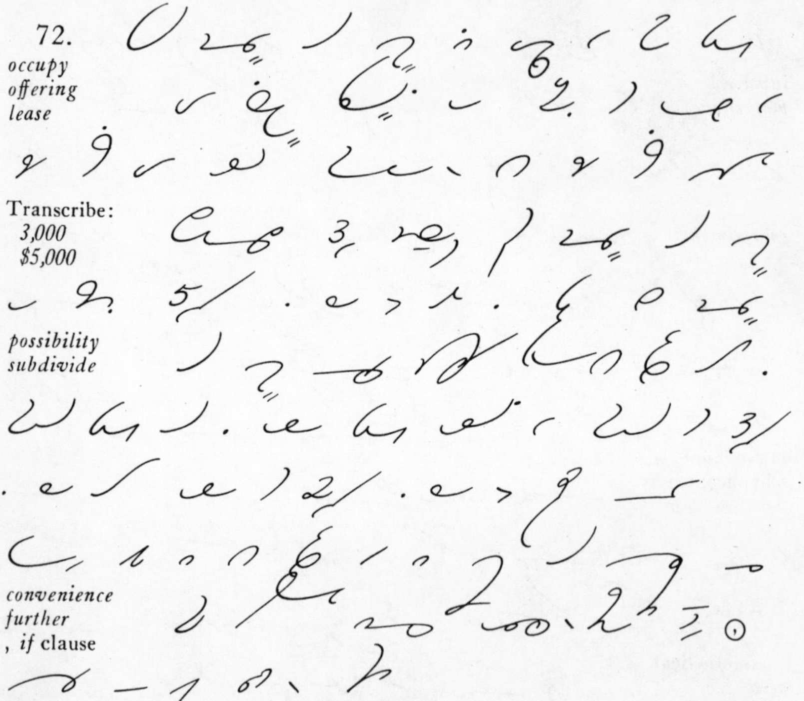

73.

example
Newark
agencies

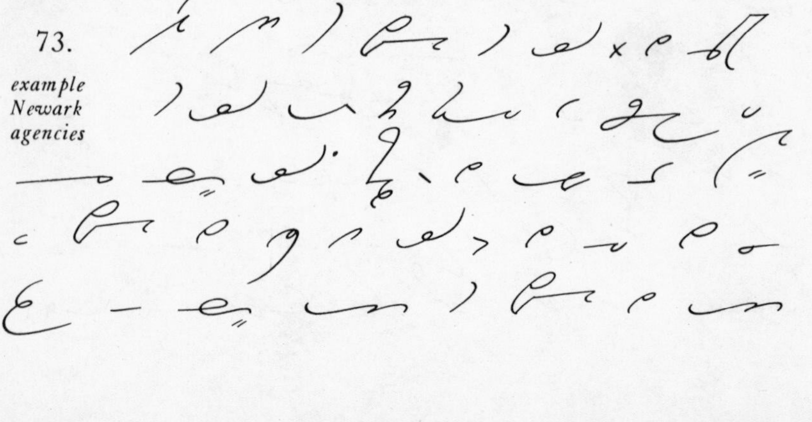

, introductory
twenty-one

ASSIGNMENT 10

74. VOCABULARY BUILDER

-XES

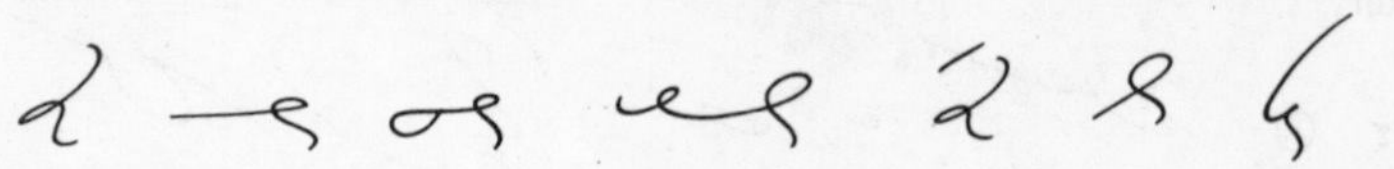

-RD

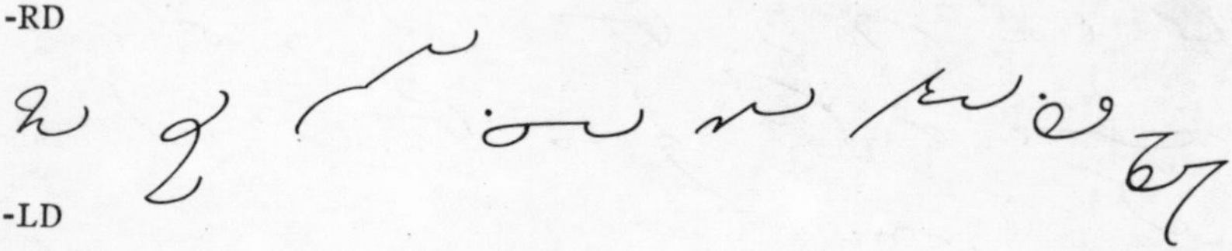

-LD

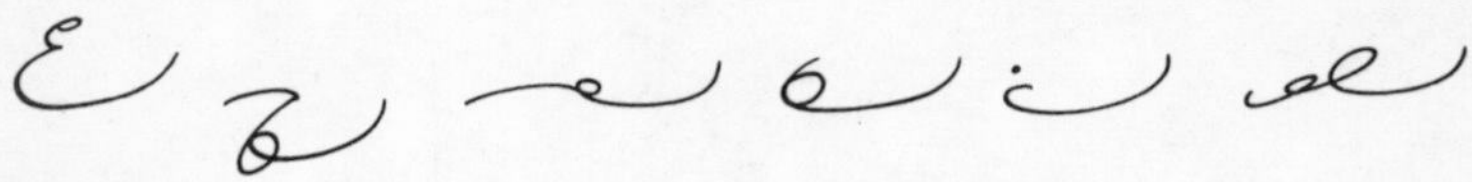

DET, TED

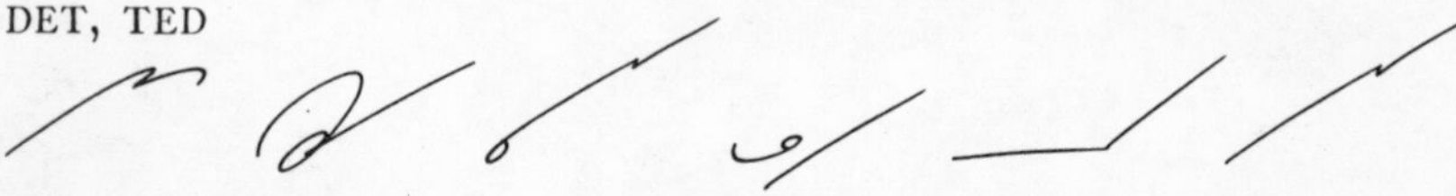

MEN

READING AND WRITING PRACTICE

75.

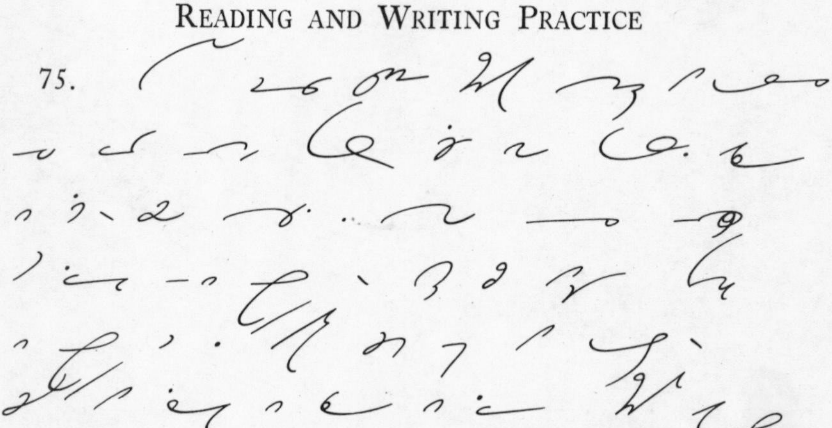

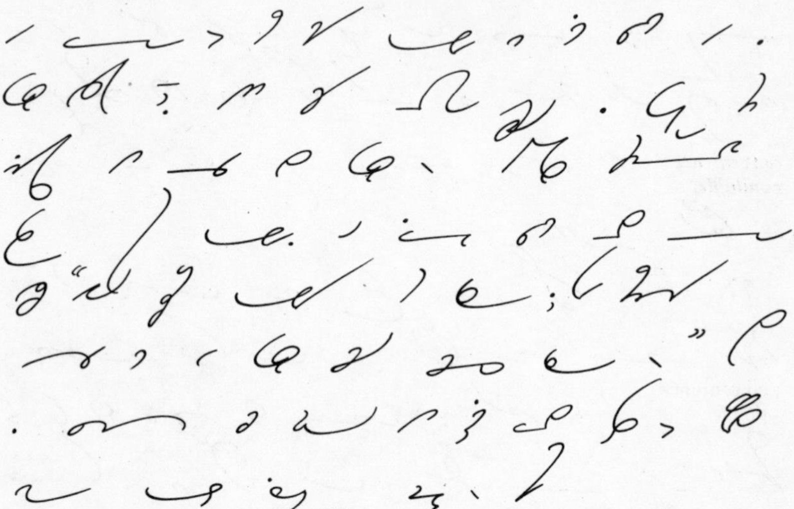

76.

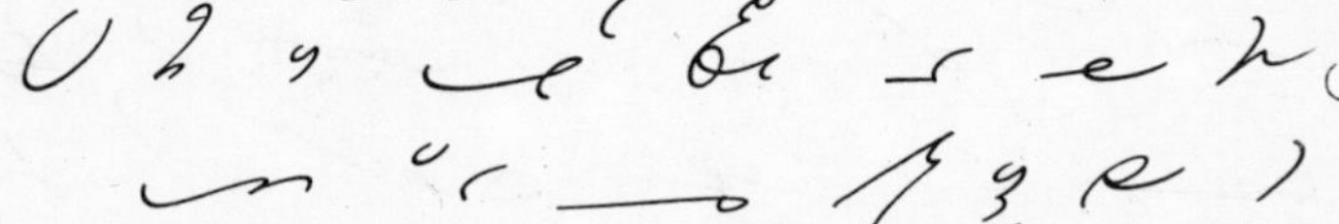

desirable
lease
, *if* clause

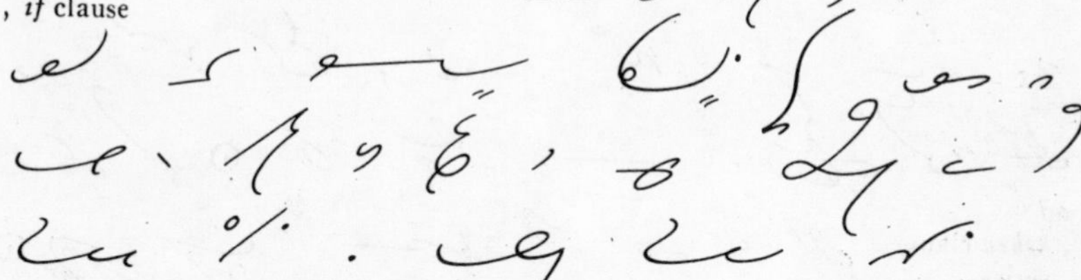

, conjunction

organizations
offices
main

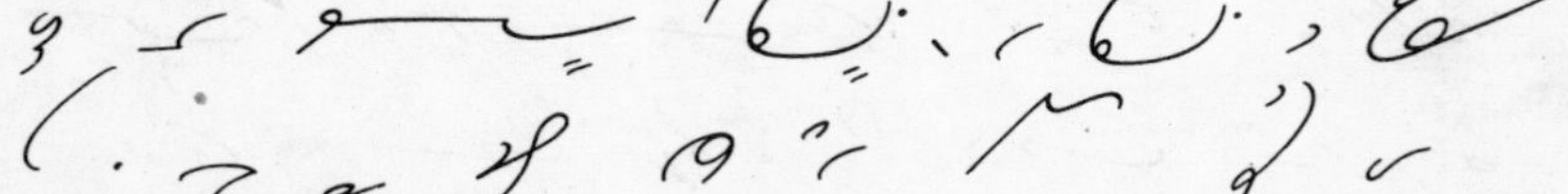

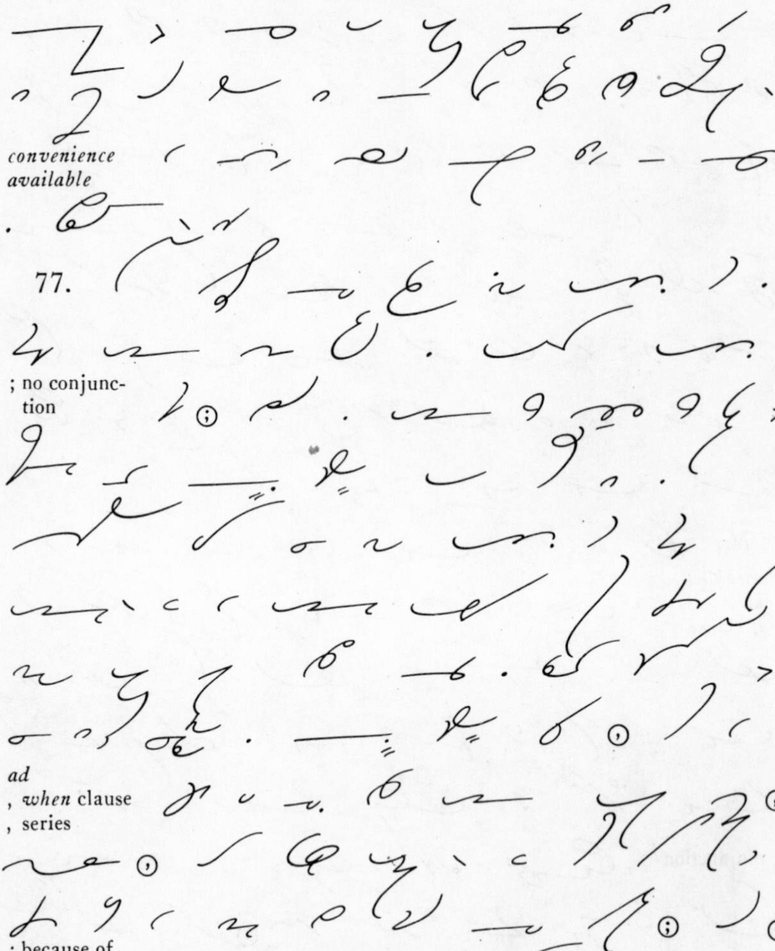

convenience
available

77.

; no conjunction

ad
, *when* clause
, series

; because of commas
, parenthetical
up-to-date hyphenated before noun

78.

, introductory
, parenthetical

, introductory
Wilson's
reaction

79.

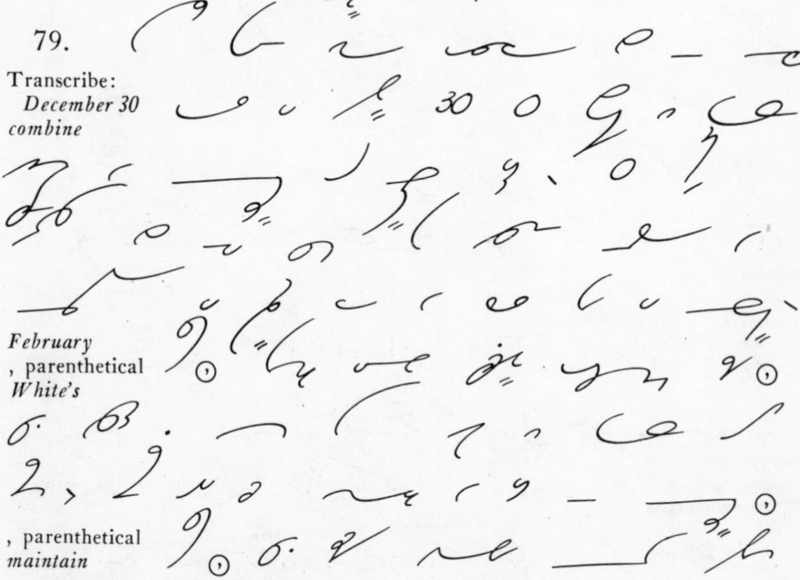

Transcribe:
December 30
combine

February
, parenthetical
White's

, parenthetical
maintain

there
, apposition

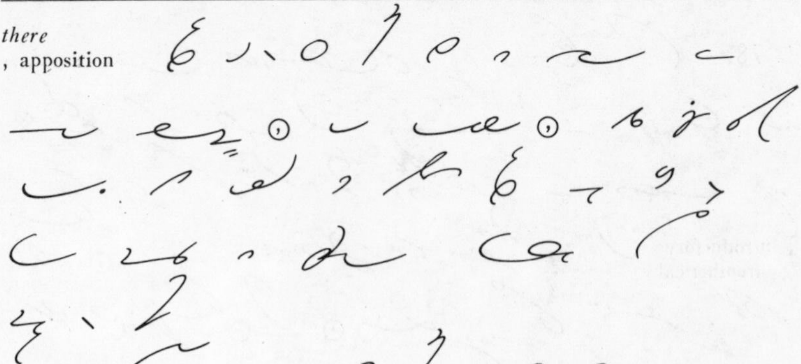

80.

, *as* clause
whether
partition

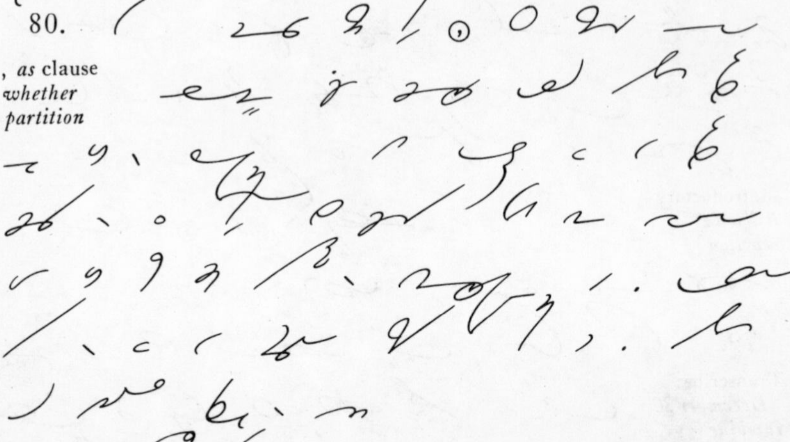

81.

enclosed
area
publicity

telephone
consented
, introductory

CHAPTER III

ASSIGNMENT 11

82. Brief-Form Chart

A B C D E F

1. 2. 3. 4. 5. 6. 7. 8. 9.

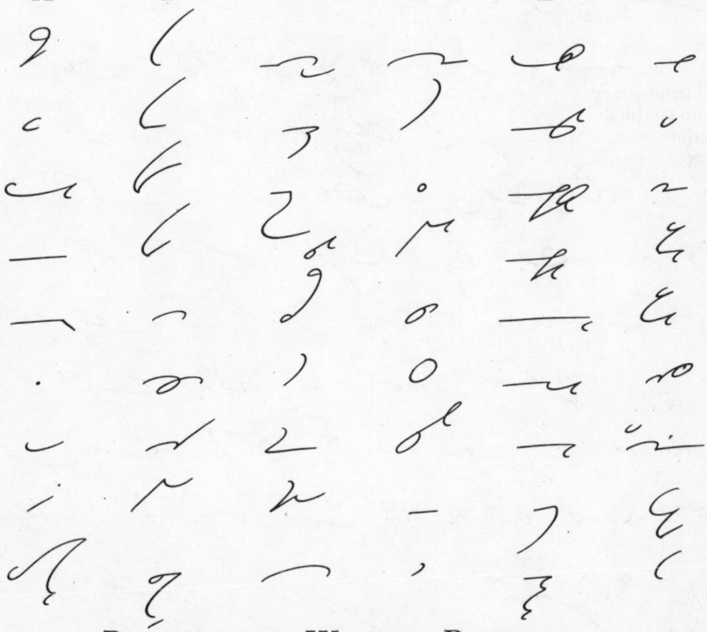

Reading and Writing Practice

83.

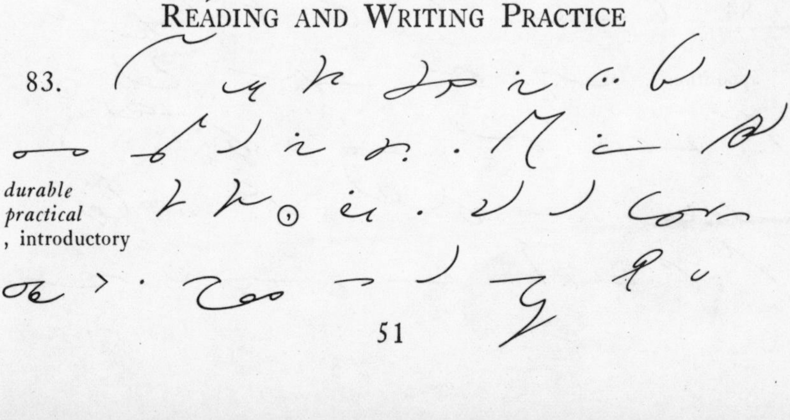

durable
practical
, introductory

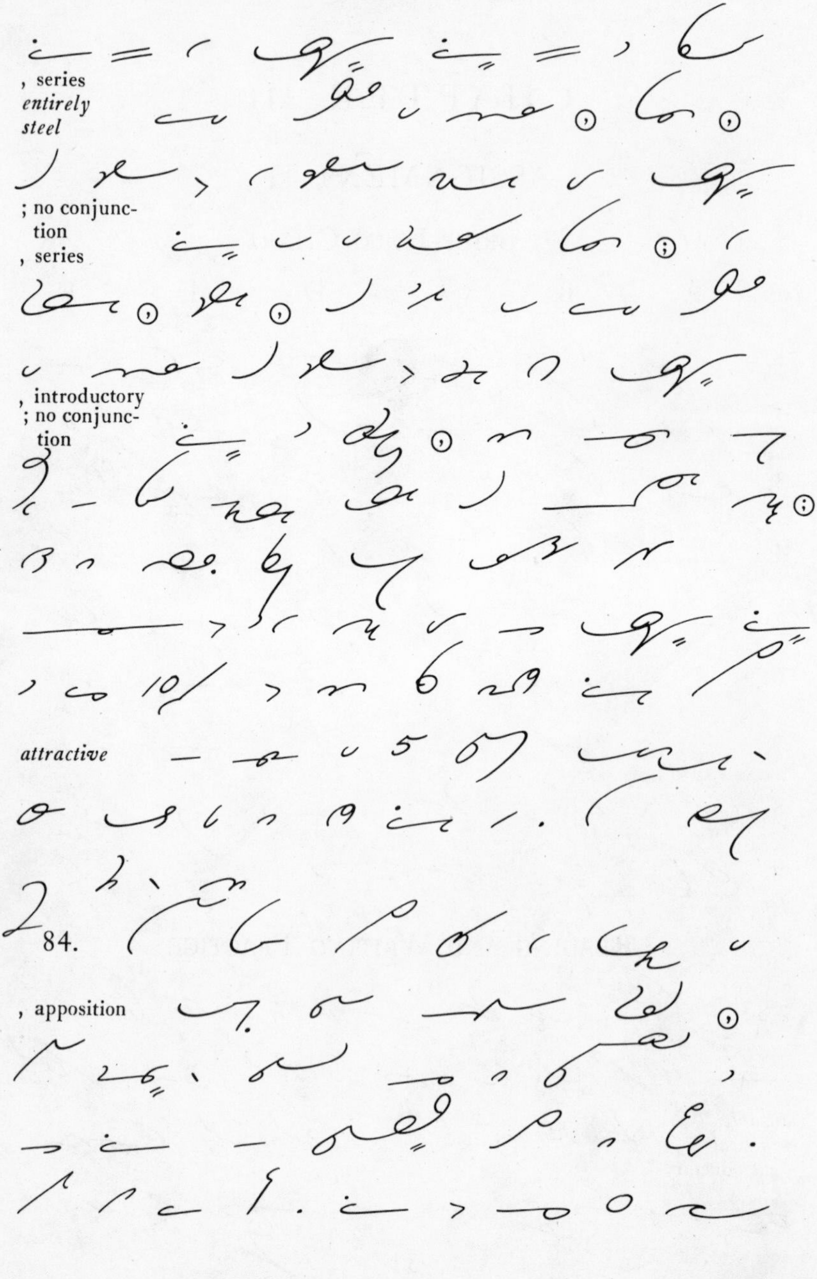

, series
entirely
steel

; no conjunction
, series

, introductory
; no conjunction

attractive

84.

, apposition

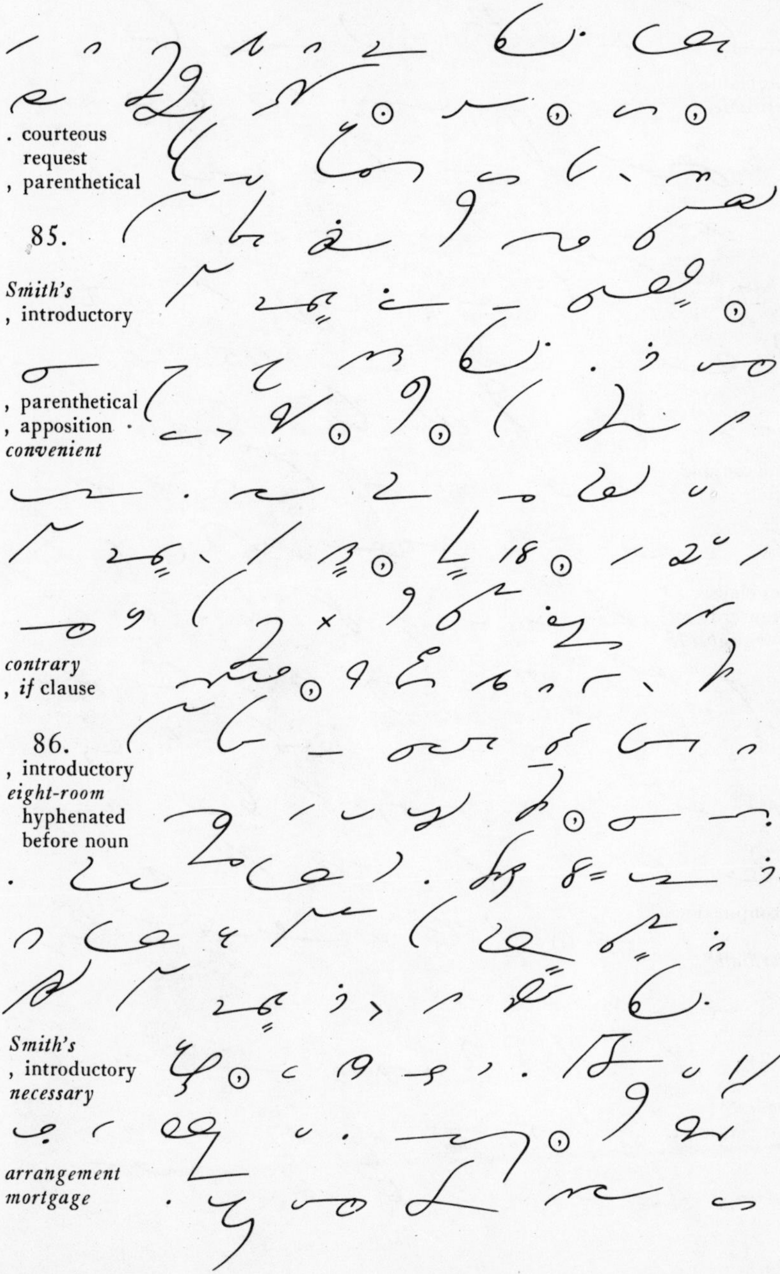

. courteous request

, parenthetical

85.

Smith's

, introductory

, parenthetical

, apposition

convenient

contrary

, *if* clause

86.

, introductory

eight-room hyphenated before noun

Smith's

, introductory

necessary

arrangement

mortgage

, *as* clause
desirable

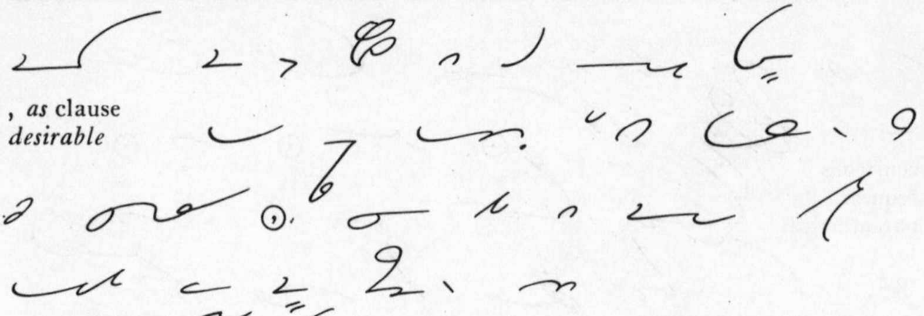

87.

; no conjunction

, *as* clause

Transcribe: *November 15.*

, conjunction

rise

Cordially

88.

request

, *as* clause

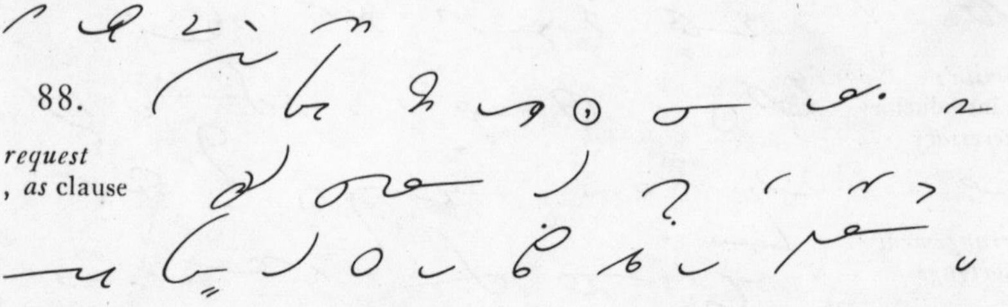

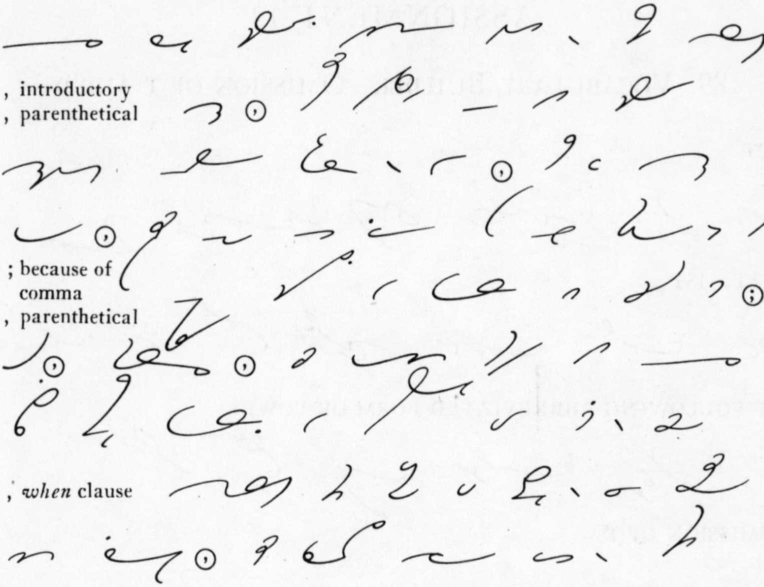
, introductory
, parenthetical
; because of comma
, parenthetical
, *when* clause

ASSIGNMENT 12

89. Vocabulary Builder—Omission of T and D

-CT

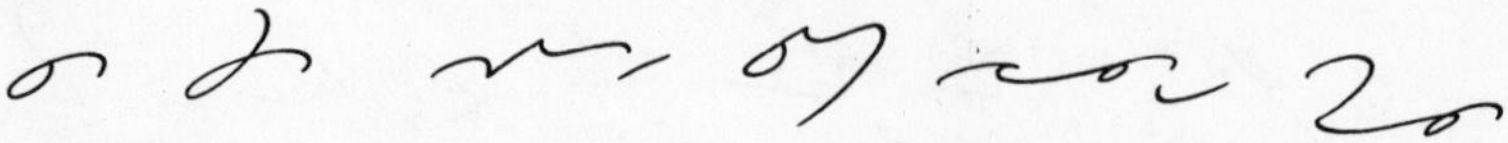

-EST, -IST

ST FOLLOWING ABBREVIATED FORM OR VOWEL

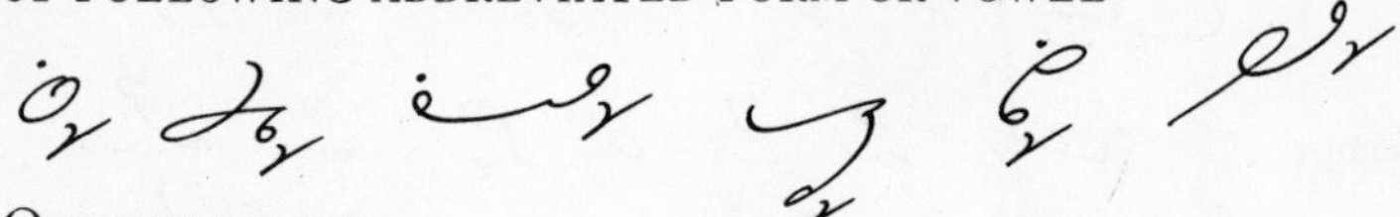

Omission of D

Reading and Writing Practice

90.

received
tenant
, apposition
effect

attention
, conjunction

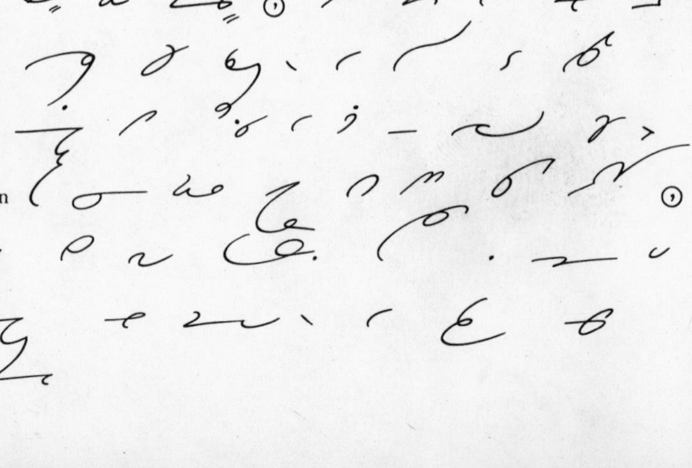

month's
; no conjunction

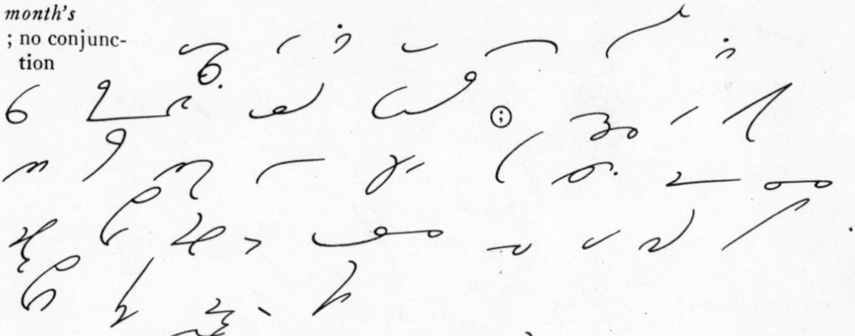

91.

, *if* clause
, parenthetical

, *if* clause
, introductory

92.

Transcribe:
$145.

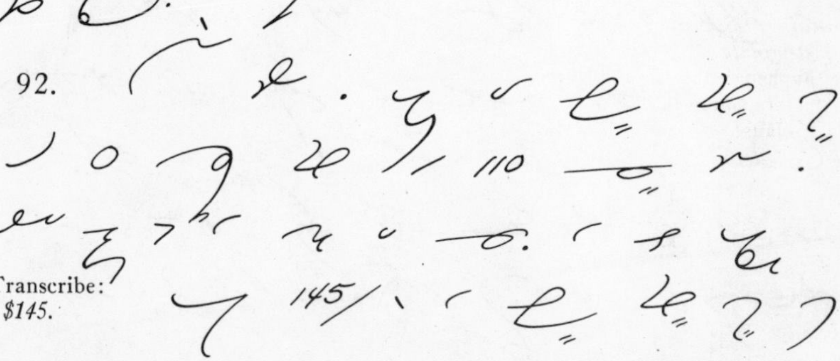

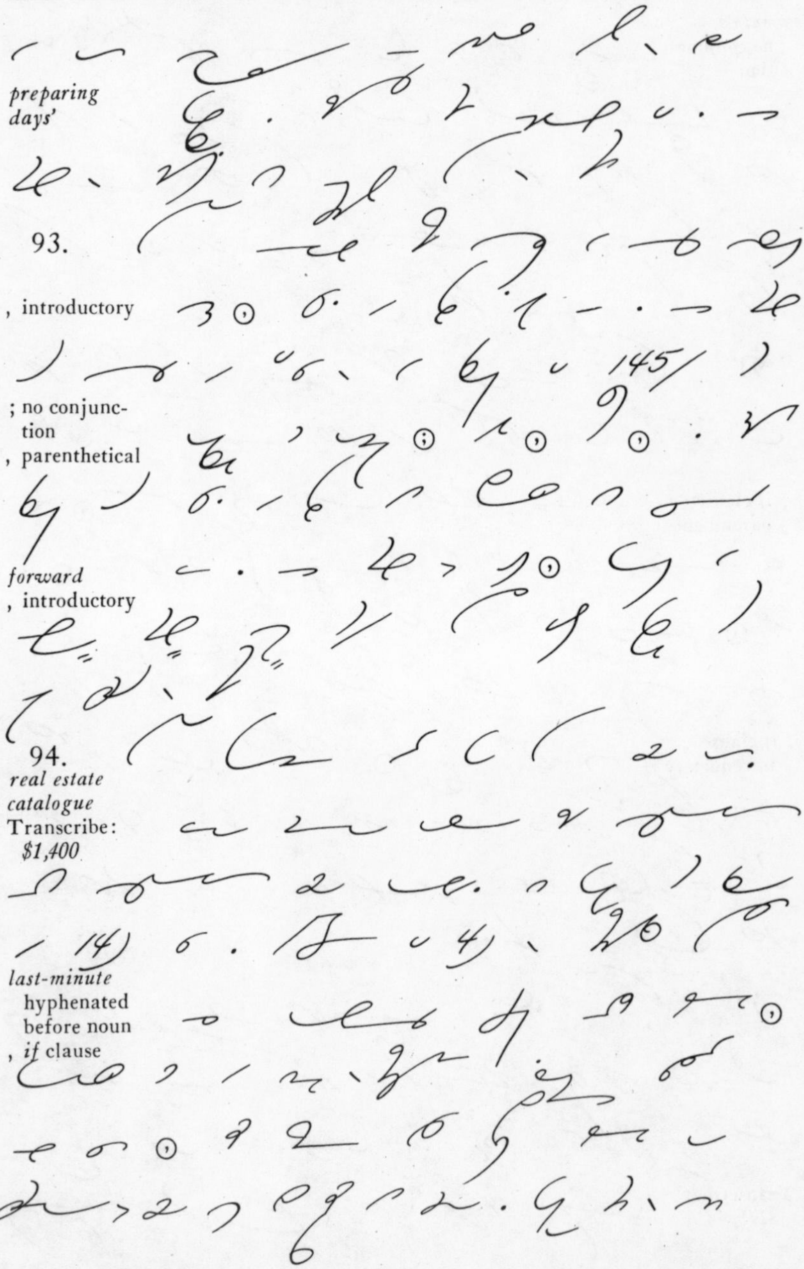

preparing
days'
93.
, introductory
; no conjunction
, parenthetical
forward
, introductory
94.
real estate
catalogue
Transcribe:
$1,400
last-minute
hyphenated before noun
, *if* clause

95.

catalogue

, parenthetical

, *as* clause

, series

; because of commas

96.

, conjunction

, *if* clause

Cordially

97.

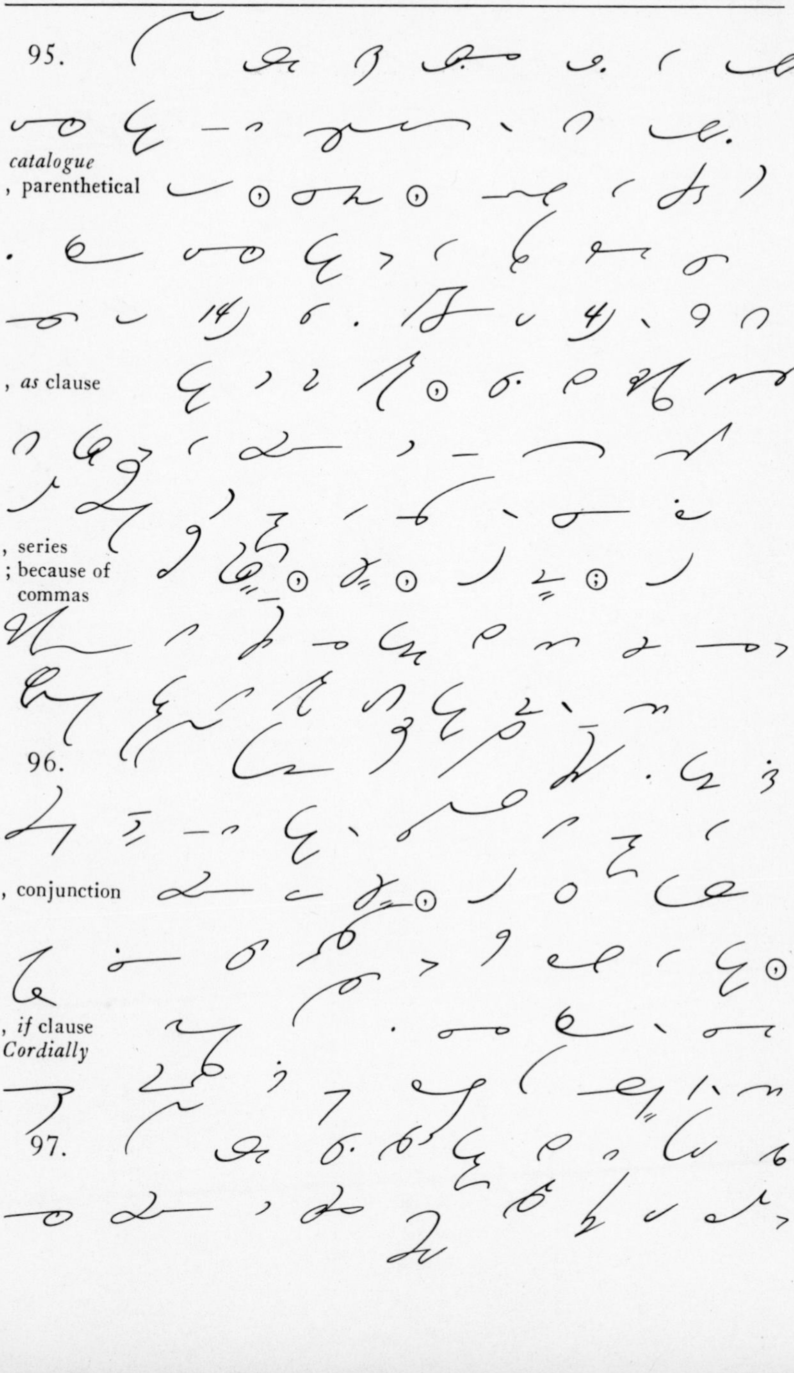

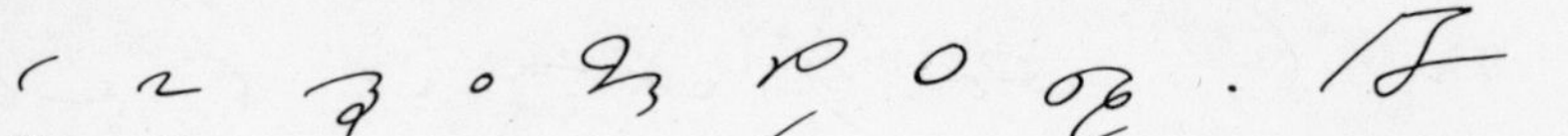

Transcribe:
$300
$400.
, *when* clause

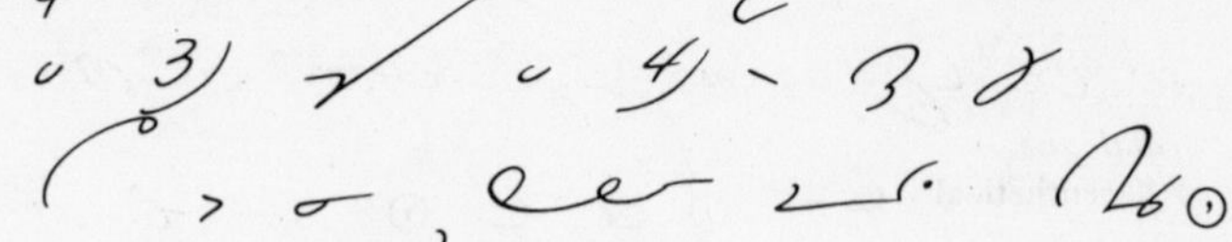

98.

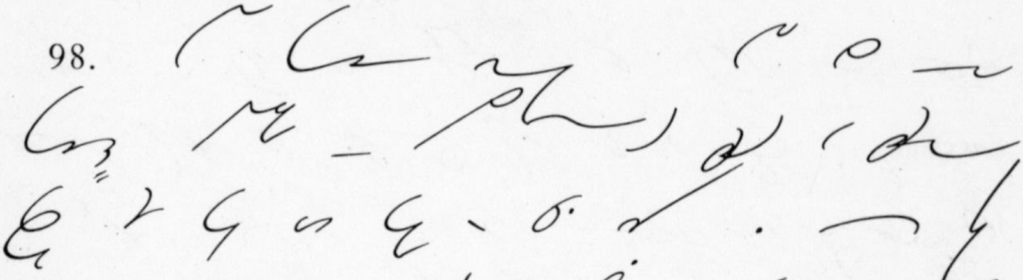

dropped
convincing

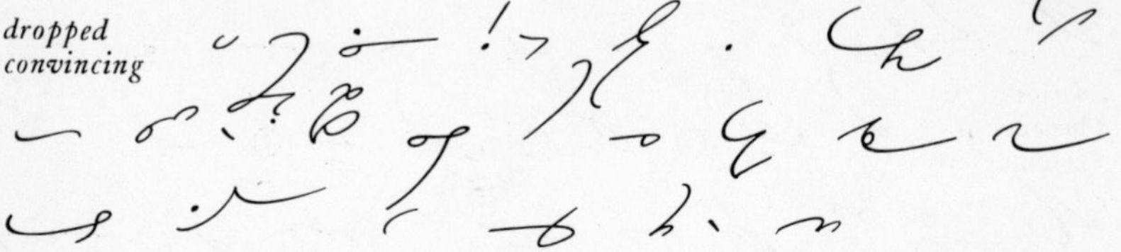

ASSIGNMENT 13

99. Most-Used Business-Letter Phrases

BY

DO

EACH

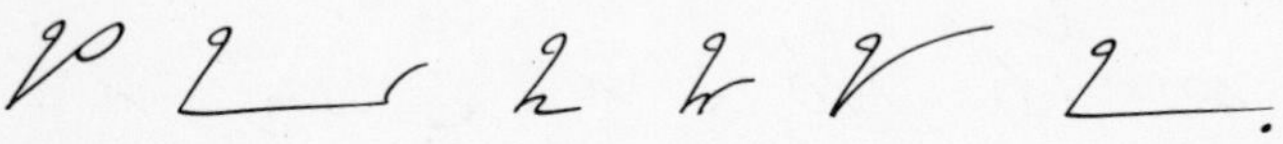

FEW

FOR

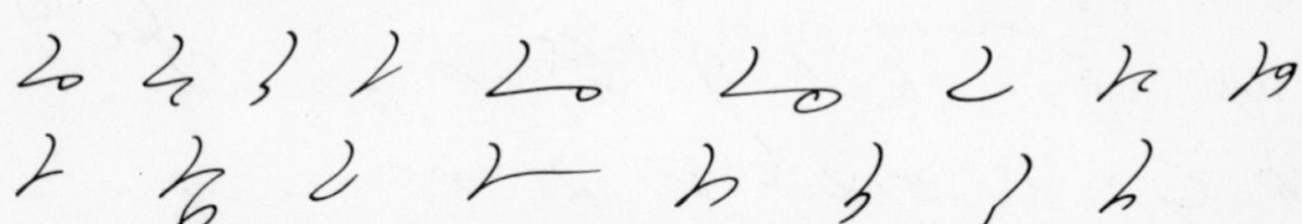

100. Geographical Expressions

Reading and Writing Practice

101.

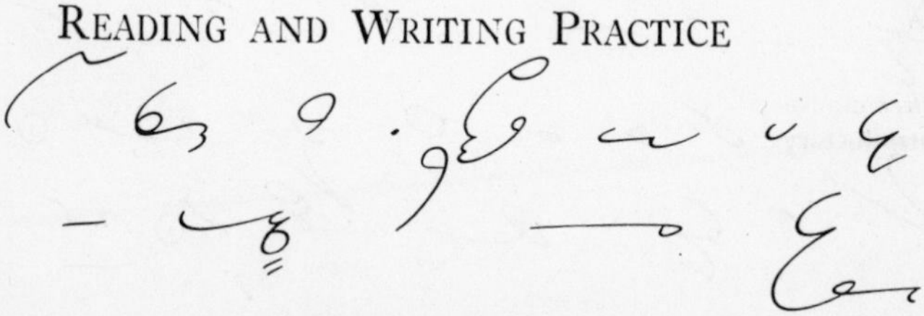

absentee
Los Angeles

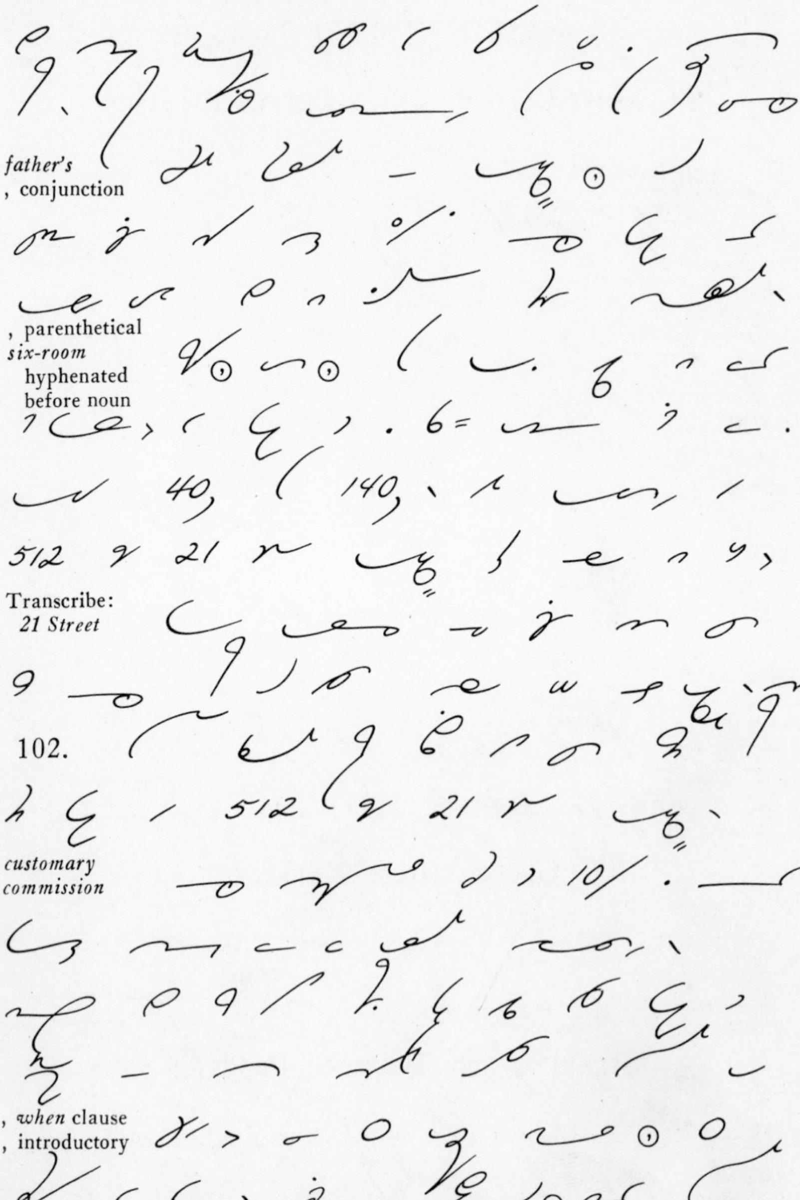

father's
, conjunction

, parenthetical
six-room
hyphenated
before noun

Transcribe:
21 Street

102.

customary
commission

, *when* clause
, introductory

attention
recent
, series

, apposition
; because of
commas

103.

, parenthetical
tenant's

, conjunction

, introductory
, *if* clause
, parenthetical

roofing
forward

104.

, *as* clause
enclosed
accept

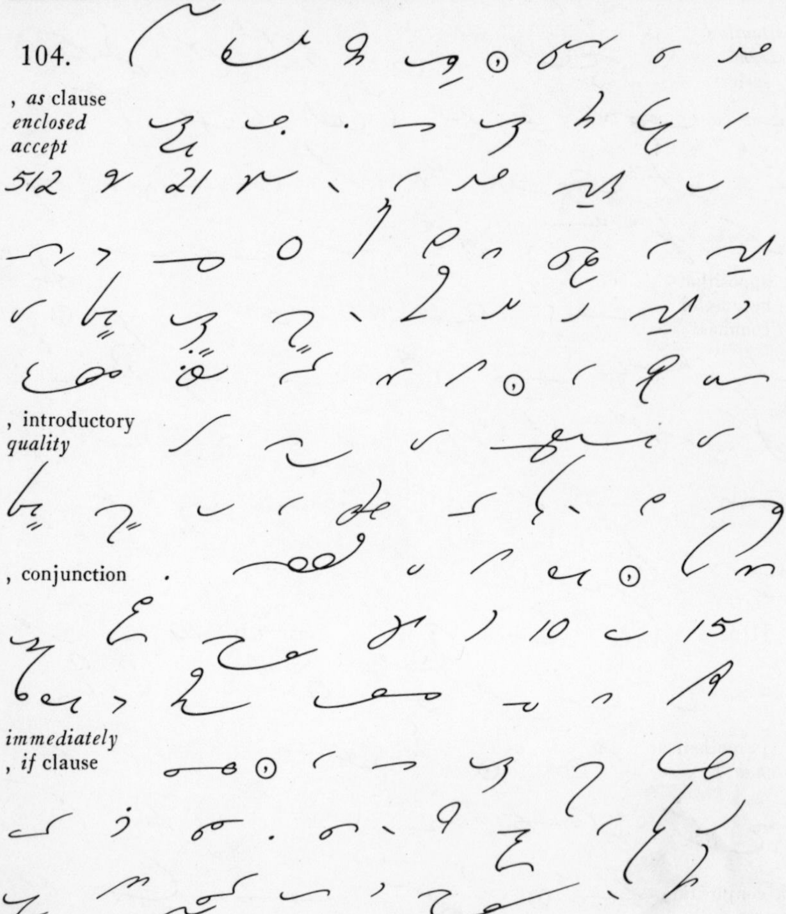

, introductory
quality

, conjunction

immediately
, *if* clause

105.

recommendation
, introductory
, parenthetical

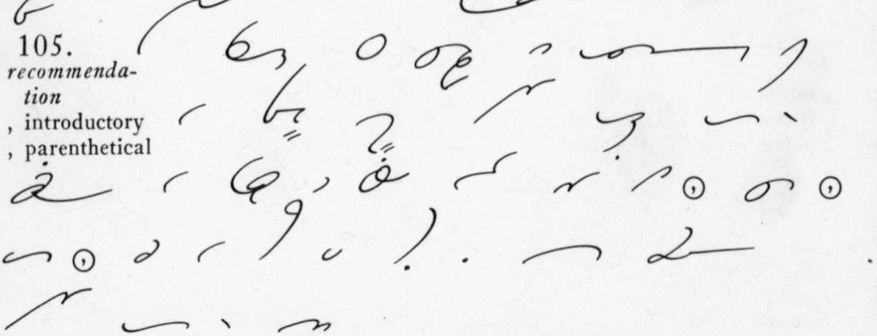

106.

; no conjunction

further

, *if* clause

ASSIGNMENT 14

107. Word Families

-NTIC

-STIC

-USE

Past Tense

Reading and Writing Practice

108.

, *when* clause
Transcribe:
January 24.
self-addressed

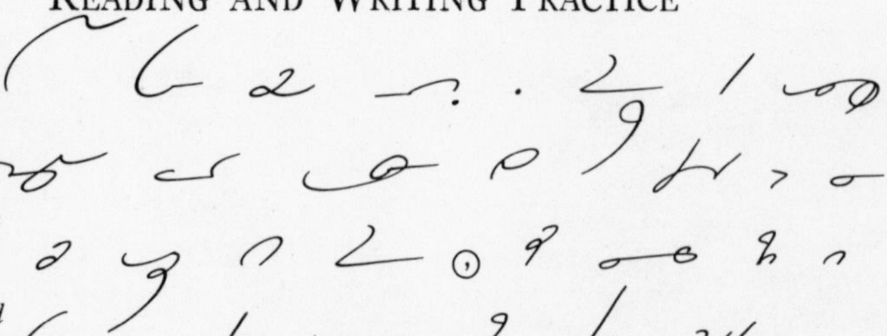

109.

bottom
son's

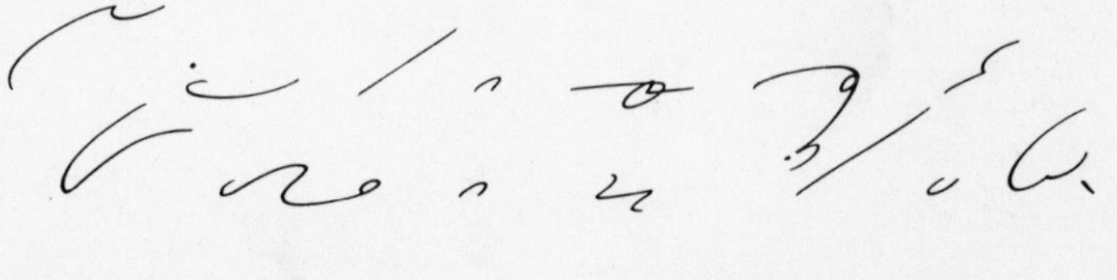

, introductory
prepaid
envelope

110.

; no conjunction
, *as* clause
, *when* clause
appreciate
opportunity

111.

, series
worthy
ambitious
, *if* clause
recommendations

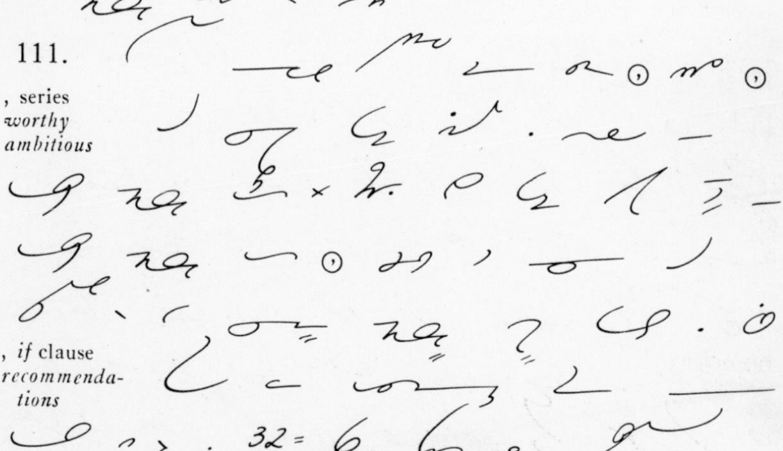

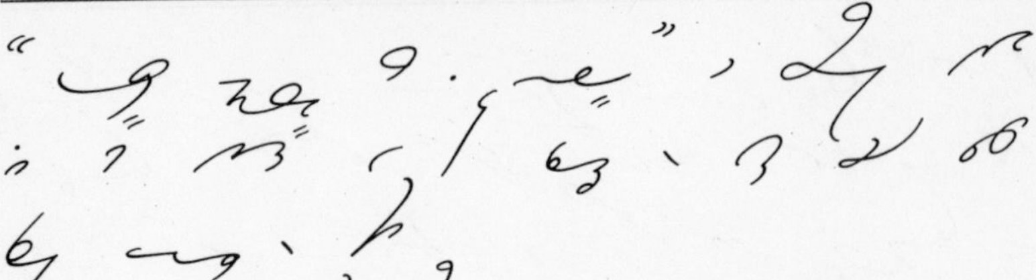

112.

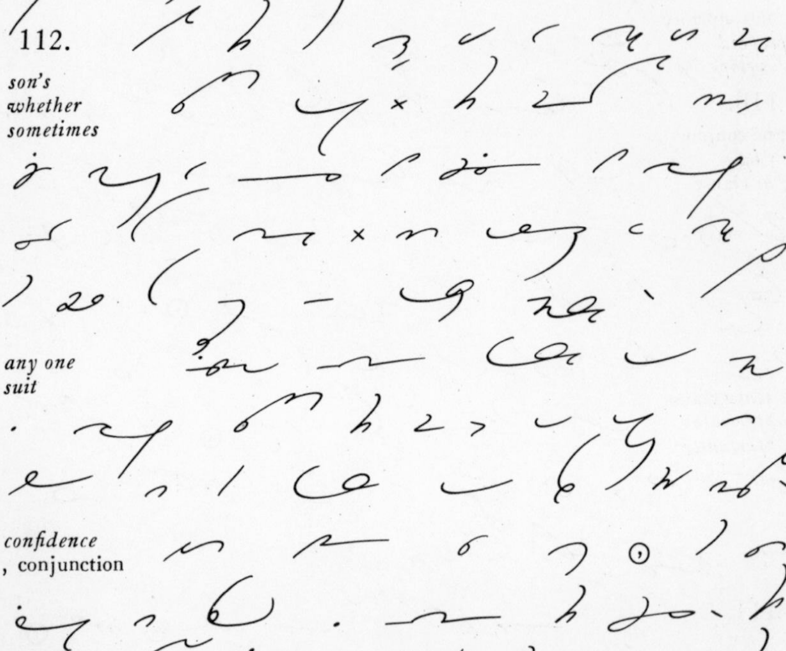

son's
whether
sometimes
any one
suit
confidence
, conjunction

113.

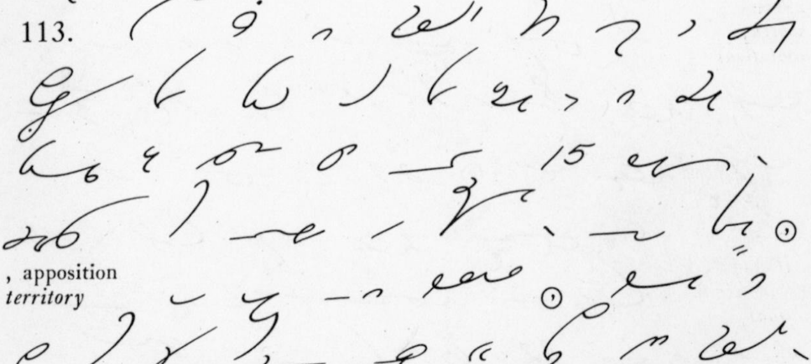

, apposition
territory

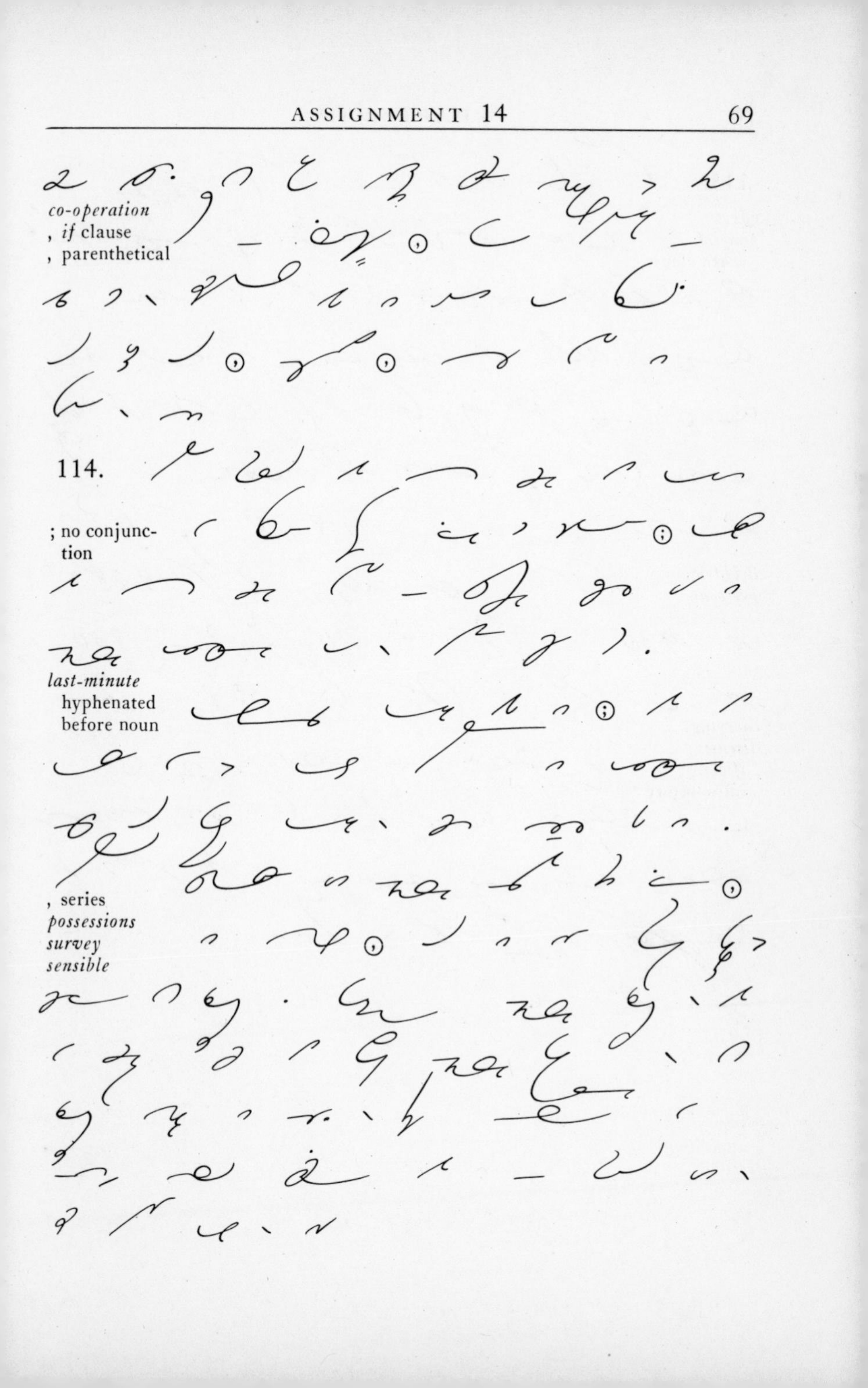

co-operation
, *if* clause
, parenthetical

114.

; no conjunction

last-minute
hyphenated before noun

, series
possessions
survey
sensible

115.

effect
policies
, *when* clause

dividend
per cent

carrying
discuss
, *if* clause
, introductory

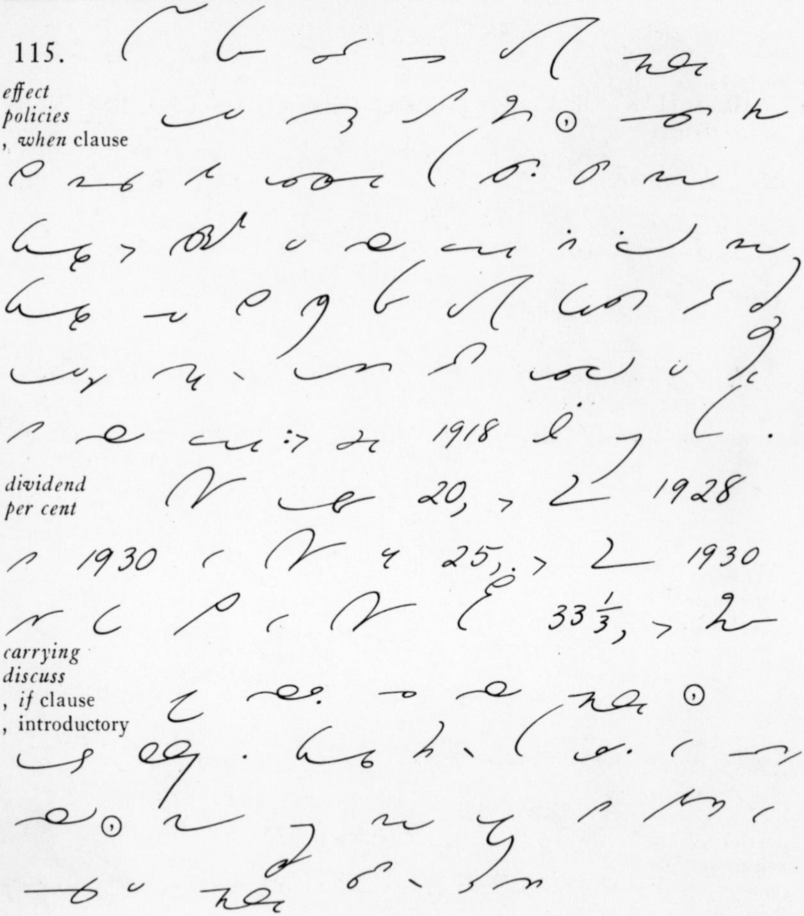

ASSIGNMENT 15

116. Chart of Word Beginnings and Word Endings

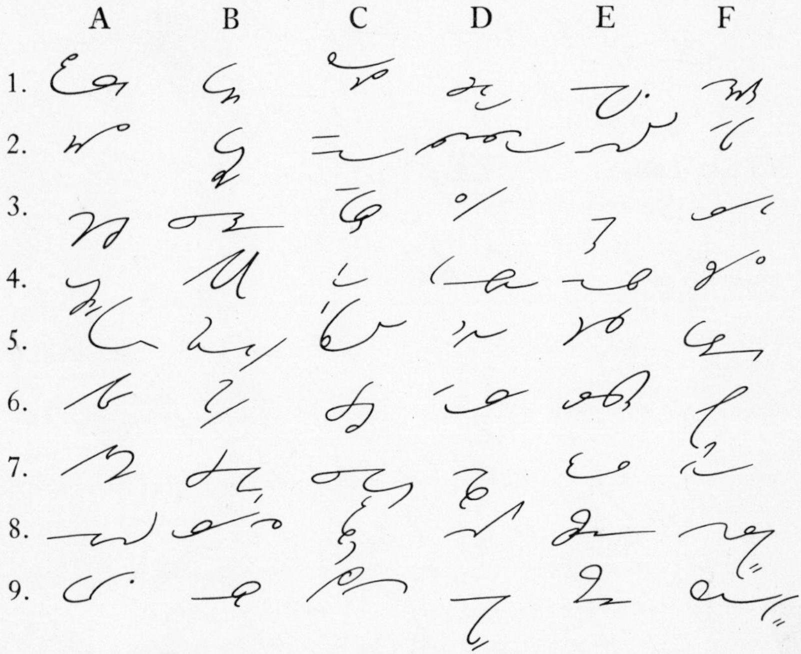

Reading and Writing Practice

117.

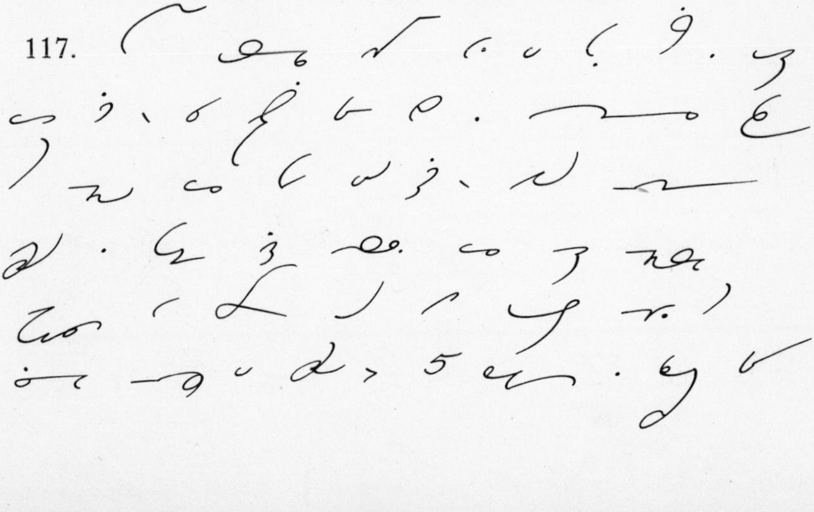

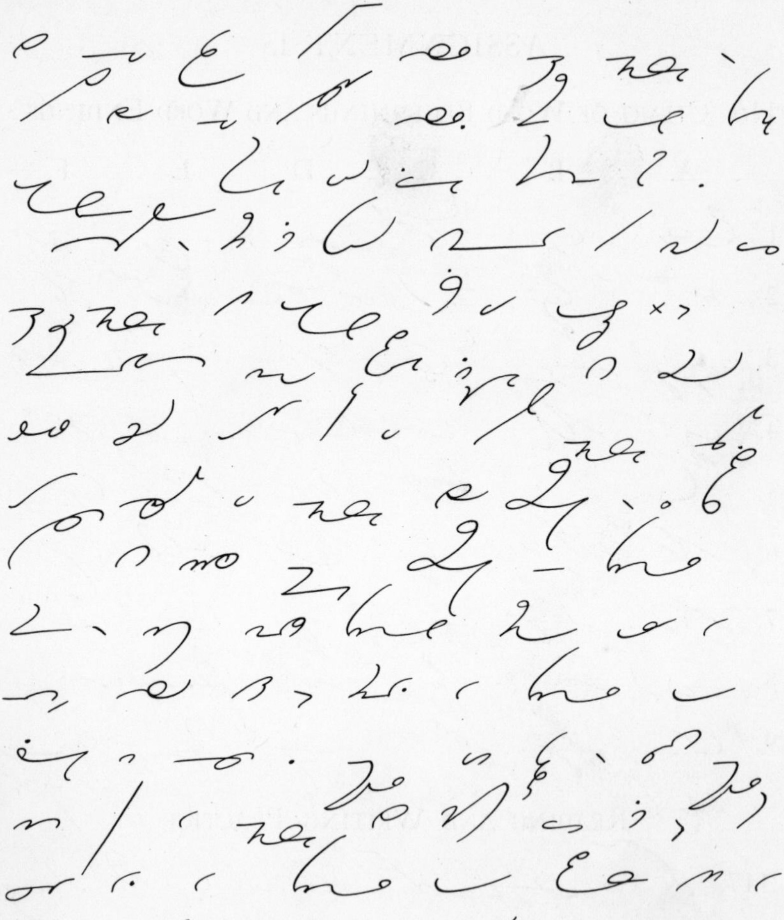

118.

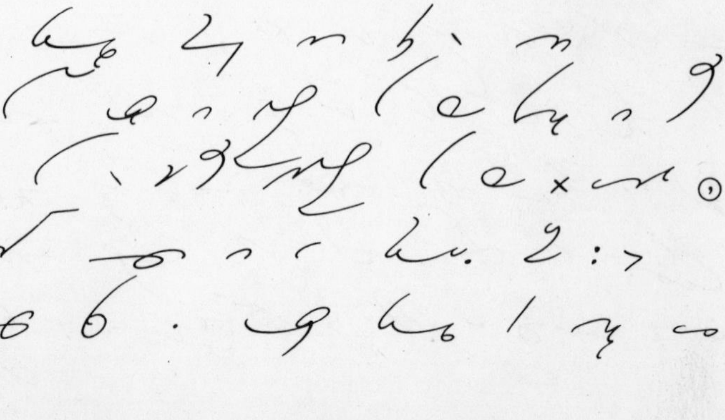

, conjunction

Transcribe:
$5
$5,000

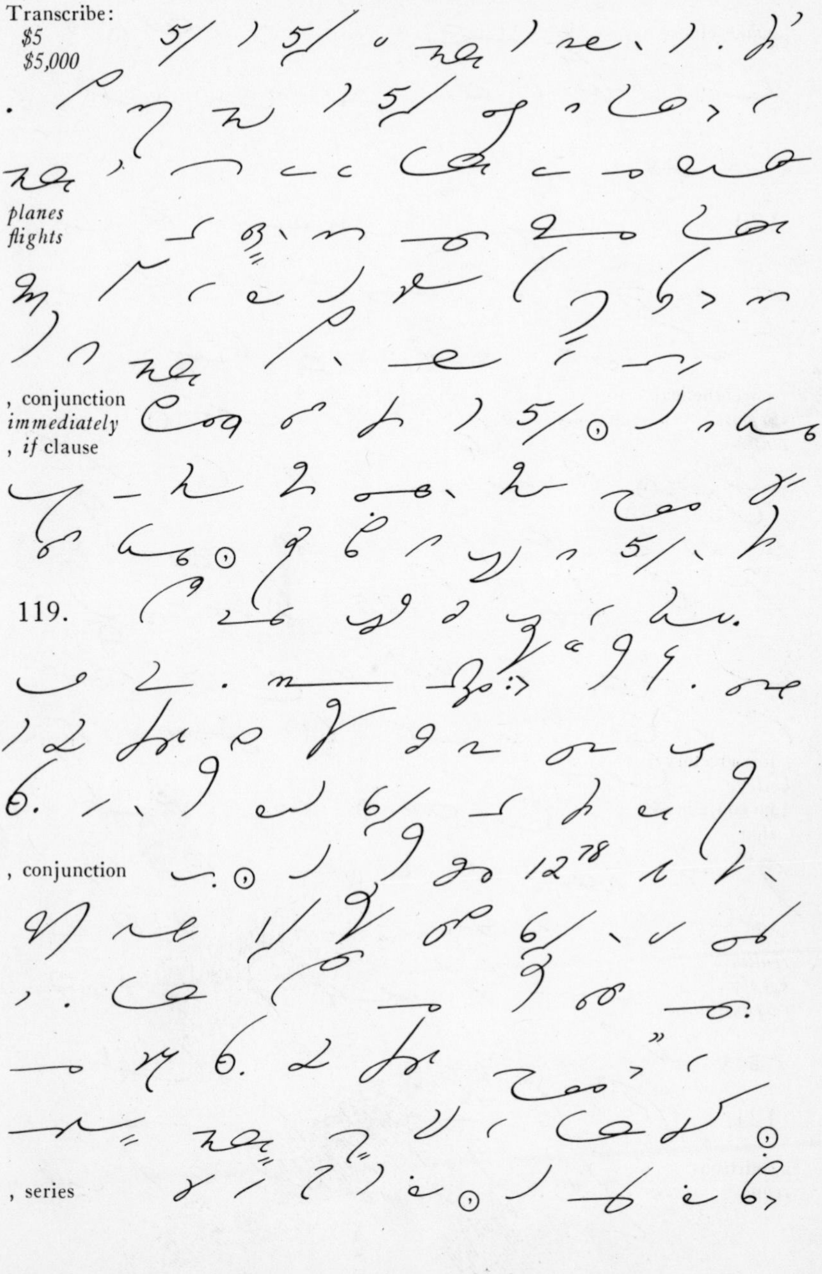

planes
flights

, conjunction
immediately
, *if* clause

119.

, conjunction

, series

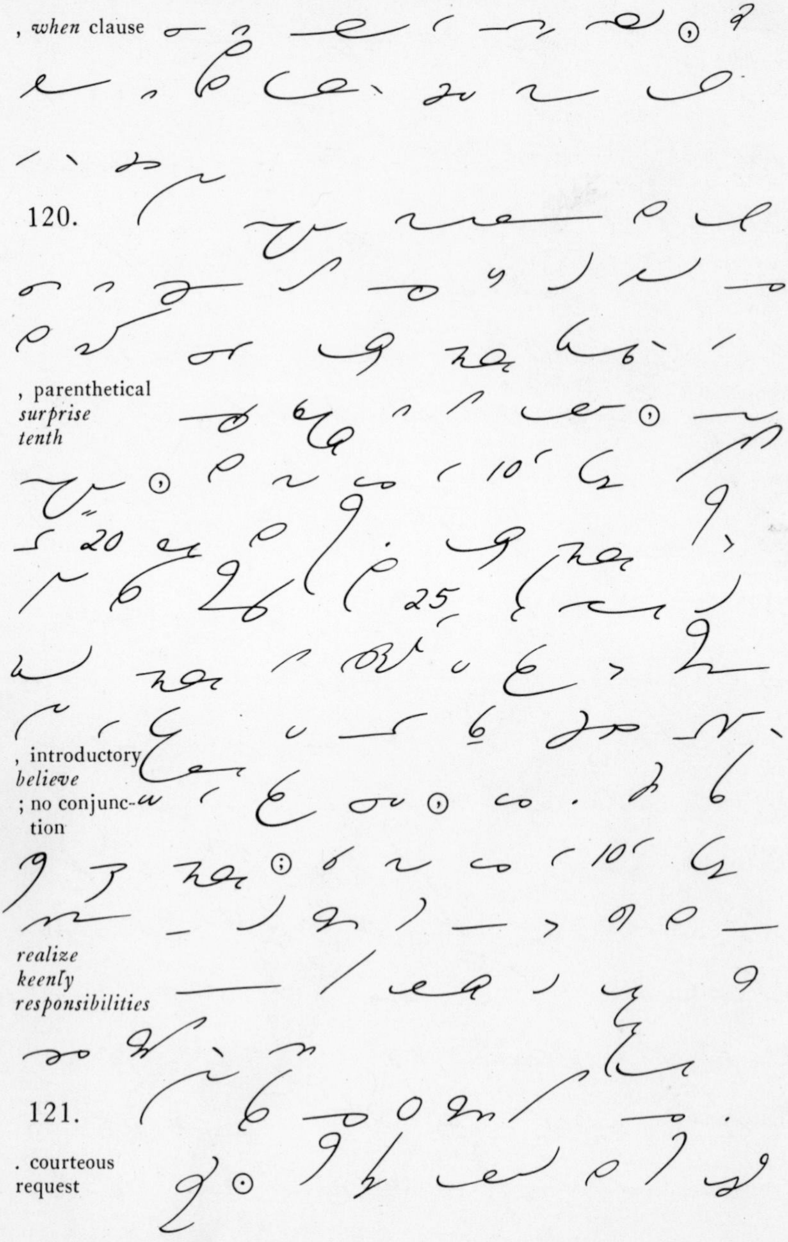

, *when* clause

120.

, parenthetical
surprise
tenth

, introductory
believe
; no conjunction

realize
keenly
responsibilities

121.

. courteous request

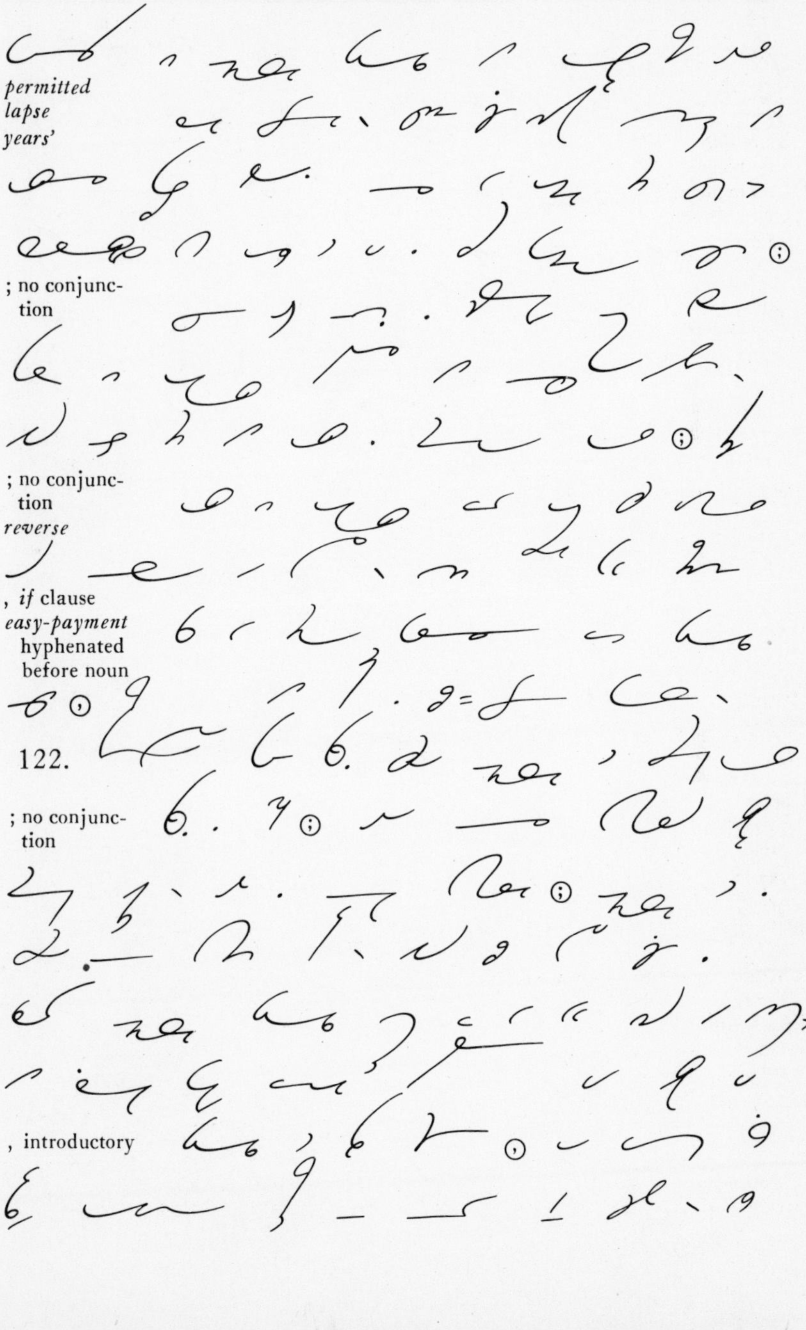

permitted
lapse
years'

; no conjunction

; no conjunction
reverse

, *if* clause
easy-payment hyphenated before noun

122.

; no conjunction

, introductory

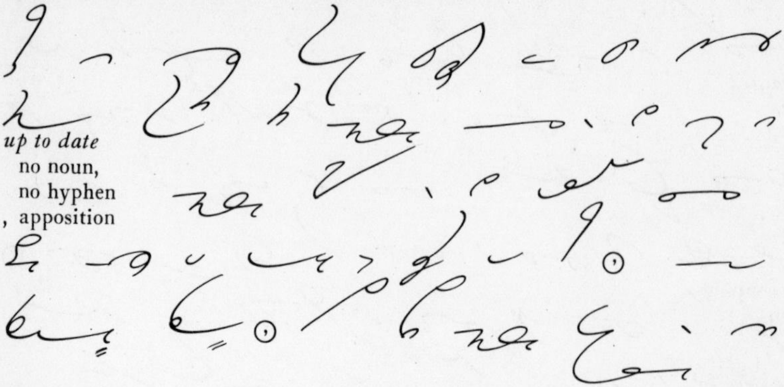

up to date
no noun,
no hyphen
, apposition

CHAPTER IV

ASSIGNMENT 16

123. Accuracy Practice

124. Vocabulary Builder

-THER

W

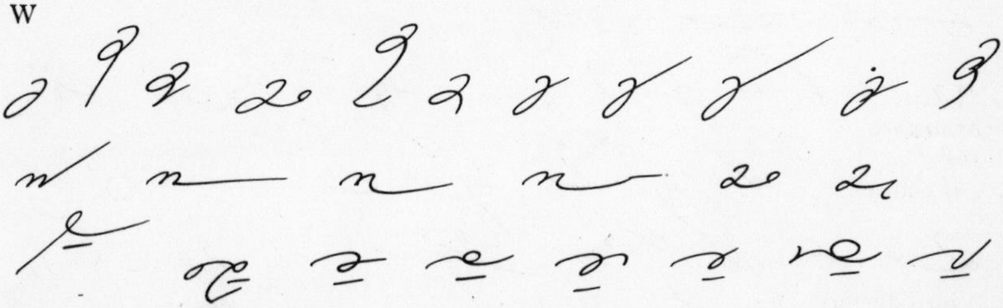

Reading and Writing Practice

125.
Dad
, *when* clause
, series
, parenthetical

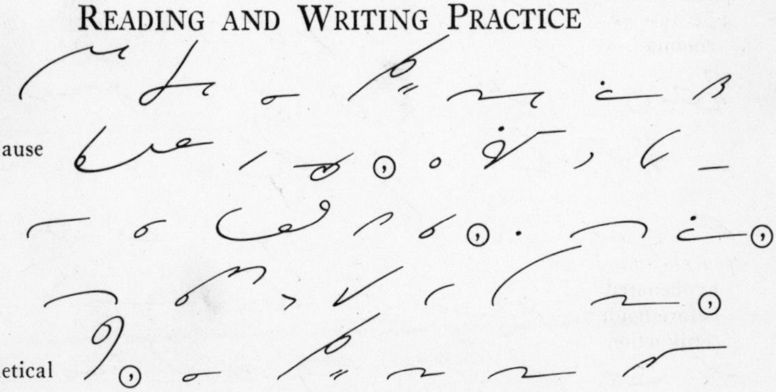

, introductory
hearts

forward
coupon
. courteous
request

126.
assurance
suffer
, *if* clause

, introductory
; because of
comma

peace-of-mind
hyphenated
before noun
, conjunction

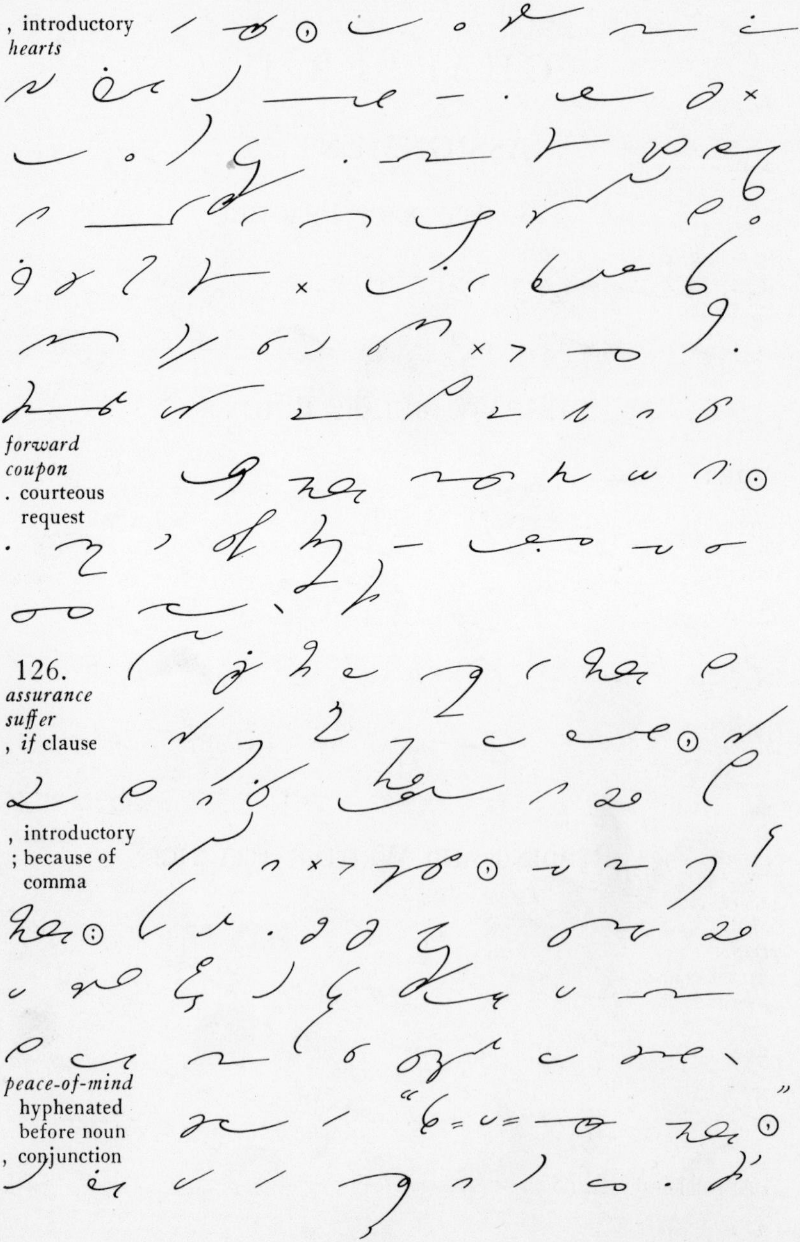

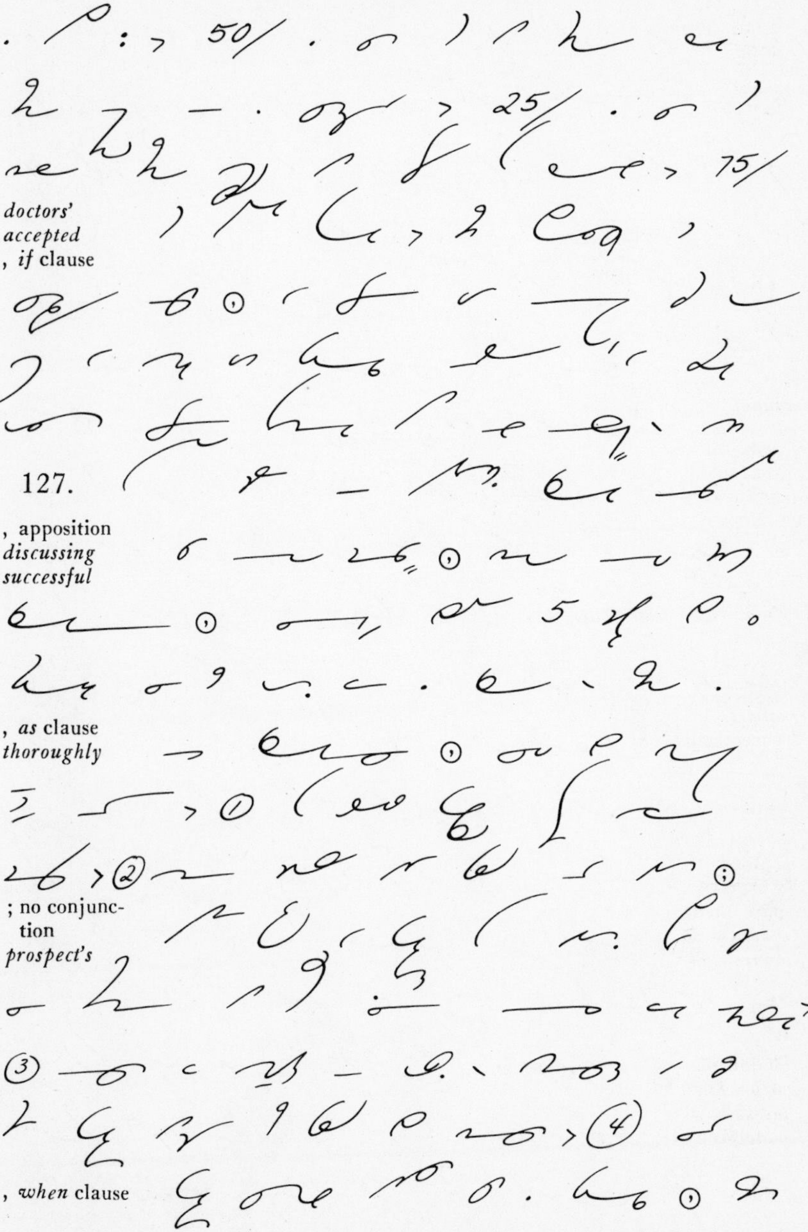

doctors'
accepted
, *if* clause

127.

, apposition
discussing
successful

, *as* clause
thoroughly

; no conjunction
prospect's

, *when* clause

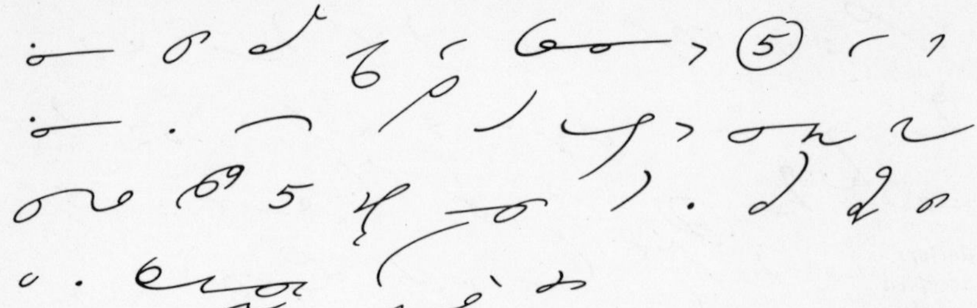

128.

annual
convention
, series

realizes
, parenthetical

, parenthetical
Governor
Connecticut

, conjunction
worth while
no noun,
no hyphen

129.

Wouldn't
comfort
receive

, conjunction
prepared

, introductory
fifty

adapted
. courteous
request

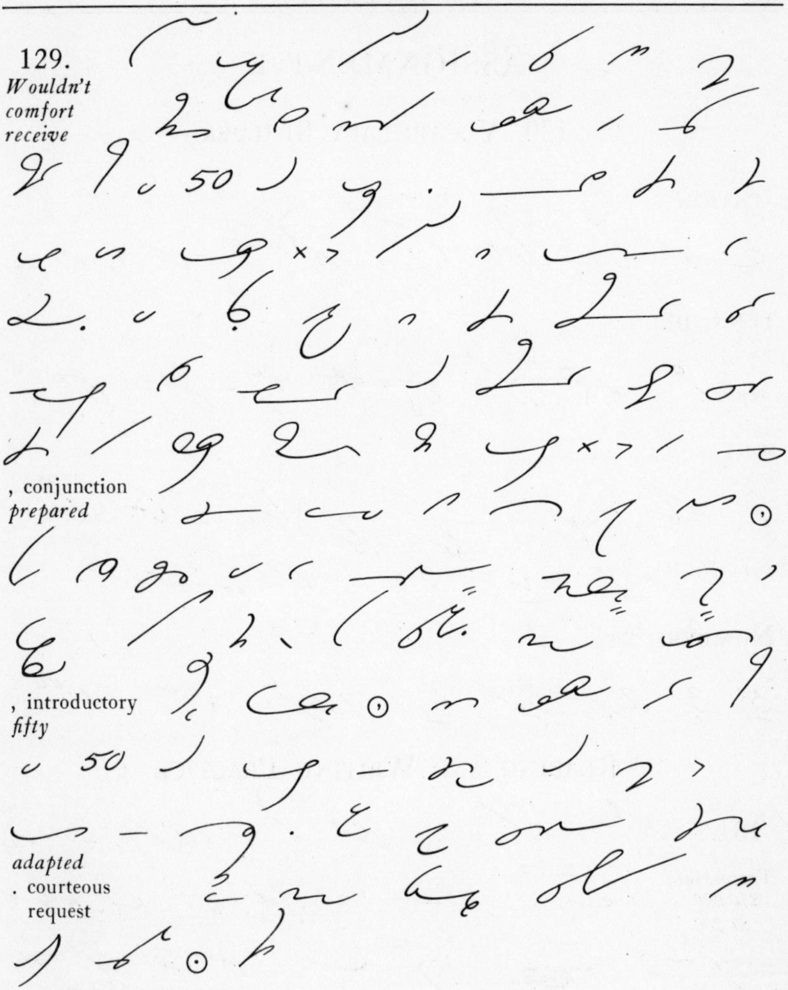

ASSIGNMENT 17

130. Vocabulary Builder

-TATION

TERN, DERN

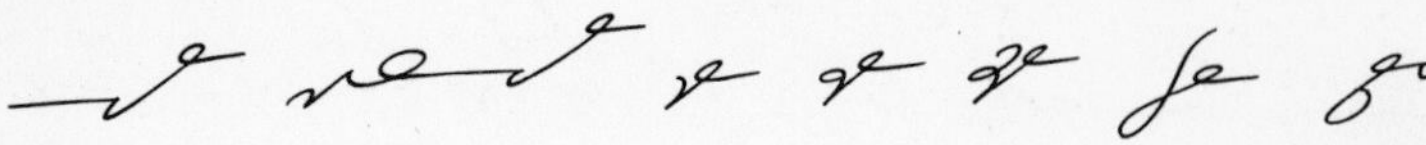

-ORT

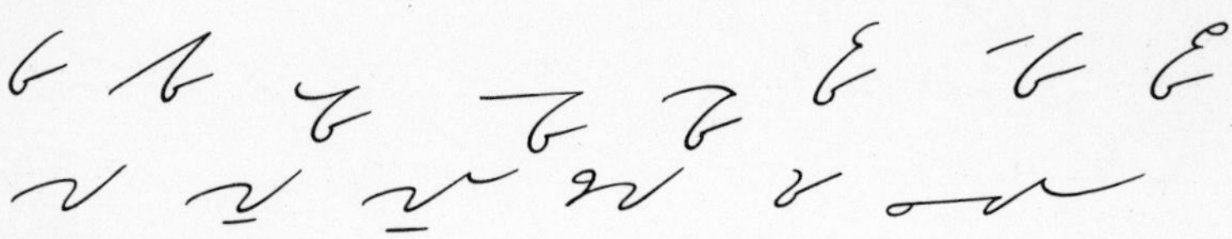

Numbers, etc.

Reading and Writing Practice

131.

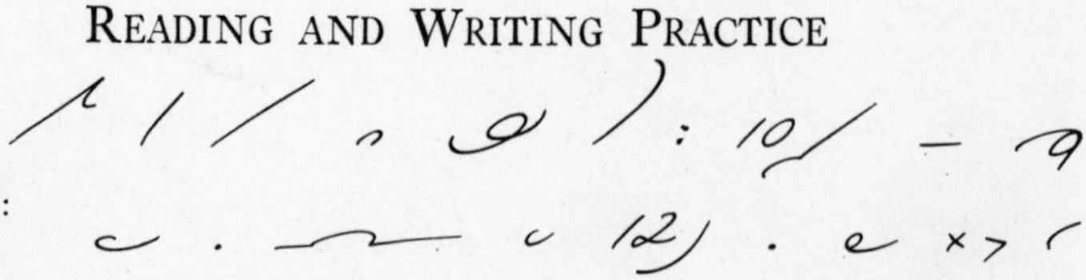

Transcribe:
$10,000
$1,200

company's
benefits
permanently

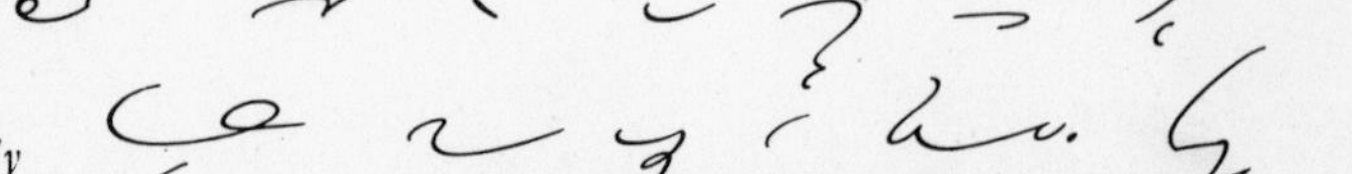

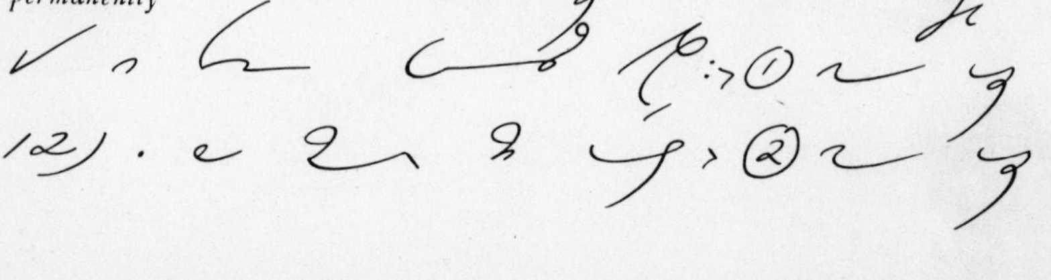

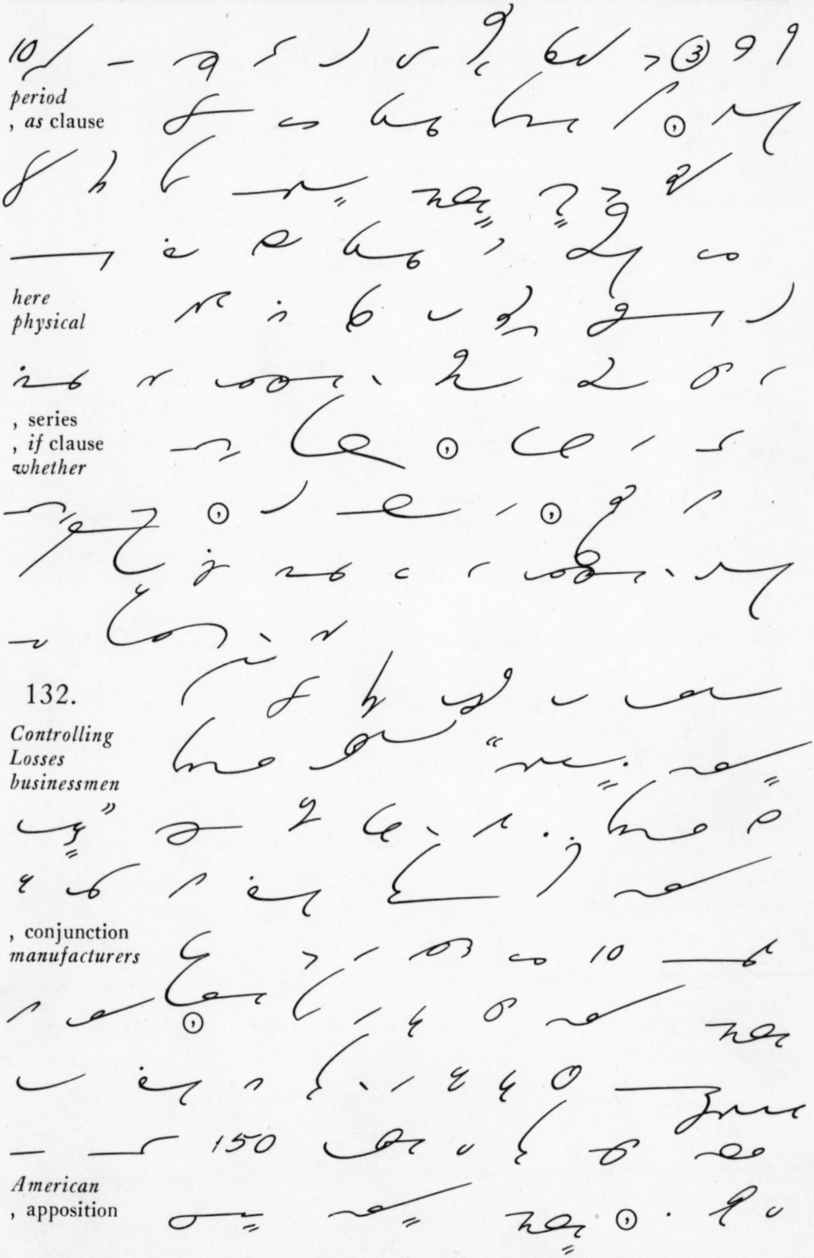

period
, *as* clause
here
physical
, series
, *if* clause
whether

132.

Controlling Losses
businessmen
, conjunction
manufacturers
American
, apposition

, *if* clause
Write
today

133.
; no conjunction
freedom

accumulated
, series

well-paying
hyphenated
before noun

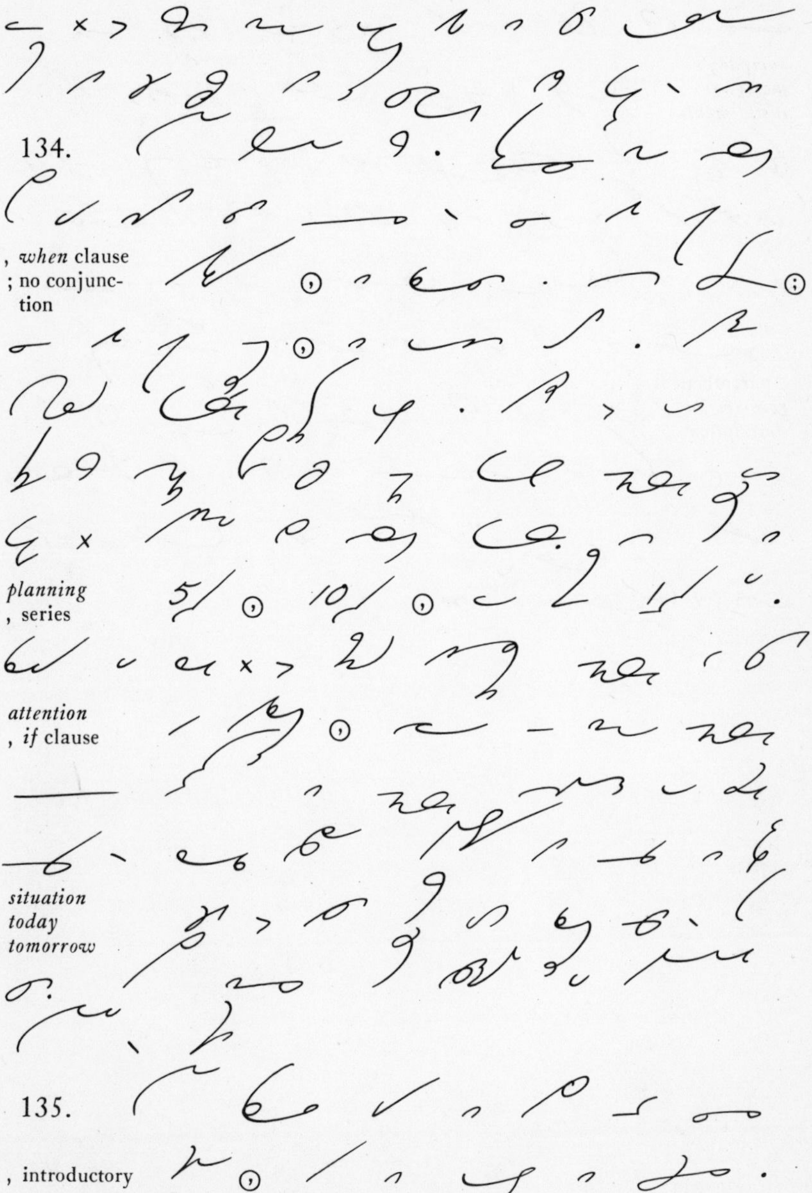

134.

, *when* clause
; no conjunction

planning
, series

attention
, *if* clause

situation
today
tomorrow

135.

, introductory

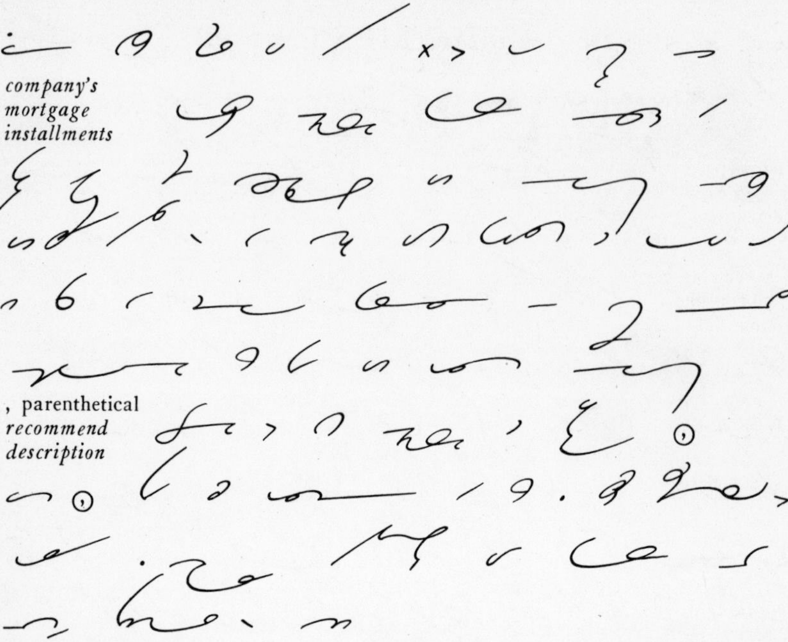

company's
mortgage
installments

, parenthetical
recommend
description

ASSIGNMENT 18

136. Most-Used Business-Letter Phrases

FROM

HAS

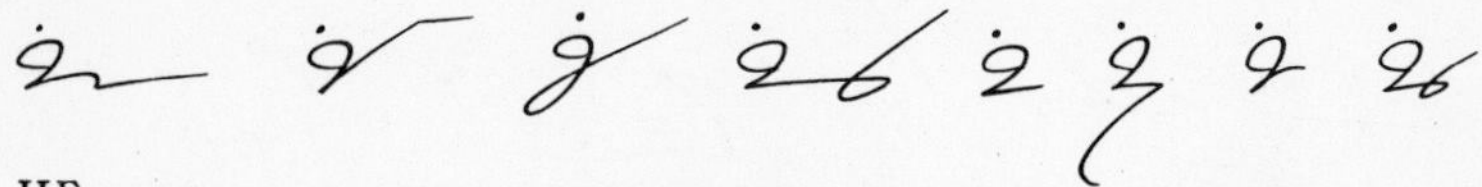

HE

I

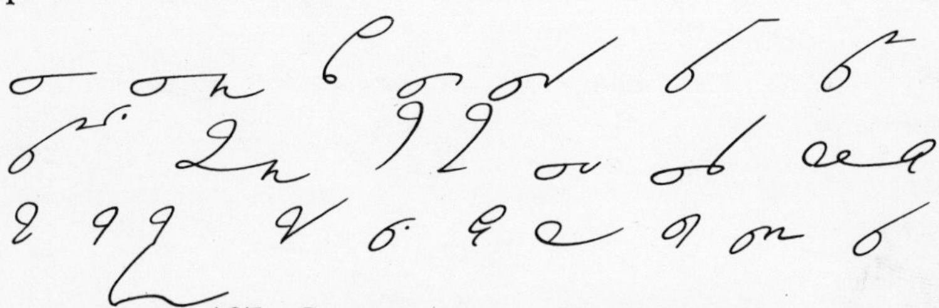

137. Geographical Expressions

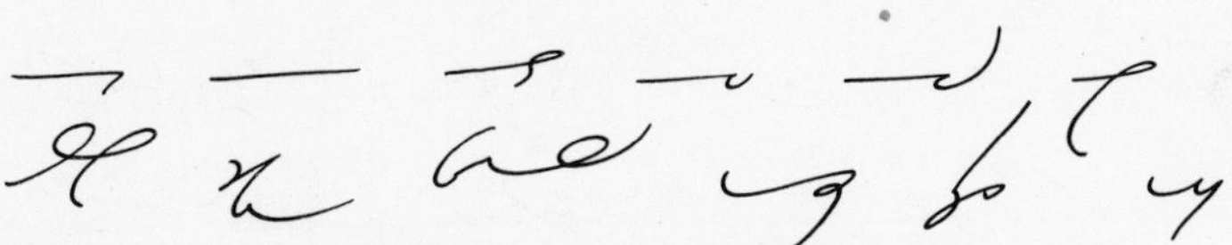

Reading and Writing Practice

138.

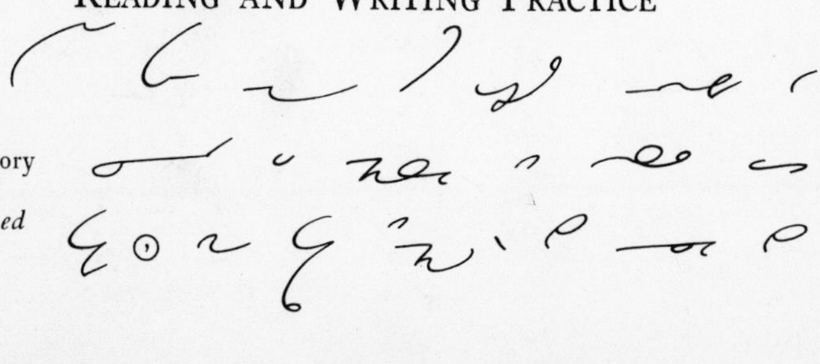

, introductory
recently
underinsured

past
, *if* clause

determining
today's
sincerely

139.

Transcribe:
April 5
cancel

, conjunction
family's
welfare

, *if* clause
, apposition
suggestion

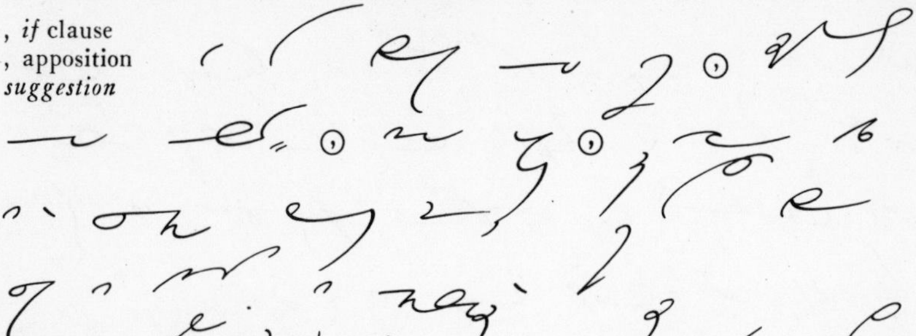

140.

abbreviated
annual
concise

Supplementing
, introductory
occasionally

; no conjunction
supplementary

141.

, *as* clause
; no conjunction

, *if* clause

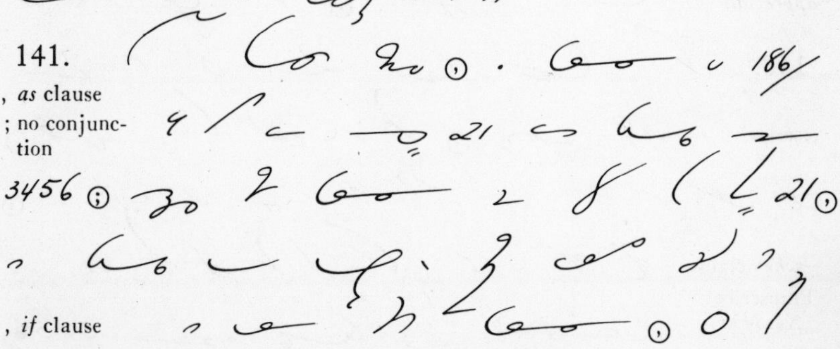

142.

, parenthetical
emergencies

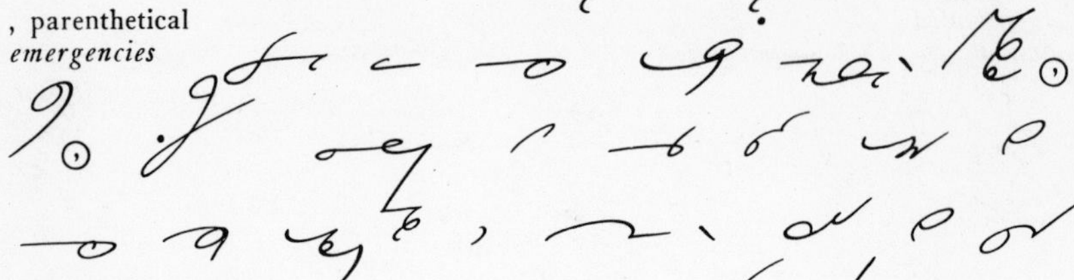

, conjunction
, parenthetical
thirty-day
hyphenated
before noun

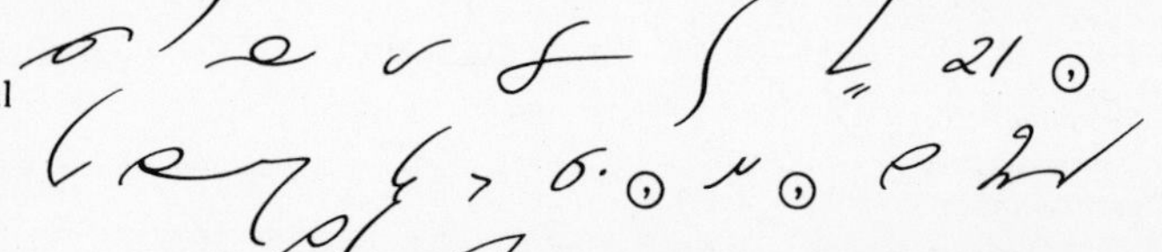

, *if* clause
appreciate

143.

, series

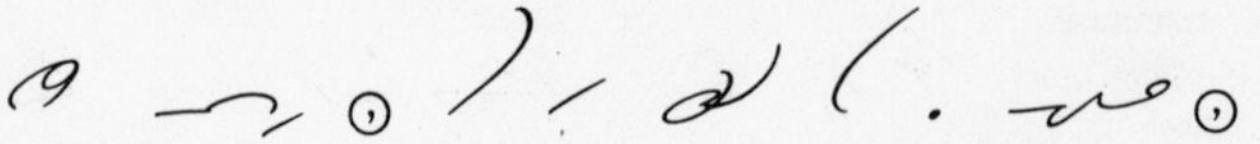

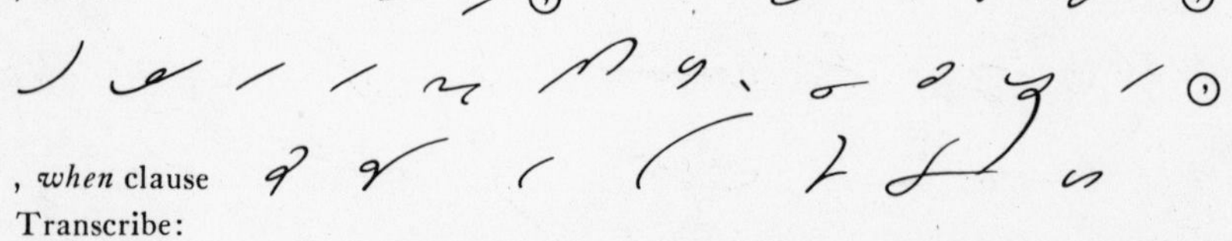

, *when* clause

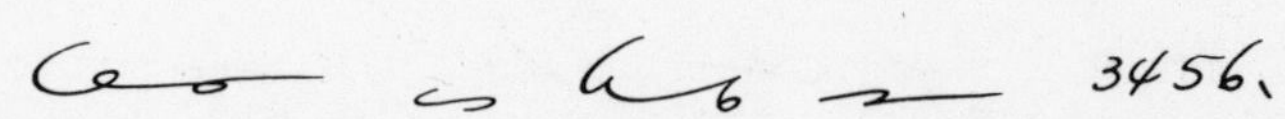

Transcribe:
No. 3456

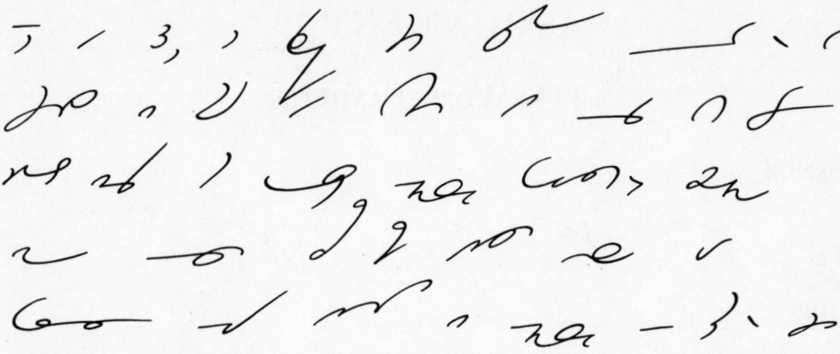

ASSIGNMENT 19

144. Word Families

-TANCE

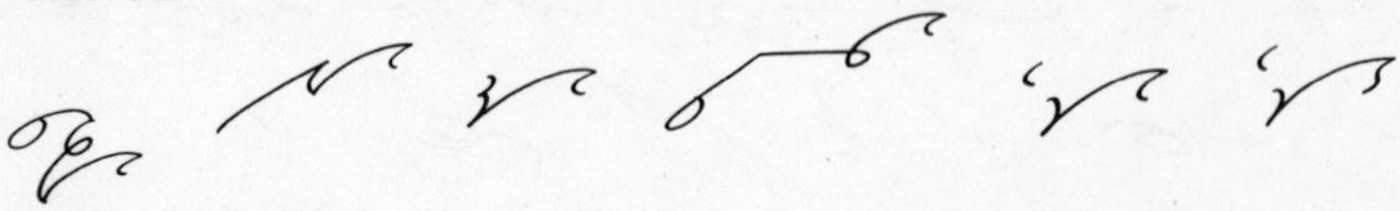

-SIDE

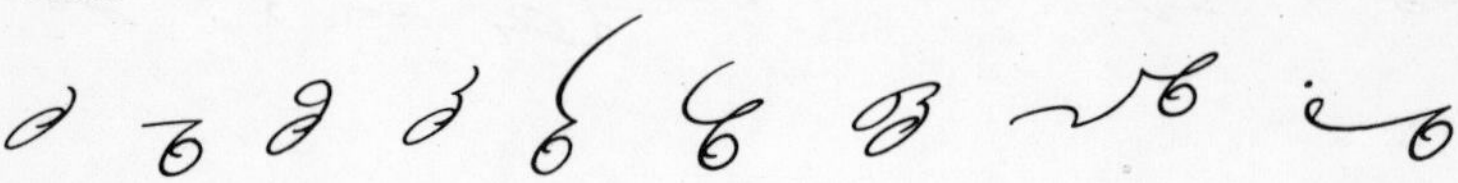

-TAKE

-PLE

UN- FOLLOWED BY VOWEL

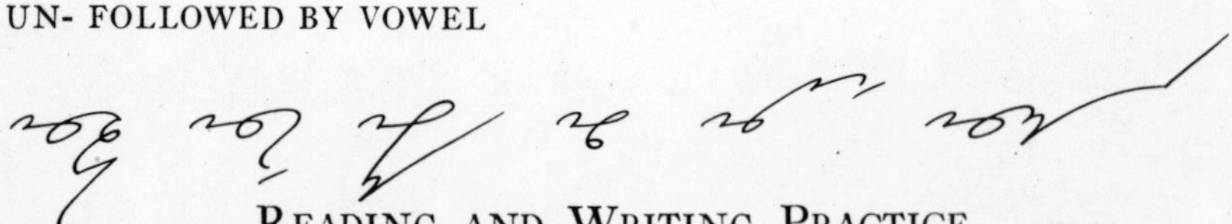

Reading and Writing Practice

145.

, parenthetical
enclosing
believe
Brown's

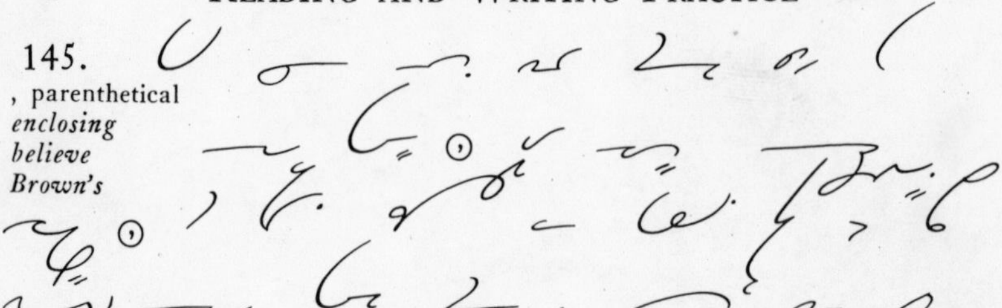

146.

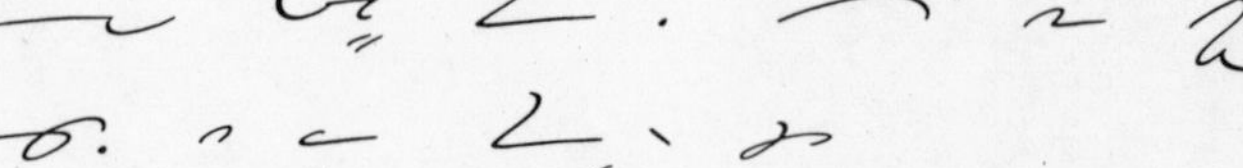

, parenthetical
skilled

management
entrust
Cordially

147.

, introductory
firm's

, parenthetical
result
, conjunction
fifty

20

50

, apposition
; because of
comma

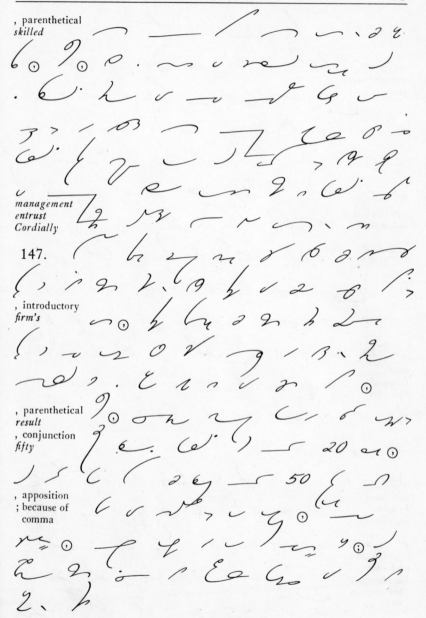

148.

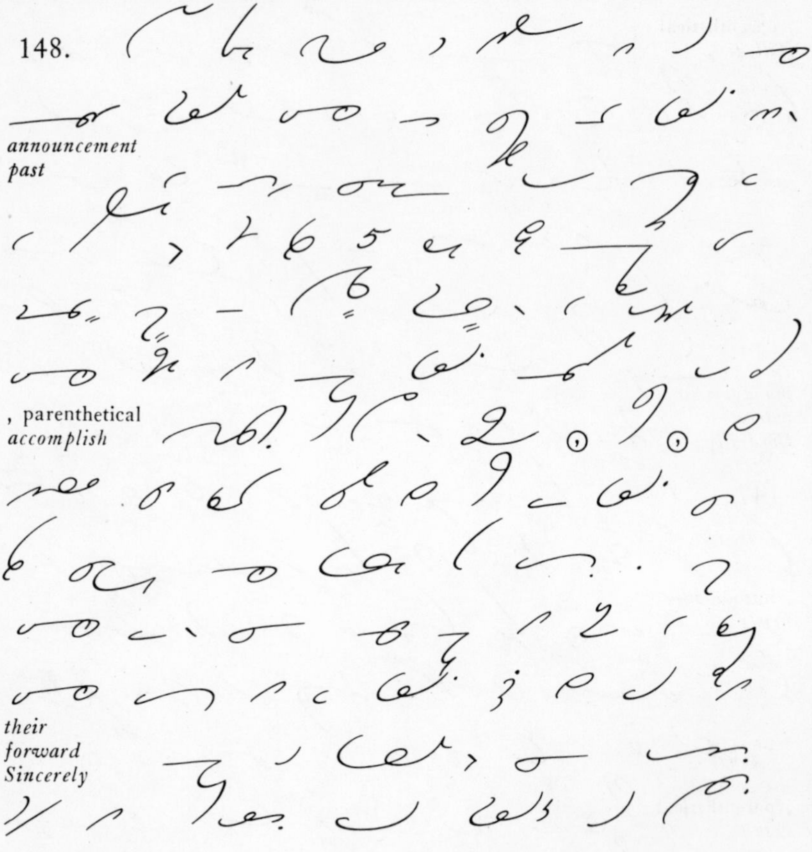

announcement
past

, parenthetical
accomplish

their
forward
Sincerely

149.

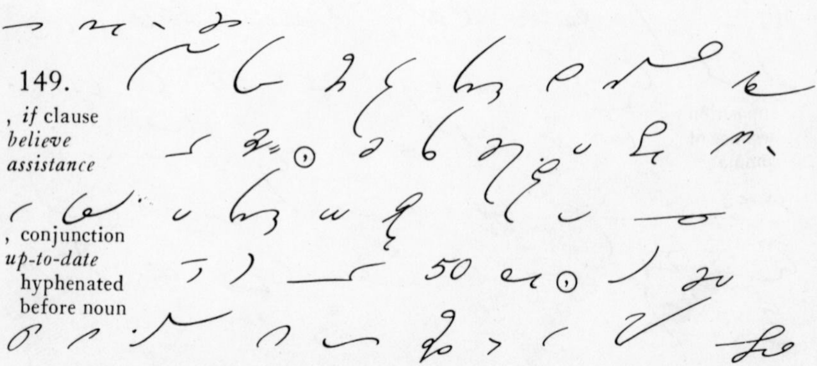

, *if* clause
believe
assistance

, conjunction
up-to-date
hyphenated
before noun

volume
experience

, series
. courteous
request

150.

everyone
equipped
appeal

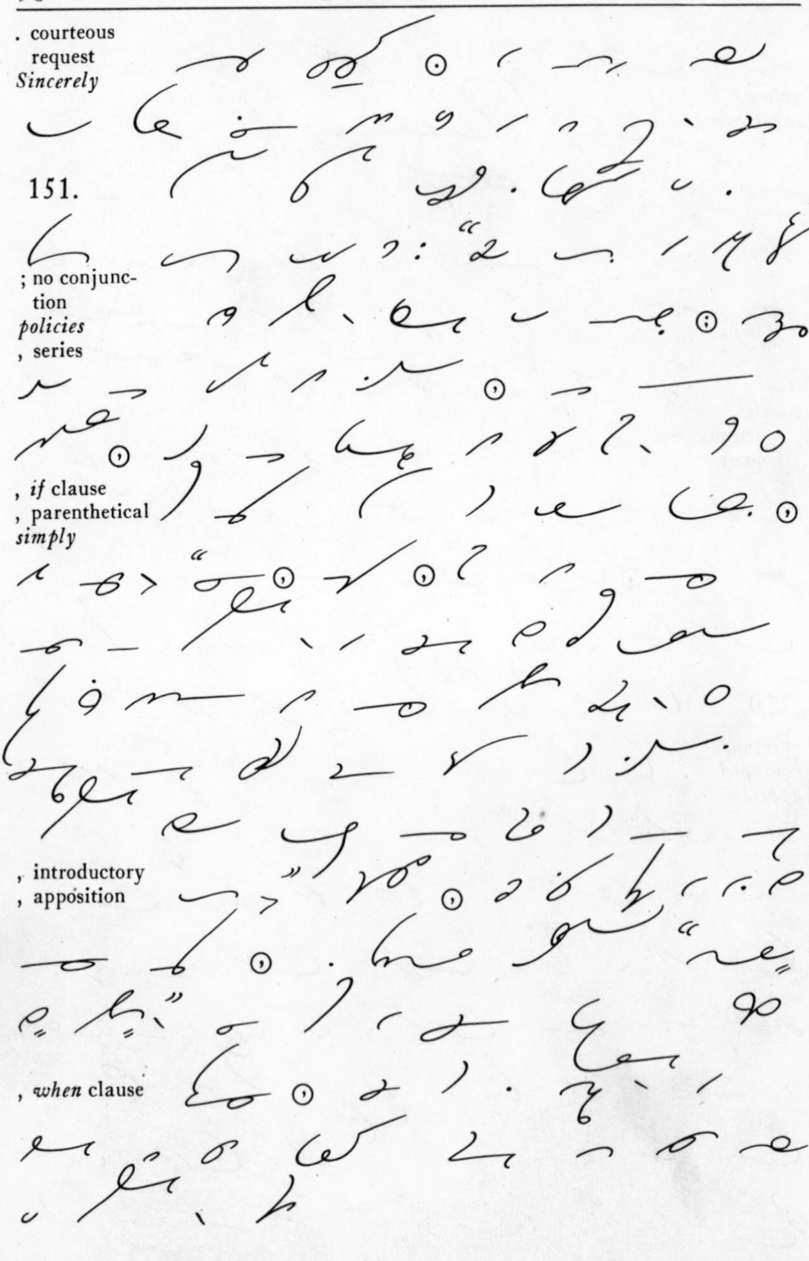

. courteous request
Sincerely

151.

; no conjunction
policies
, series

, *if* clause
, parenthetical
simply

, introductory
, apposition

, *when* clause

ASSIGNMENT 20

152. Vocabulary Builder

NT

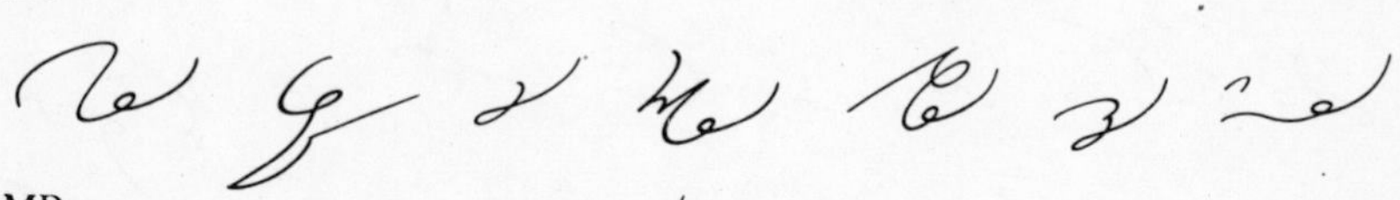

MD

GENT, PEND

TIVE, DEF

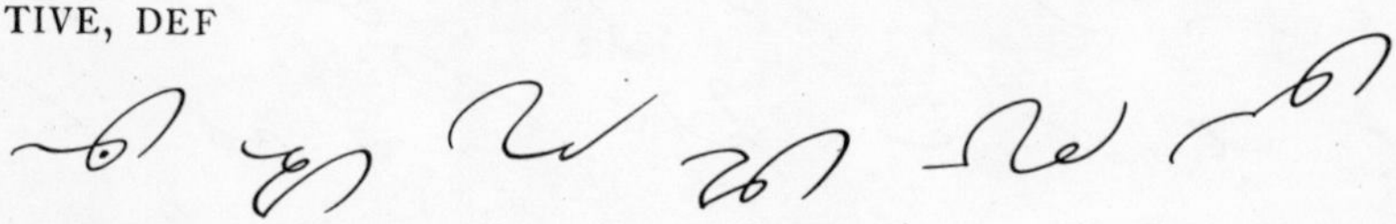

TEN, DEN

TEM, DEM

Reading and Writing Practice

153.

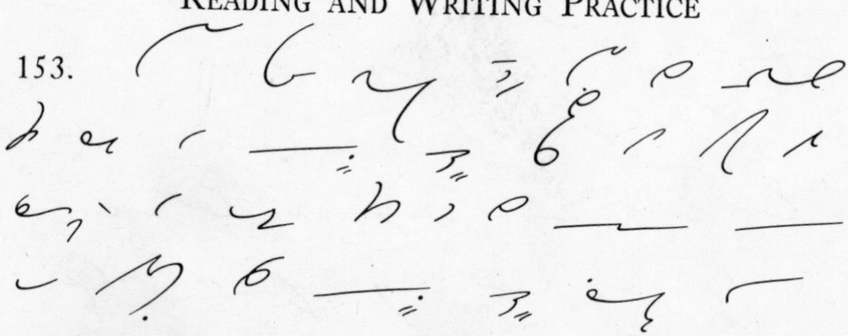

154.

, introductory
possible

, introductory
; no conjunction

high-quality
hyphenated before noun

agencies
workmanship
, series

appreciate
whether
, *if* clause

155.
; no conjunction
, parenthetical

Forty
different

, series
twenty-five
here

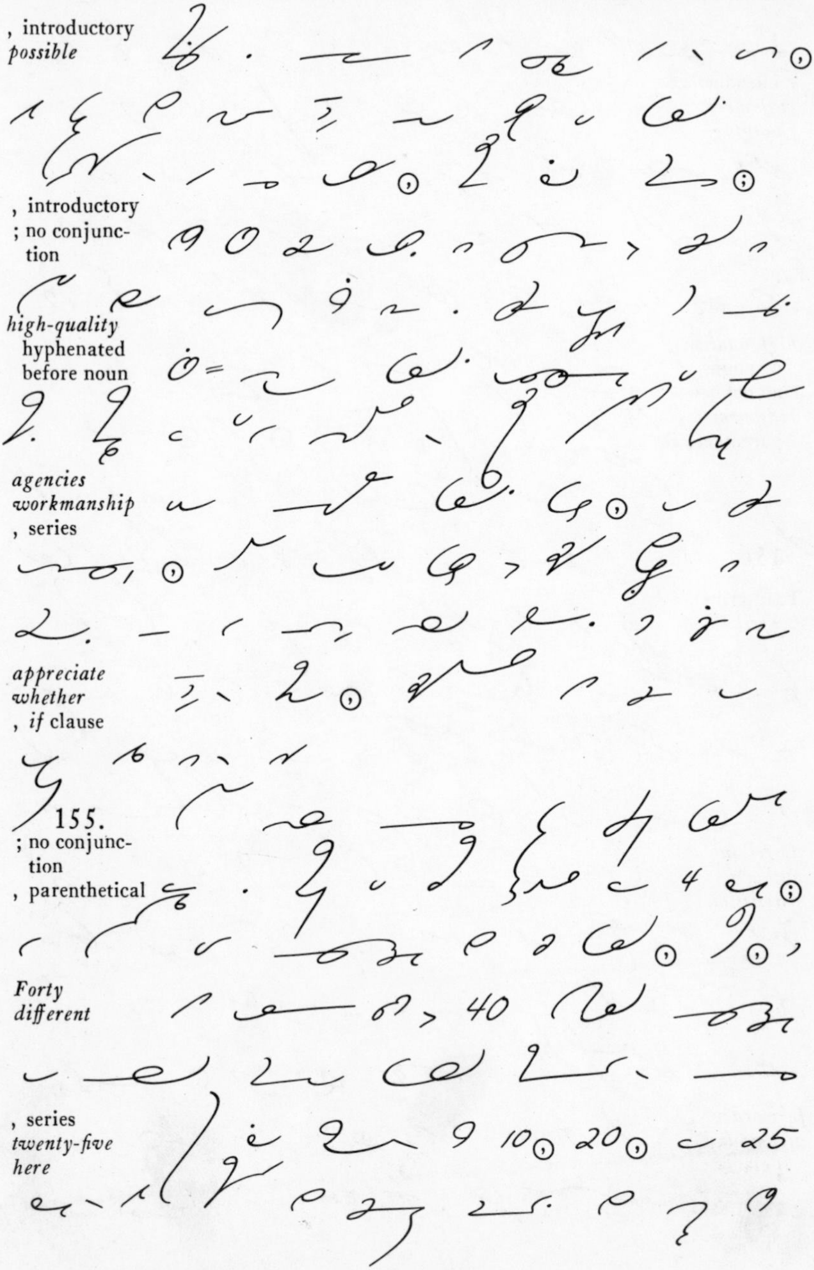

, introductory
customers'
changing

high quality
no noun,
no hyphen
judgment
, parenthetical

156.

Transcribe:
April 18.

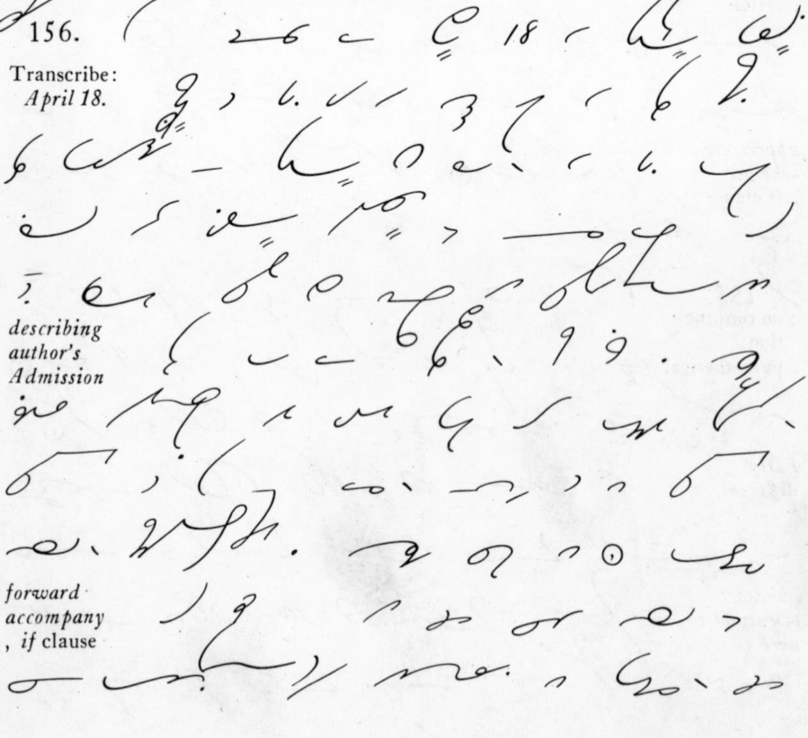

describing
author's
Admission

forward
accompany
, *if* clause

157.

, apposition
Chicago

, *if* clause
co-operation

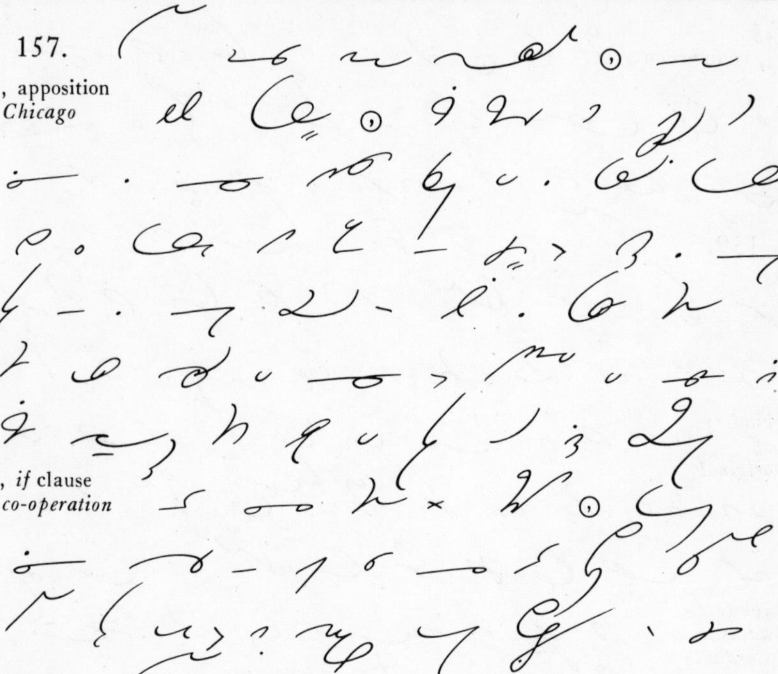

158.

concern
situation
, introductory

fifty
; no conjunction

off
, conjunction

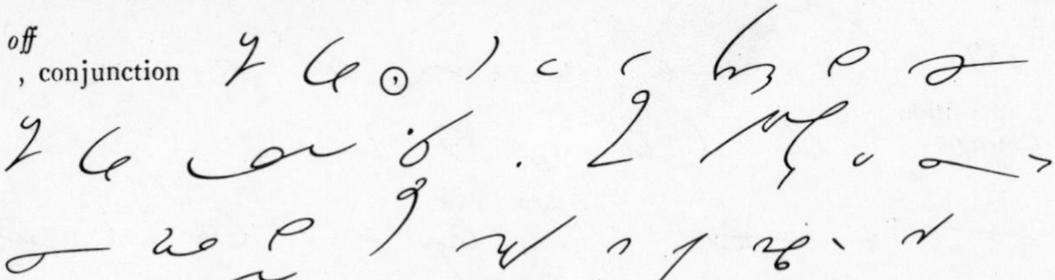

159.

bindery
off
original

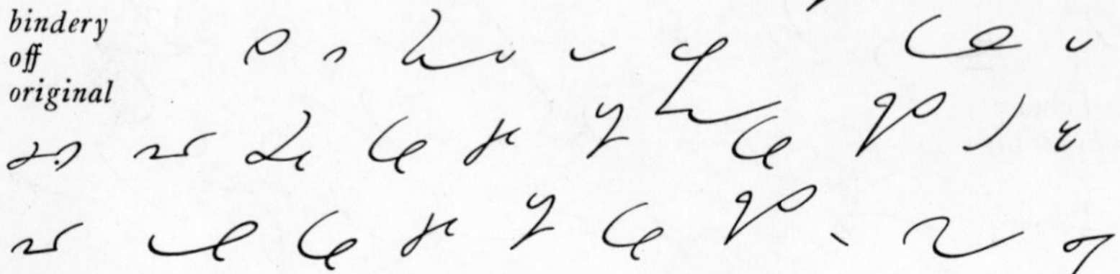

color
adjustment
Cordially

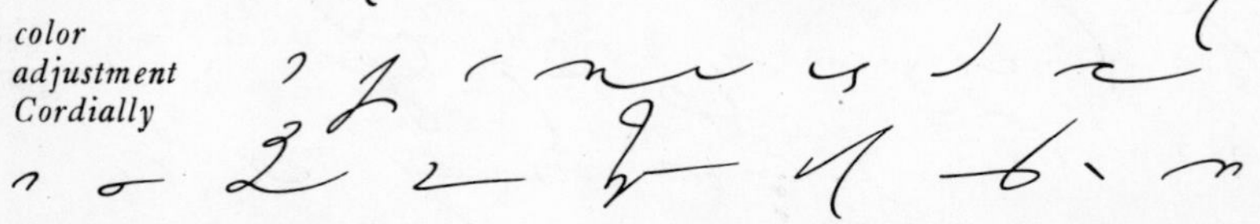

CHAPTER V

ASSIGNMENT 21

160. Brief-Form Chart

A B C D E F

1. 2. 3. 4. 5. 6. 7. 8. 9.

Reading and Writing Practice

161.

Society
year's
, introductory

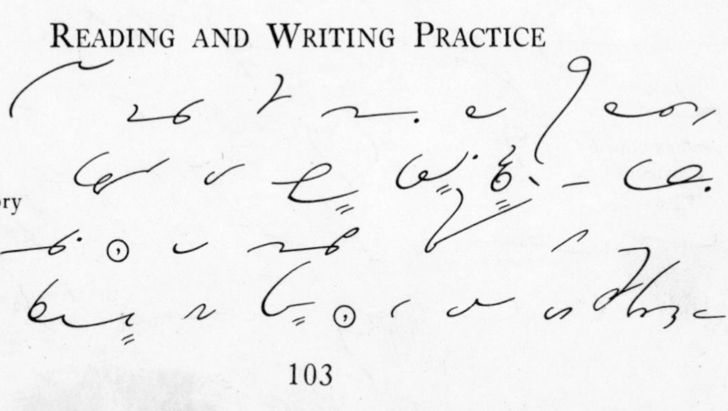

, apposition
principal

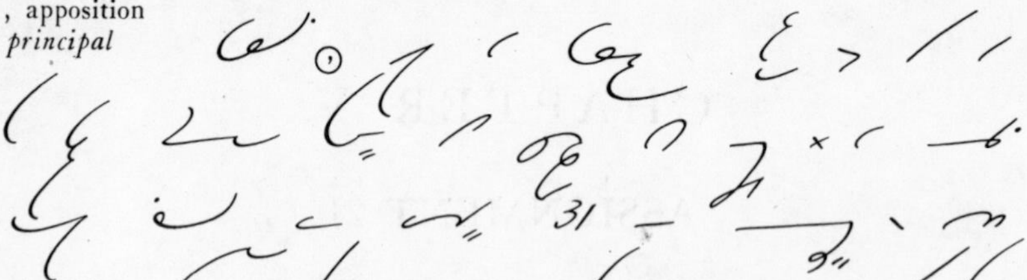

162.

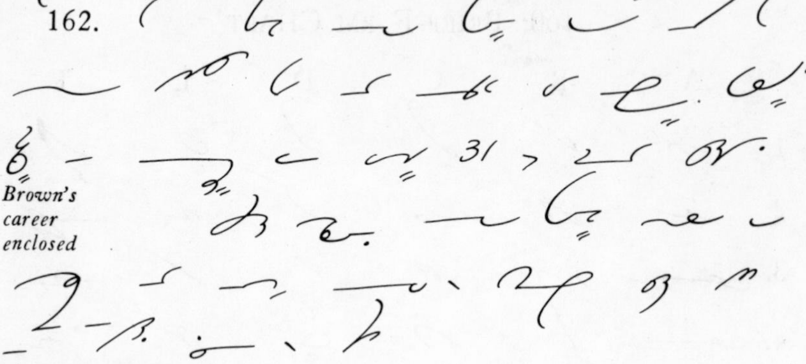

Brown's
career
enclosed

163.

Philadelphia
, parenthetical

, *when* clause
. courteous
request

164.

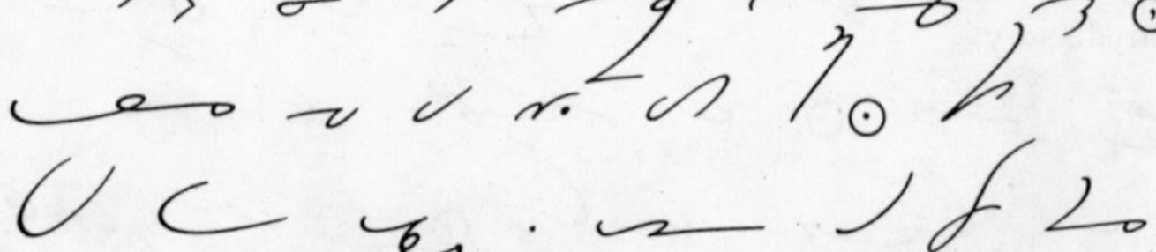

, series
, introductory

annual

165.
overlooking
, introductory
, series

comfortable
Transcribe:
$4

166.

, conjunction

, introductory
past
; no conjunction

167.

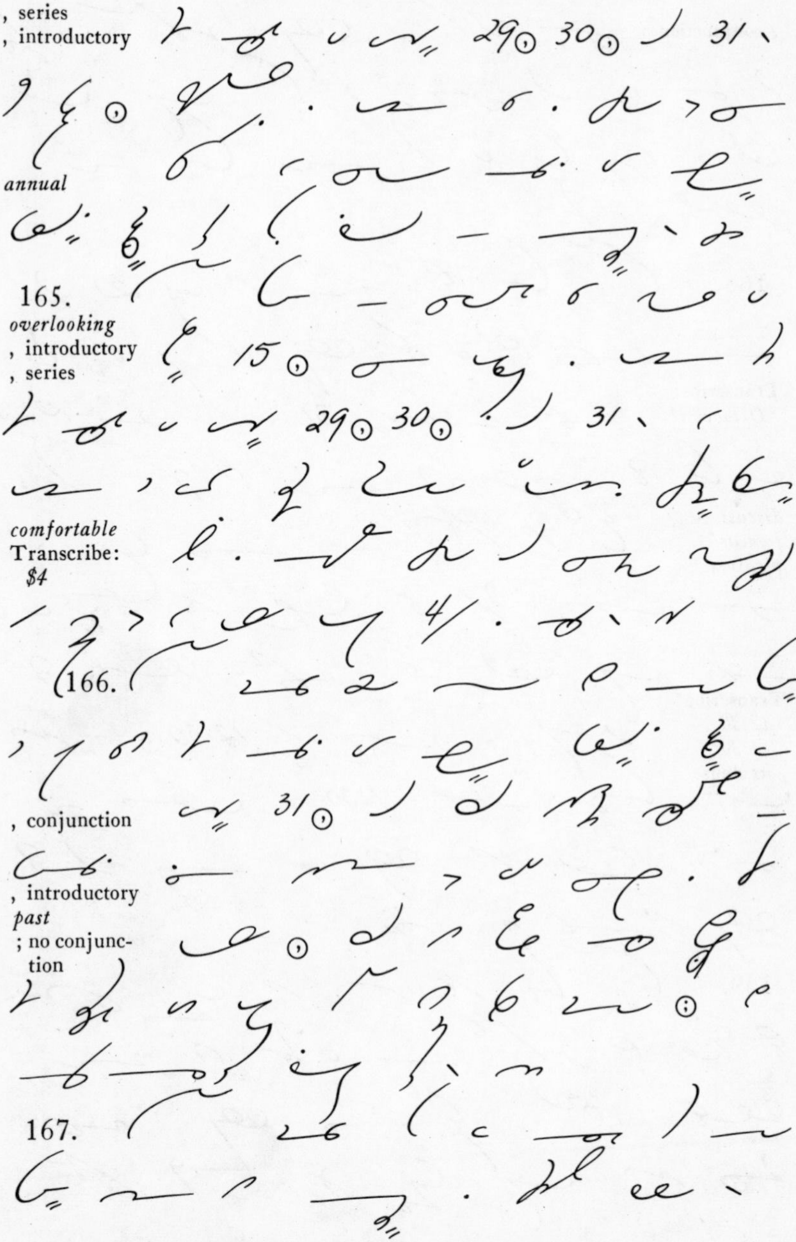

, conjunction

168.

Transcribe:
October 31

discuss
forward
pleasure

Transcribe:
12:30
1:30
, *as* clause

169.

contrary
, *if* clause
forty-five-minute
hyphenated before noun
, conjunction
indications

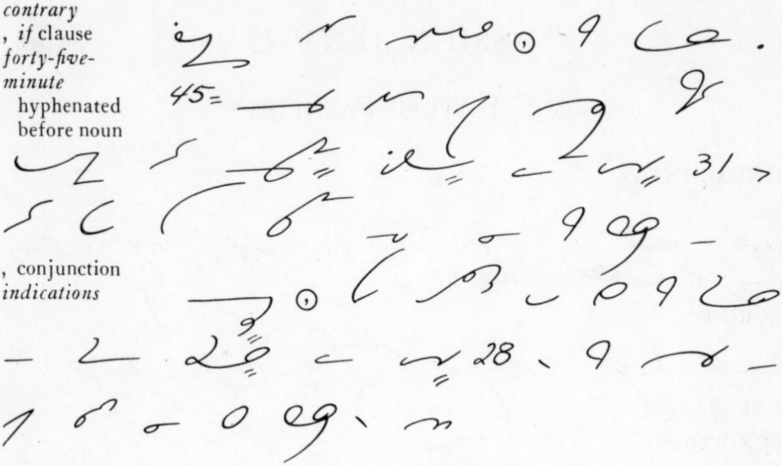

ASSIGNMENT 22

170. Word Families

UNEX-, INEX-

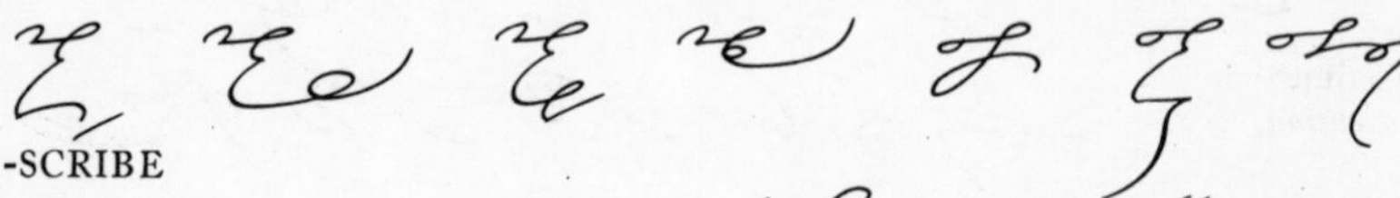

-SCRIBE

-SCRIPTION

-ANCE

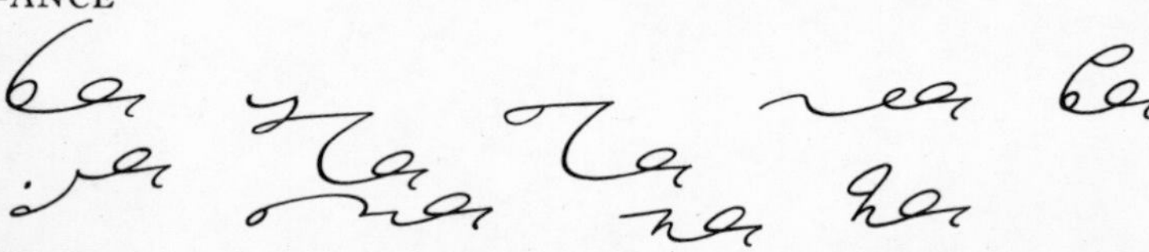

Reading and Writing Practice

171.

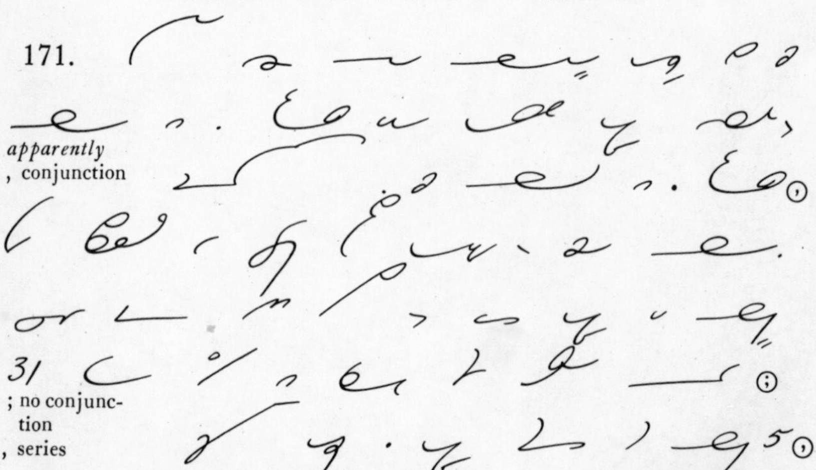

apparently
, conjunction

31

; no conjunction

, series

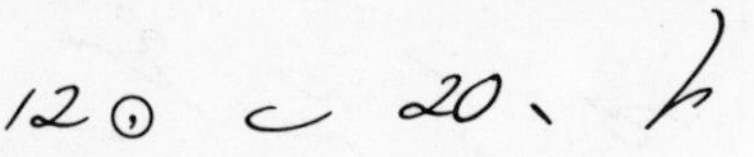

172.

accept
compliments
up-to-the-minute
hyphenated before noun

underneath
pleasure

173.

, conjunction
reminder
missed

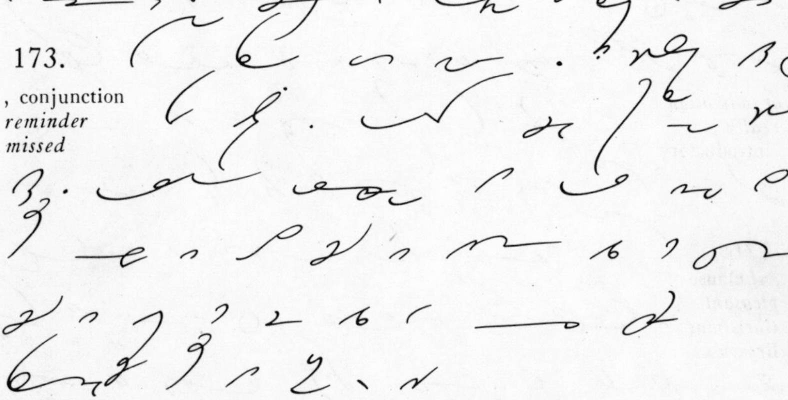

174.

apparent
wouldn't
, *if* clause

, conjunction

, *if* clause
won't
. courteous request

175.

customers'
, parenthetical

organization
really
, introductory

176.

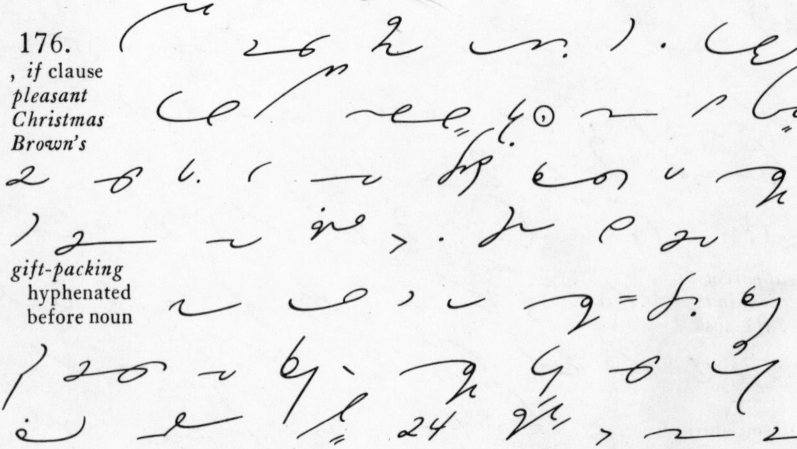

, *if* clause
pleasant
Christmas
Brown's

gift-packing hyphenated before noun

177.

season
happiest
thoughts

, parenthetical
sincere

178.
, conjunction
, introductory
; because of
commas

, apposition

179.

Chicago
annual

fascinating
, *if* clause

, series
Simply

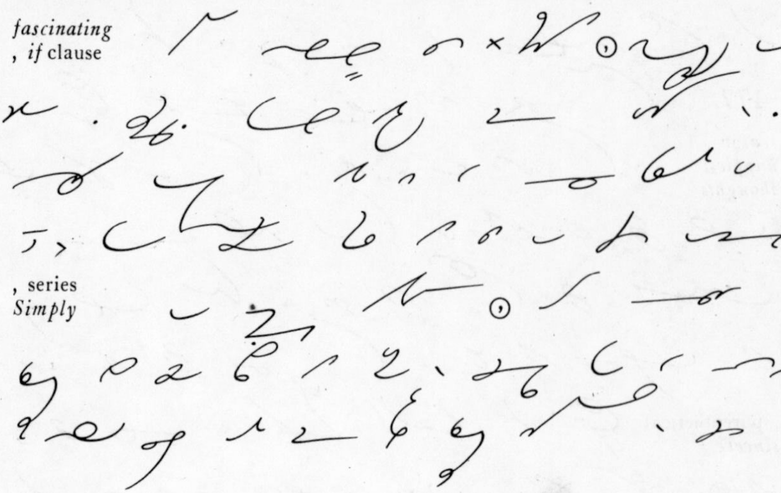

ASSIGNMENT 23

180. Most-Used Business-Letter Phrases

IF

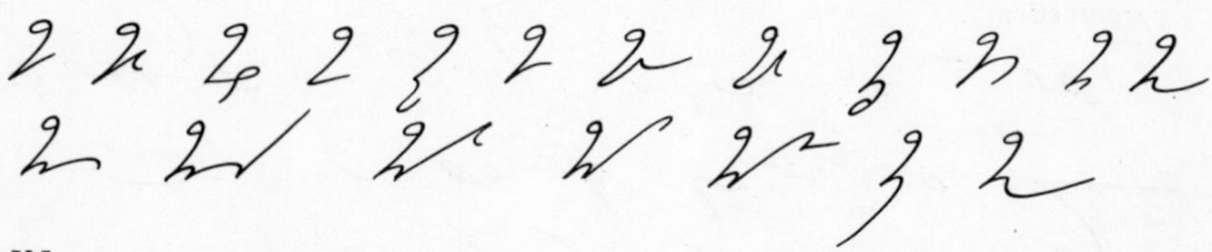

IN

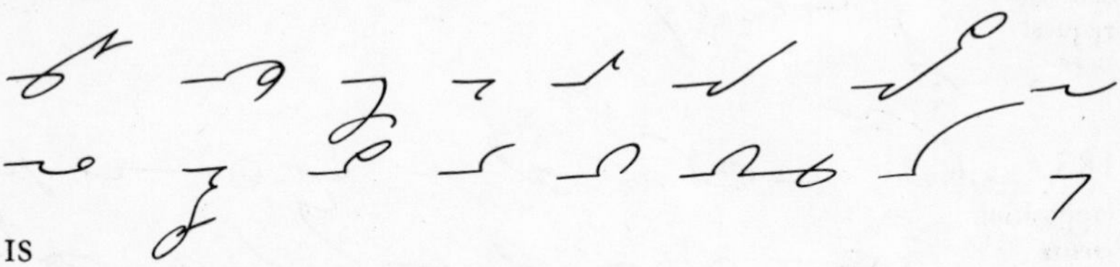

IS

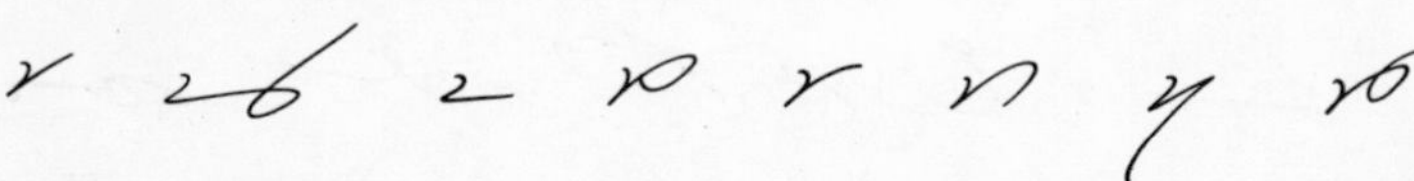

IT

181. Geographical Expressions

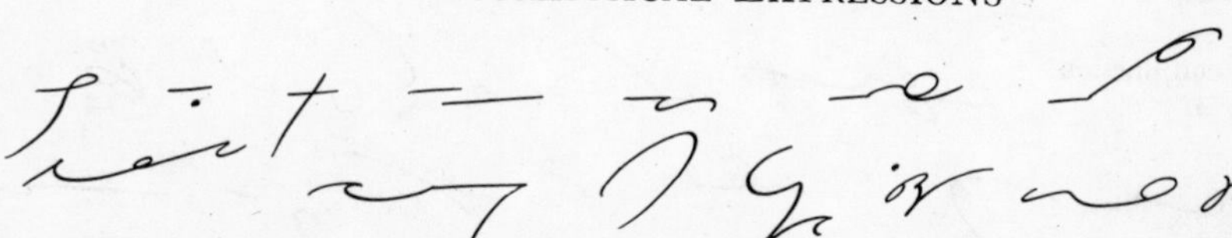

Reading and Writing Practice

182.

Here
Christmas
crammed

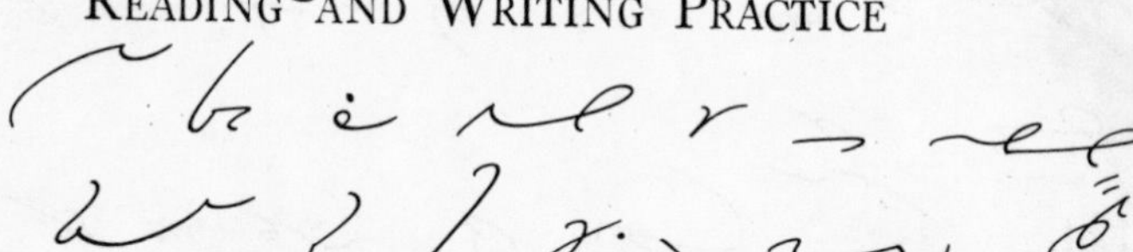

16

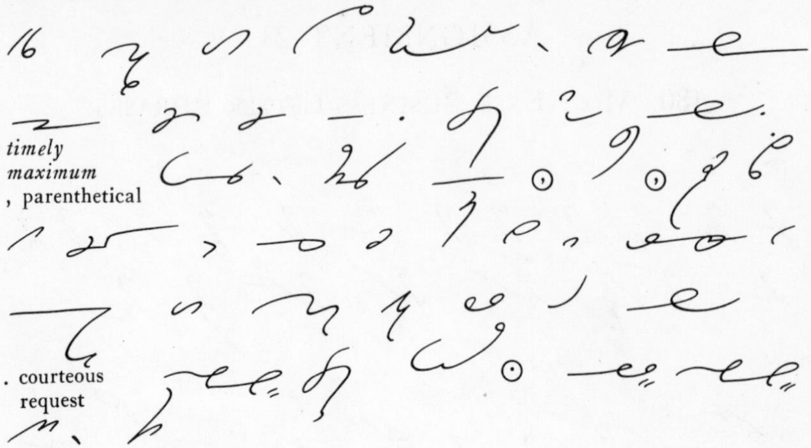

timely
maximum
, parenthetical

. courteous
request

183.

, apposition
discuss
steel

, *as* clause
sellers
materials

, conjunction
trial

184.

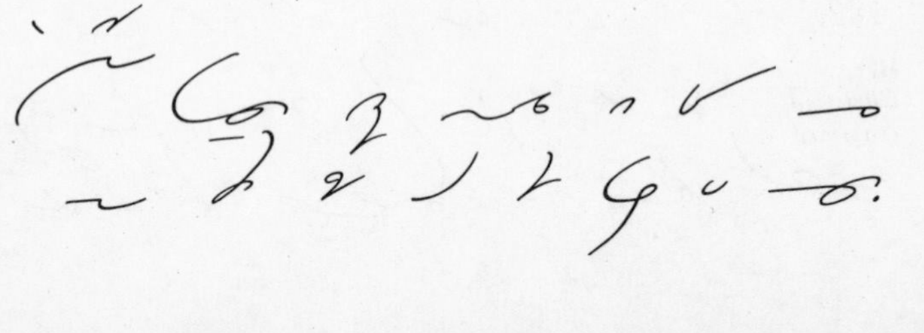

courtesy
privilege
estimate

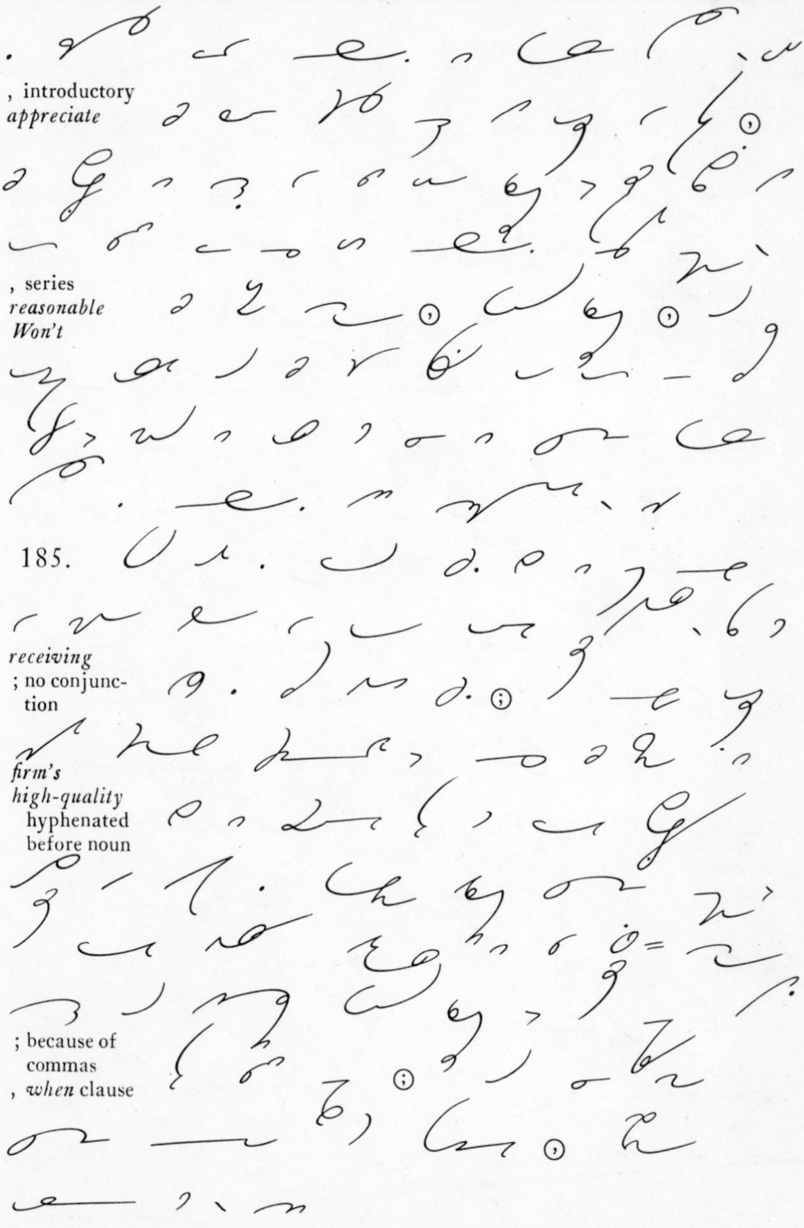

, introductory
appreciate

, series
reasonable
Won't

185.

receiving
; no conjunction

firm's
high-quality hyphenated before noun

; because of commas
, *when* clause

186.

close
pleasant

, parenthetical
welfare

, introductory

187.

salesmen's
channels

, *if* clause
, apposition

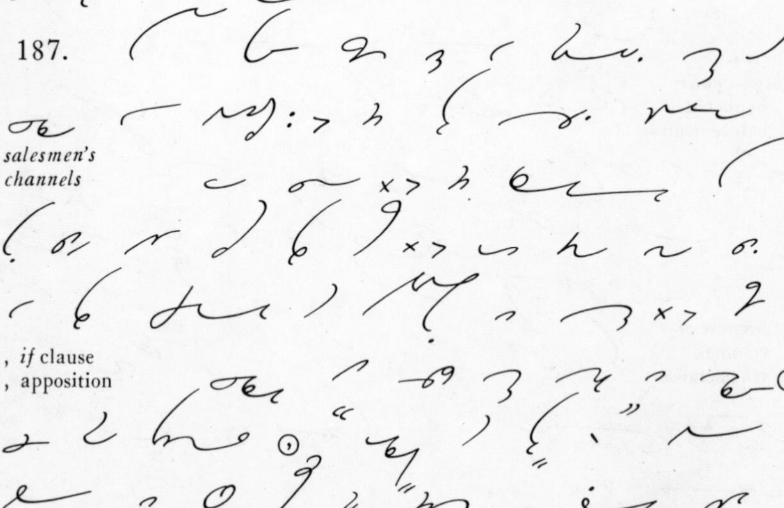

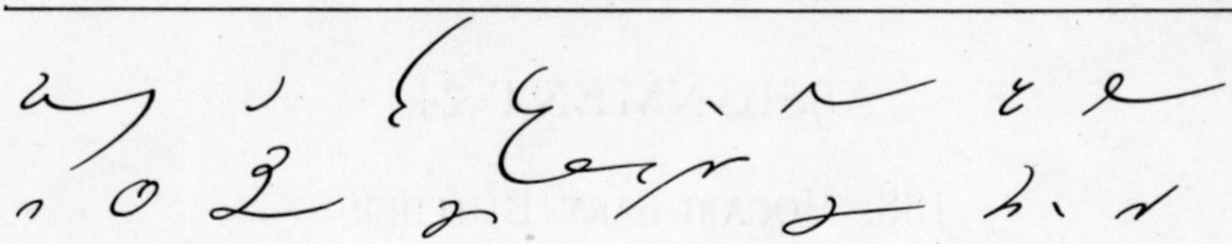

ASSIGNMENT 24

188. Vocabulary Builder

TH

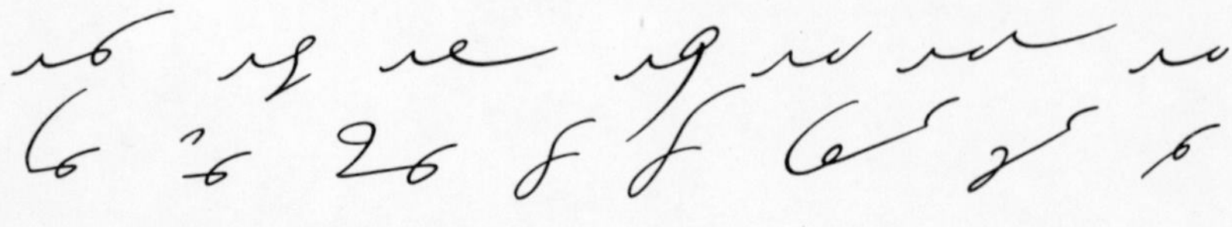

-TION, -TIAL

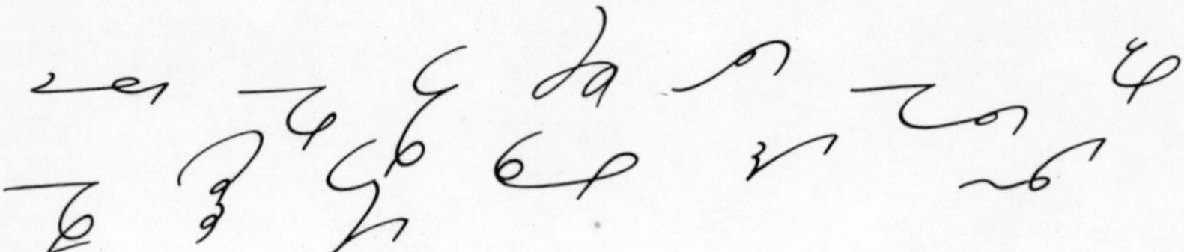

OI

I

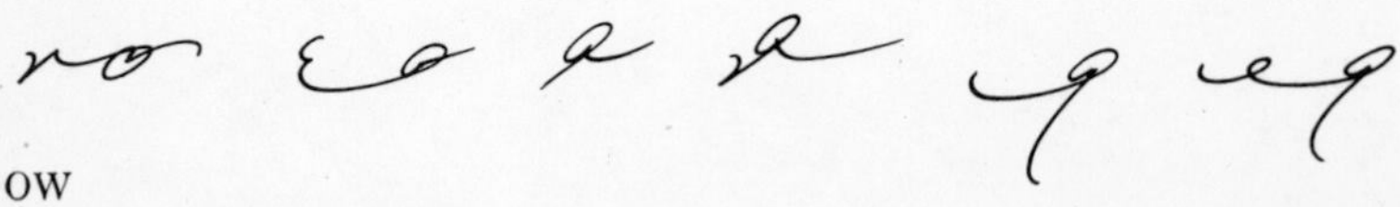

OW

U

Reading and Writing Practice

189.
Here
answer
Christmas

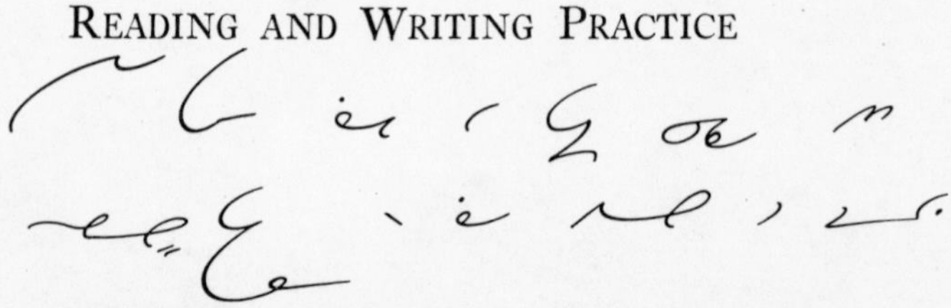

, apposition
public's approval

, series
; no conjunction

Transcribe: *$20.*

190.

sometimes
, conjunction

forget
, conjunction

son's
cameras
selection

191.

, apposition
confident
delicious
peaches

; no conjunction
, parenthetical

192.
, introductory
handling

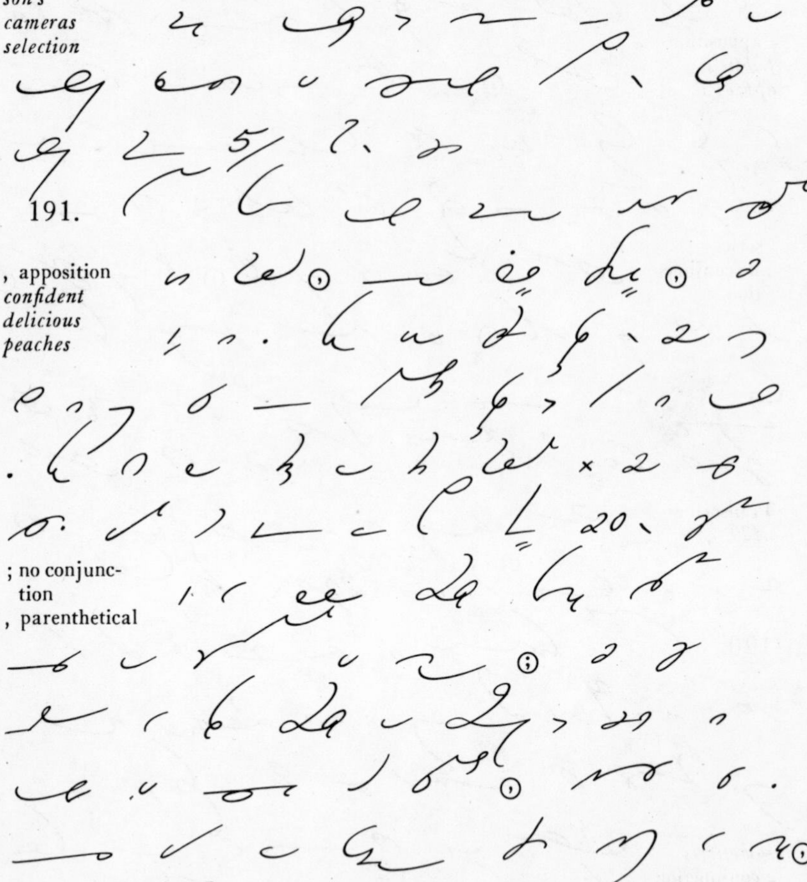

, conjunction
commercial
Millions

193.

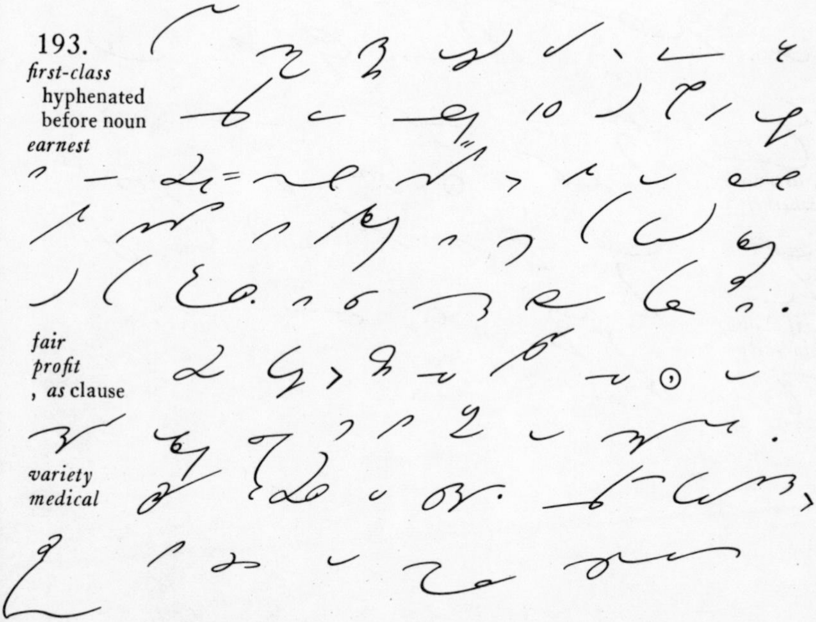

first-class
hyphenated
before noun
earnest

fair
profit
, *as* clause

variety
medical

post card

194.

received
businessmen
, introductory

, *as* clause
whether

, *if* clause
sincerely

ASSIGNMENT 25

195. Chart of Word Beginnings and Word Endings

A B C D E F

1.
2.
3.
4.
5.
6.
7.
8.
9.

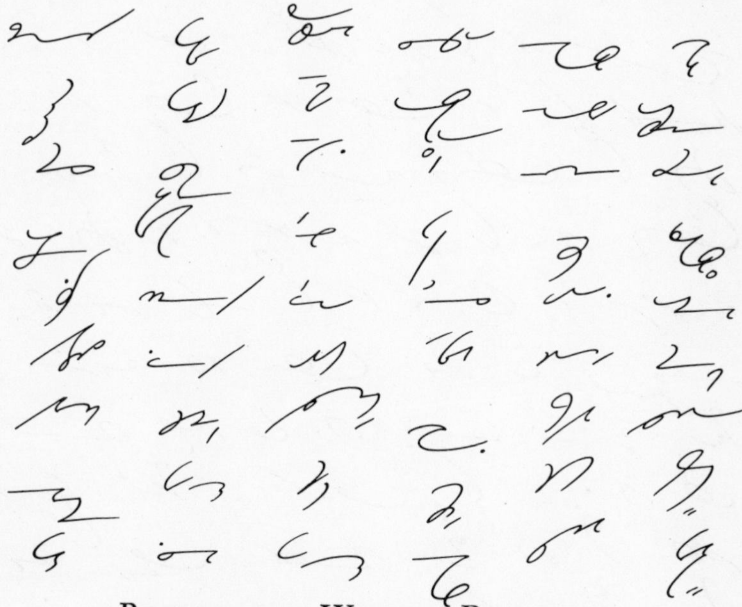

Reading and Writing Practice

196.

197.

; no conjunction
idea
, conjunction
sales
angle
; no conjunction
, series

well-planned
hyphenated
before noun

, *if* clause
, apposition

198.

Company's
their
, *when* clause

, conjunction
reason
impression

customer's
, introductory

well trained
no noun,
no hyphen

, *if* clause

199.

catalogue
, *as* clause

pencils
retailer
features

, introductory

, parenthetical

200.

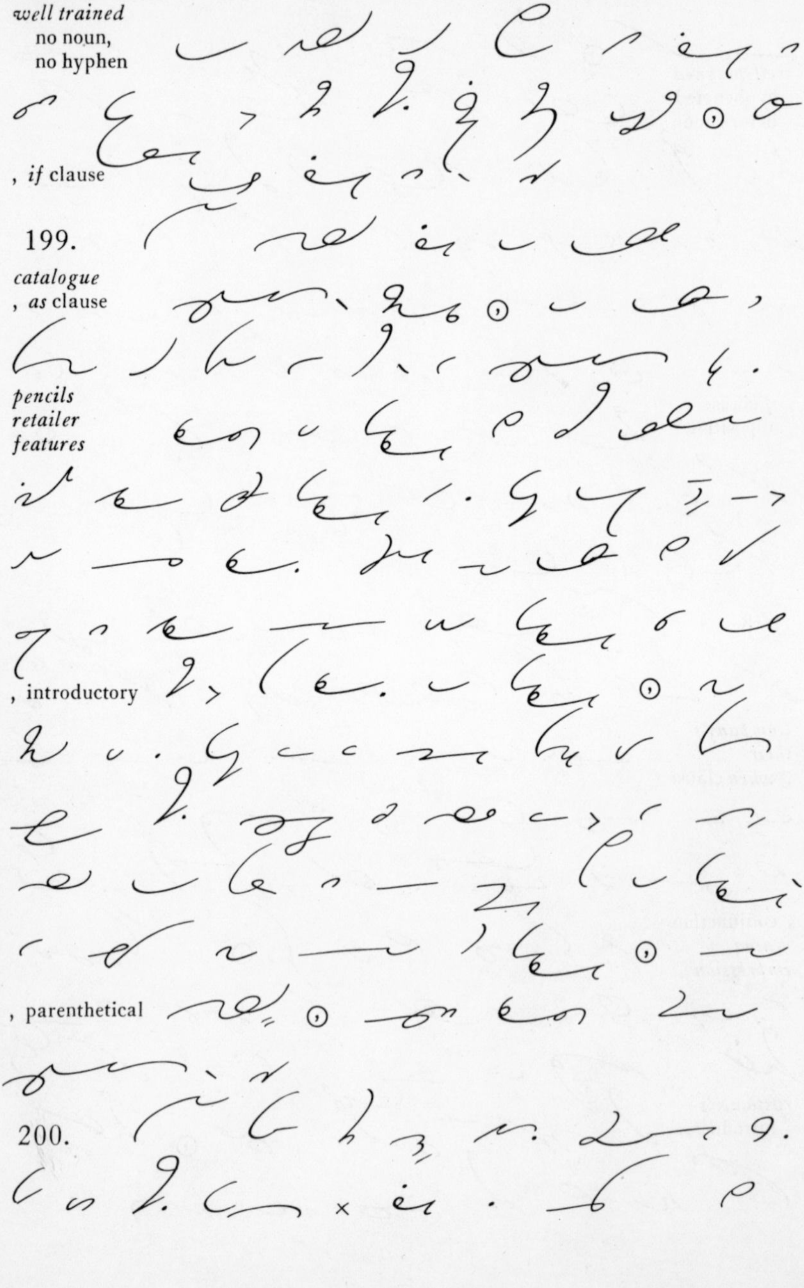

, introductory
, *when* clause
budget

201.

agreeably
columns
, conjunction

, *as* clause
; because of
comma
Transcribe:
$40,000 worth

202.

receive
pieces

envelopes
material

CHAPTER VI

ASSIGNMENT 26

203. Accuracy Practice

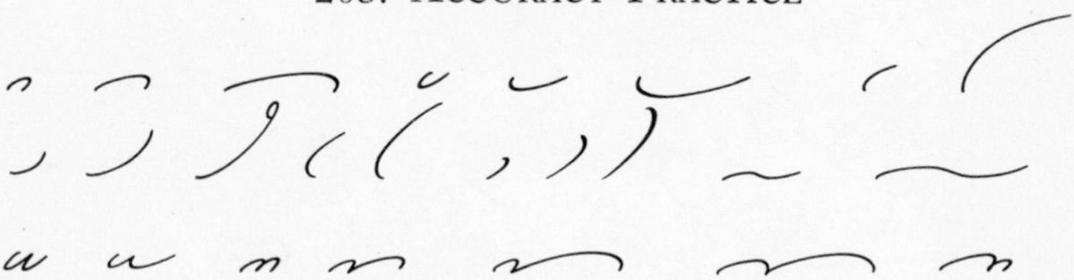

204. Vocabulary Builder

NG

NGK

Months of the Year

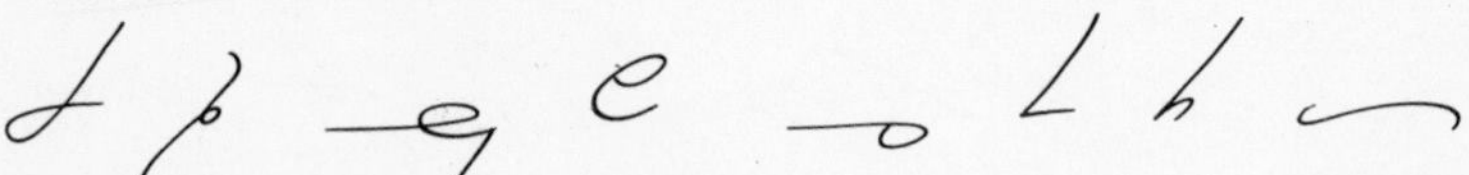

Special Business Phrases

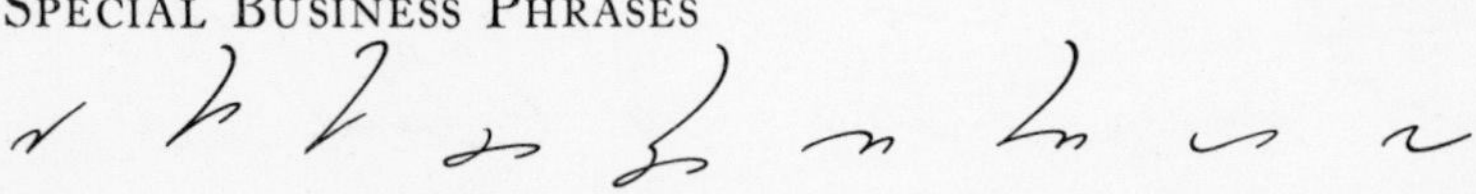

Reading and Writing Practice

205. 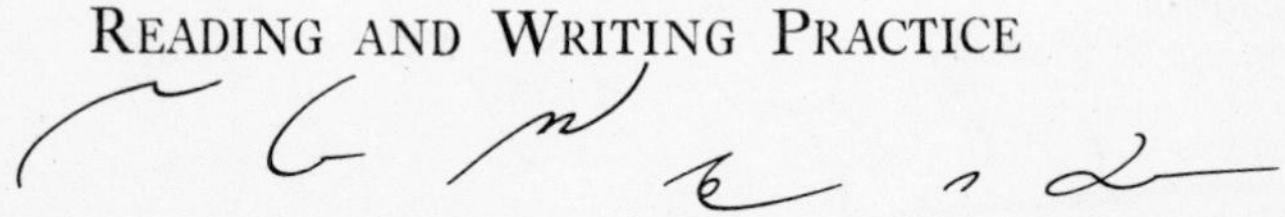

, apposition
; because of
comma
, introductory

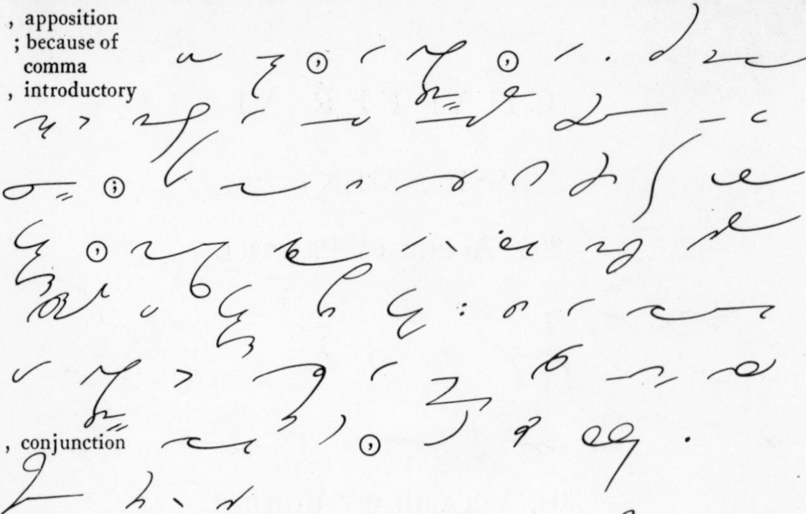

, conjunction

206.

colors

advertise
. courteous request

207.

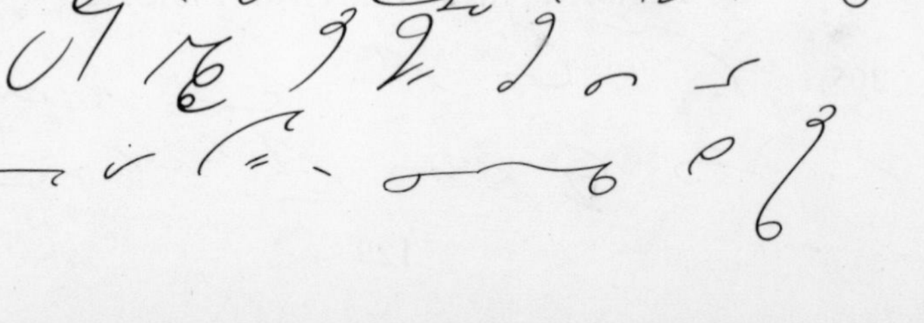

week
offered
steadily

208.

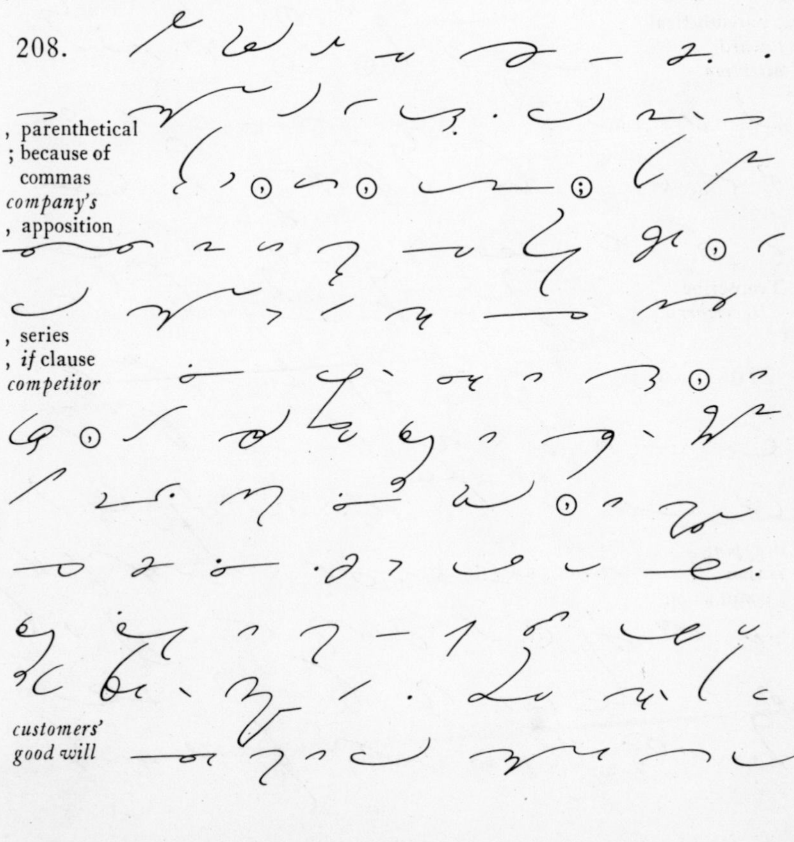

, parenthetical
; because of
commas
company's
, apposition

, series
, *if* clause
competitor

customers'
good will

209.

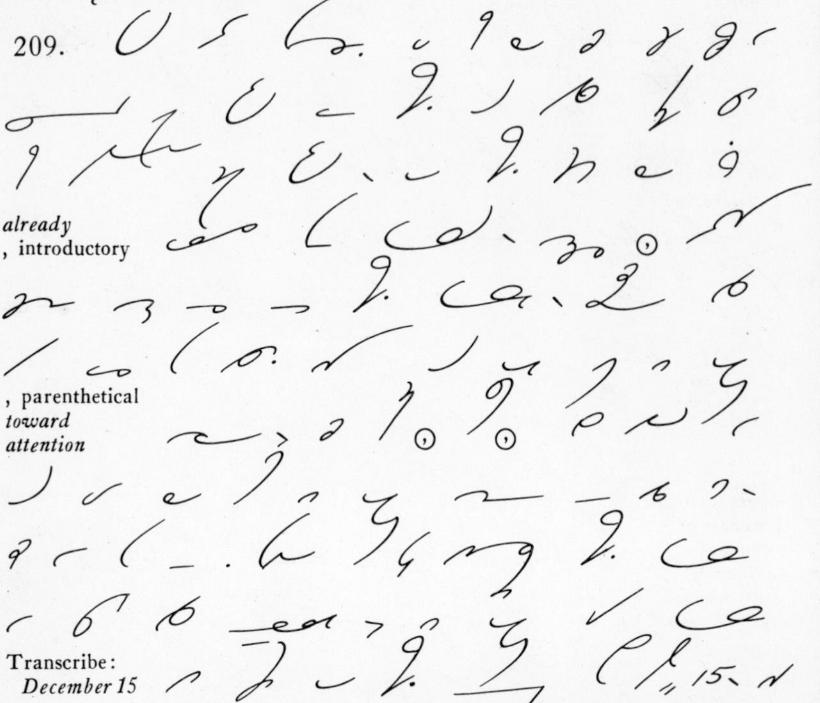

already
, introductory

, parenthetical
toward
attention

Transcribe:
December 15

210.

dropping
reason
, conjunction

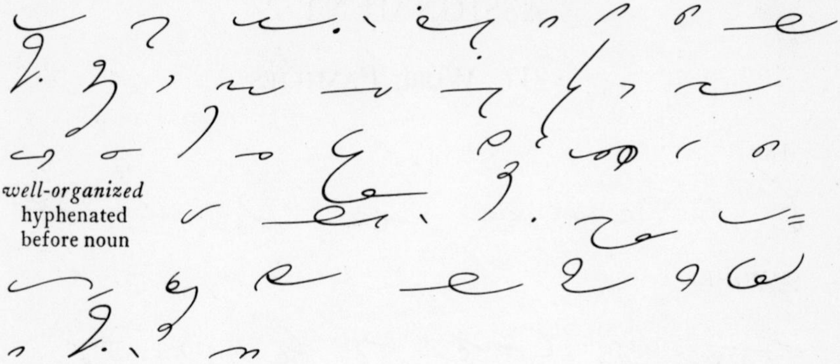

well-organized
hyphenated
before noun

ASSIGNMENT 27

211. Word Families

-IER

-SHIONER

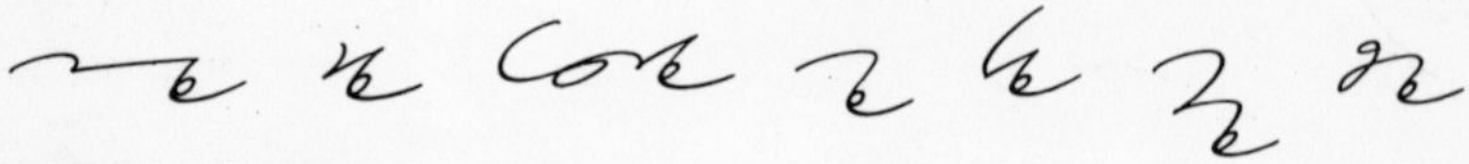

-SURE, -JURE

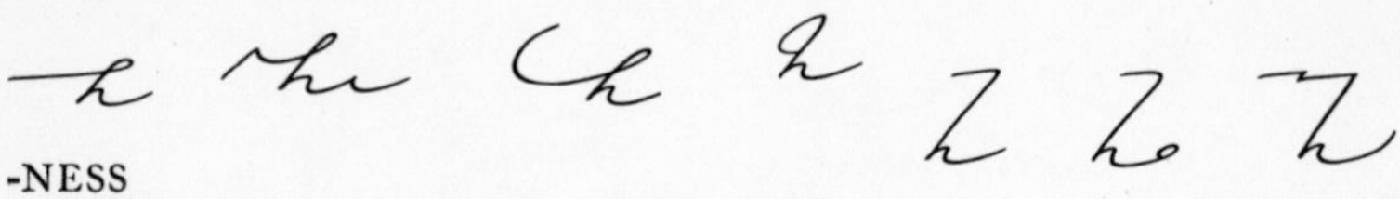

-NESS

-UOUS

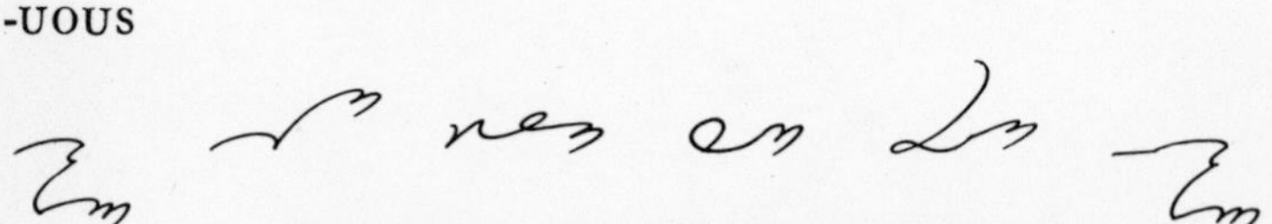

Reading and Writing Practice

212. *Here likely*

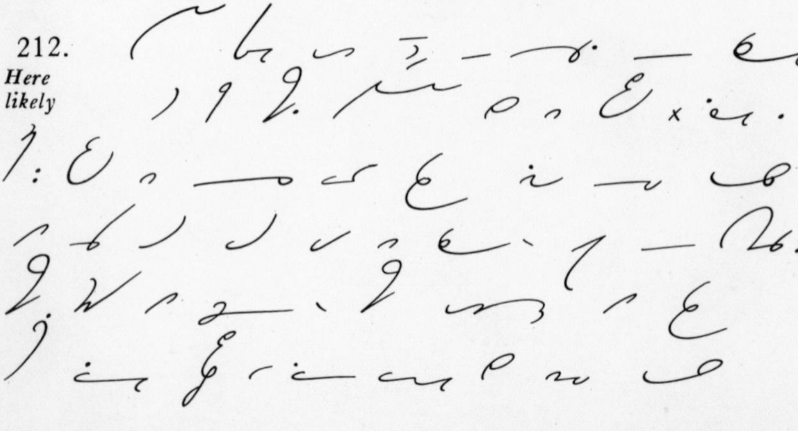

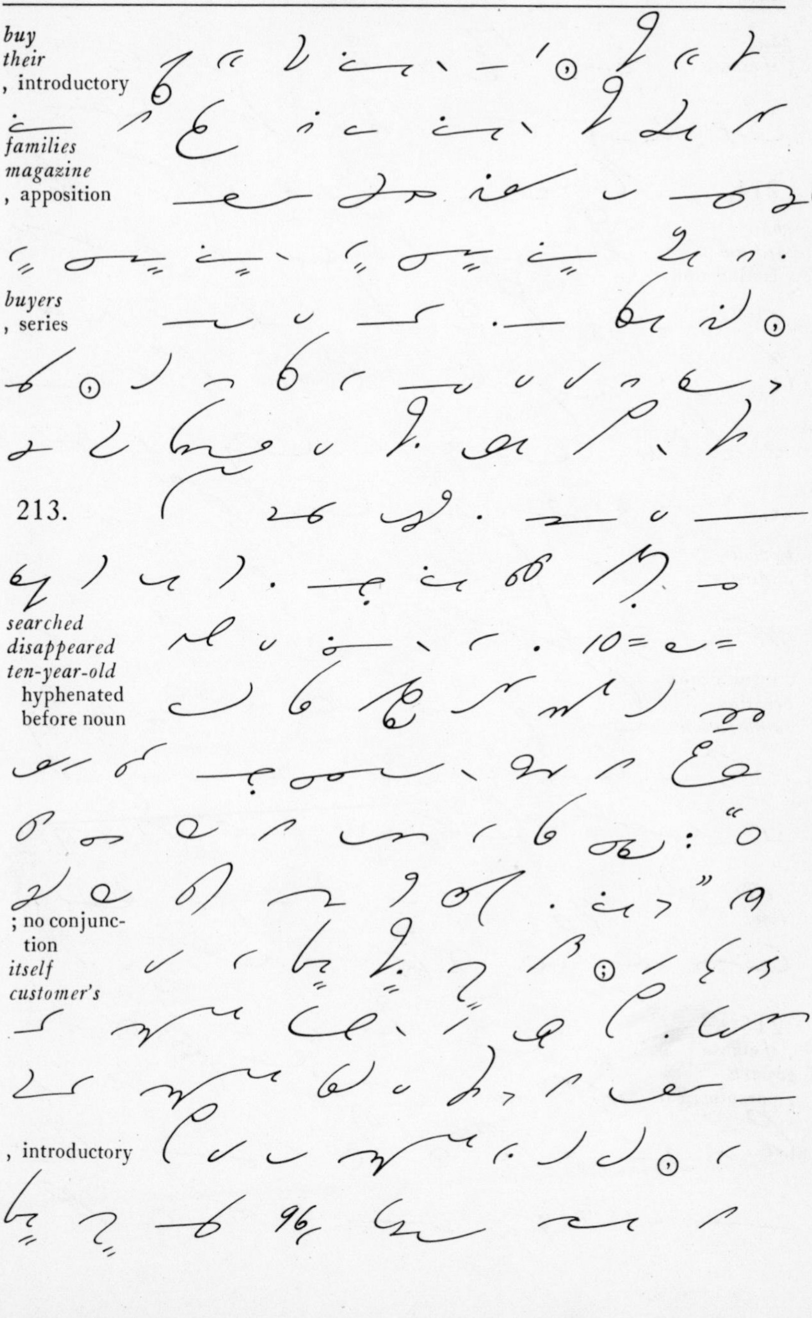

buy
their
, introductory
families
magazine
, apposition
buyers
, series

213.

searched
disappeared
ten-year-old
hyphenated before noun

; no conjunction
itself
customer's

, introductory

past
, *if* clause

214.

chose
medium
, conjunction

obvious
audience

, introductory
occasion
co-operation

215.
, *if* clause
women
, parenthetical

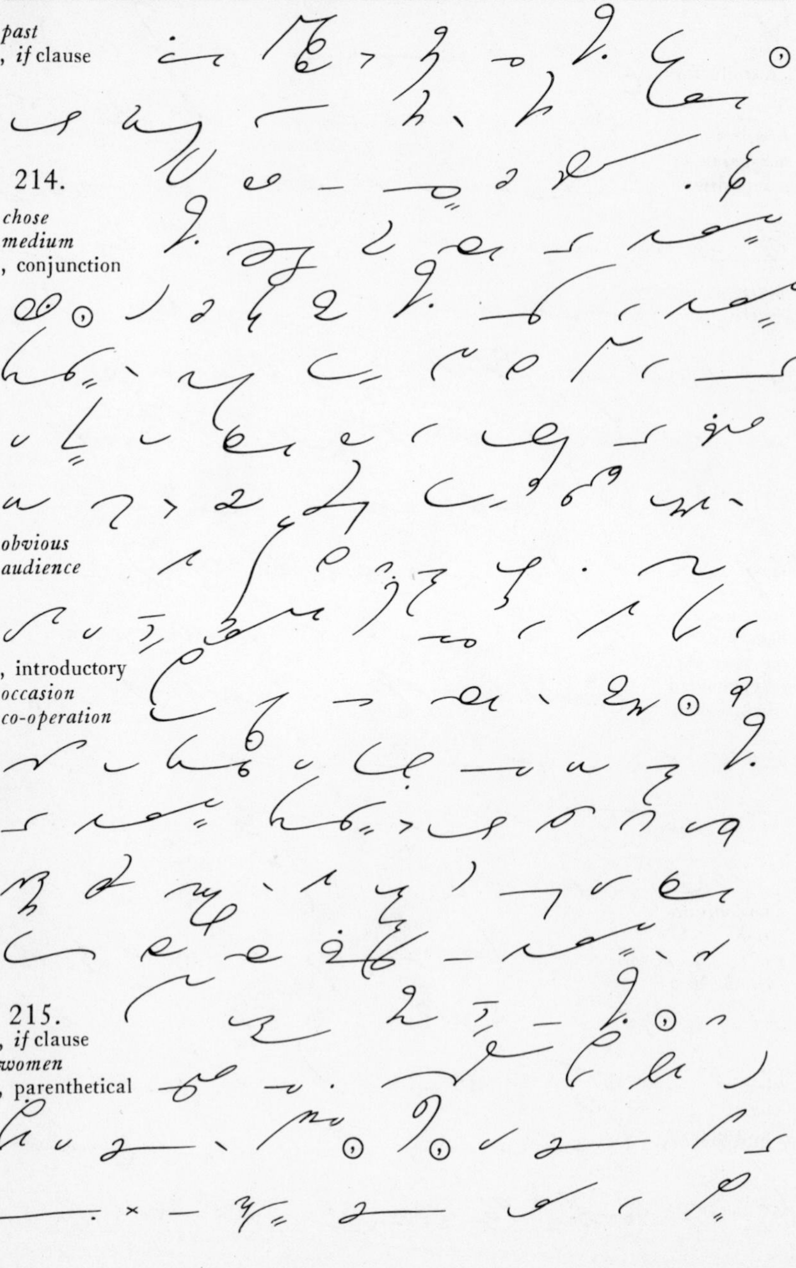

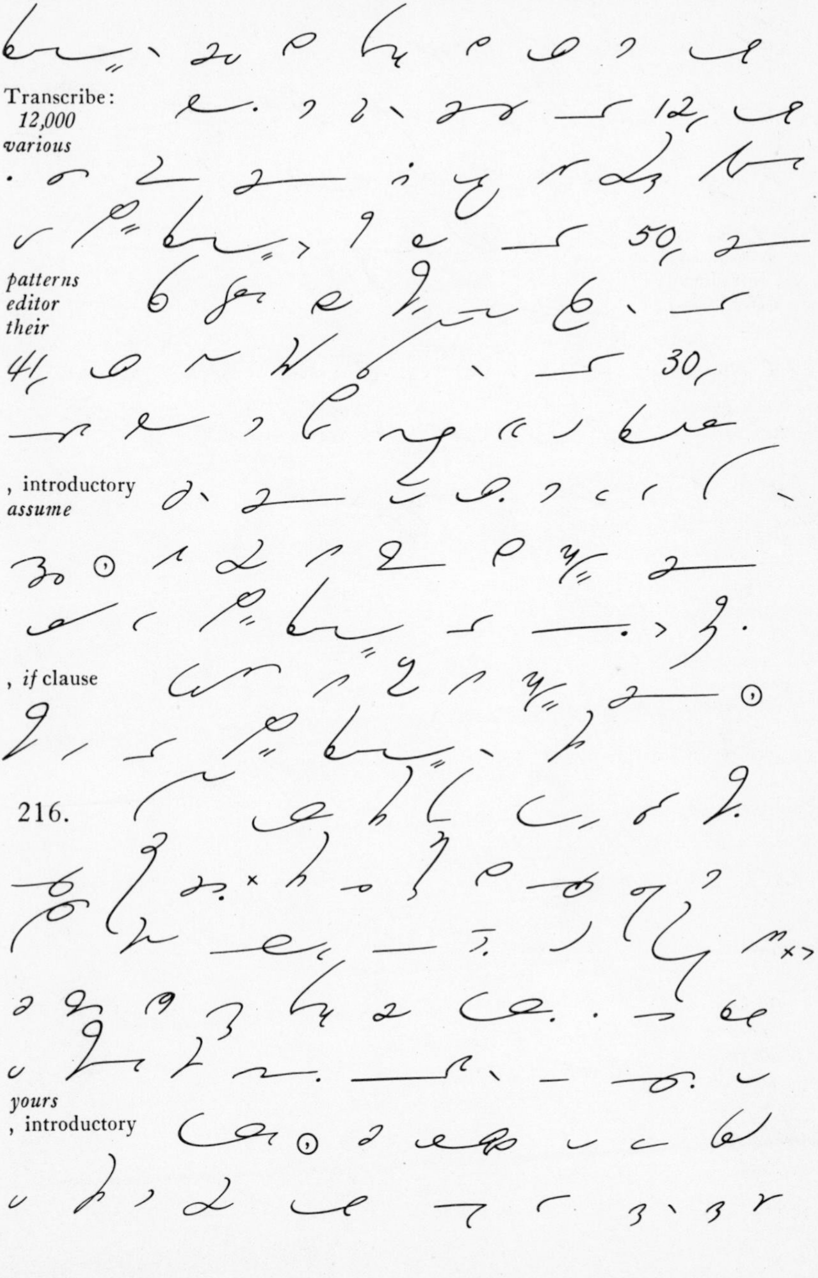

Transcribe:
12,000
various

patterns
editor
their

, introductory
assume

, *if* clause

216.

yours
, introductory

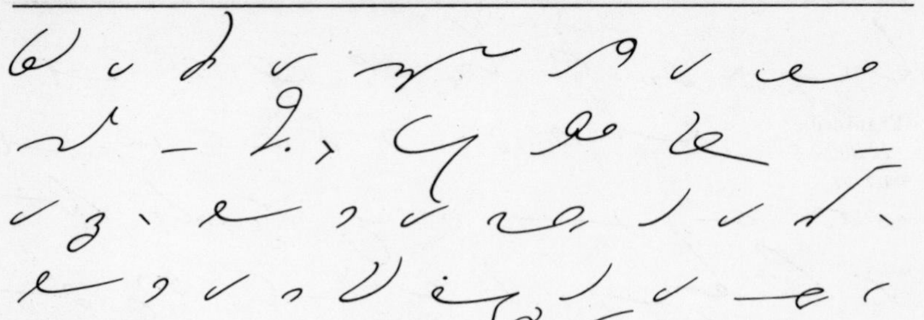

, introductory
self-addressed

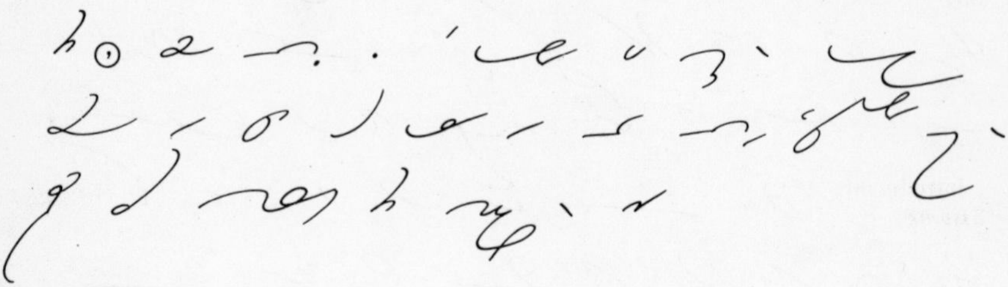

ASSIGNMENT 28

217. Most-Used Business-Letter Phrases

MANY

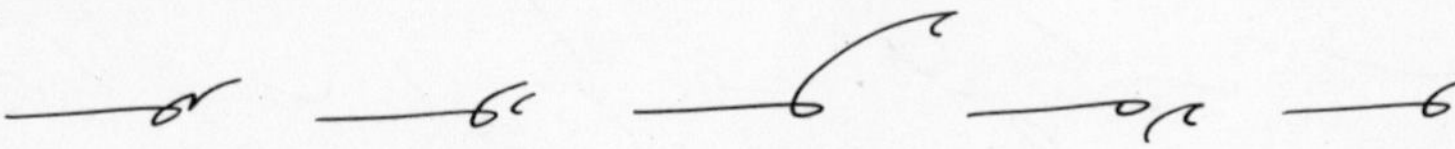

OF

ON

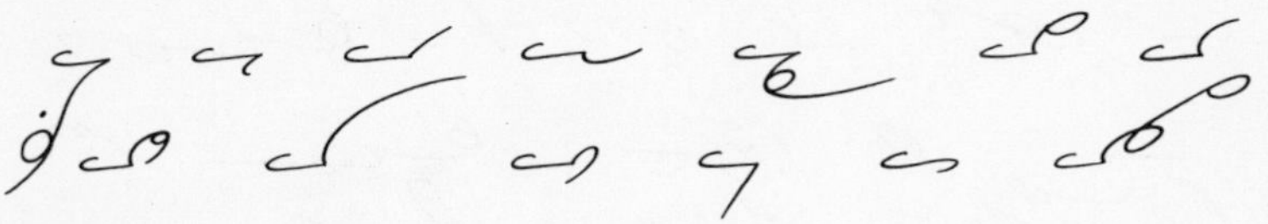

PLEASE

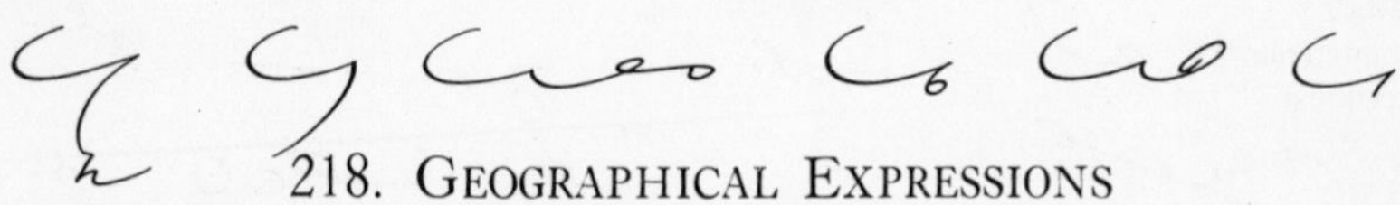

218. Geographical Expressions

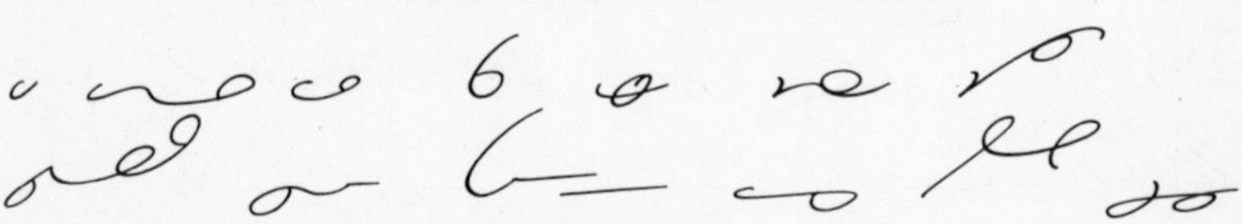

Reading and Writing Practice

219.

everybody's

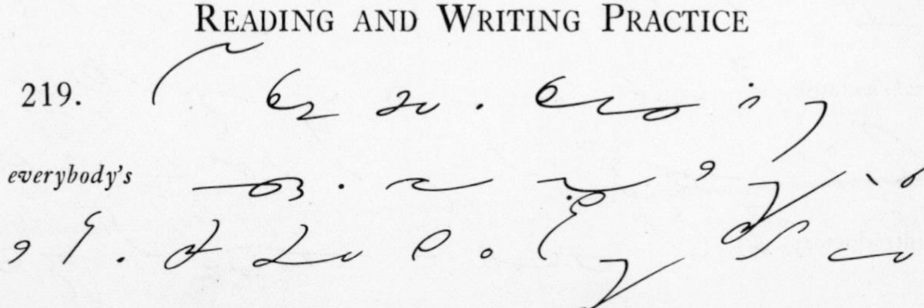

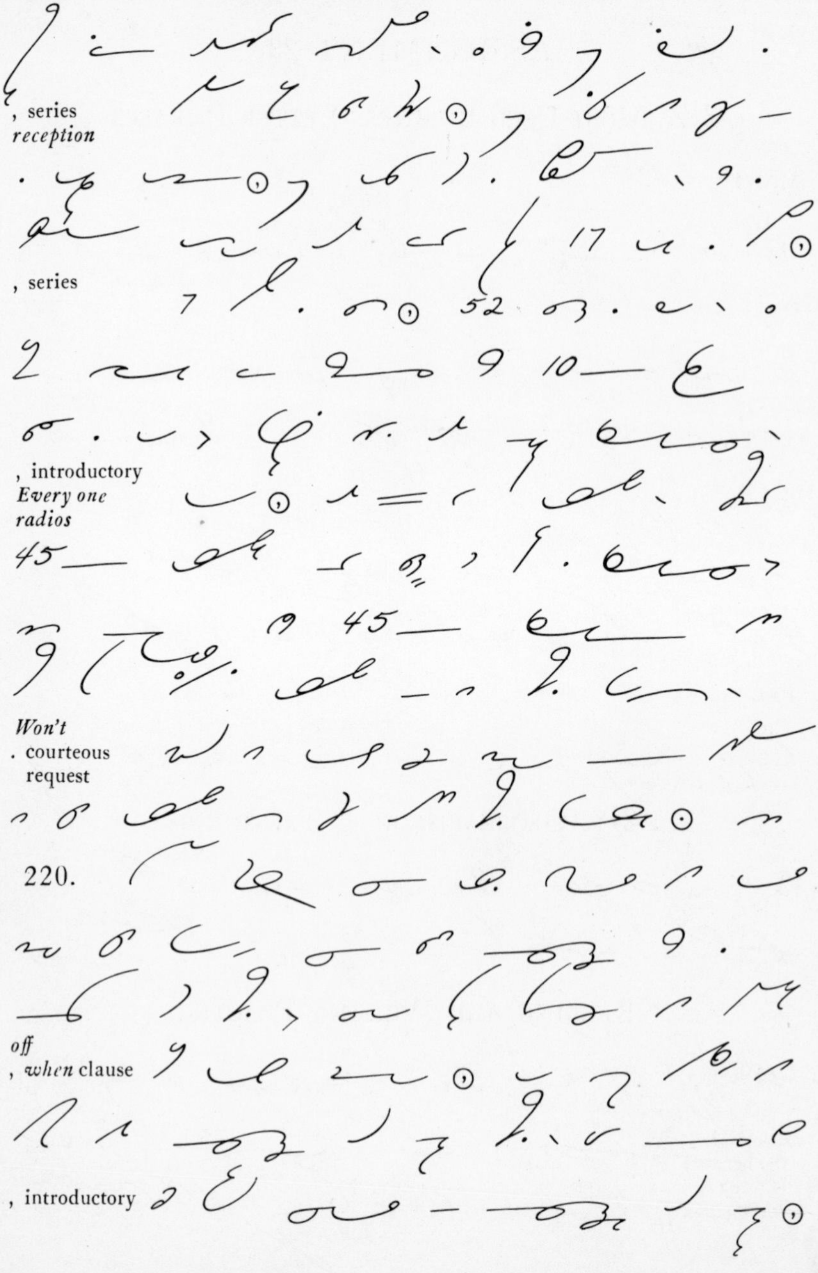

, series
reception

, series

, introductory
Every one
radios

Won't
. courteous request

220.

off
, *when* clause

, introductory

, introductory
, parenthetical

per cent
territory

221.

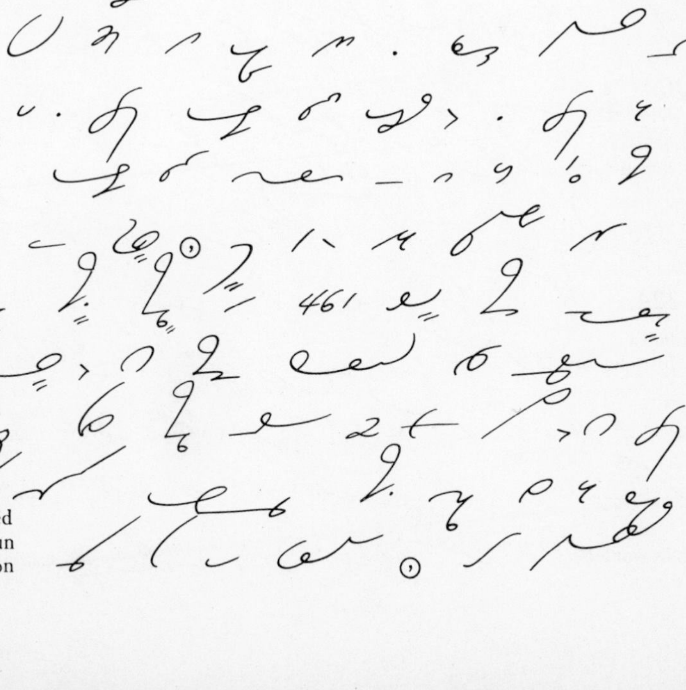

Transcribe:
8 p.m.
, apposition

last-minute
hyphenated
before noun
, conjunction

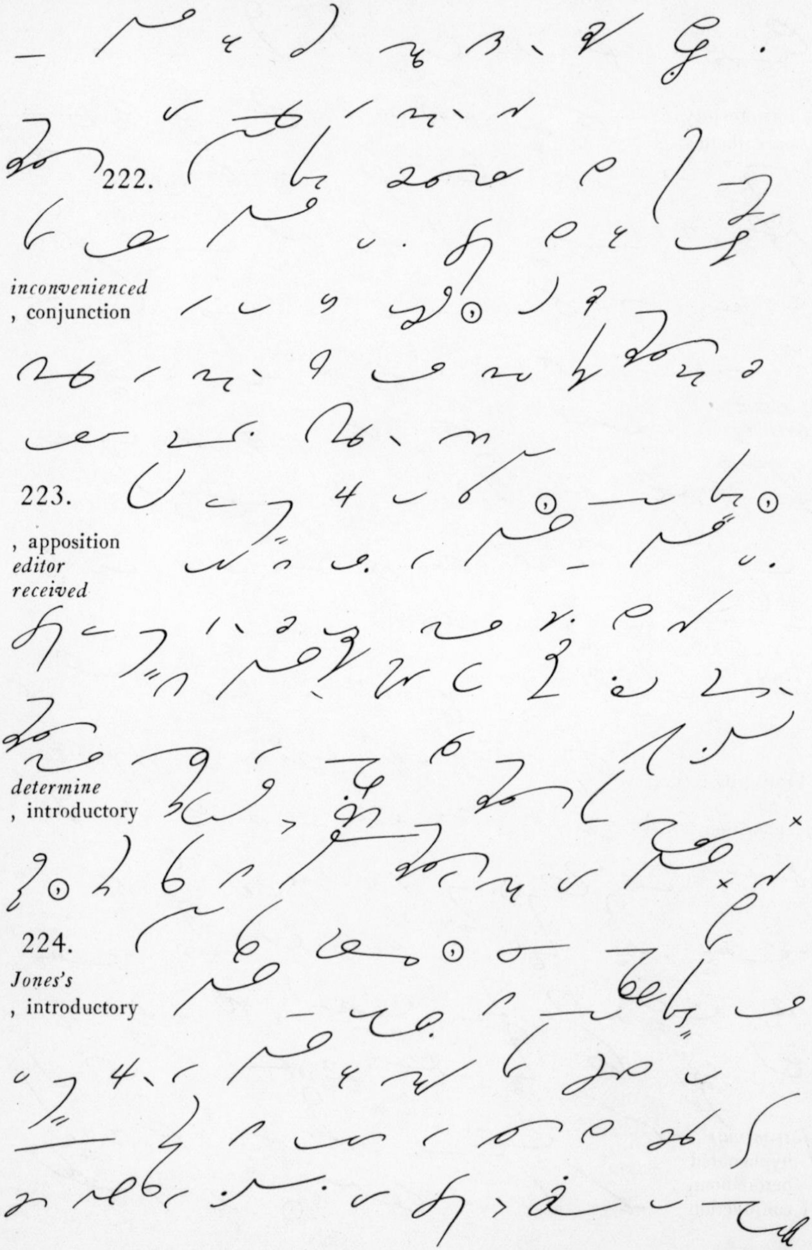

222.

inconvenienced

, conjunction

223.

, apposition

editor

received

determine

, introductory

224.

Jones's

, introductory

, introductory
; because of
commas

, *when* clause

ASSIGNMENT 29

225. Vocabulary Builder—Omission of Vowels

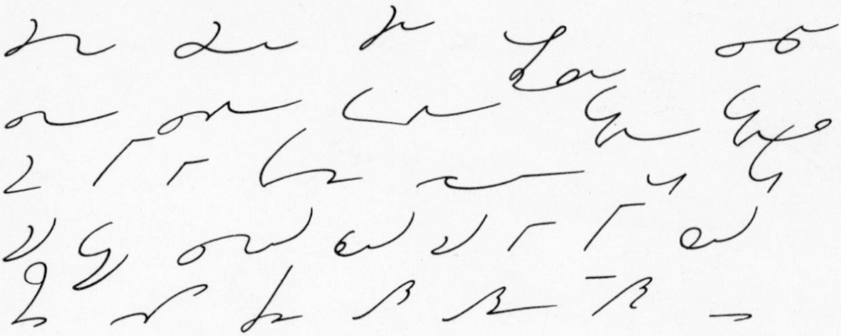

Reading and Writing Practice

226.

response
vacation
completely

227.

Recently
announcement
flight

timetable
, parenthetical

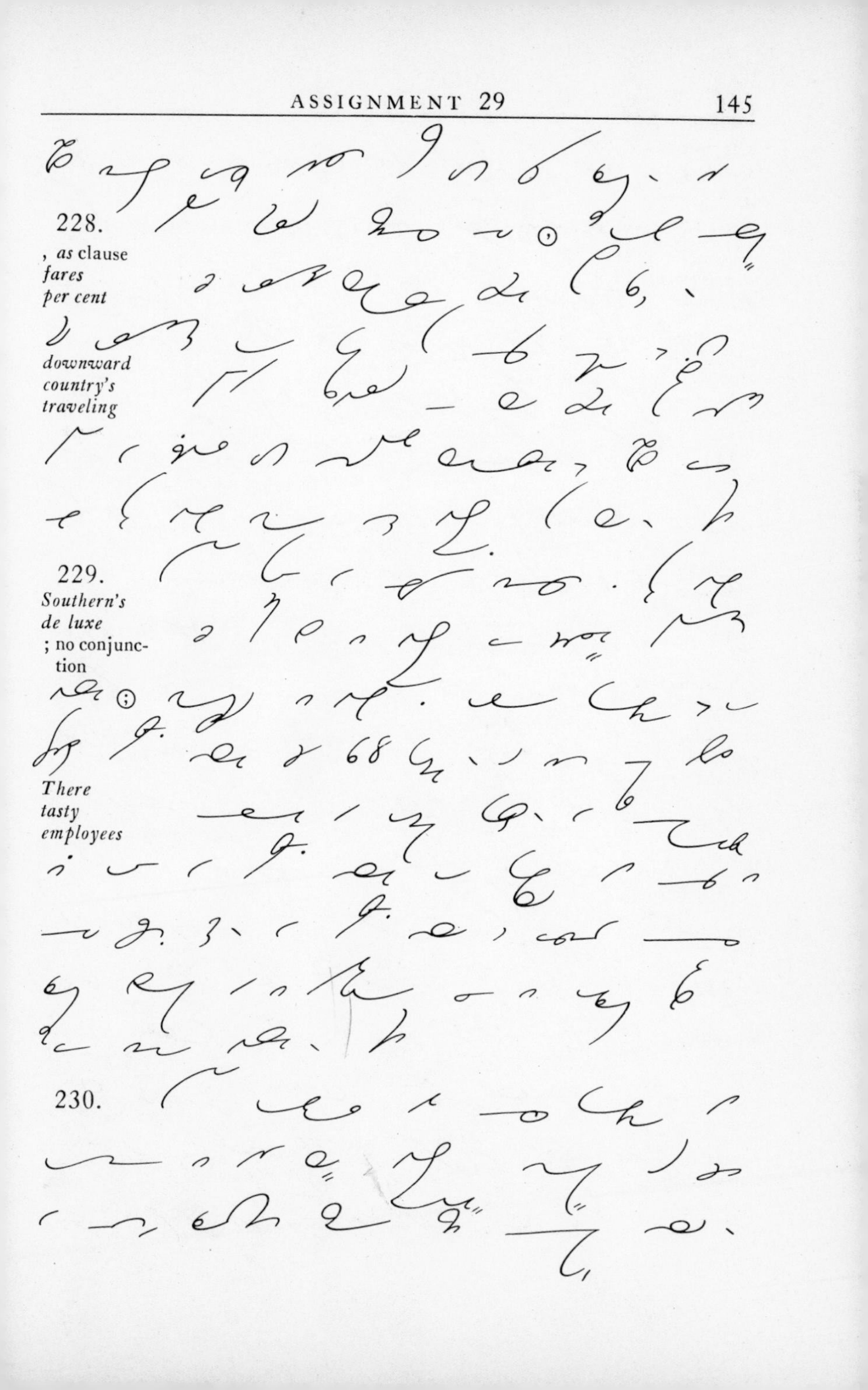

228.
, *as* clause
fares
per cent

downward
country's
traveling

229.
Southern's
de luxe
; no conjunction

There
tasty
employees

230.

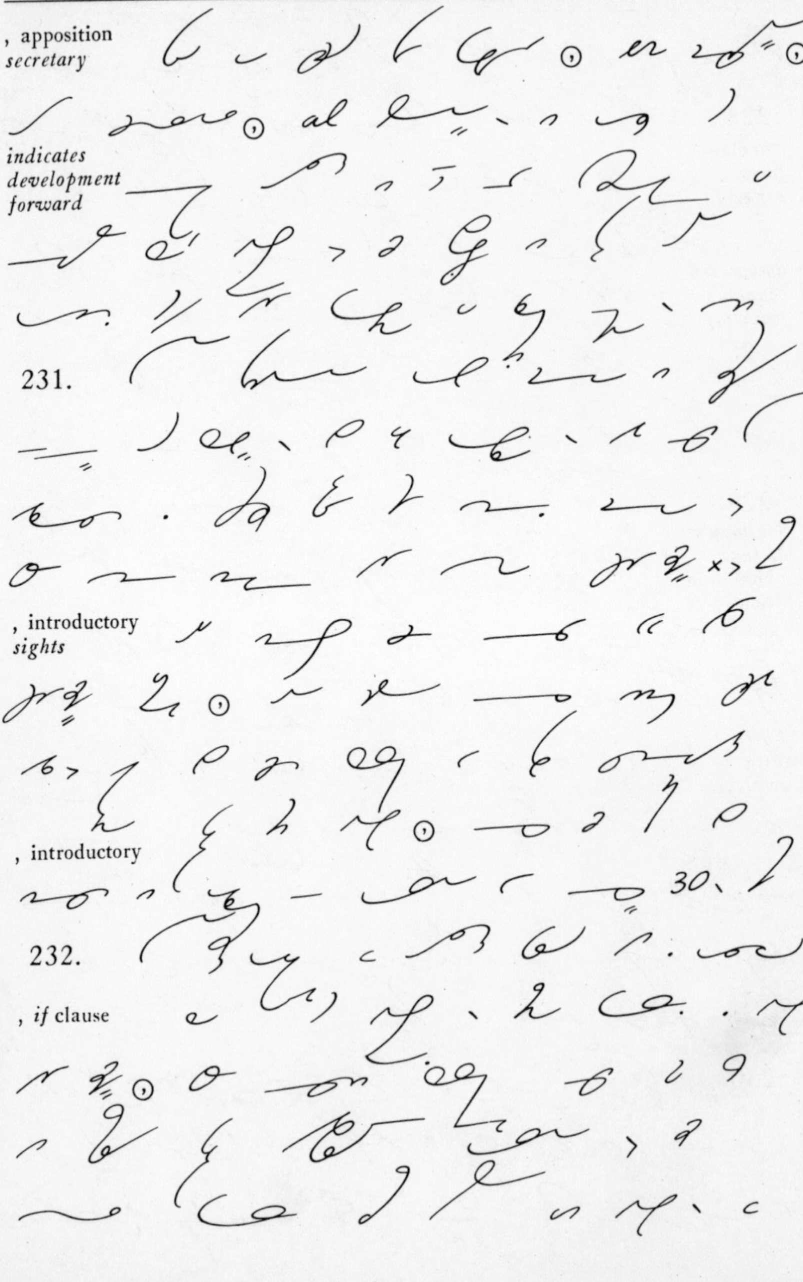

, apposition
secretary

indicates
development
forward

231.

, introductory
sights

, introductory

232.

, *if* clause

, conjunction
, introductory
foreign

233.
women
tiresome
, series
, introductory
four-hour
hyphenated
before noun
nonstop

ASSIGNMENT 30

234. Vocabulary Builder

SES

-RD

-LD

DET, TED

MEN

Reading and Writing Practice

235.

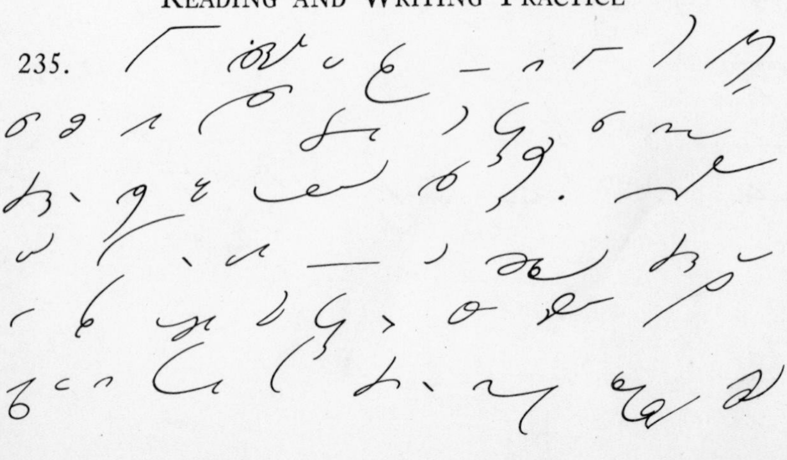

236.

, series
, introductory
Brown's
up-to-the-minute
hyphenated
before noun

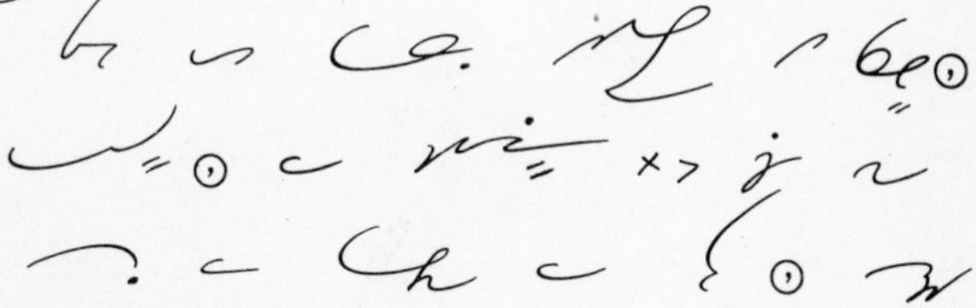

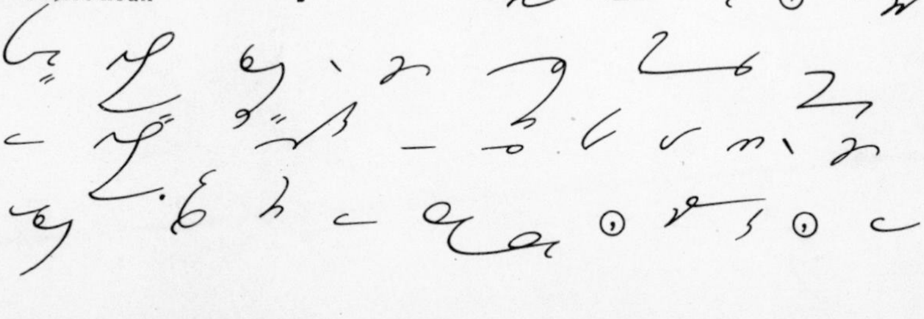

Transcribe:
13 Street.
, *if* clause

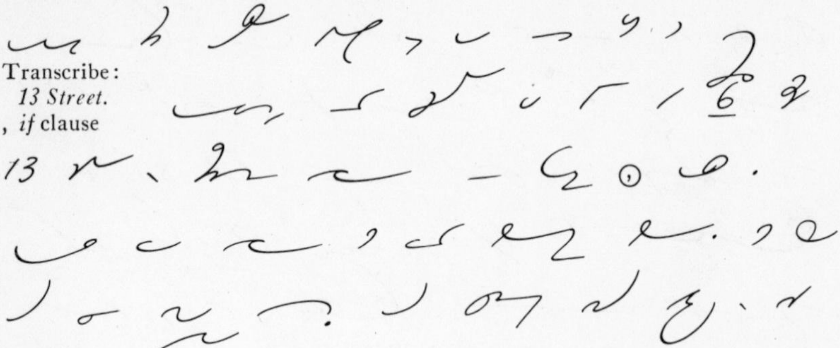

237.

, apposition
Hawaii
assistance

current
schedule
fares

238.

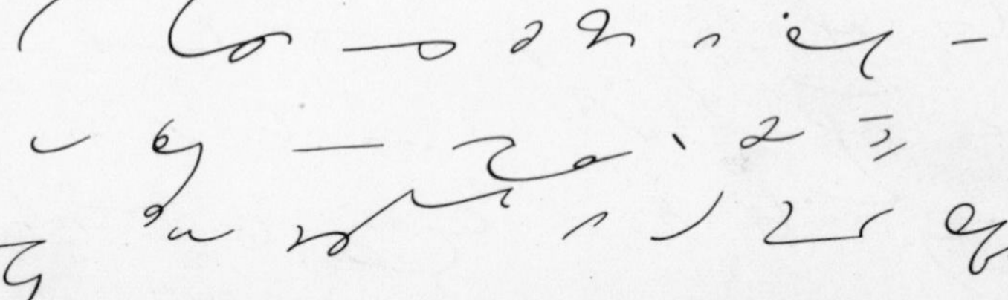

area
intelligently
, introductory

postal card
co-operation

239.

past
distance
; no conjunction

nation's
fascinating
country's

240.
; no conjunction
, parenthetical

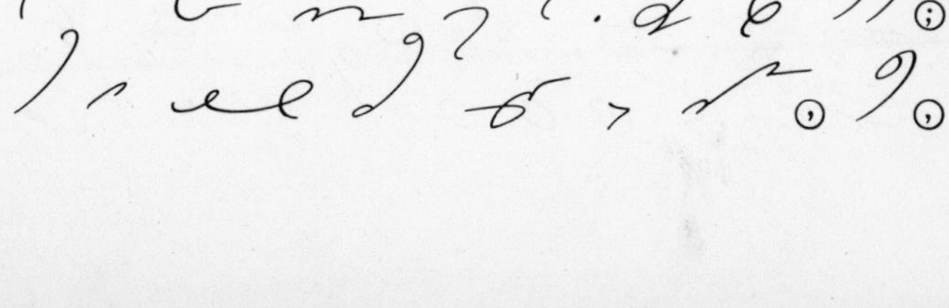

surface
Pacific

various
routes
schedules

241.

, *if* clause
believe
enclosed

two
, conjunction

, *if* clause
practical

CHAPTER VII

ASSIGNMENT 31

242. Brief-Form Chart

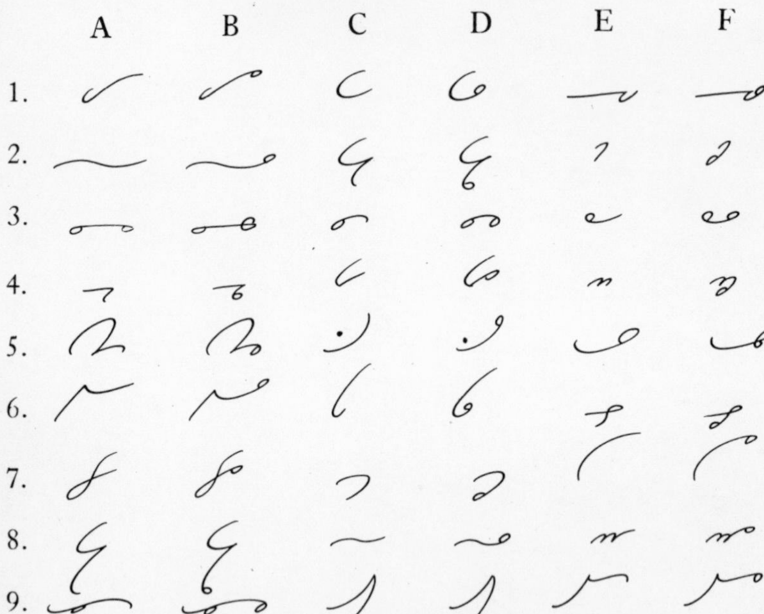

Reading and Writing Practice

243.
; no conjunction
, parenthetical

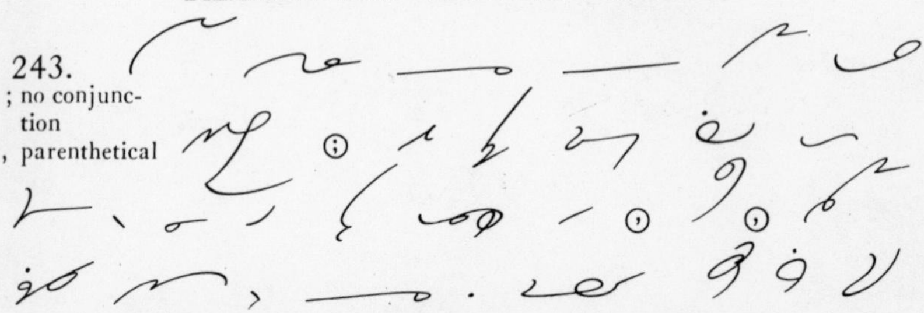

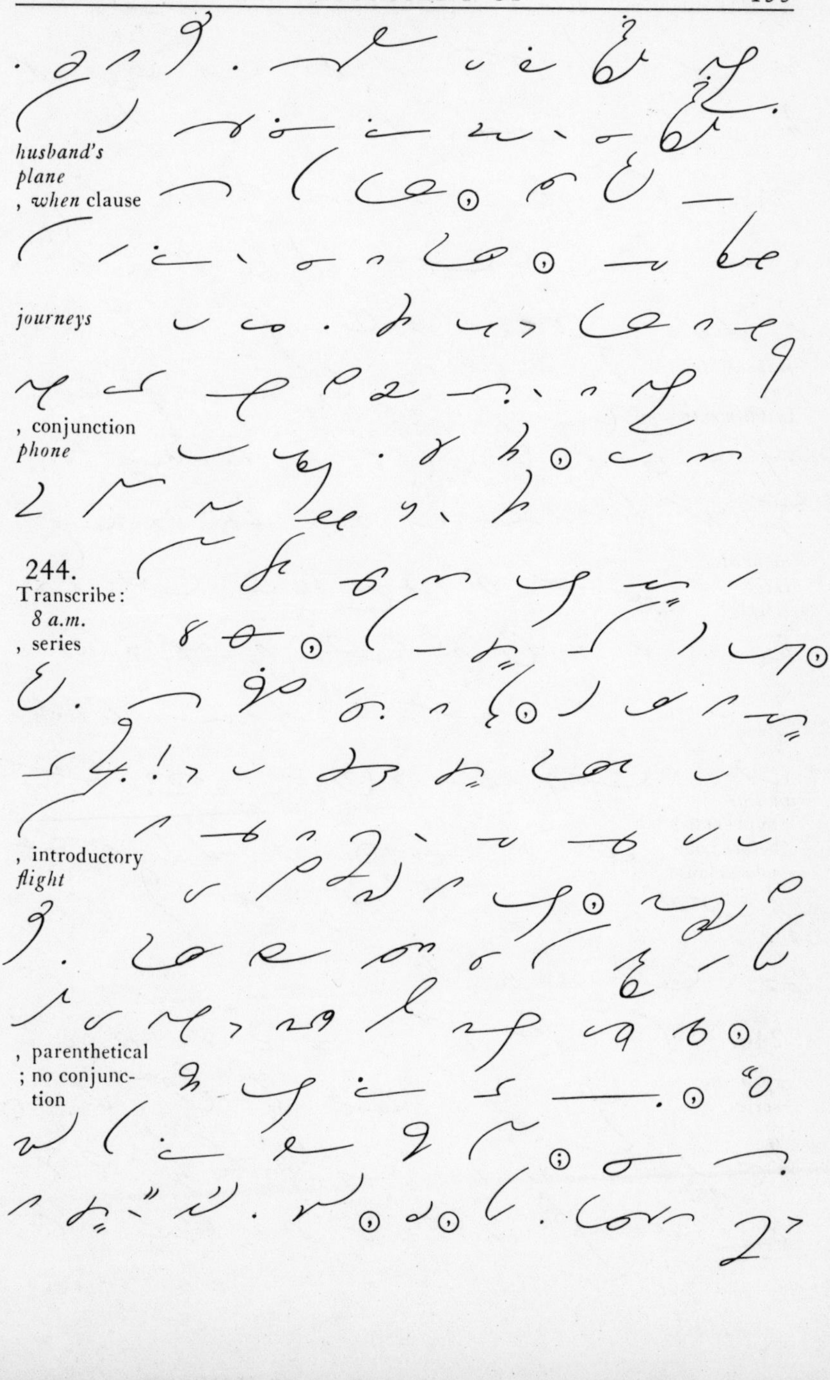

husband's
plane
, *when* clause

journeys

, conjunction
phone

244.
Transcribe:
8 a.m.
, series

, introductory
flight

, parenthetical
; no conjunction

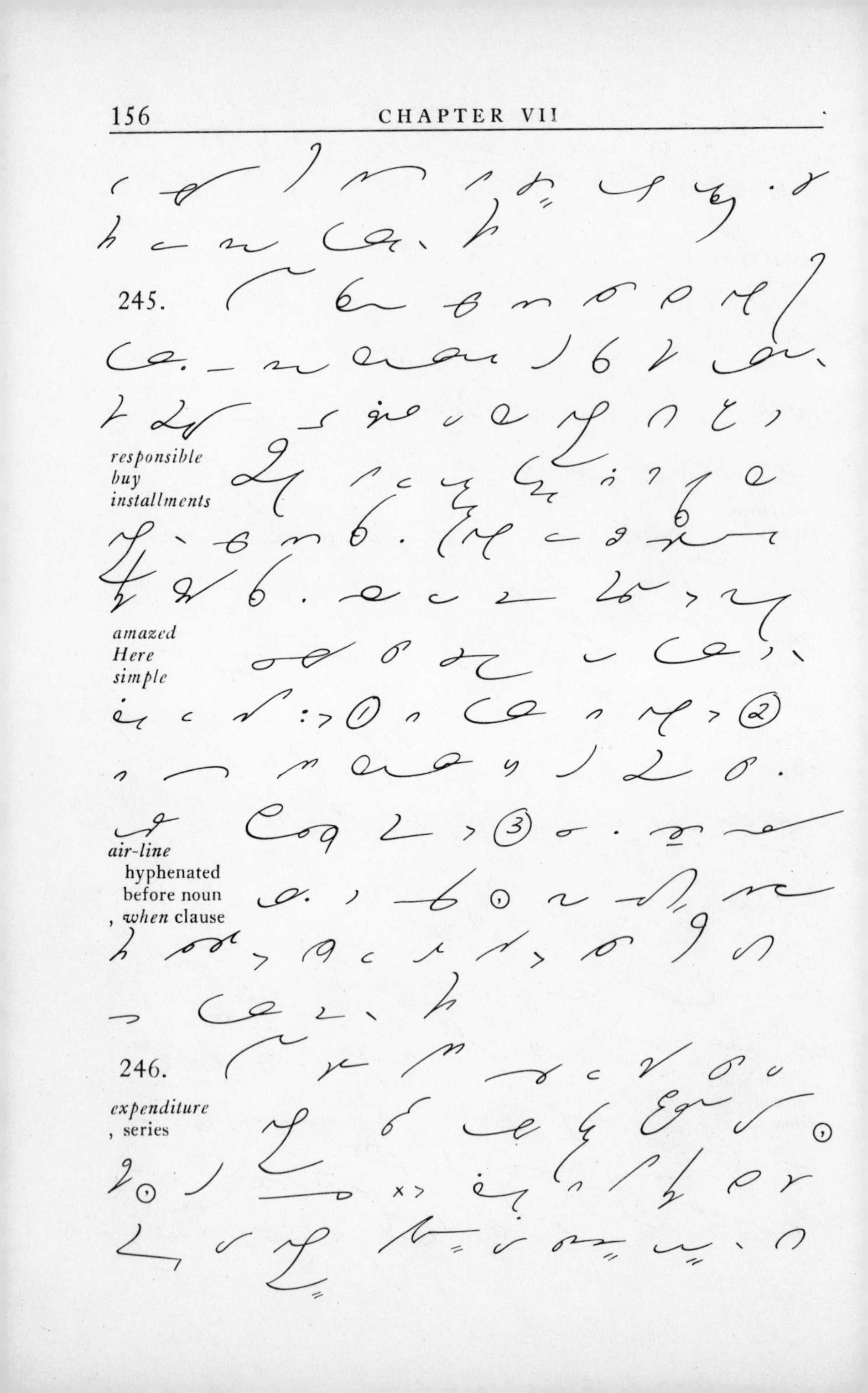

245.

responsible
buy
installments

amazed
Here
simple

air-line
hyphenated
before noun
, *when* clause

246.

expenditure
, series

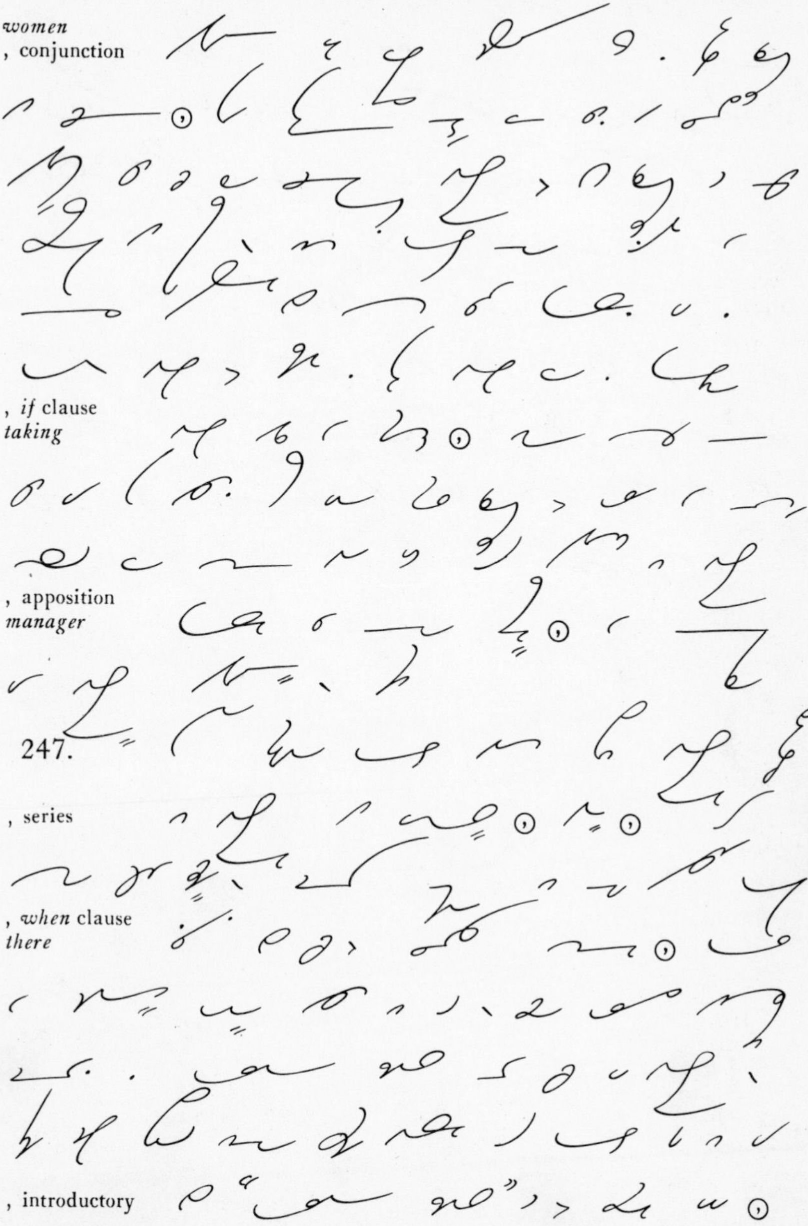

women
, conjunction
, *if* clause
taking
, apposition
manager
247.
, series
, *when* clause
there
, introductory

nation's
scenic

ASSIGNMENT 32

248. VOCABULARY BUILDER—OMISSION OF T AND D

-CT

-IST, -EST

ST FOLLOWING ABBREVIATED FORM OR VOWEL

OMISSION OF D

READING AND WRITING PRACTICE

249.

, series
forward

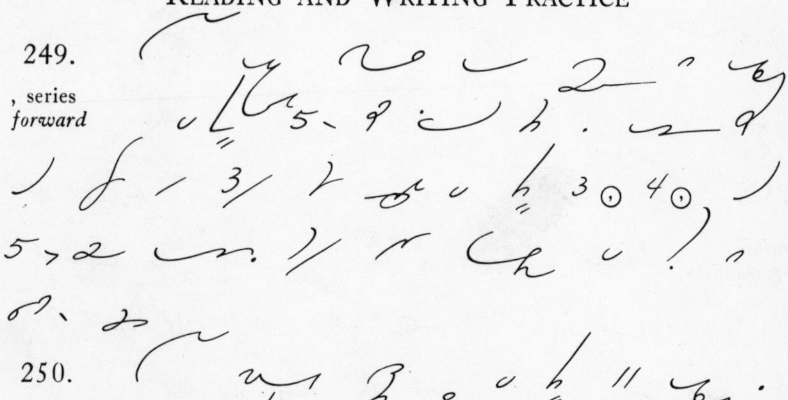

250.

, conjunction

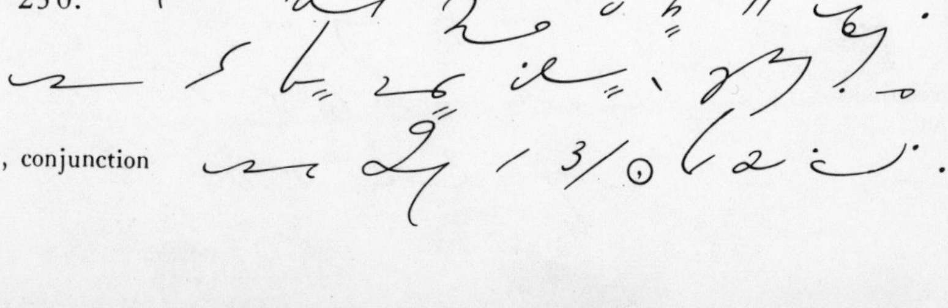

contrary
, introductory

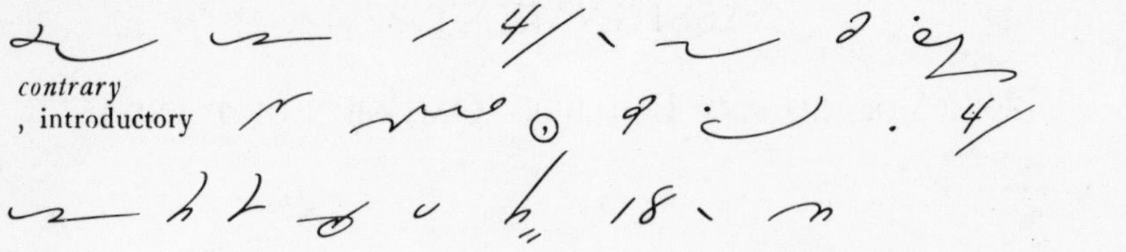

251.

occasion
compliment
received
, parenthetical
organization's
, introductory
decorating

252.

Enclosed
opportunities
; no conjunction

253.

, apposition
headquarters

, parenthetical
facilities
their

, conjunction

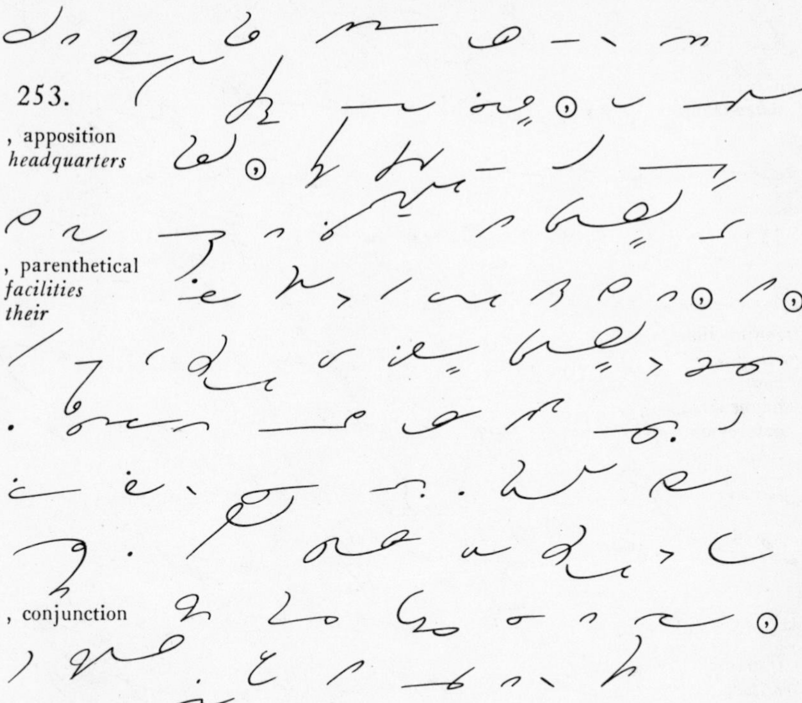

254.

, introductory
passed
guests'

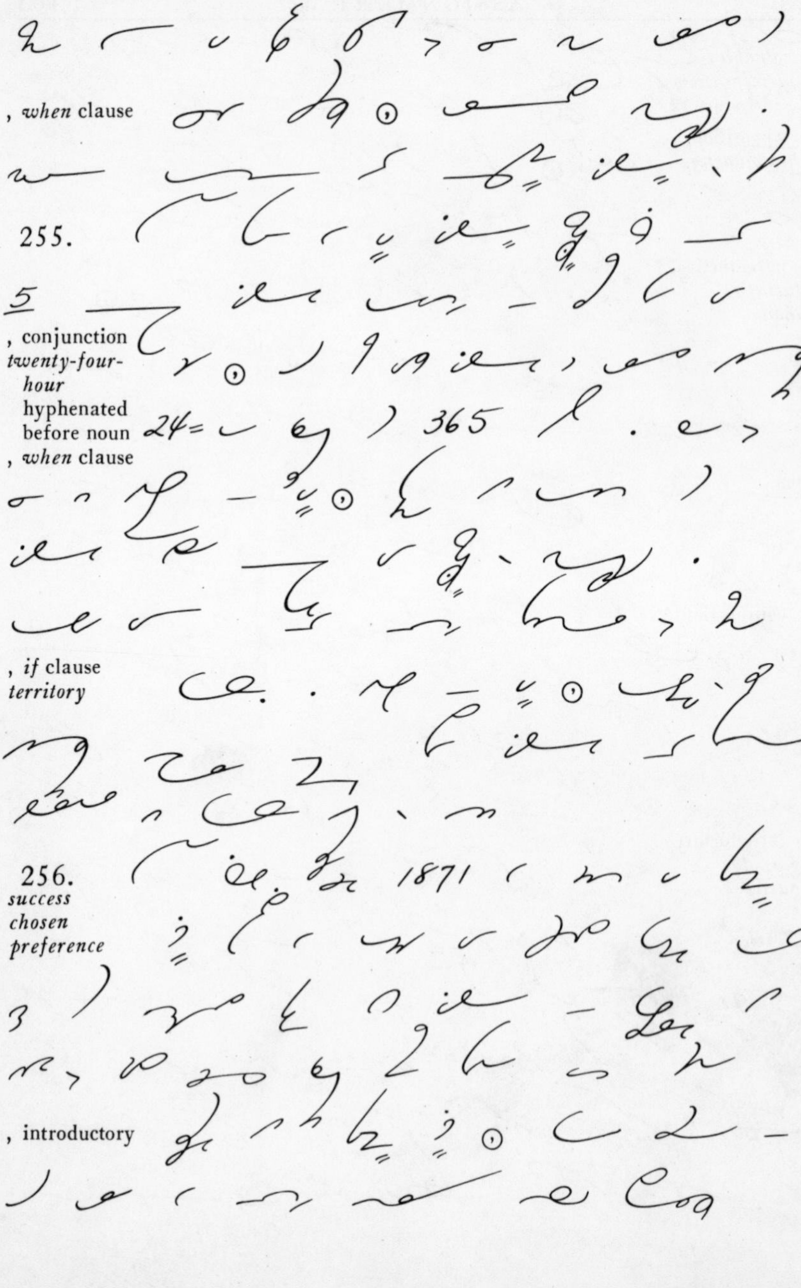

, *when* clause

255.

5

, conjunction

twenty-four-hour hyphenated before noun

, *when* clause

, *if* clause

territory

256.

success

chosen

preference

, introductory

valuable
identification
, introductory

ASSIGNMENT 33

257. Most-Used Business-Letter Phrases

SEVERAL

SO

THANK

THAT

THERE

258. Geographical Expressions

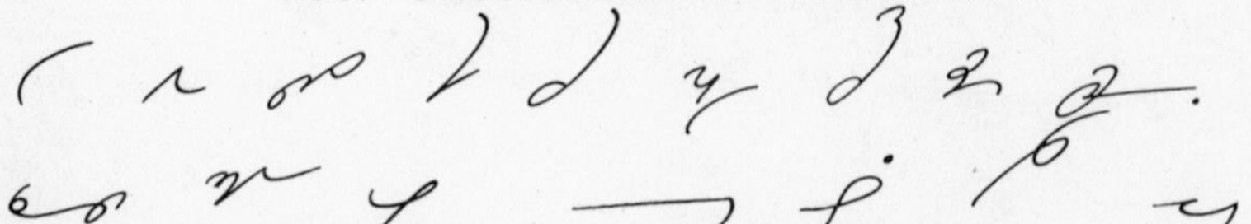

Reading and Writing Practice

259.

recent

, apposition

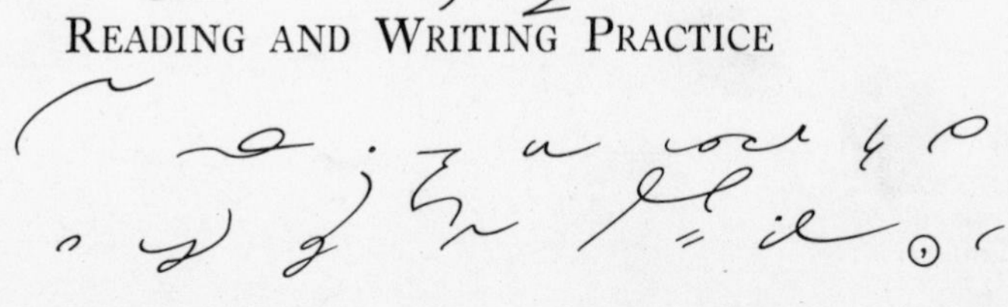

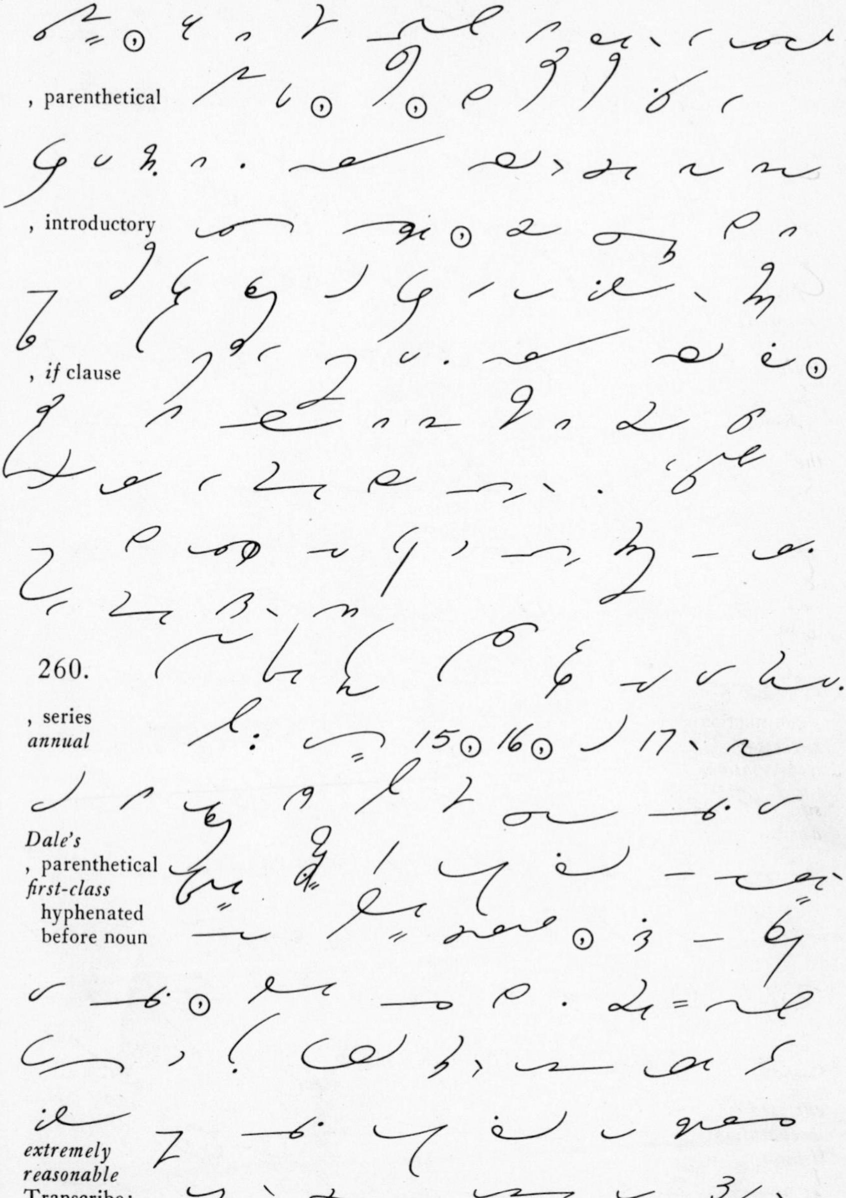

, parenthetical

, introductory

, *if* clause

260.

, series

annual

Dale's

, parenthetical

first-class

hyphenated before noun

extremely

reasonable

Transcribe: *$3.*

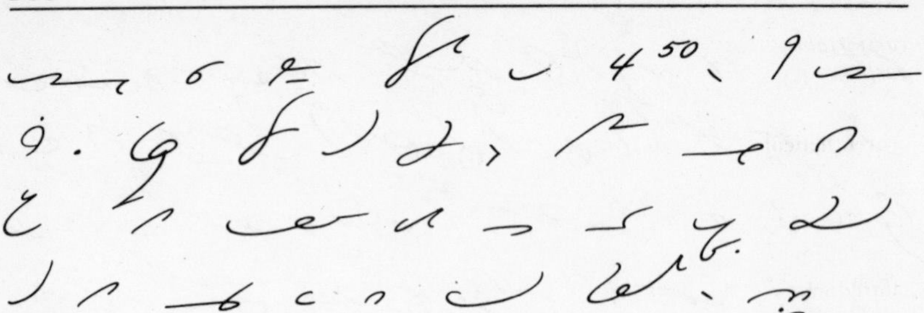

261.

honored
Chicago
their

, conjunction
success
appreciation

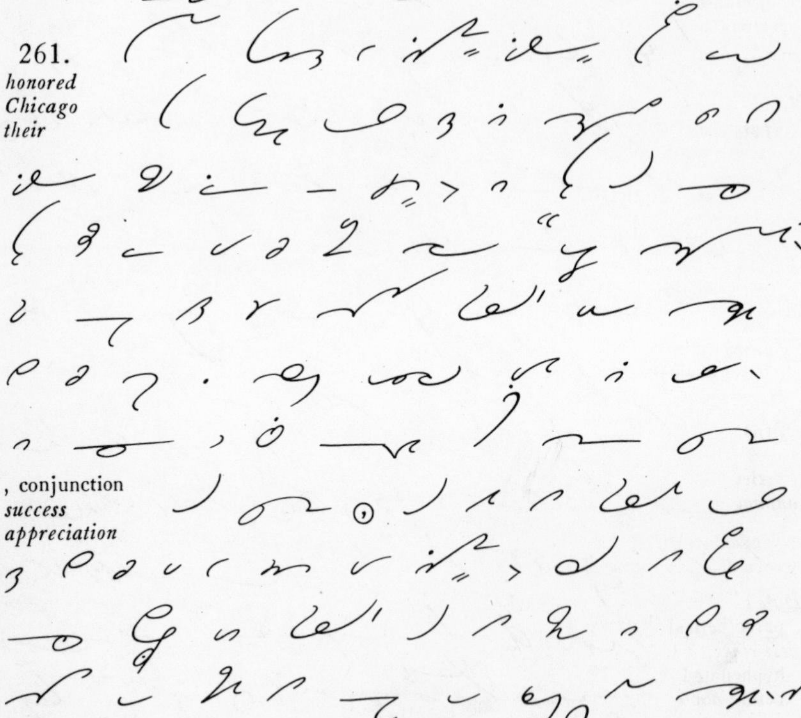

262.

enclosed
preparation
season

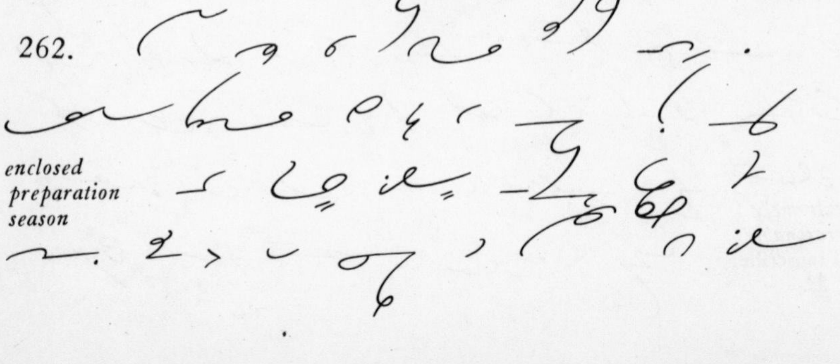

comfortable
earlier

; no conjunction
, *if* clause
fortune

263.

, *when* clause
, parenthetical
Here

, introductory
choose
won't

; no conjunction
, parenthetical

, series

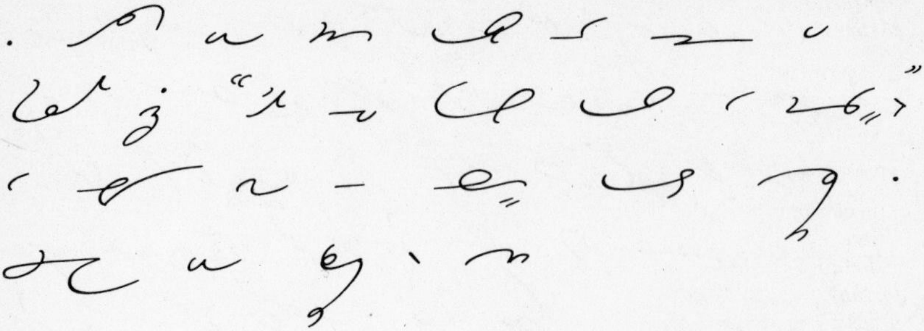

ASSIGNMENT 34

264. Word Families

-SULT

-DENT

-TENT

COUNT

MOST

Reading and Writing Practice

265.

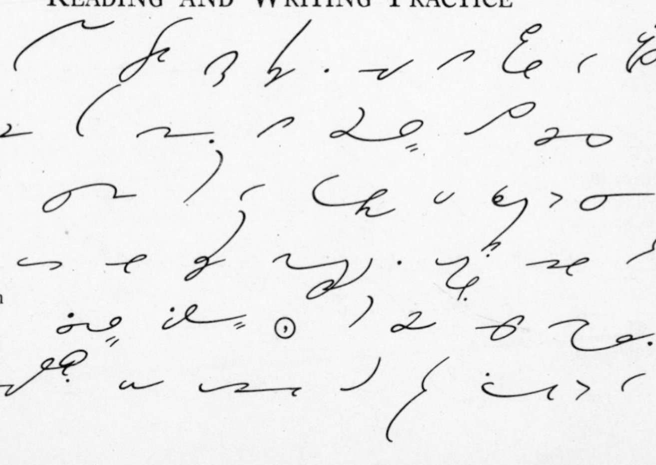

Philadelphia
pleasure

, conjunction
completing
modernizing

, conjunction
forward
greeting

266.

hotel's
forty-eight

48

everyone
, introductory

24

equipped
Transcribe:
February 1.

accommodate
past
disappoint

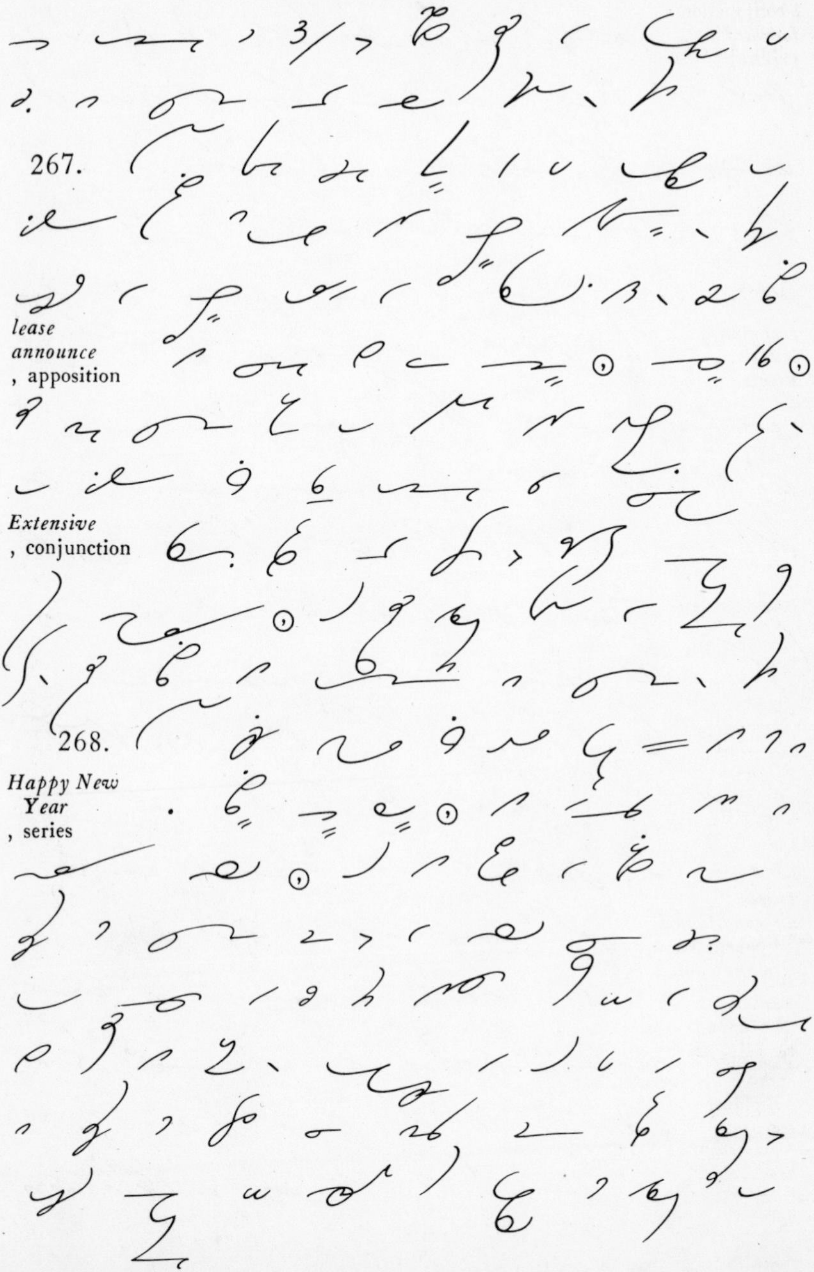

267.

lease
announce
, apposition

Extensive
, conjunction

268.

Happy New Year
, series

guests'
appreciate
, introductory

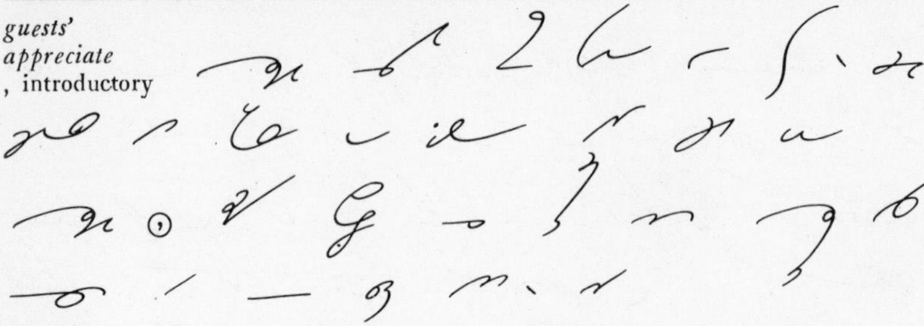

269.

, *as* clause
length
assume

quiet
air-conditioned
hyphenated before noun

, *if* clause
Cordially

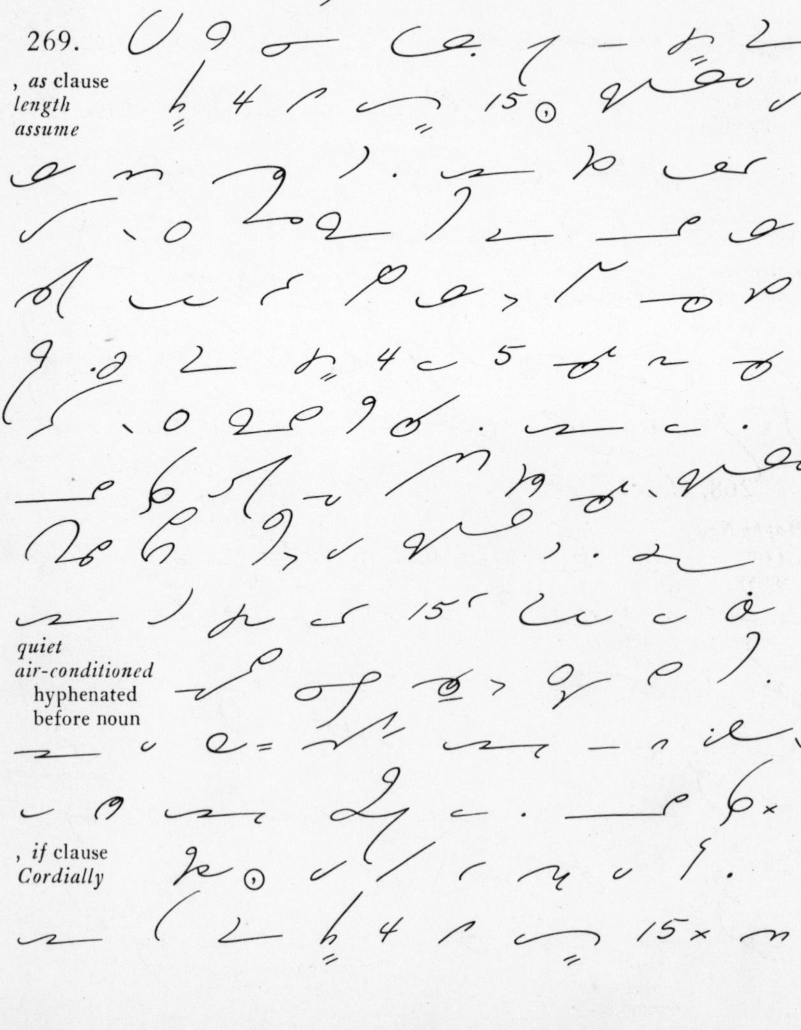

270.

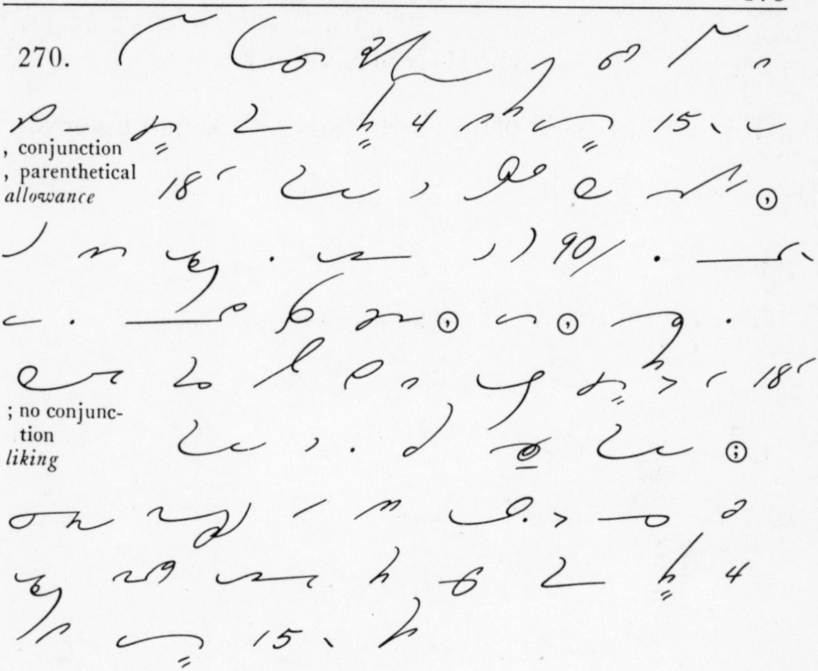

, conjunction
, parenthetical
allowance

; no conjunction
liking

ASSIGNMENT 35

271. Chart of Word Beginnings and Word Endings

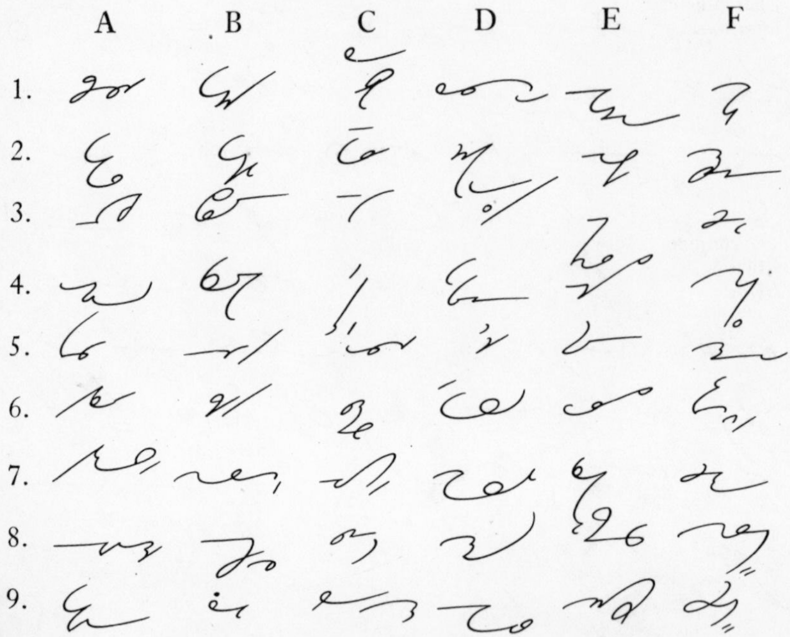

Reading and Writing Practice

272.

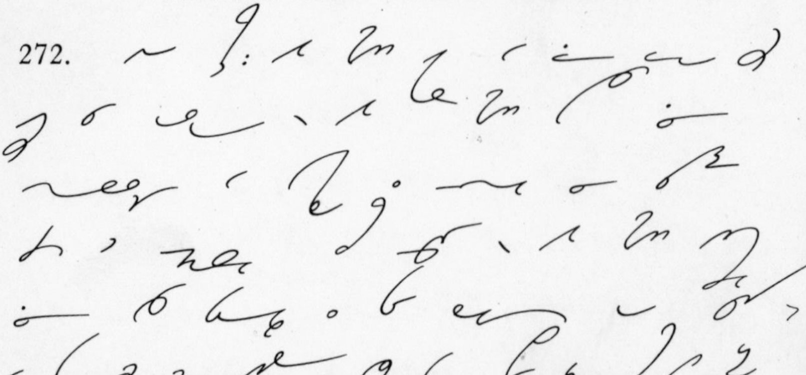

273.

buy

, *when* clause

, series

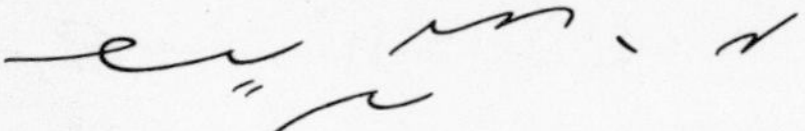

274.

, apposition
receive

well equipped
no noun,
no hyphen

275.

, introductory
information

, series
self-addressed

exceed
year's

276.

occurred

discussion
adjust
, introductory

277.
; no conjunction
, introductory

, conjunction
, parenthetical

278.

, introductory
past

whether
, *as* clause

, conjunction
guarantee
, *if* clause

Won't
. courteous
request

279.

year's
financing
whether

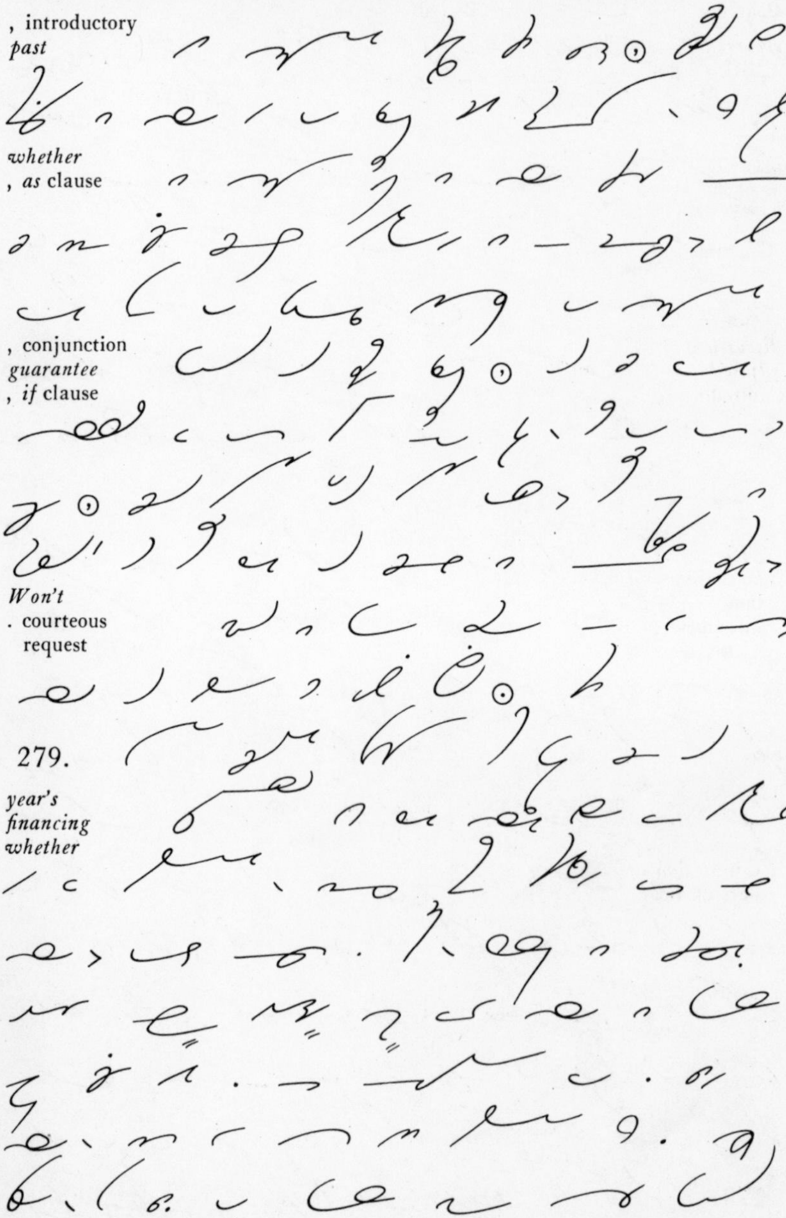

280.

air-conditioning hyphenated before noun

CHAPTER VIII

ASSIGNMENT 36

281. Accuracy Practice

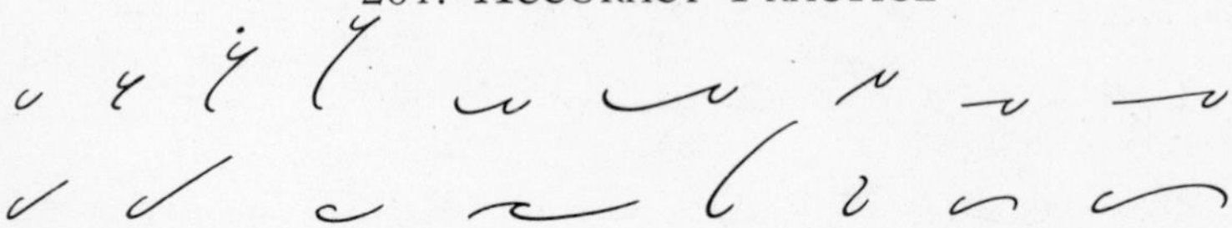

282. Vocabulary Builder

-THER

W

Reading and Writing Practice

283.

experiences
trailers

territory
, conjunction

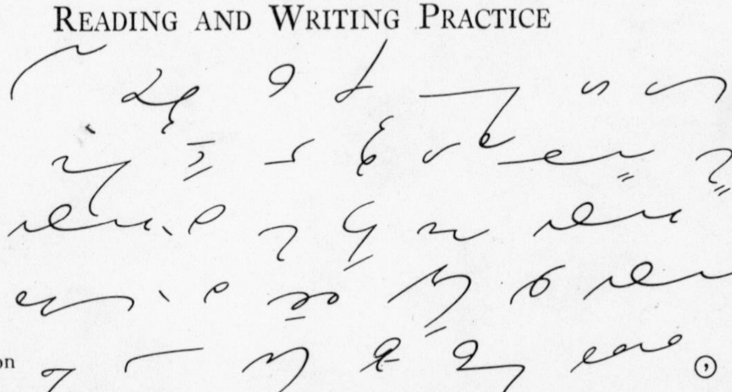

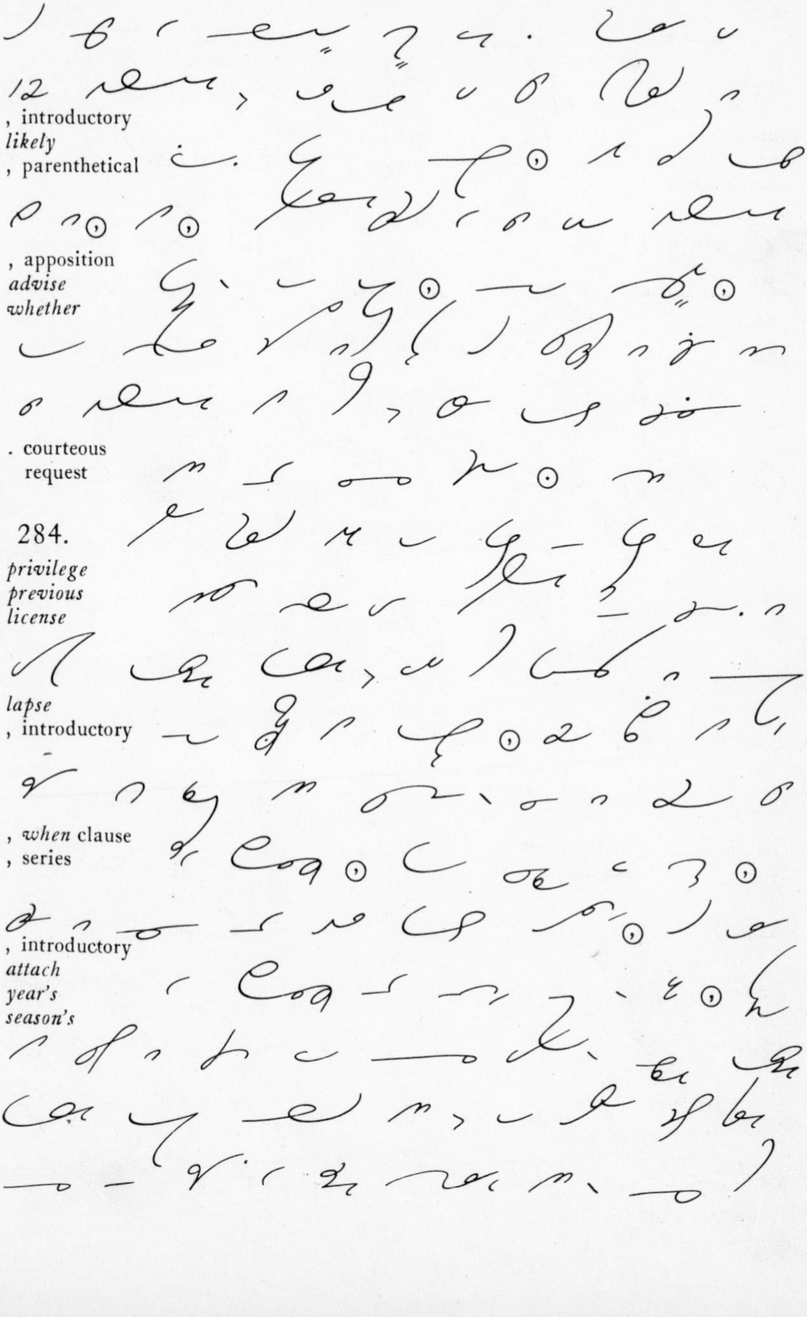

, introductory
likely
, parenthetical

, apposition
advise
whether

. courteous
request

284.
privilege
previous
license

lapse
, introductory

, *when* clause
, series

, introductory
attach
year's
season's

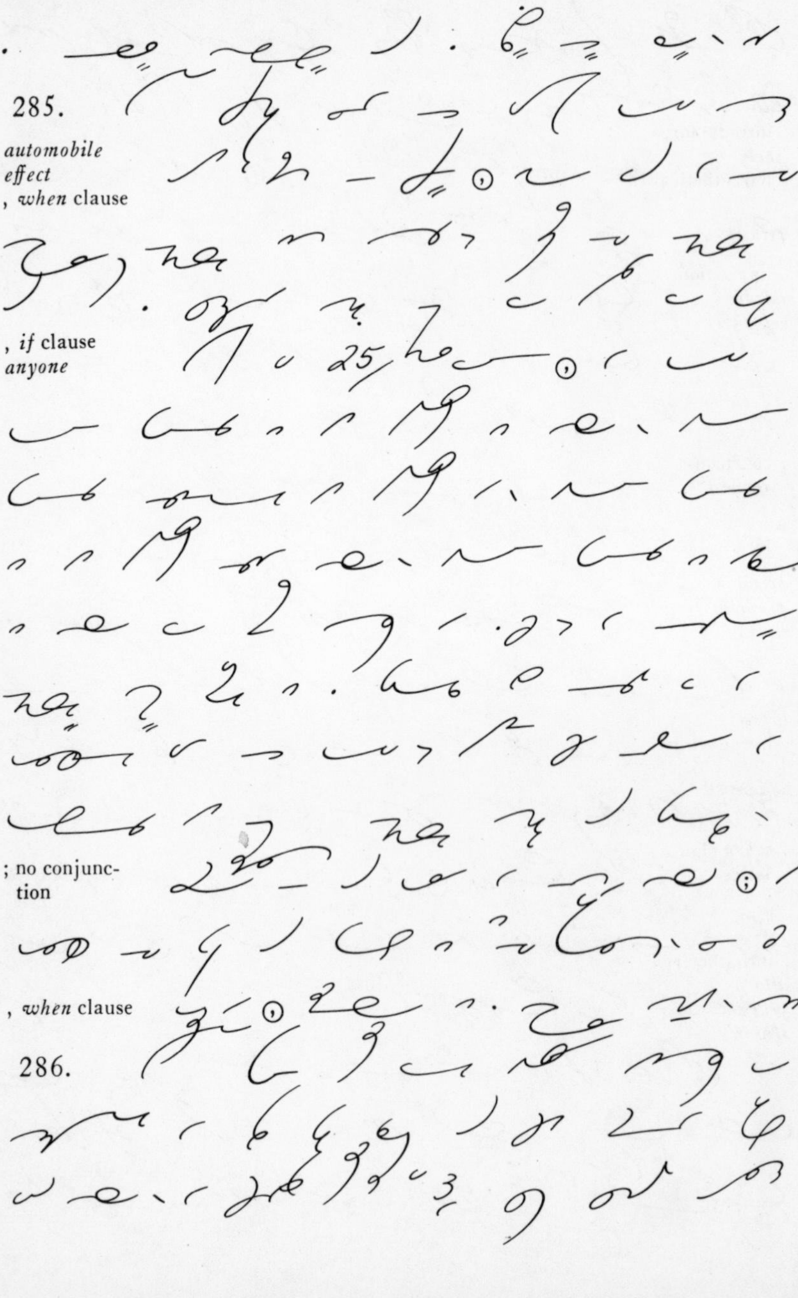

285.

automobile
effect
, *when* clause

, *if* clause
anyone

; no conjunction

, *when* clause

286.

although

pickup

effect
privilege

287.

qualified
experience

urge
deliberately
profitable

low-priced
hyphenated
before noun
, *if* clause

ASSIGNMENT 37

288. Vocabulary Builder

-TATION, ETC.

TERM, THERN

-ORT

NUMBERS, ETC.

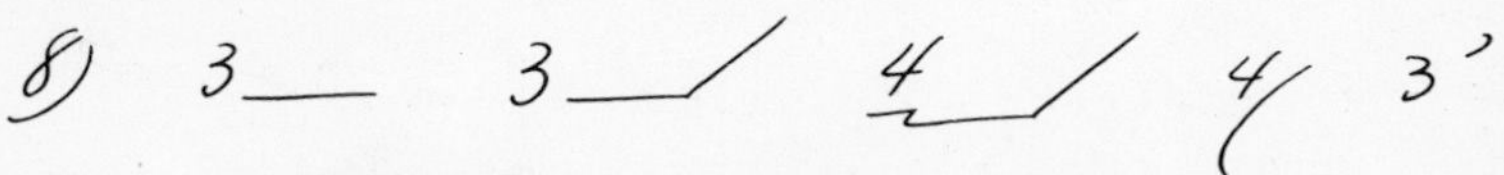

Reading and Writing Practice

289.

successful
, *if* clause

year's
, introductory

quiet
, parenthetical

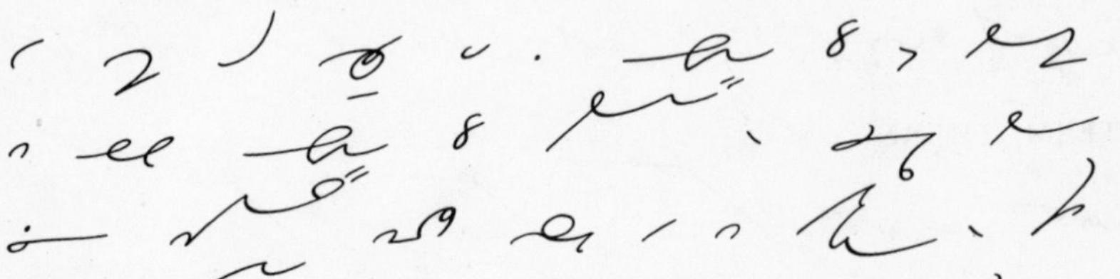

290.

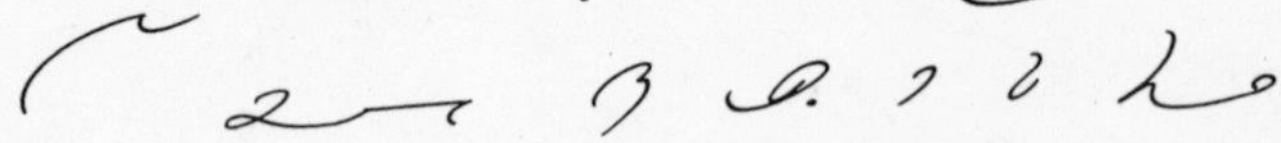

canceling
pleasant

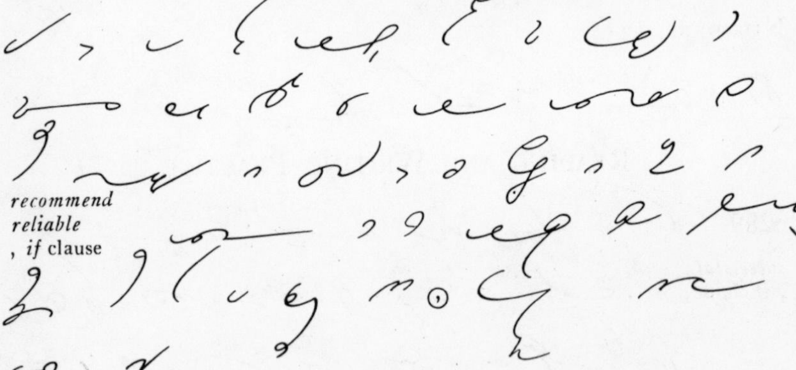

recommend
reliable
, *if* clause

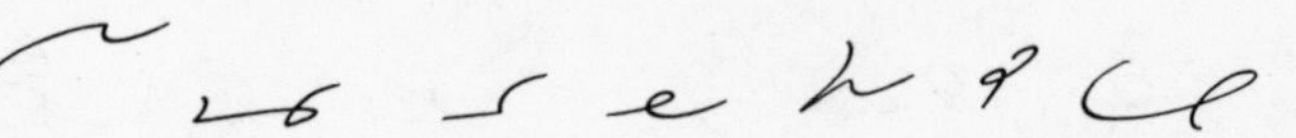

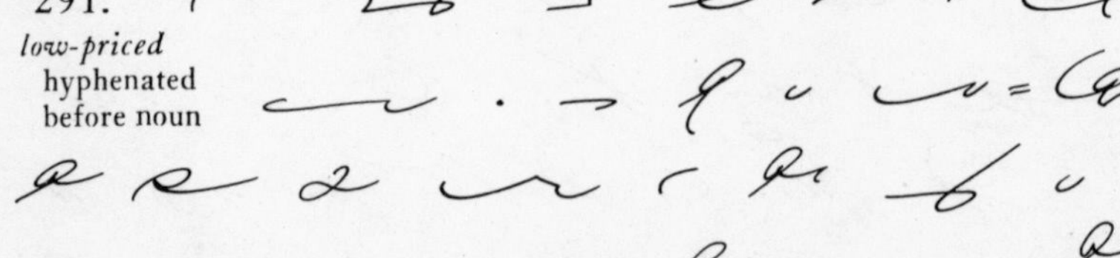

291.

low-priced
hyphenated
before noun

usage
rough
research
, introductory
safety
equipped
, *as* clause
; because of comma

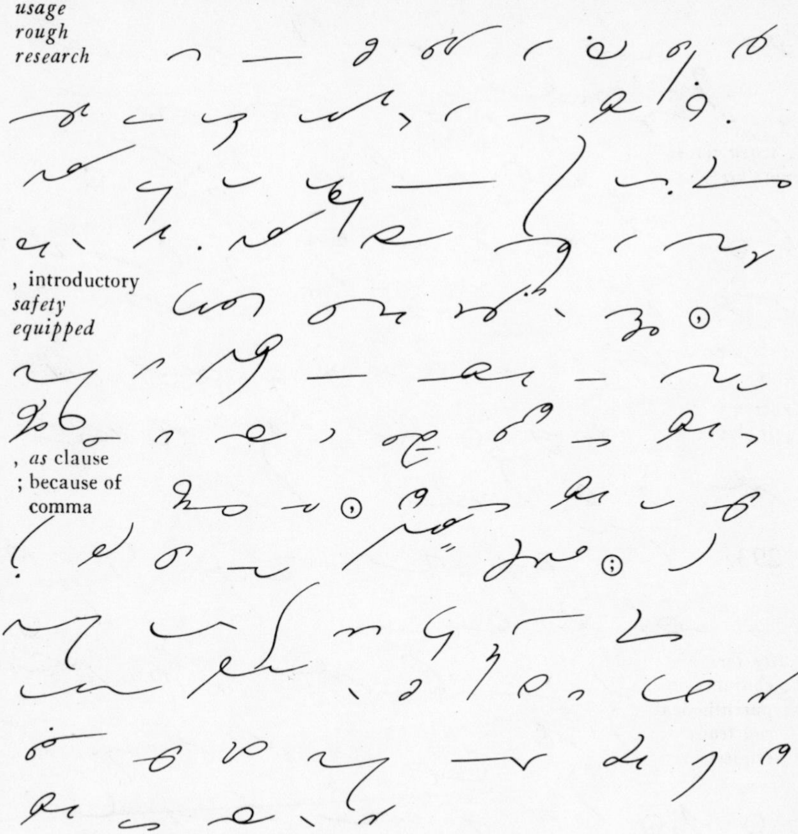

292.

, *when* clause
profitable
, series
; because of commas

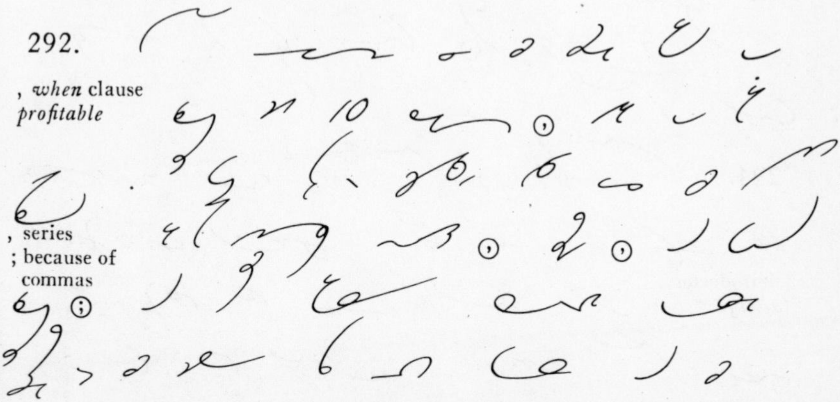

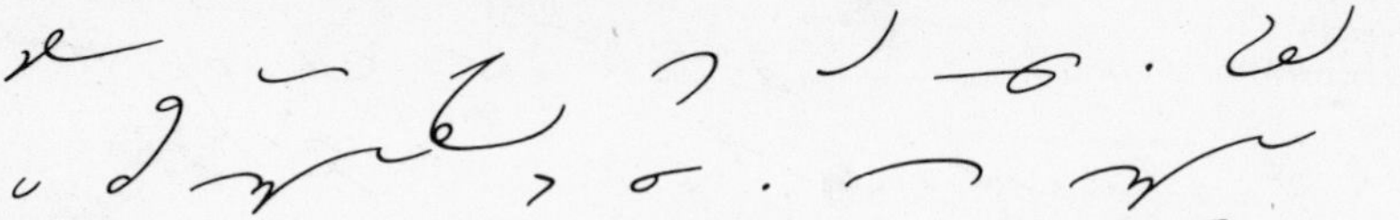

, *when* clause
whether

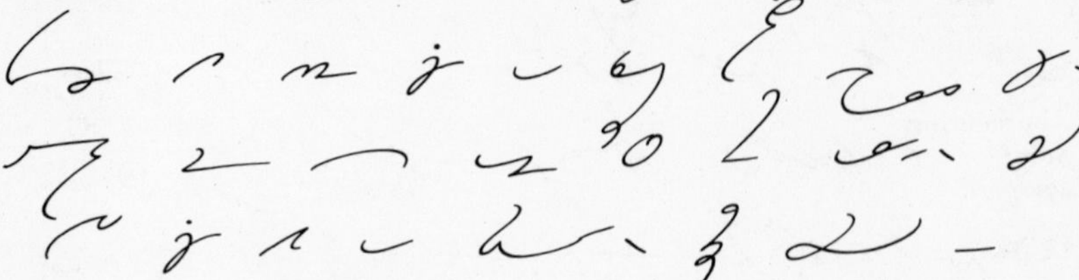

reason
, *if* clause

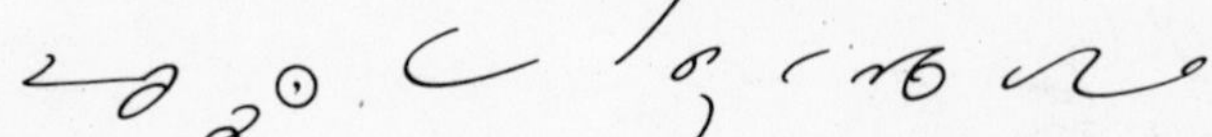

293.

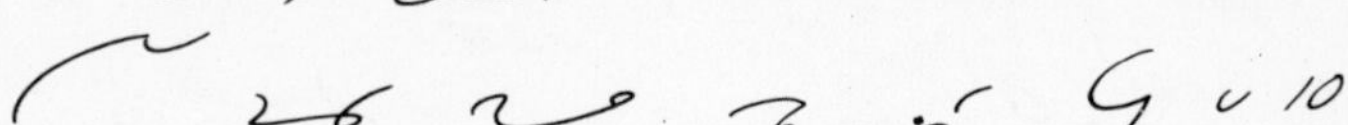

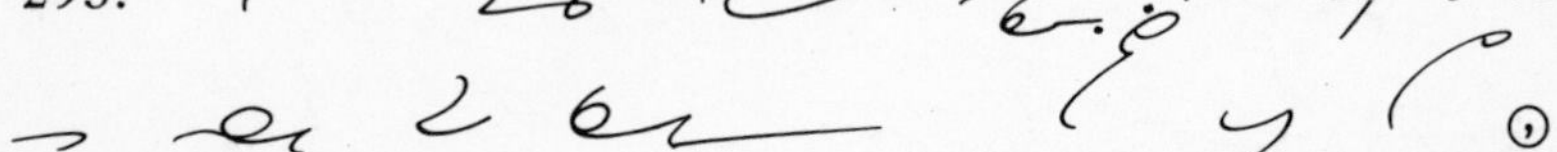

directors
, conjunction
, parenthetical
. courteous
request

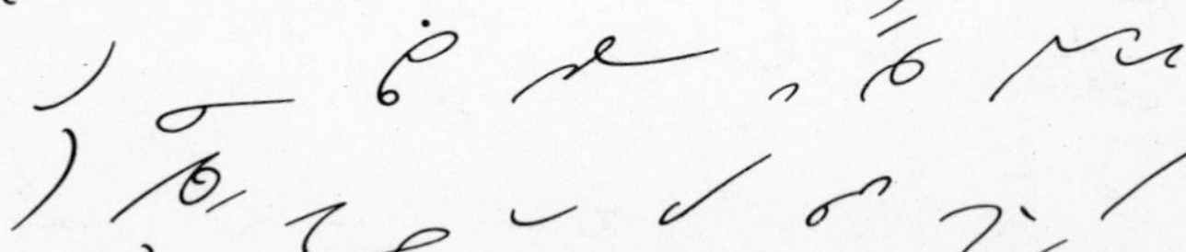

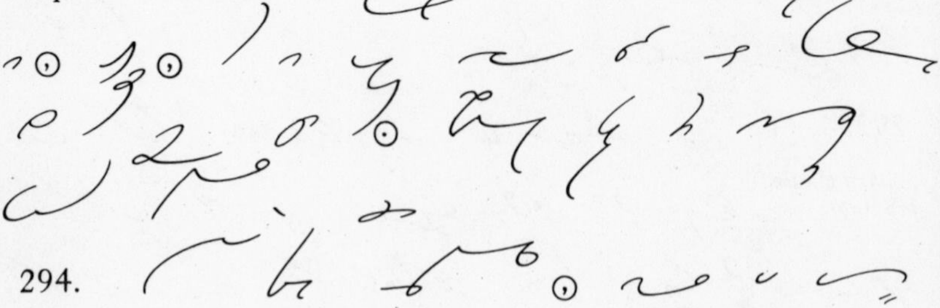

294.

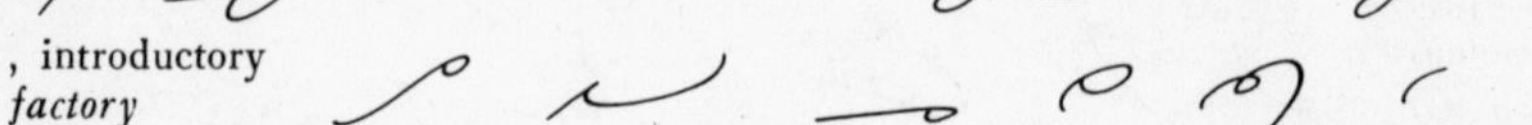

, introductory
factory

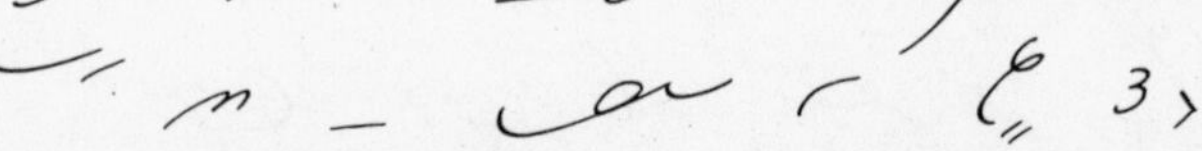

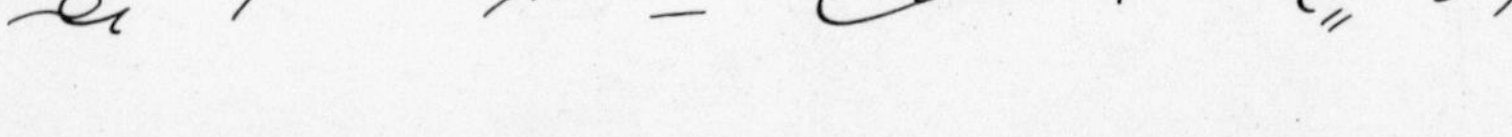

, apposition
territory

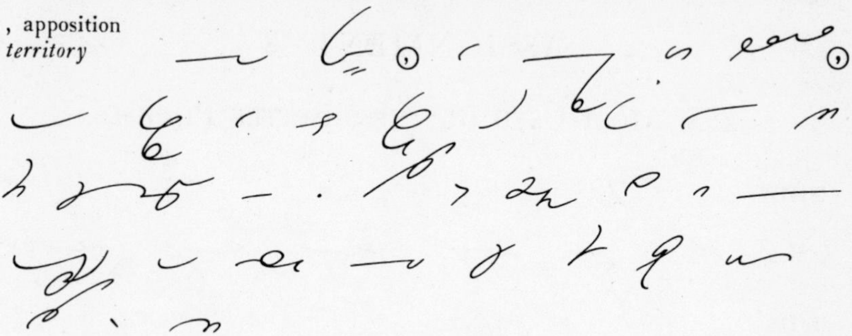

ASSIGNMENT 38

295. MOST-USED BUSINESS-LETTER PHRASES

THEY

THIS

TO

296. GEOGRAPHICAL EXPRESSIONS

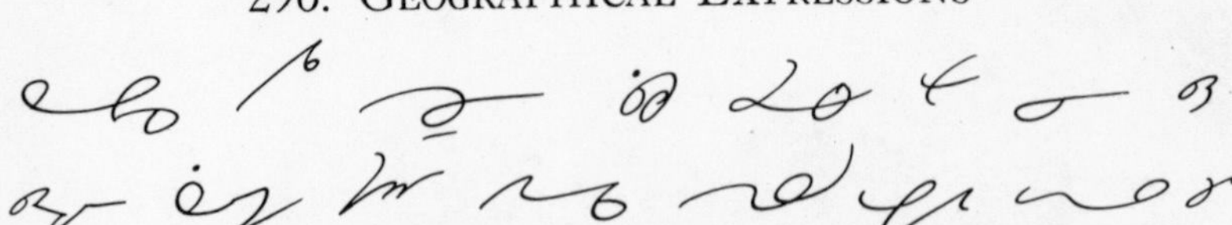

READING AND WRITING PRACTICE

297.

Thanksgiving
, introductory

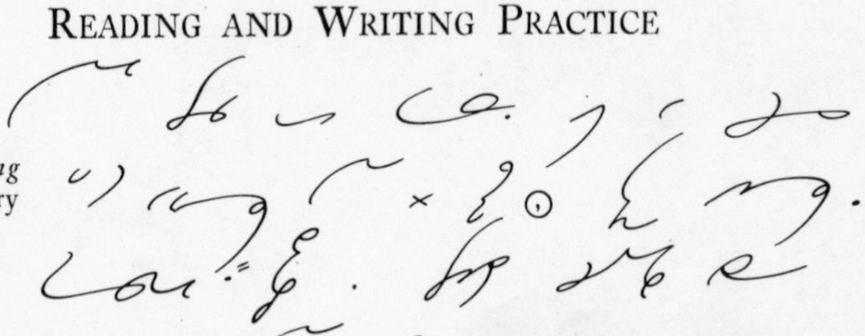

, introductory

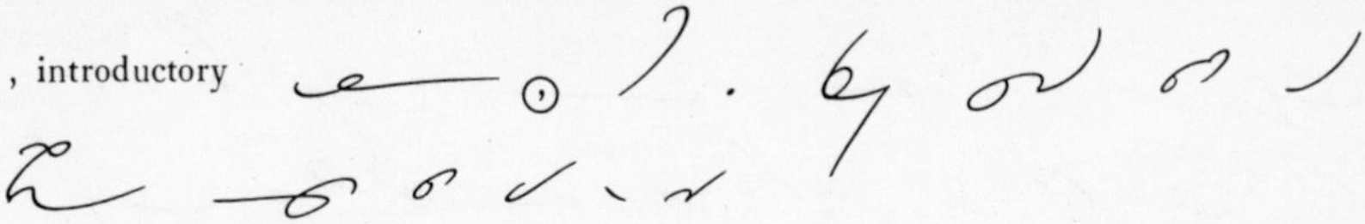

298.

, apposition
twenty-five

past
, *as* clause

sometime
, series

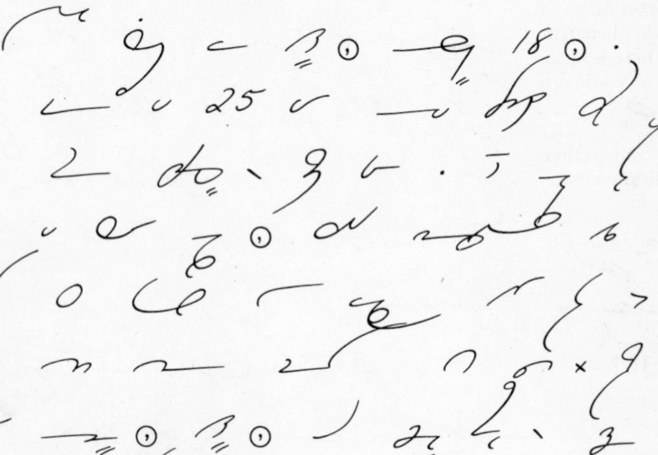

299.

raise
maintenance

, *as* clause

economical
, *as* clause

receipt
remittance
, introductory

300.

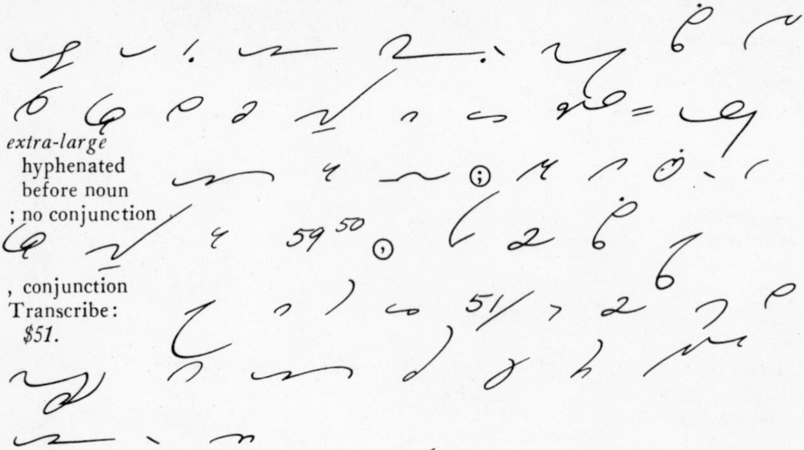

extra-large
hyphenated
before noun
; no conjunction
, conjunction
Transcribe:
$51.

301.

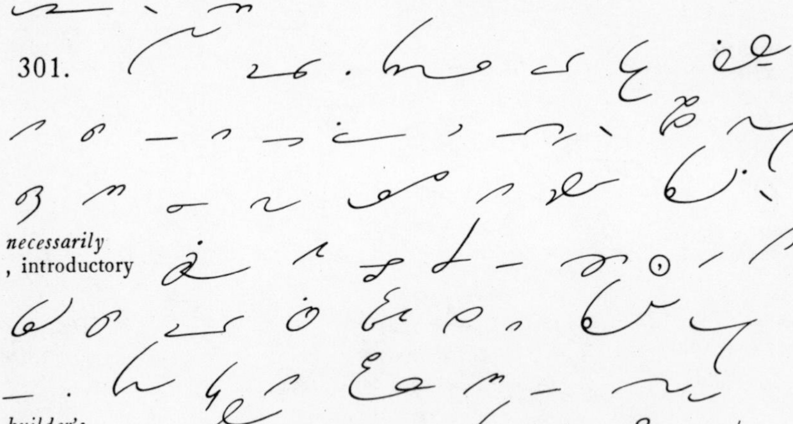

necessarily
, introductory
builder's
source
adventure

302.

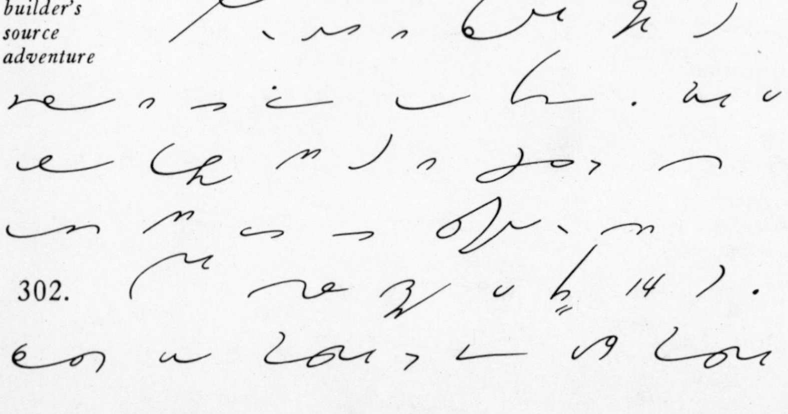

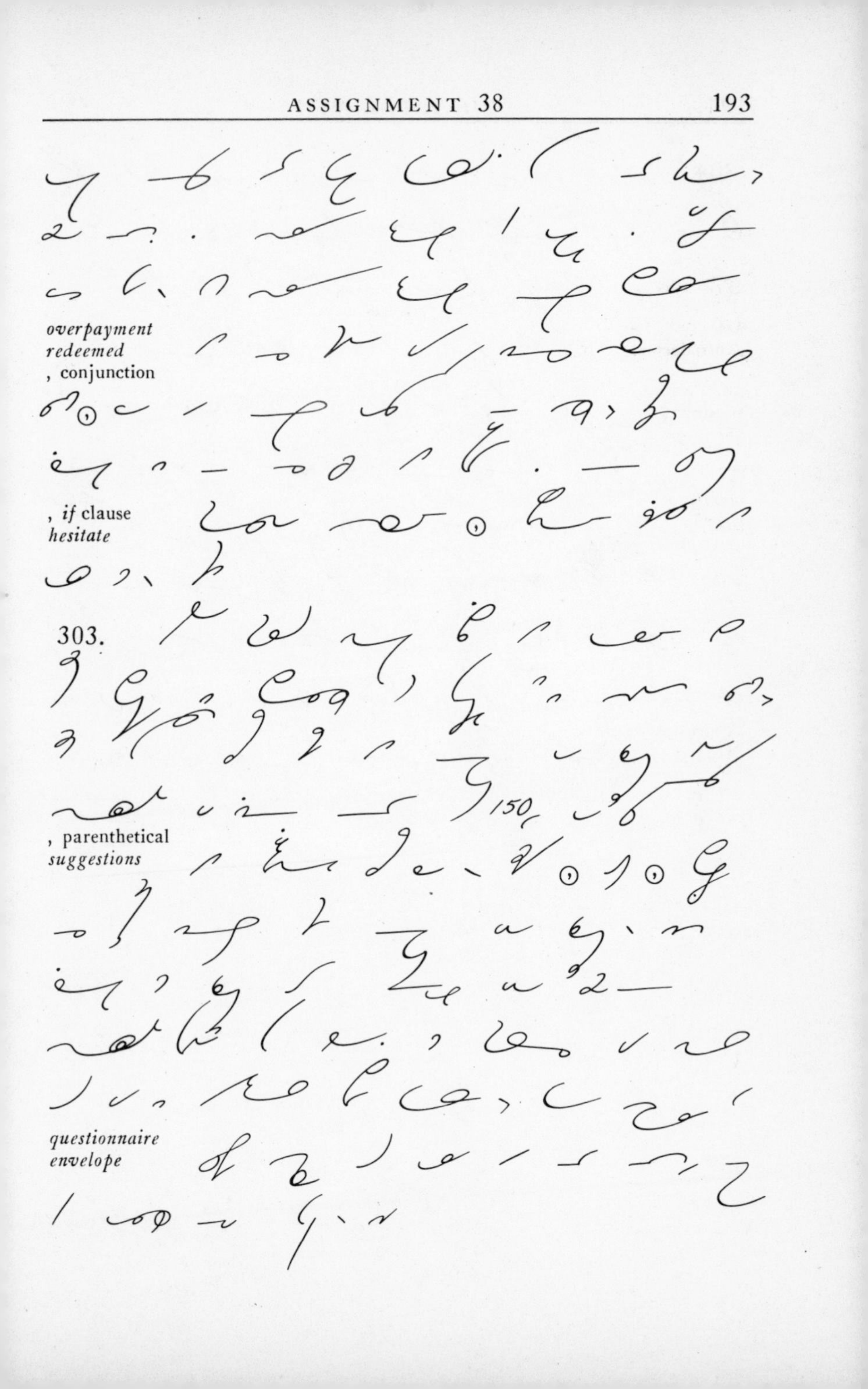

overpayment
redeemed
, conjunction

, *if* clause
hesitate

303.

, parenthetical
suggestions

questionnaire
envelope

304.

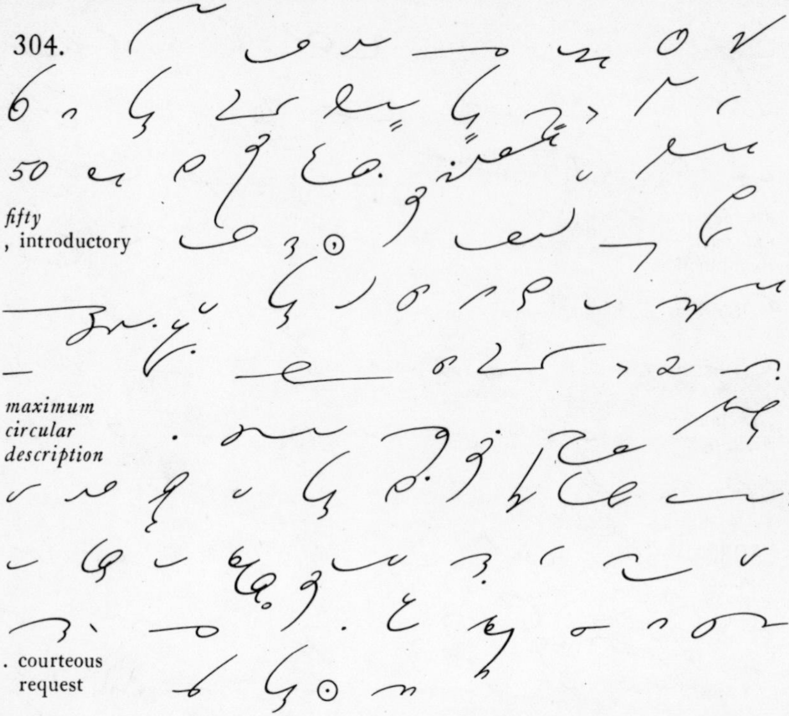

50

fifty

, introductory

maximum
circular
description

. courteous
request

ASSIGNMENT 39

305. Word Families

-WAY

-CY, -SY

CENTR-

DISA-

-IAL, -EAL

Reading and Writing Practice

306.
recently
, apposition
, conjunction

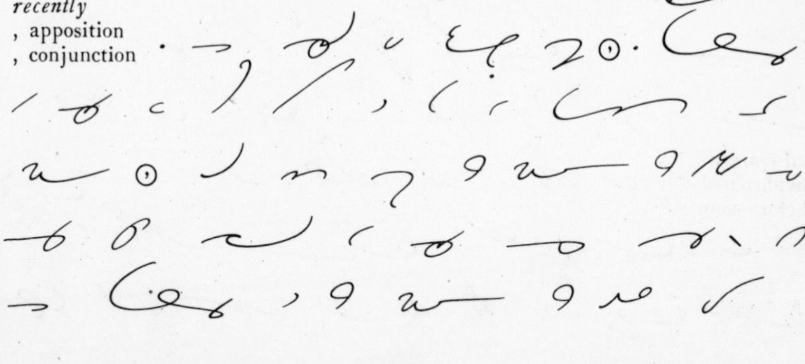

weighs
; no conjunction

beforehand
neighborhood
, *if* clause

307.
centuries
oriental
, conjunction

, parenthetical
difference

well-trained
hyphenated before noun

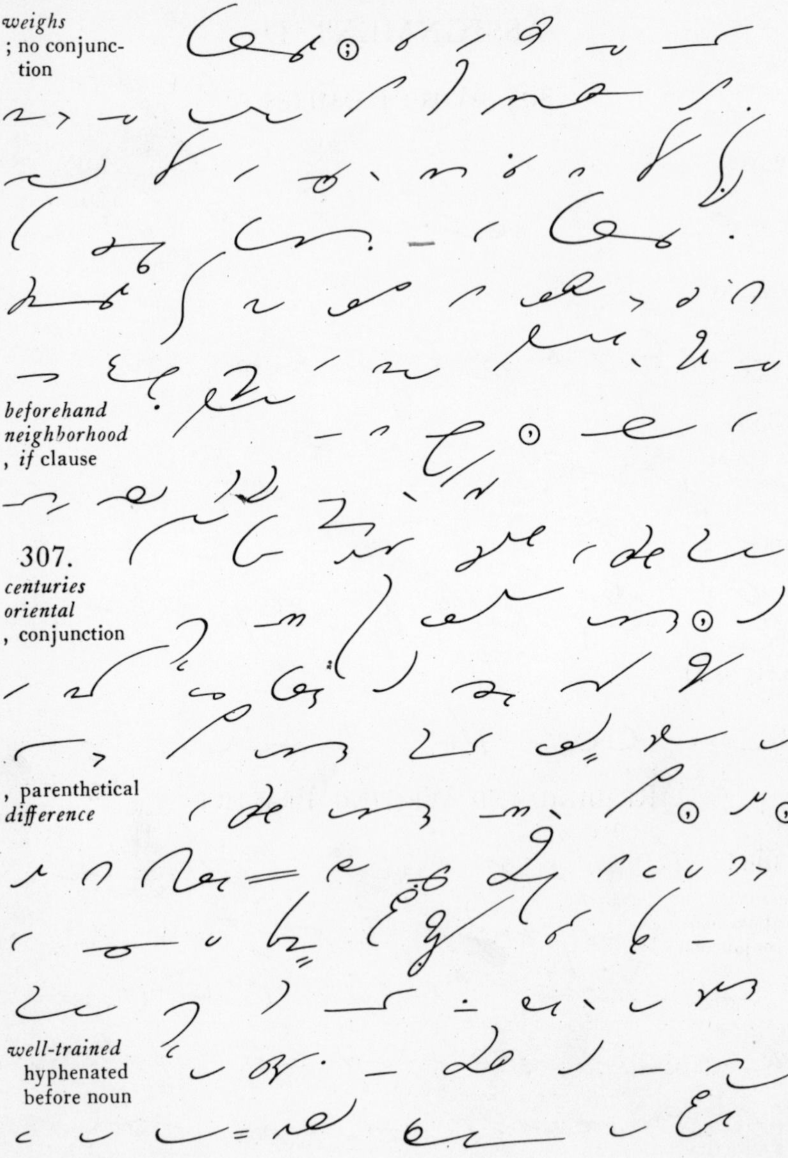

Won't
. courteous request

308.

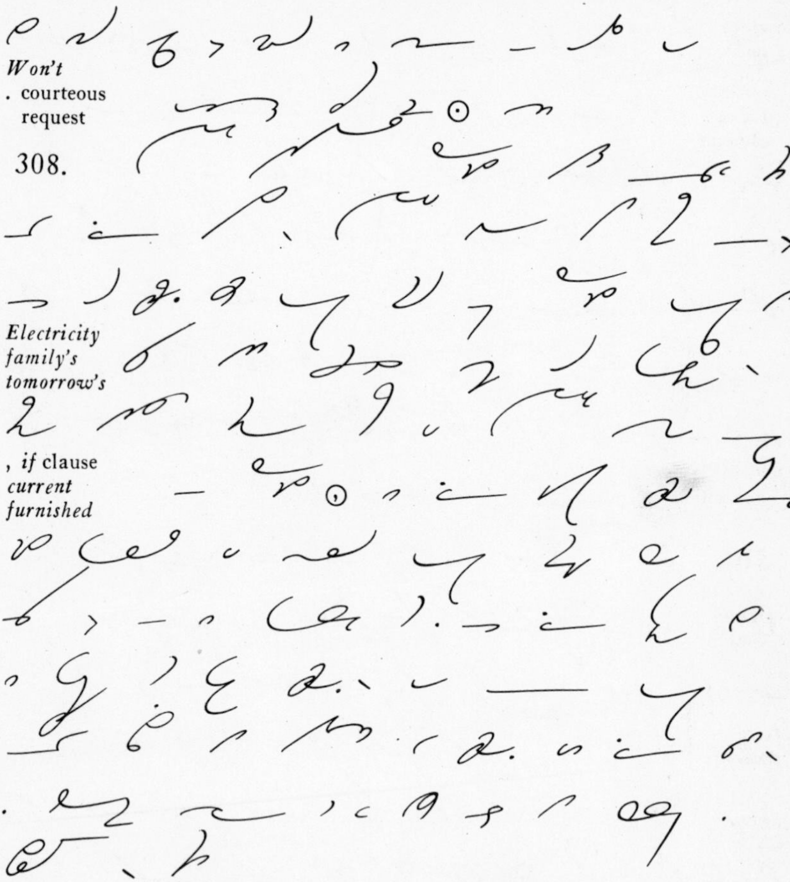

Electricity
family's
tomorrow's

, *if* clause
current
furnished

309.

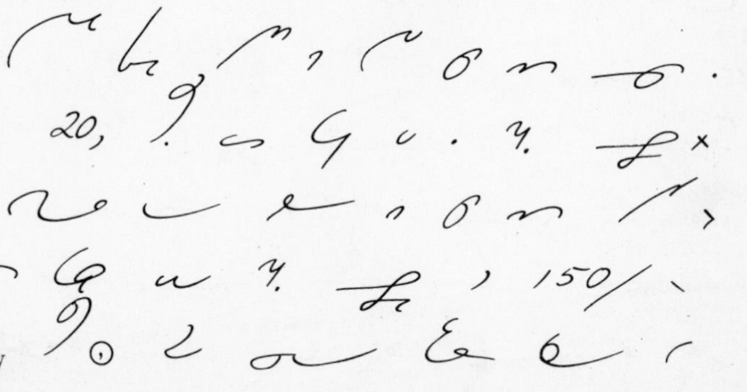

, *if* clause

Transcribe:
$150.
, introductory

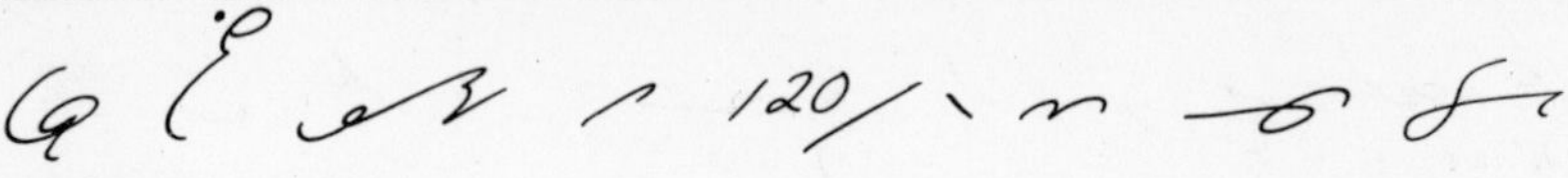

, series
; because of
commas

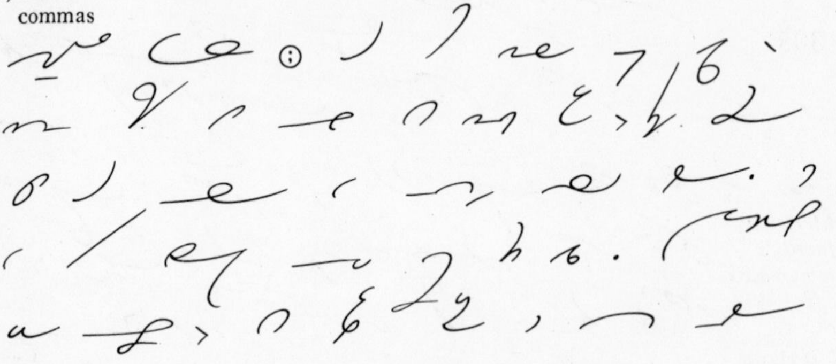

, apposition

310.

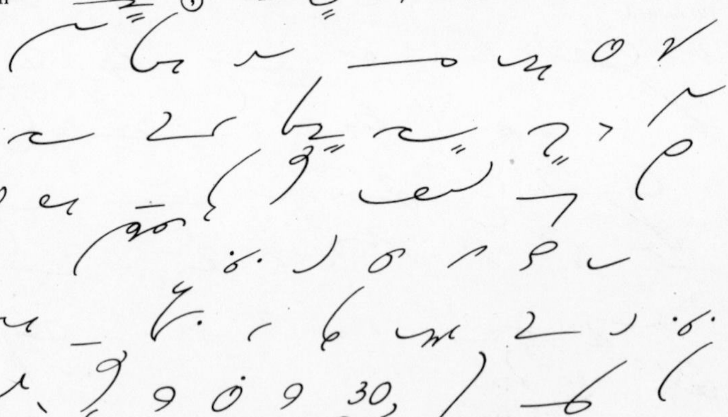

forty
domestic

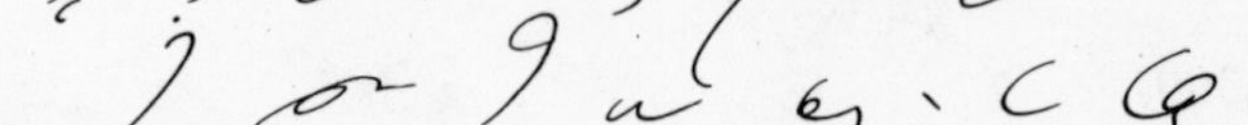

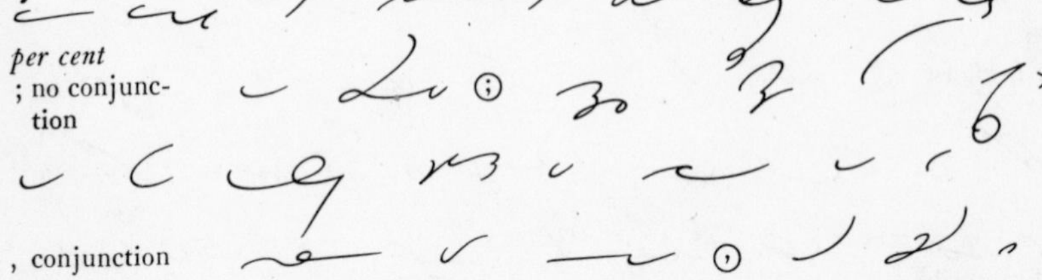

per cent
; no conjunc-
tion

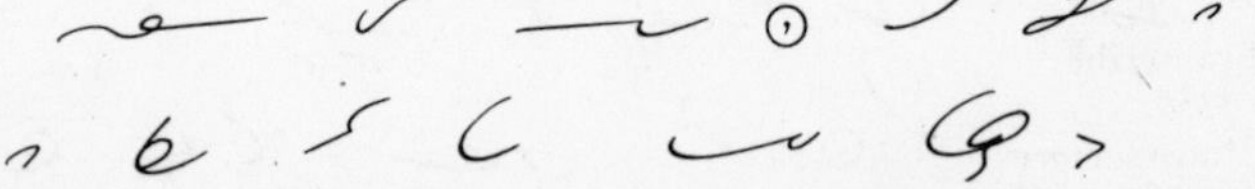

, conjunction

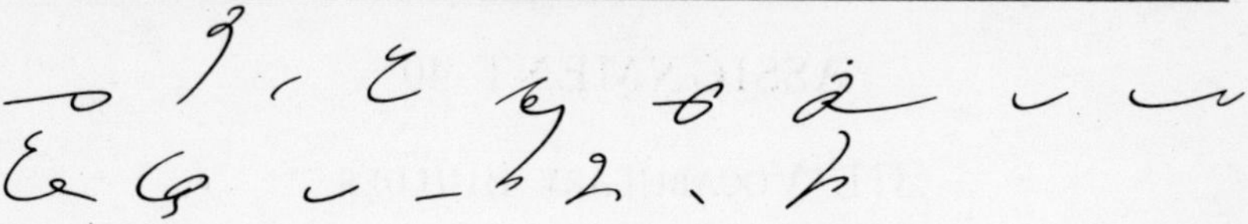

ASSIGNMENT 40

311. Vocabulary Builder

NT, ND

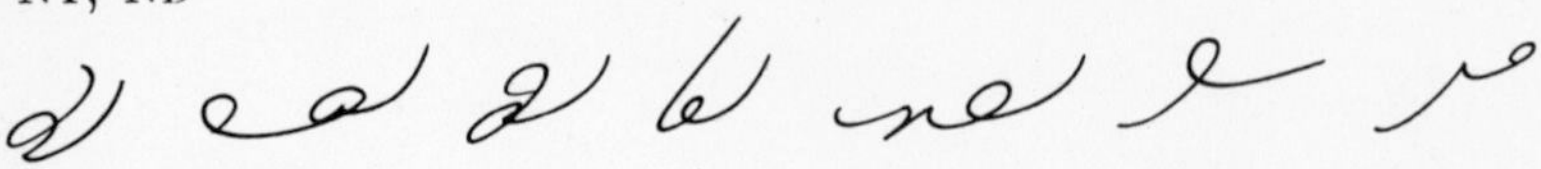

MD

GENT, PEND

DIV, TIVE

TAIN

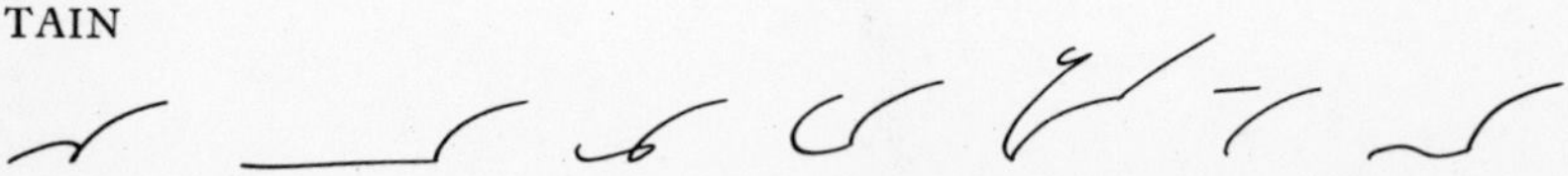

TEM, DEM

Reading and Writing Practice

312.

313.

, parenthetical
beautify
repaired

hand-cleaning
hyphenated
before noun

reliable
companies
assistance

314.

Transcribe:
$475

, *if* clause
privilege

315.
five-day
hyphenated
before noun

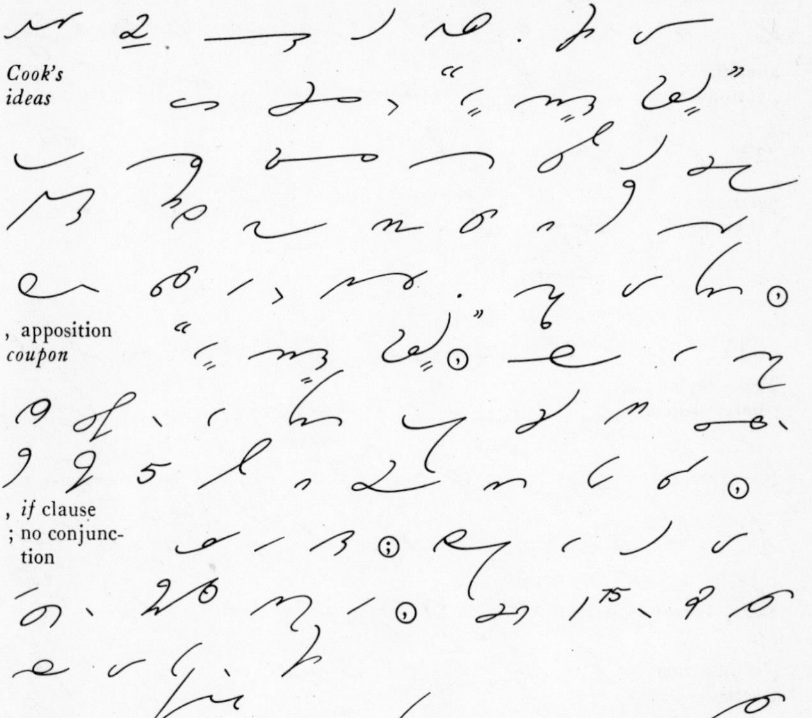

Cook's ideas

, apposition
coupon

, *if* clause
; no conjunction

316.

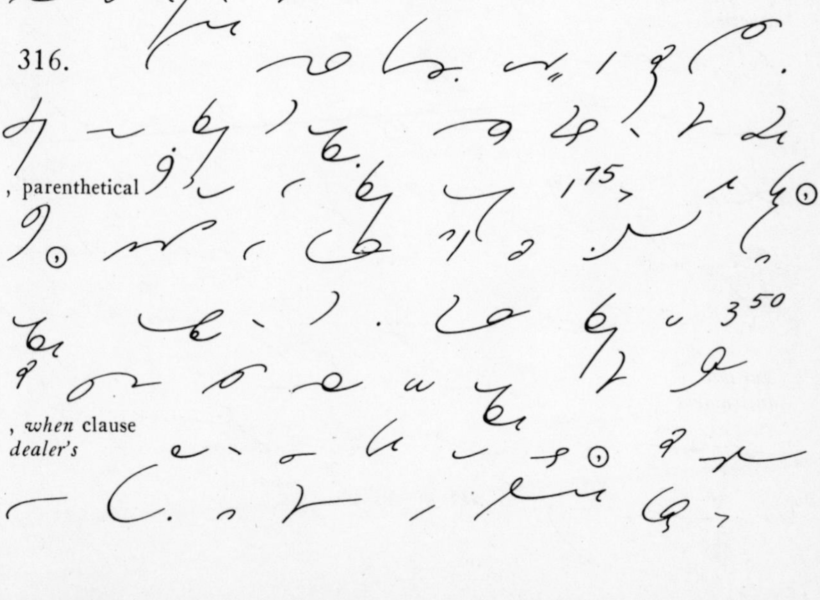

, parenthetical

, *when* clause
dealer's

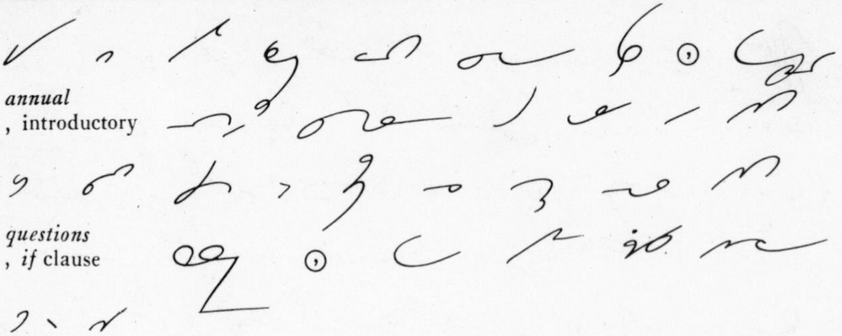

annual
, introductory

questions
, *if* clause

317.

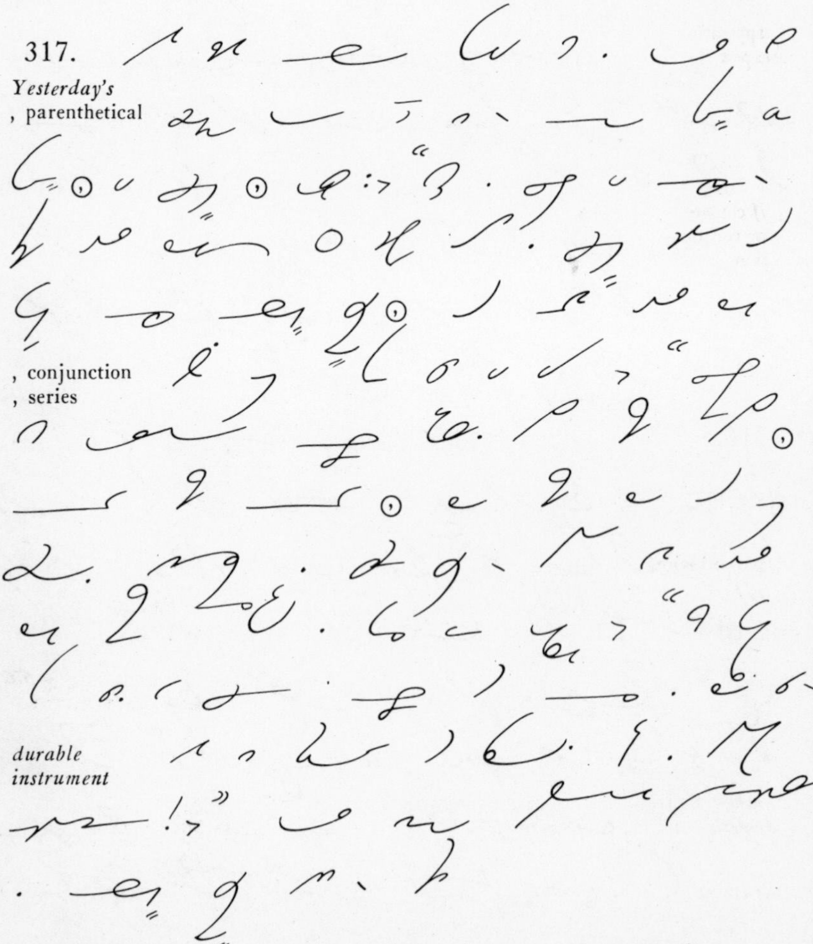

Yesterday's
, parenthetical

, conjunction
, series

durable
instrument

CHAPTER IX

ASSIGNMENT 41

318. Brief-Form Chart

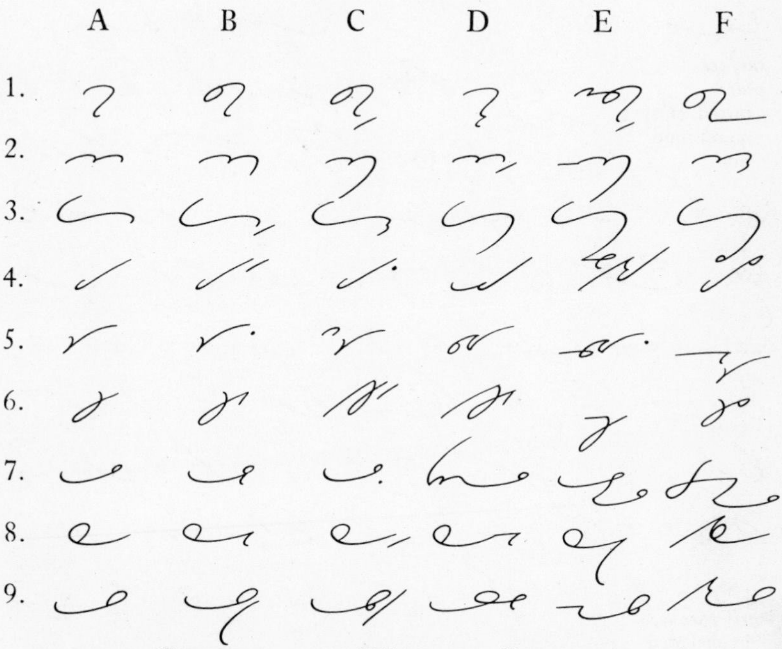

Reading and Writing Practice

319.

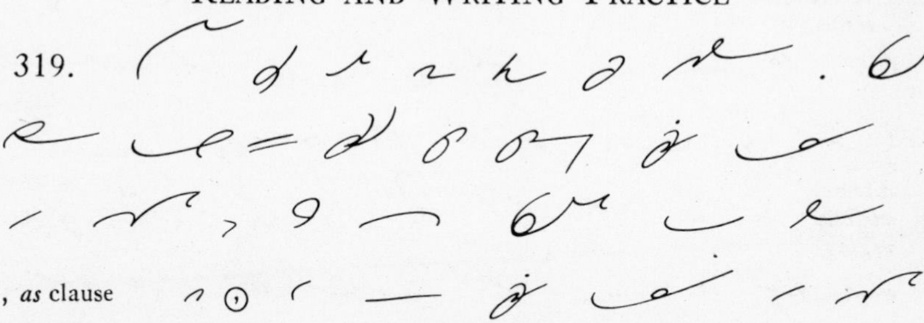

per cent
Brill's
, apposition

surface
years'
, introductory
; no conjunction

320.
well-planned
hyphenated before noun
, series

diseases
vicinity
urging

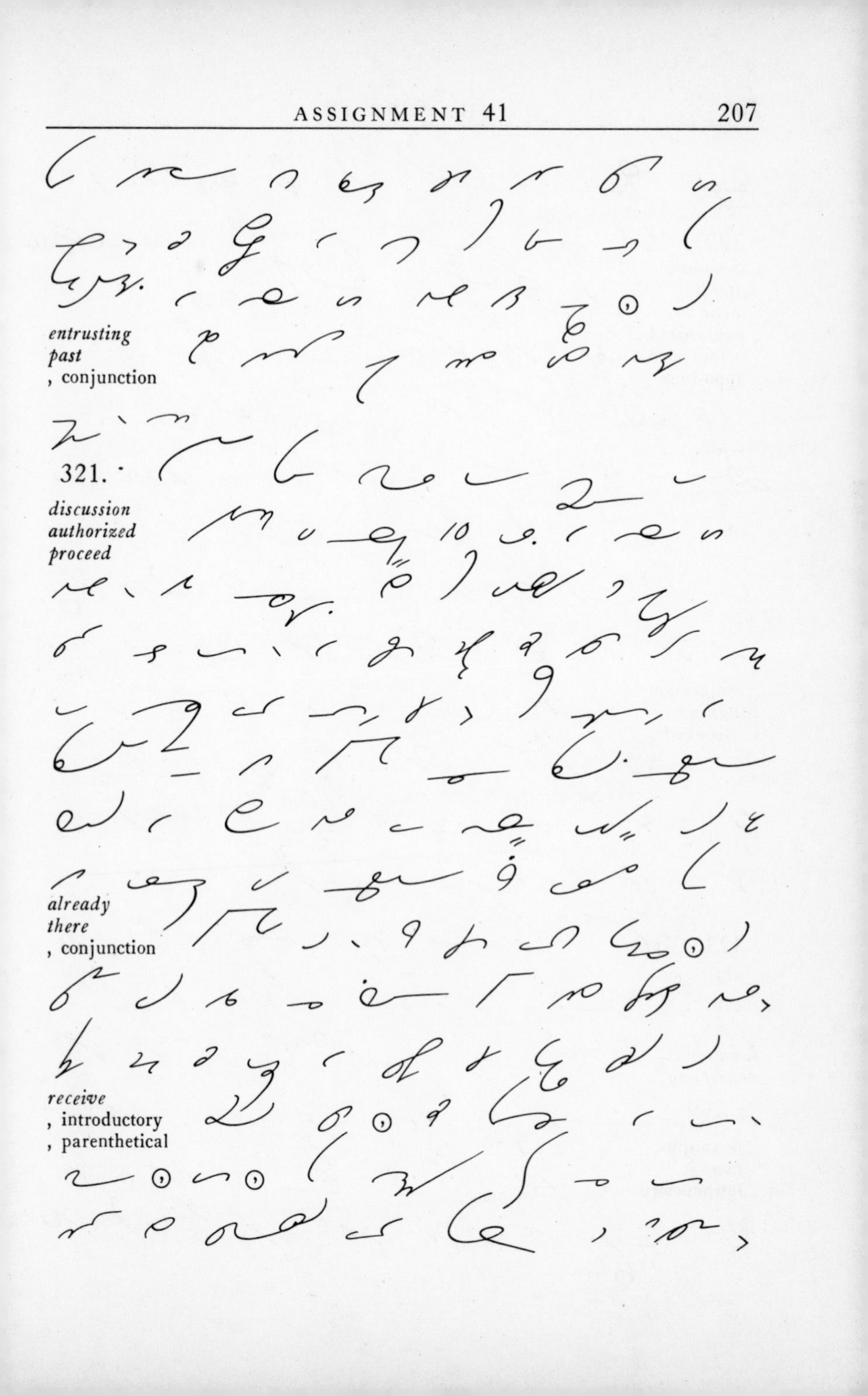

entrusting
past
, conjunction

321.

discussion
authorized
proceed

already
there
, conjunction

receive
, introductory
, parenthetical

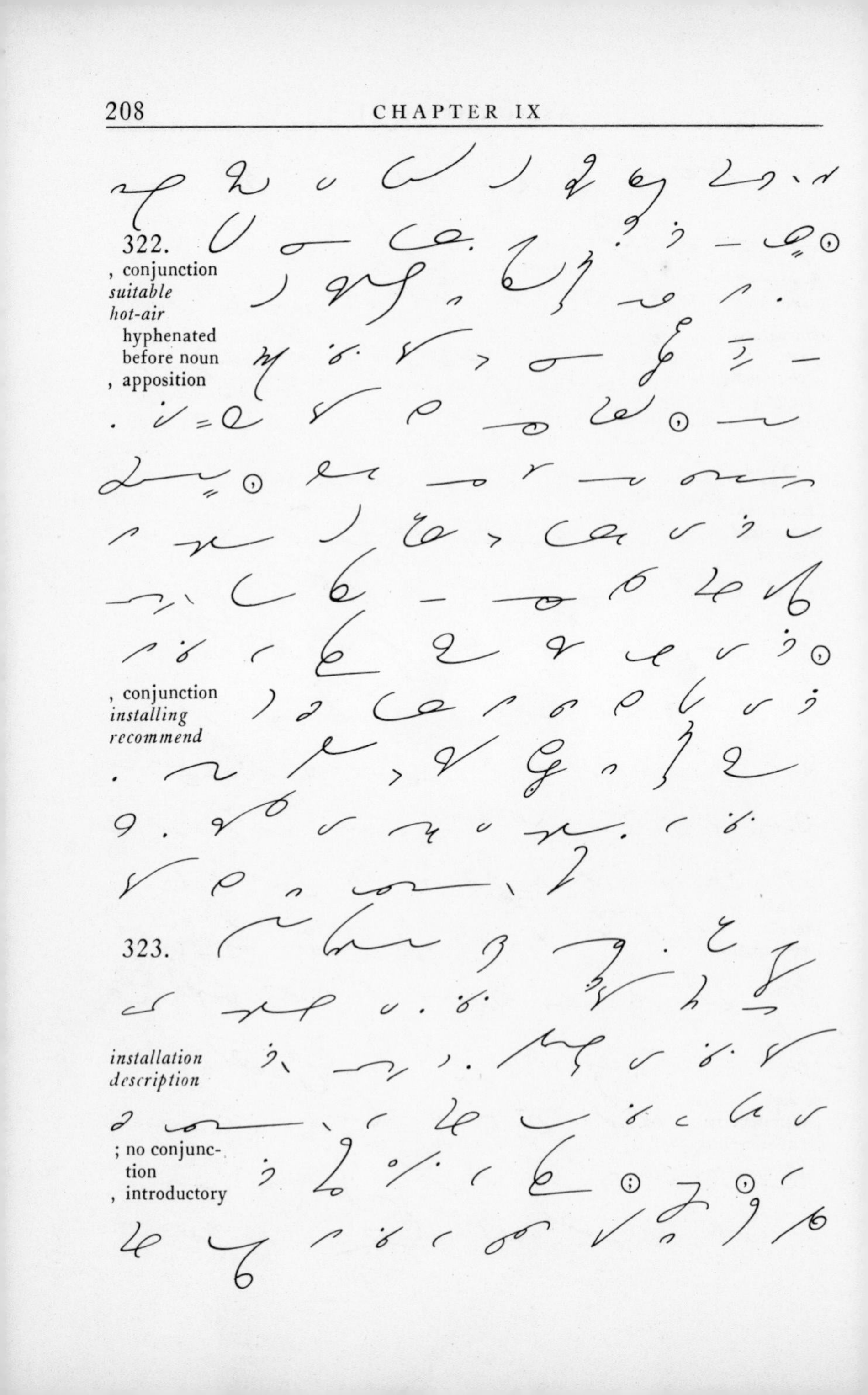

322.

, conjunction
suitable
hot-air
hyphenated before noun
, apposition

, conjunction
installing
recommend

323.

installation
description

; no conjunction
, introductory

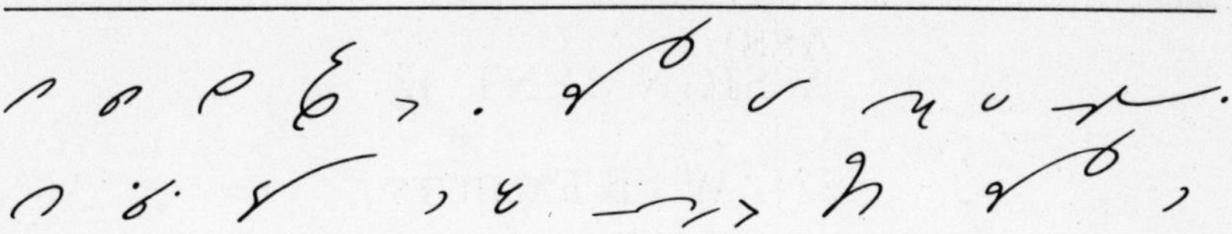

, *if* clause

ASSIGNMENT 42

324. Word Families

-TIME

-FORM

-SIGN

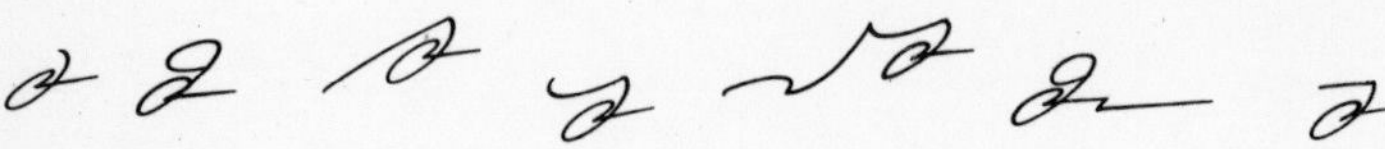

-NCTION

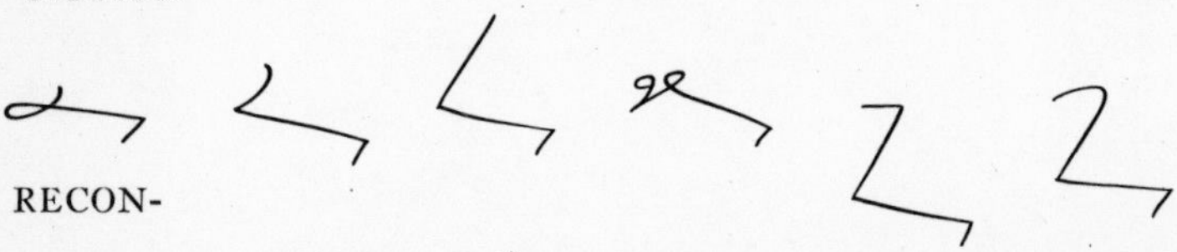

RECON-

Reading and Writing Practice

325.

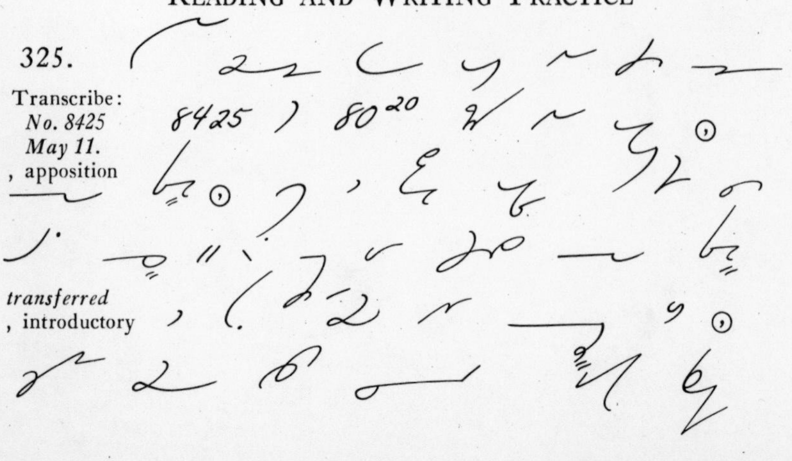

Transcribe:
No. 8425
May 11.
, apposition

transferred
, introductory

326.

, *when* clause
bank's

relieve
worrying
, *if* clause

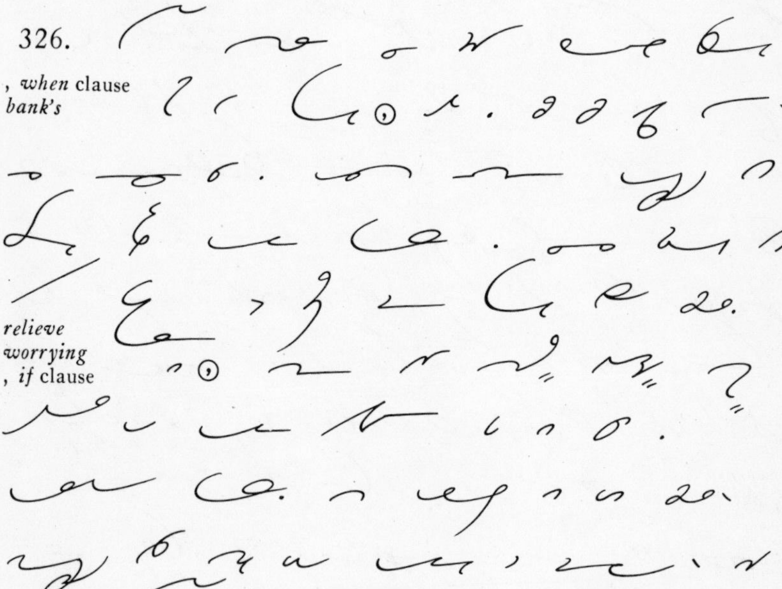

327.

companies
volume
foreign

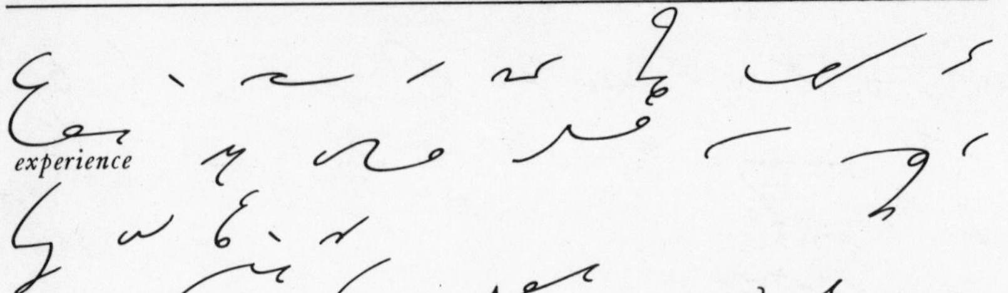

experience

328.

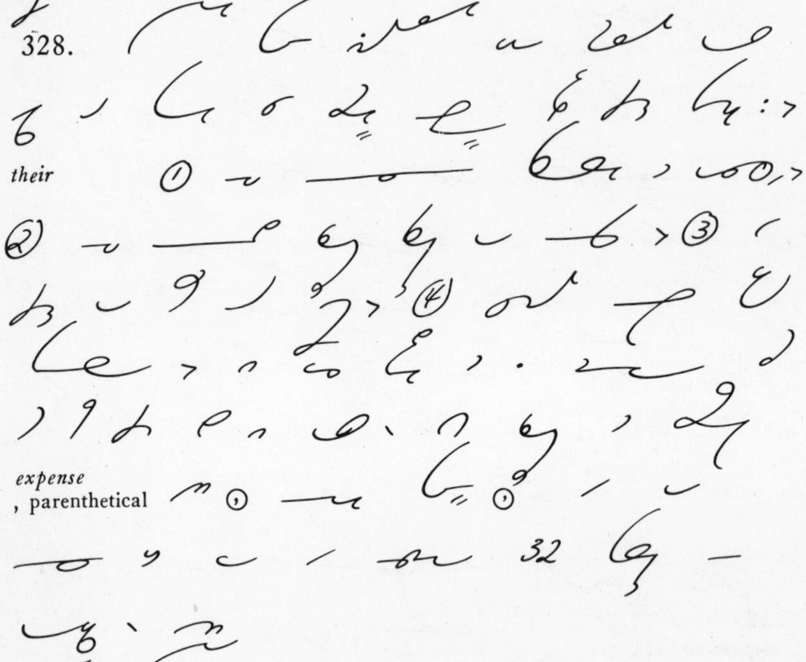

their

expense

, parenthetical

329.

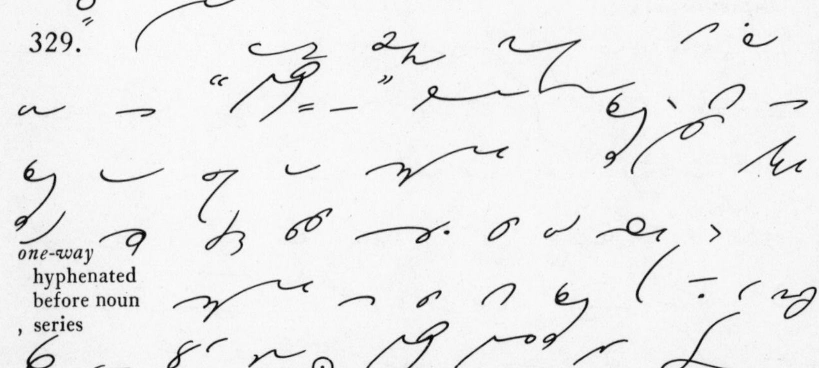

one-way

hyphenated before noun

, series

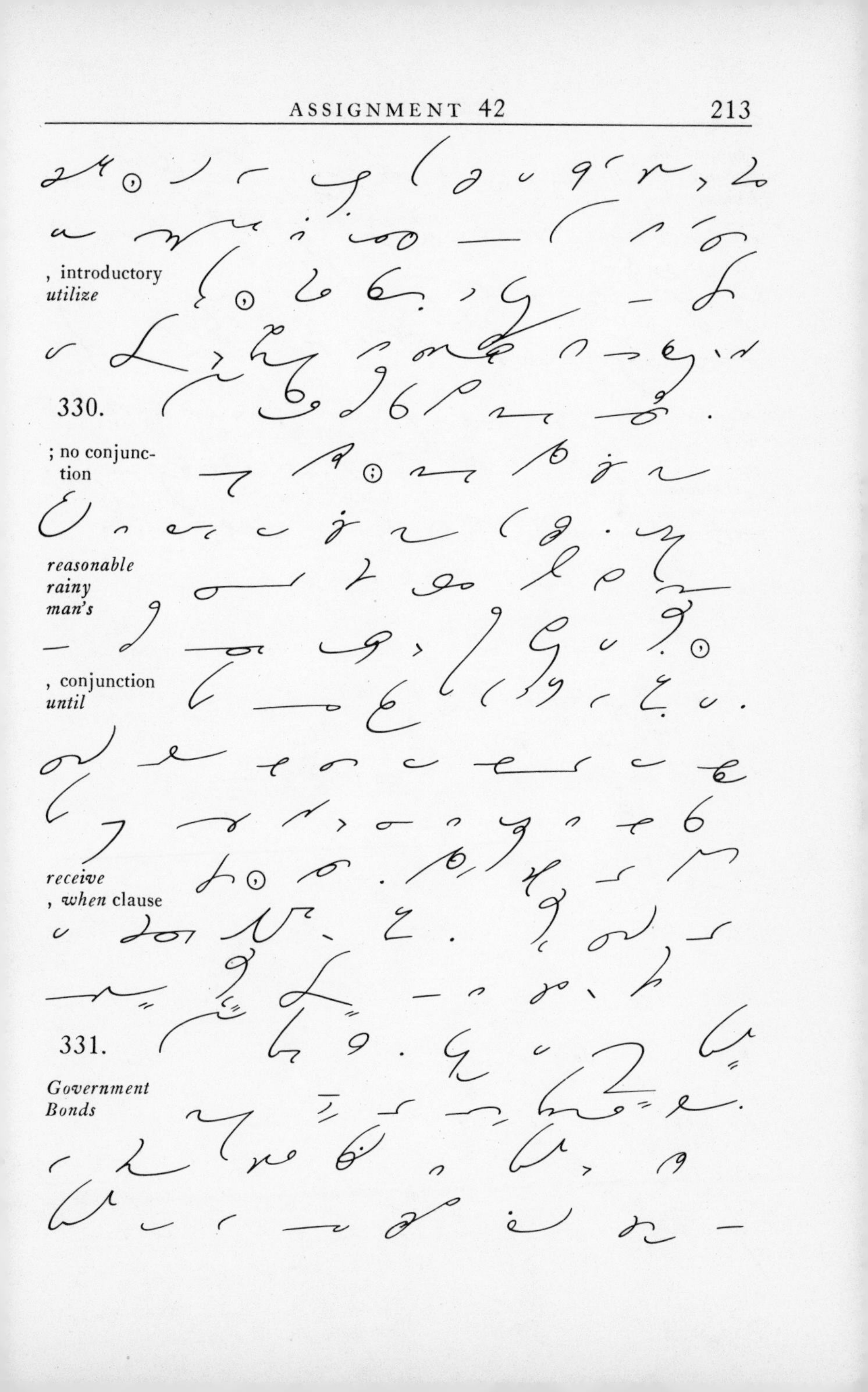

, introductory
utilize

330.

; no conjunction

reasonable
rainy
man's

, conjunction
until

receive
, *when* clause

331.

Government
Bonds

, conjunction
response
issuance
, *if* clause

ASSIGNMENT 43

332. Most-Used Business-Letter Phrases

VERY

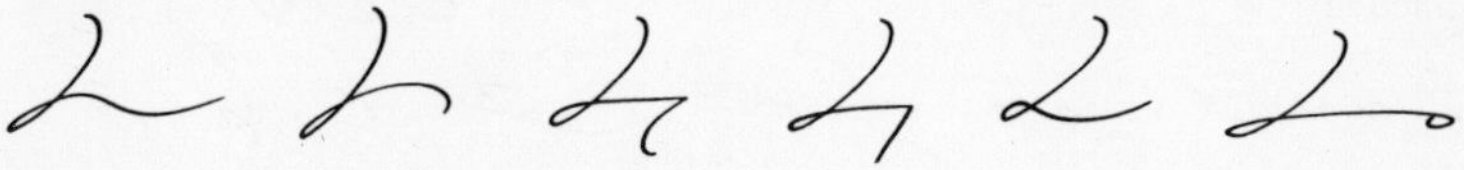

WE

WHICH

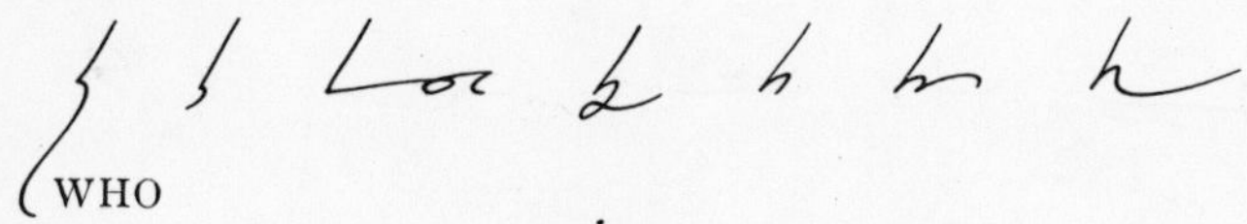

WHO

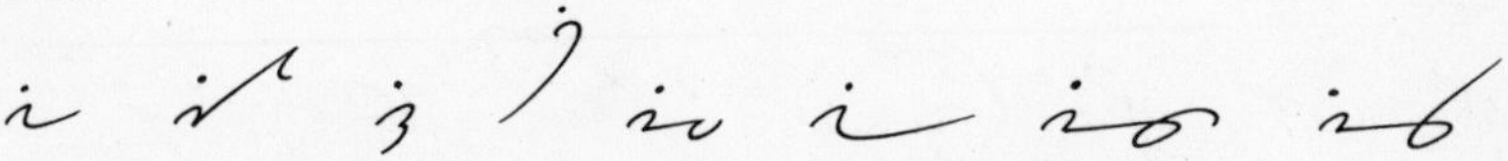

333. Geographical Expressions

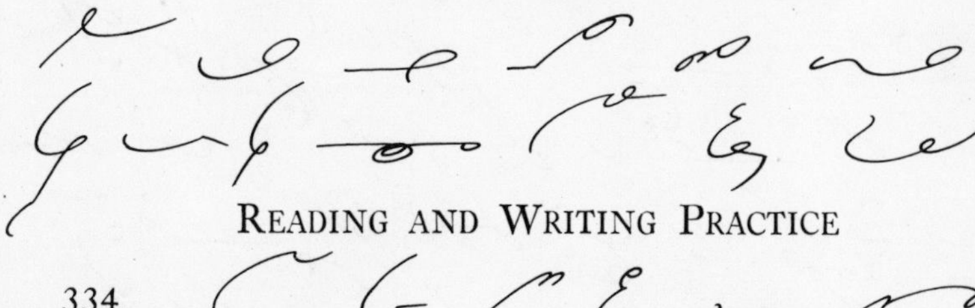

Reading and Writing Practice

334.

farther
puzzles

, conjunction

, apposition
elaborate
bookkeeping

335.

, introductory

preparing
attendance
filed

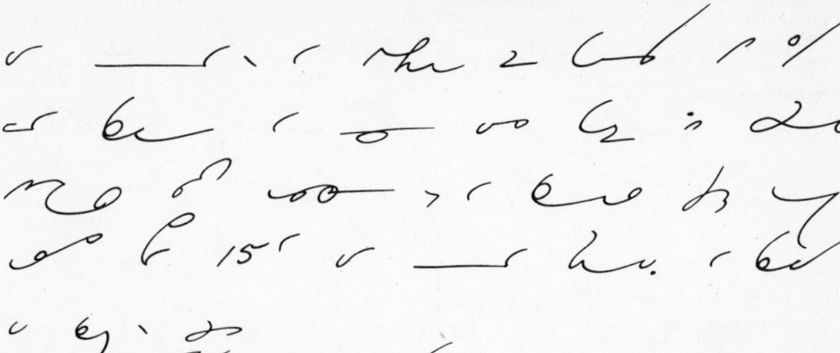

336.

toward
, series

, *if* clause
attention

337.

pay-roll hyphenated before noun

twentieth

exception

; no conjunction

, introductory

338.

birth

experiencing

, parenthetical

expense

Doctors'

nurses'

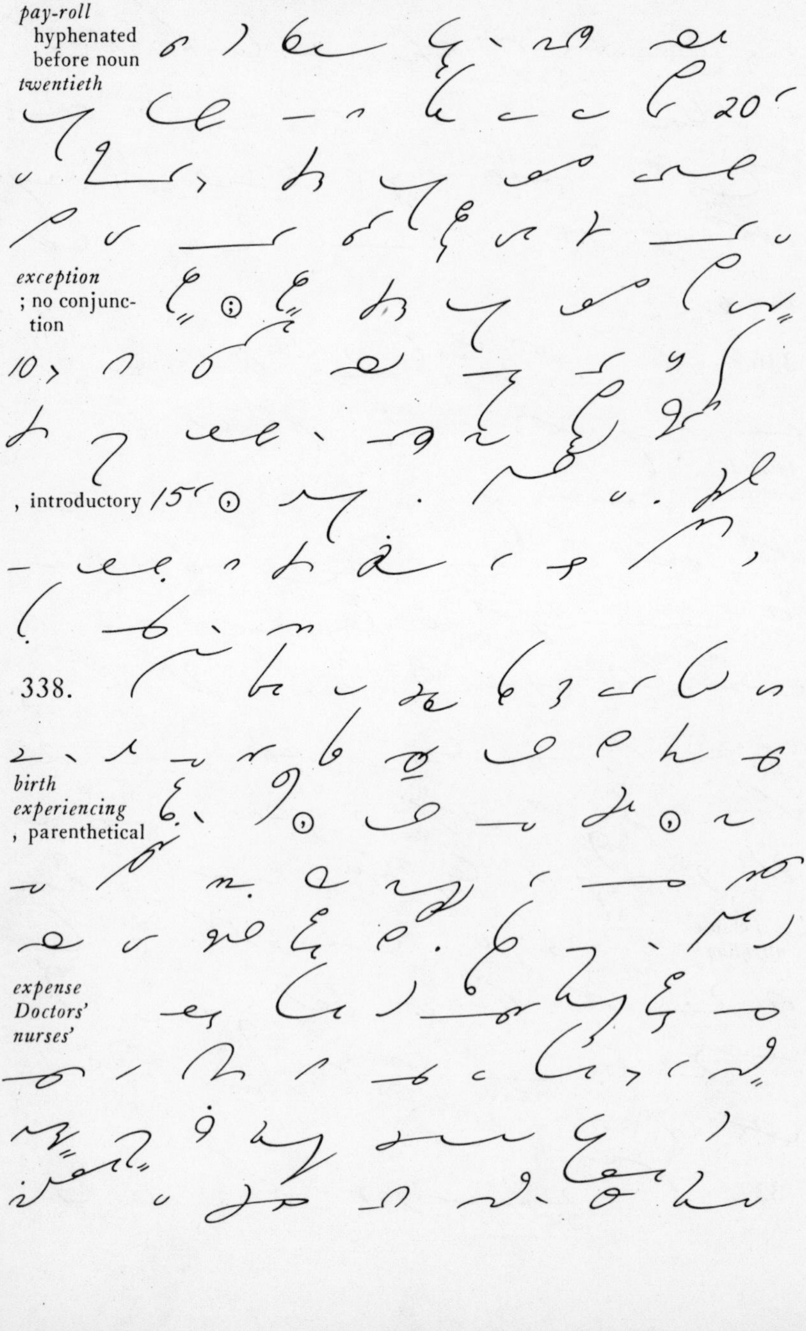

low-cost
hyphenated before noun
, conjunction

339.

opinion
per cent

, series
promptly
available

, conjunction

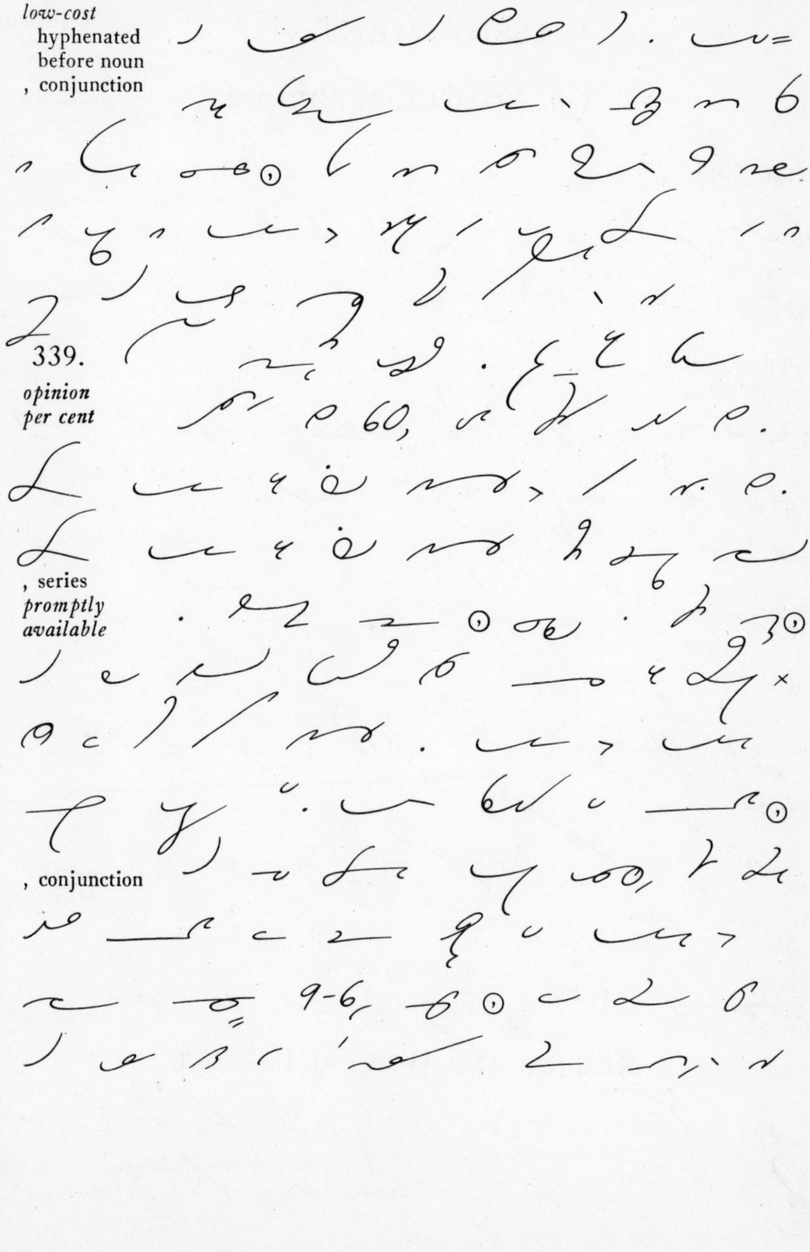

ASSIGNMENT 44

340. Vocabulary Builder

TH

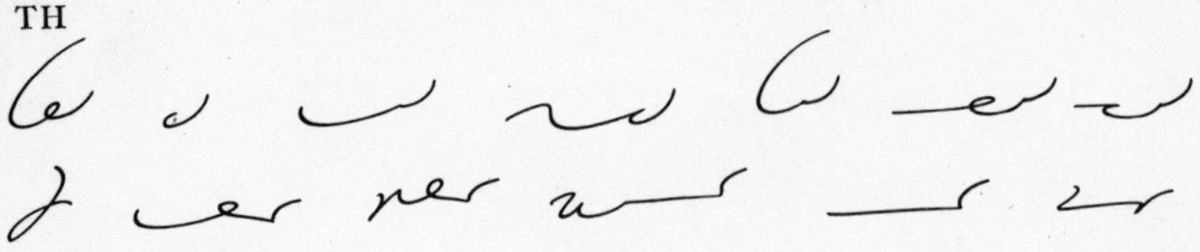

-TION, -TIAL

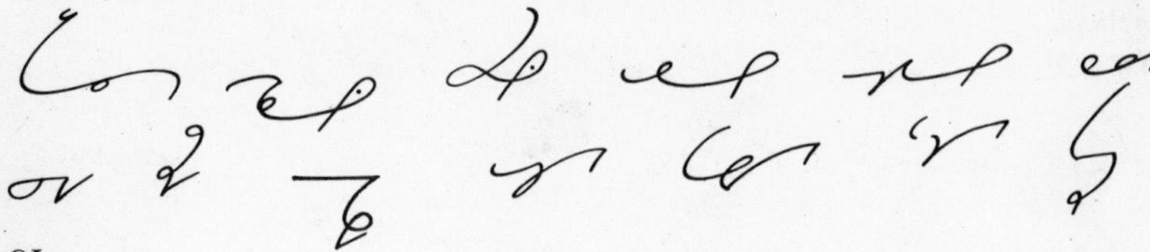

OI

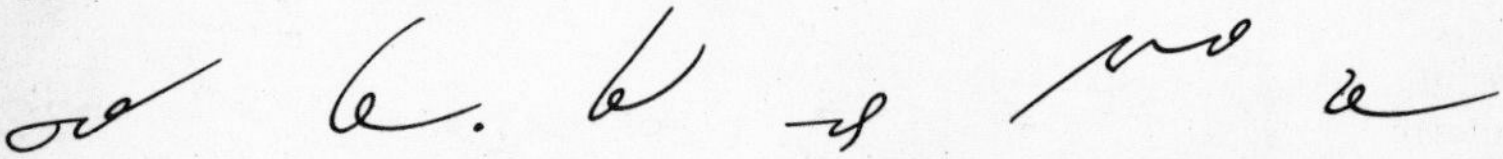

I

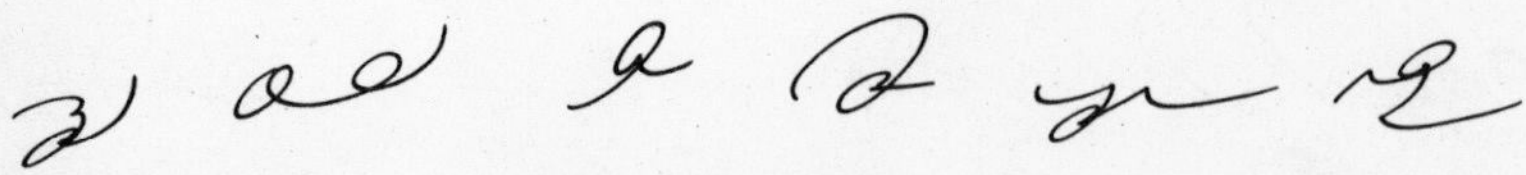

OW

U

Reading and Writing Practice

341.

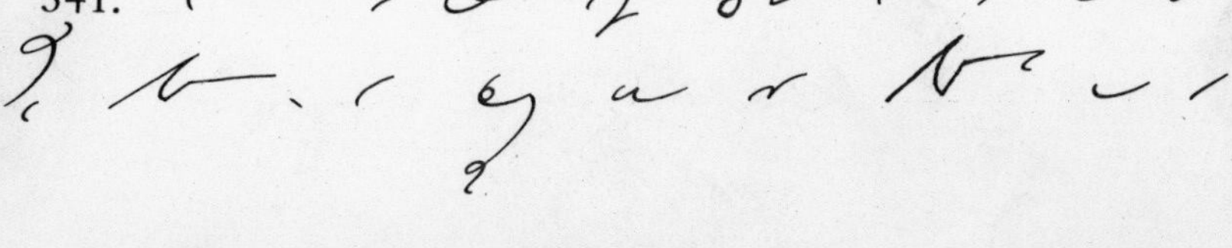

recommendations
per cent

, introductory
hesitation

pleasant
, conjunction

342.
friend's
, *when* clause
; because of comma

, introductory

; no conjunction
believe
, conjunction
, introductory

343.

, introductory

, introductory

discuss
company's

344.

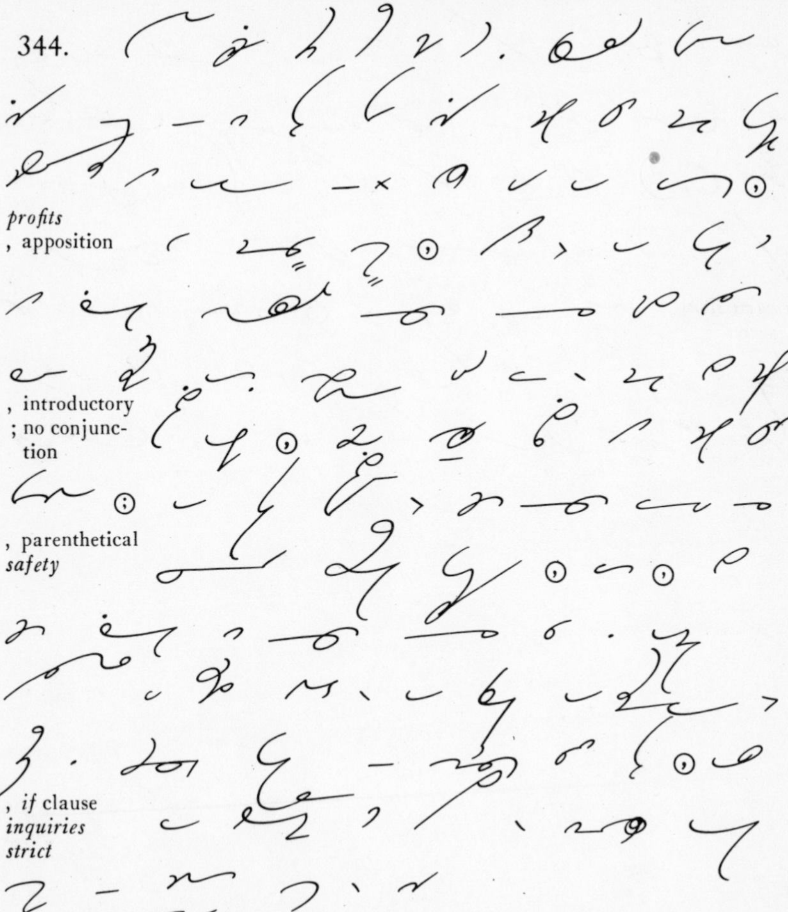

profits
, apposition
, introductory
; no conjunction
, parenthetical
safety
, *if* clause
inquiries
strict

345.

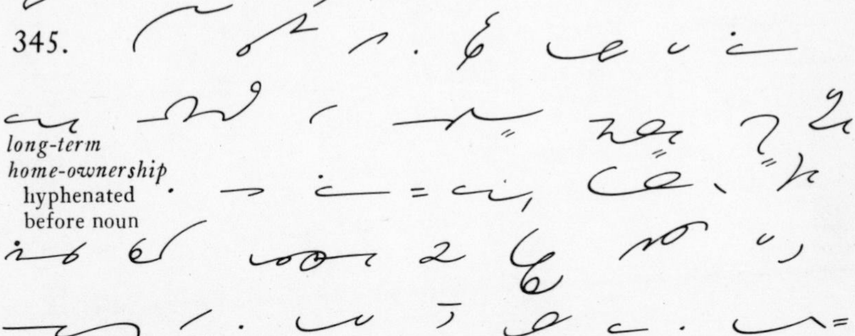

long-term
home-ownership
hyphenated before noun

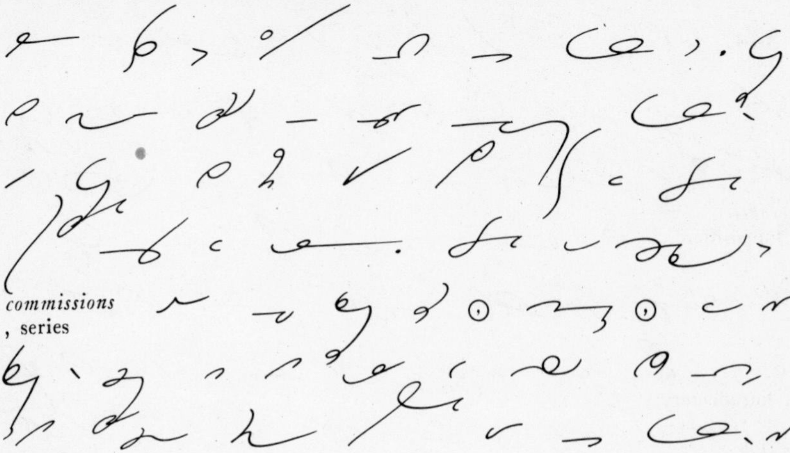

commissions
, series

ASSIGNMENT 45

346. Chart of Word Beginnings and Word Endings

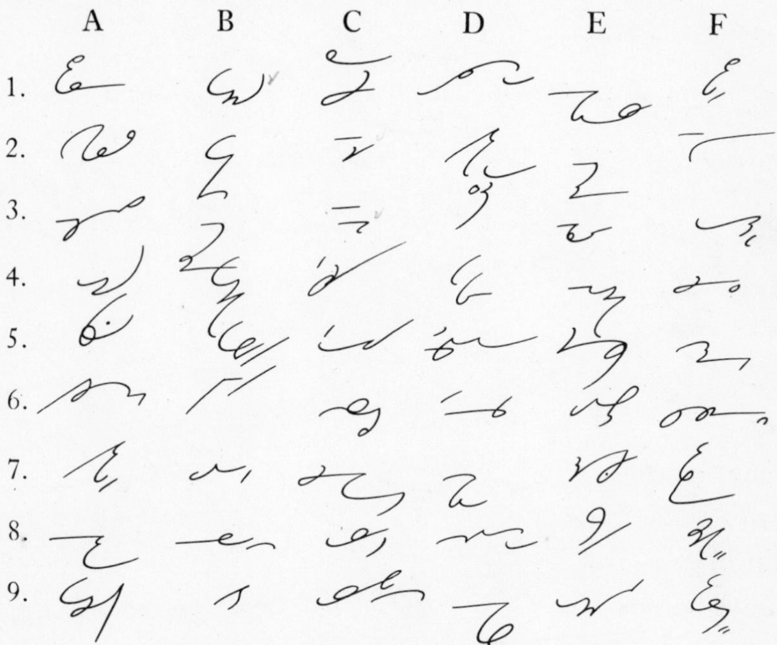

Reading and Writing Practice

347.

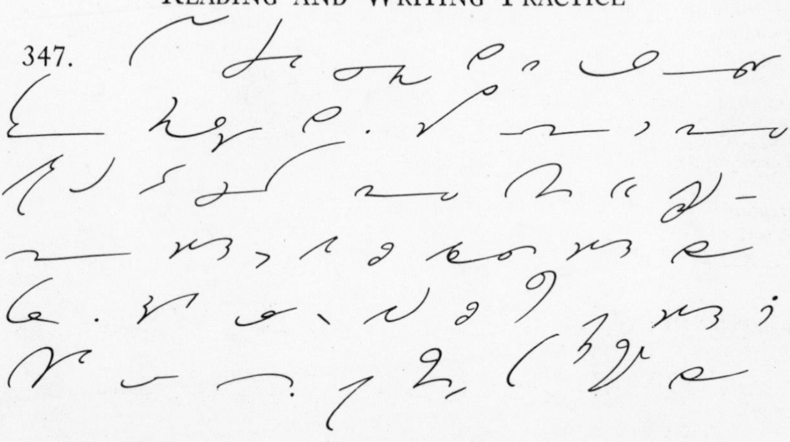

348.

bank's
deposits
per cent

, parenthetical
; because of commas

; no conjunction
mutual
, series

, introductory

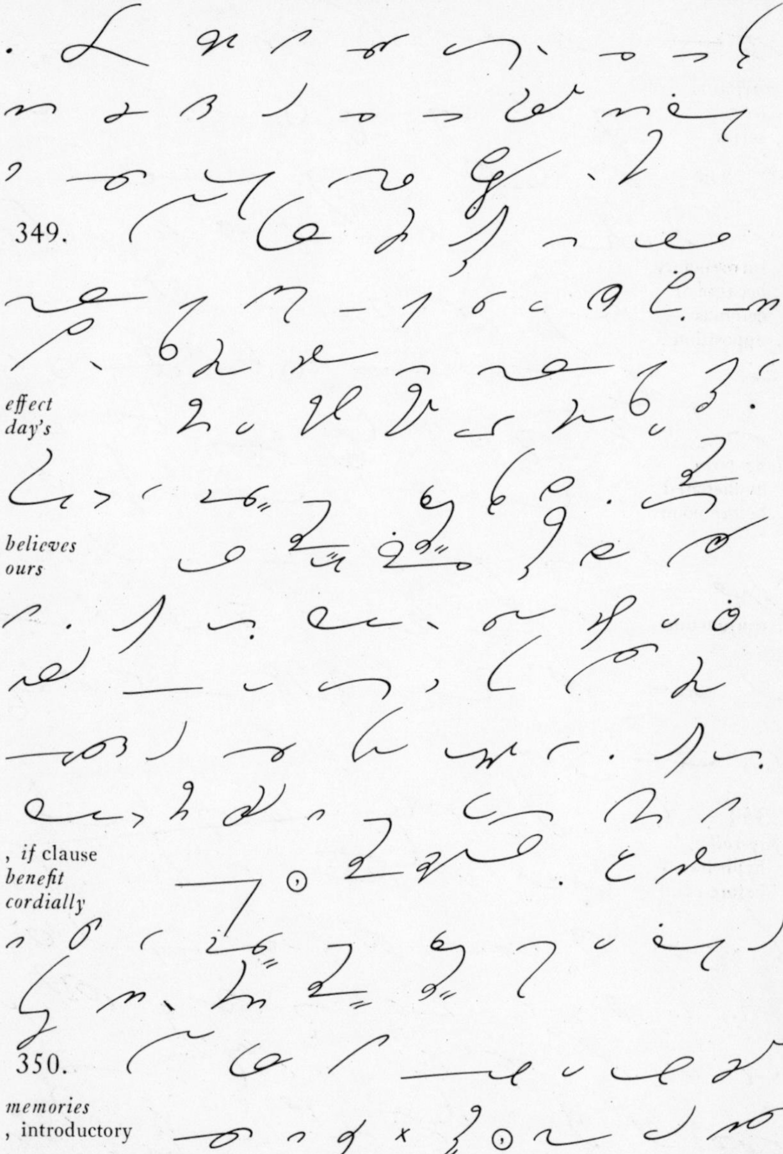

349.

effect
day's

believes
ours

, *if* clause
benefit
cordially

350.

memories
, introductory

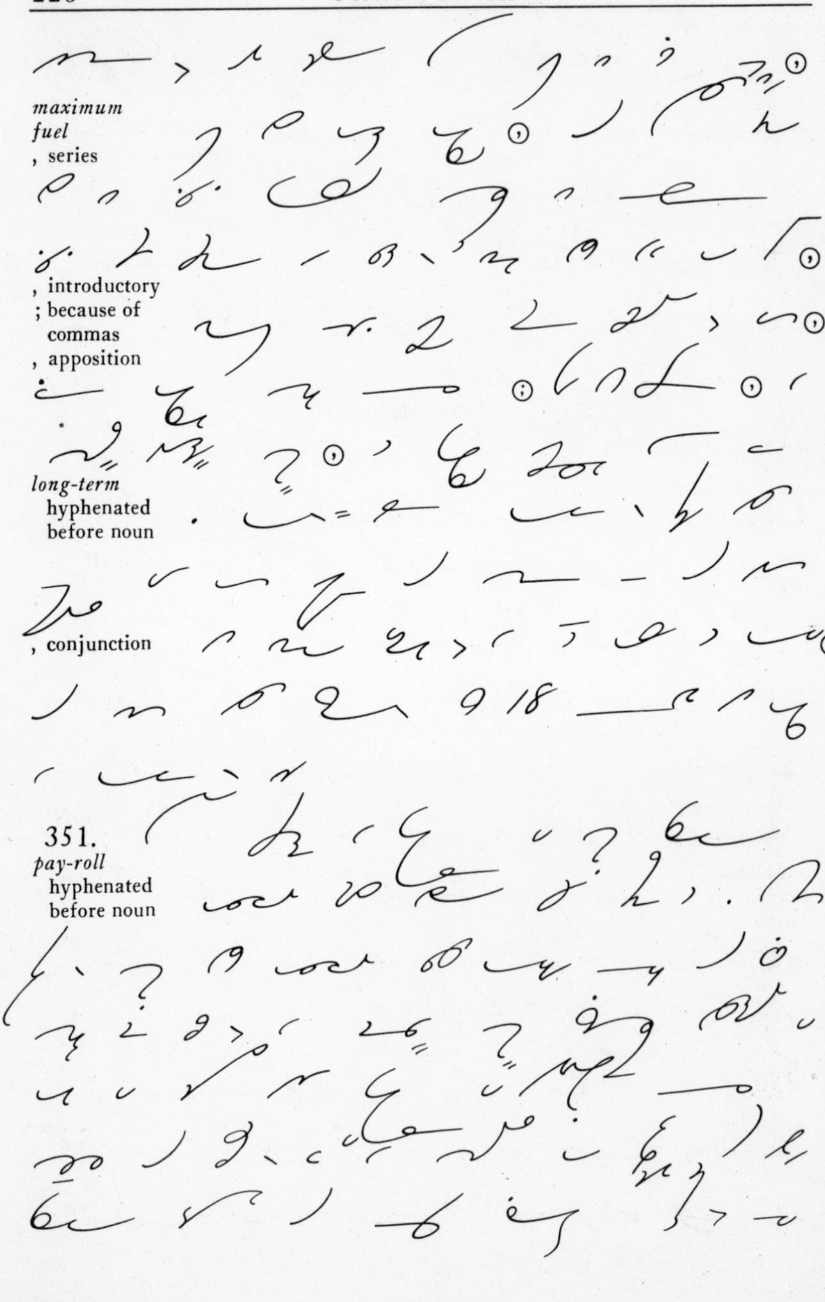

maximum
fuel
, series

, introductory
; because of
commas
, apposition

long-term
hyphenated
before noun

, conjunction

351.
pay-roll
hyphenated
before noun

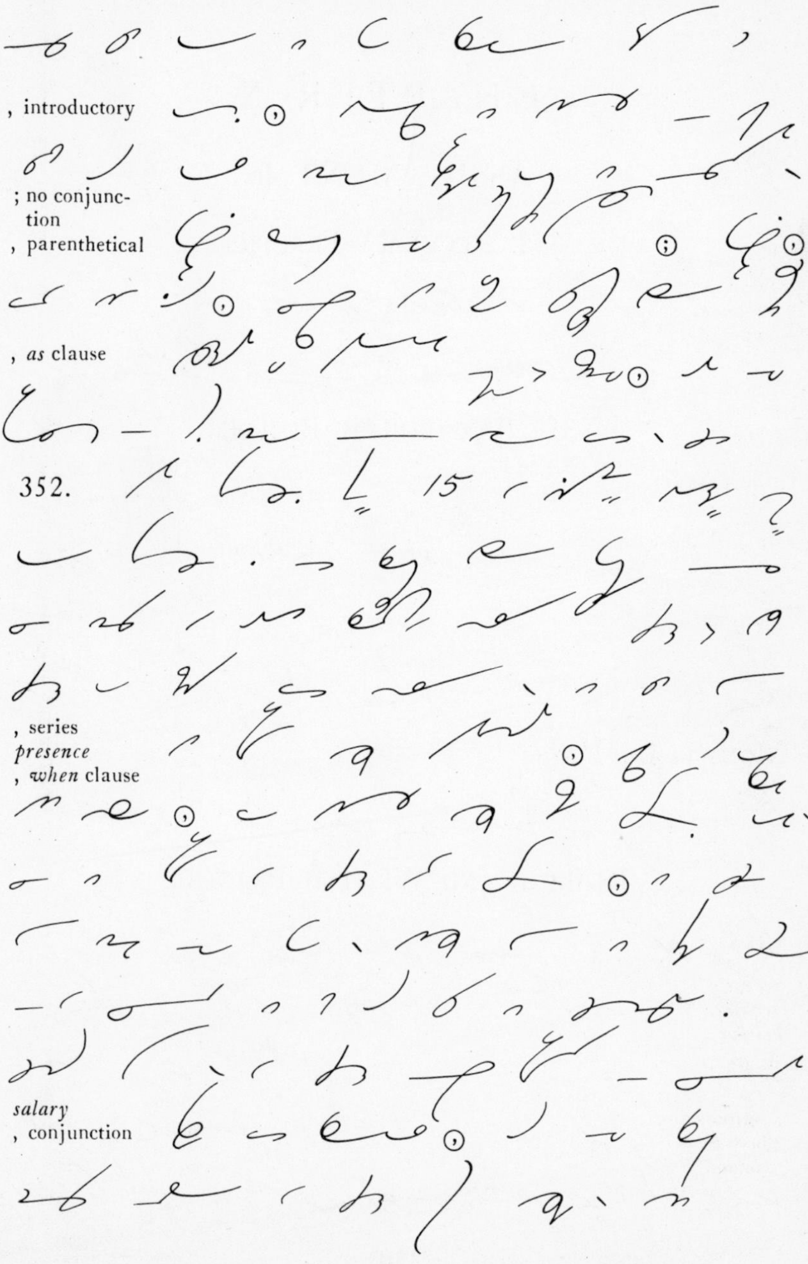

, introductory

; no conjunction

, parenthetical

, *as* clause

352.

, series

presence

, *when* clause

salary

, conjunction

CHAPTER X

ASSIGNMENT 46

353. Accuracy Practice

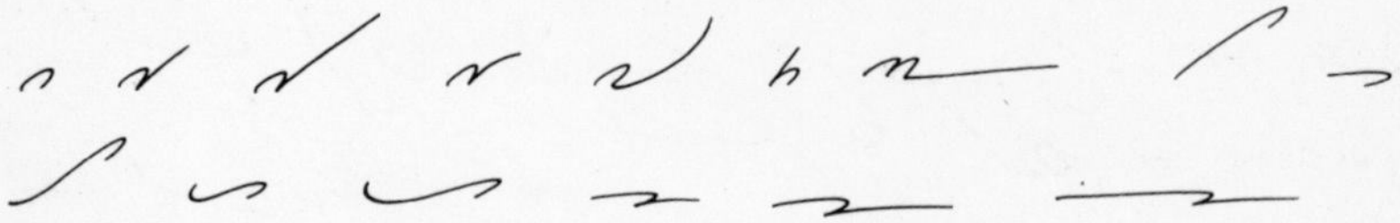

354. Vocabulary Builder

NG

NGK

Months and Days

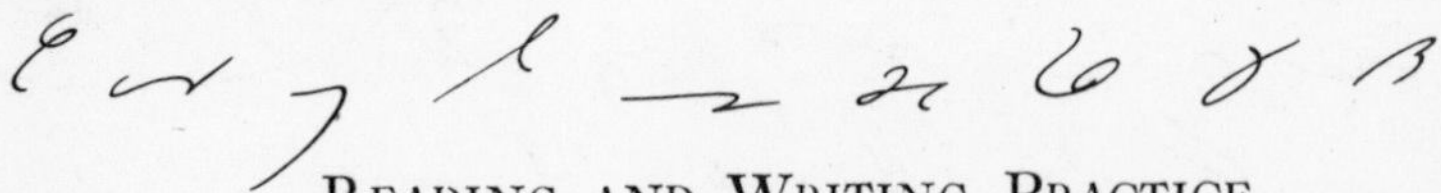

Reading and Writing Practice

355.

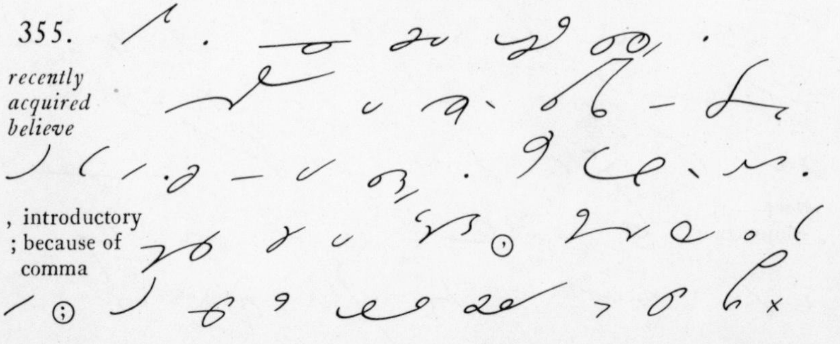

recently
acquired
believe

, introductory
; because of comma

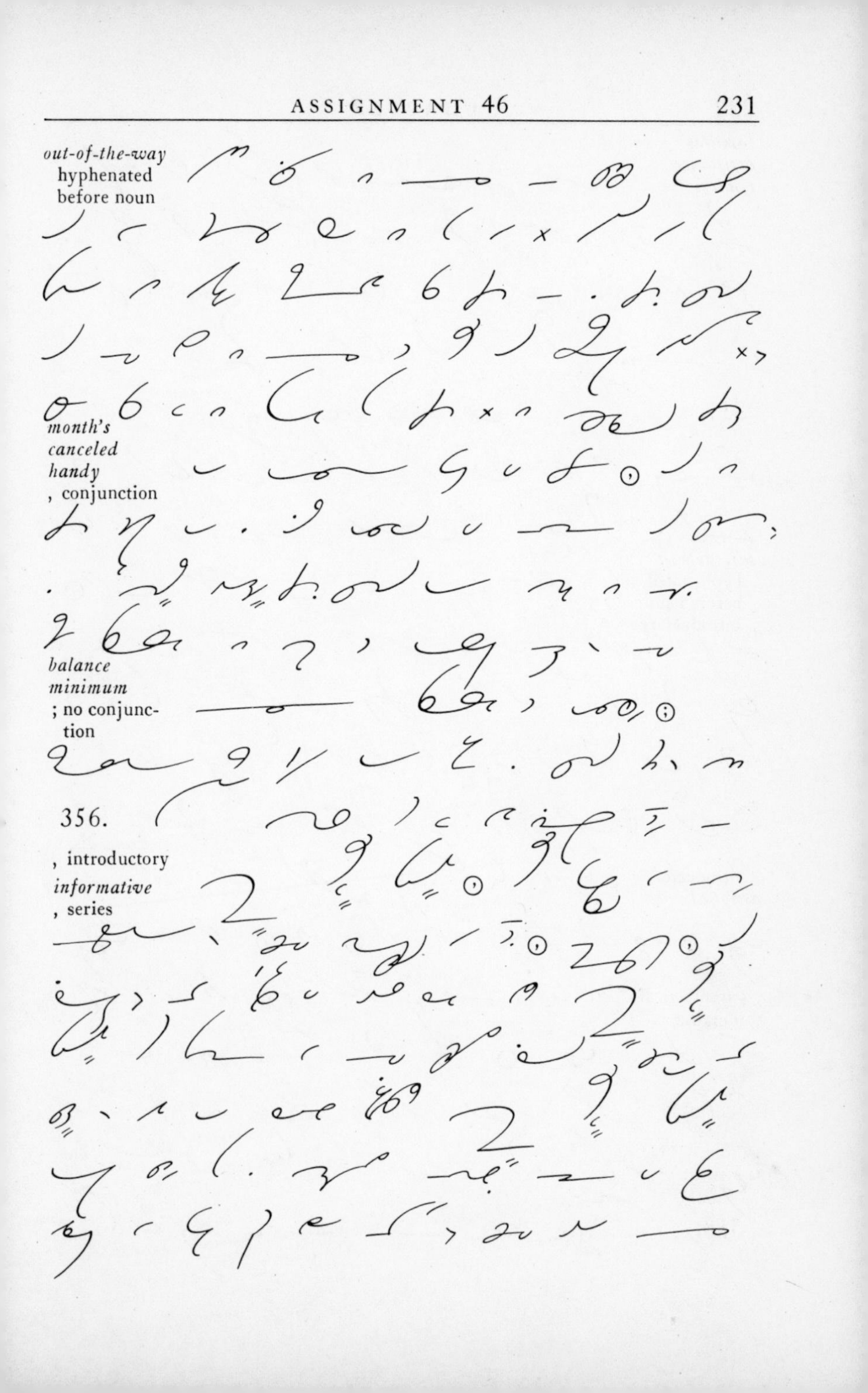

out-of-the-way
hyphenated
before noun

month's
canceled
handy
, conjunction

balance
minimum
; no conjunction

356.

, introductory
informative
, series

familiar
assistance
readers'

357.

safe-deposit hyphenated before noun
, introductory

, introductory
assigned

, parenthetical
, *if* clause

358.

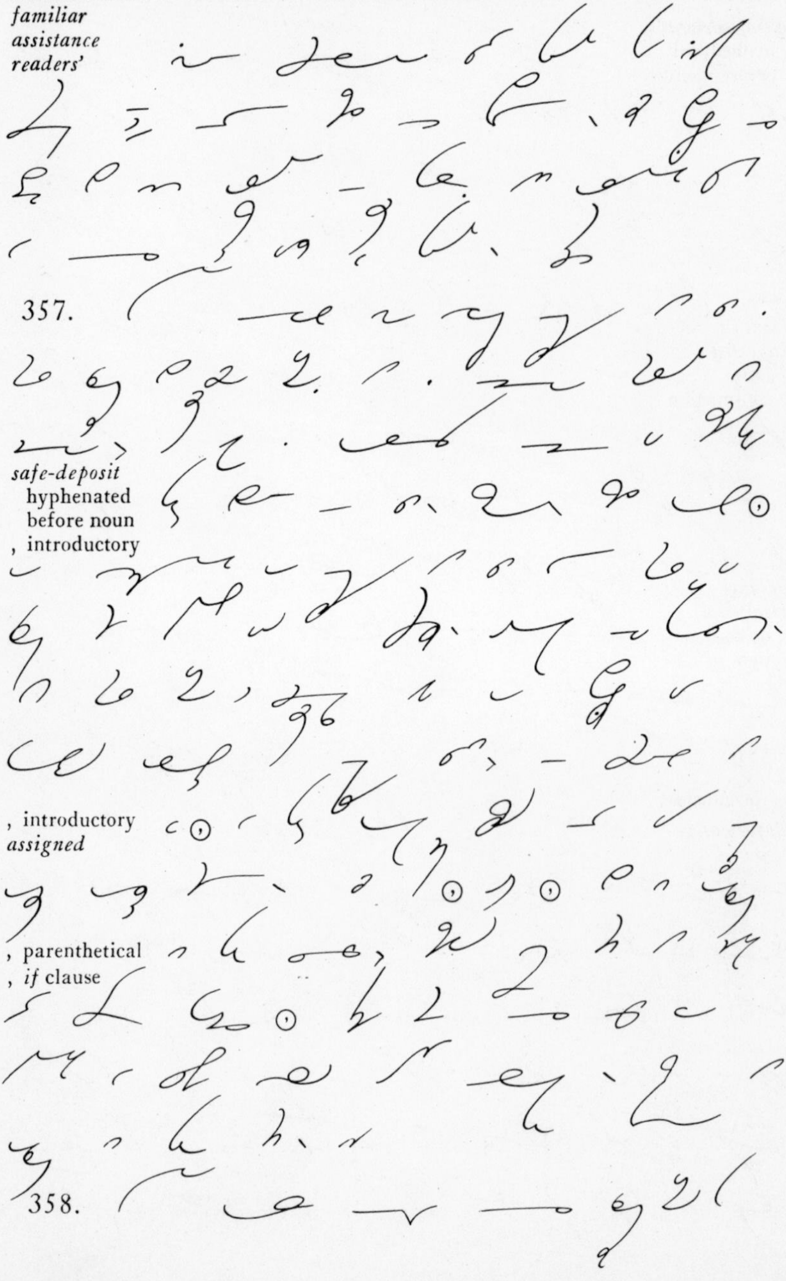

personal-loan
hyphenated
before noun

Transcribe:
9 a.m.
3 p.m.

inconvenient
here
, introductory

, *if* clause
welcome

359.
elsewhere
policies
, *if* clause

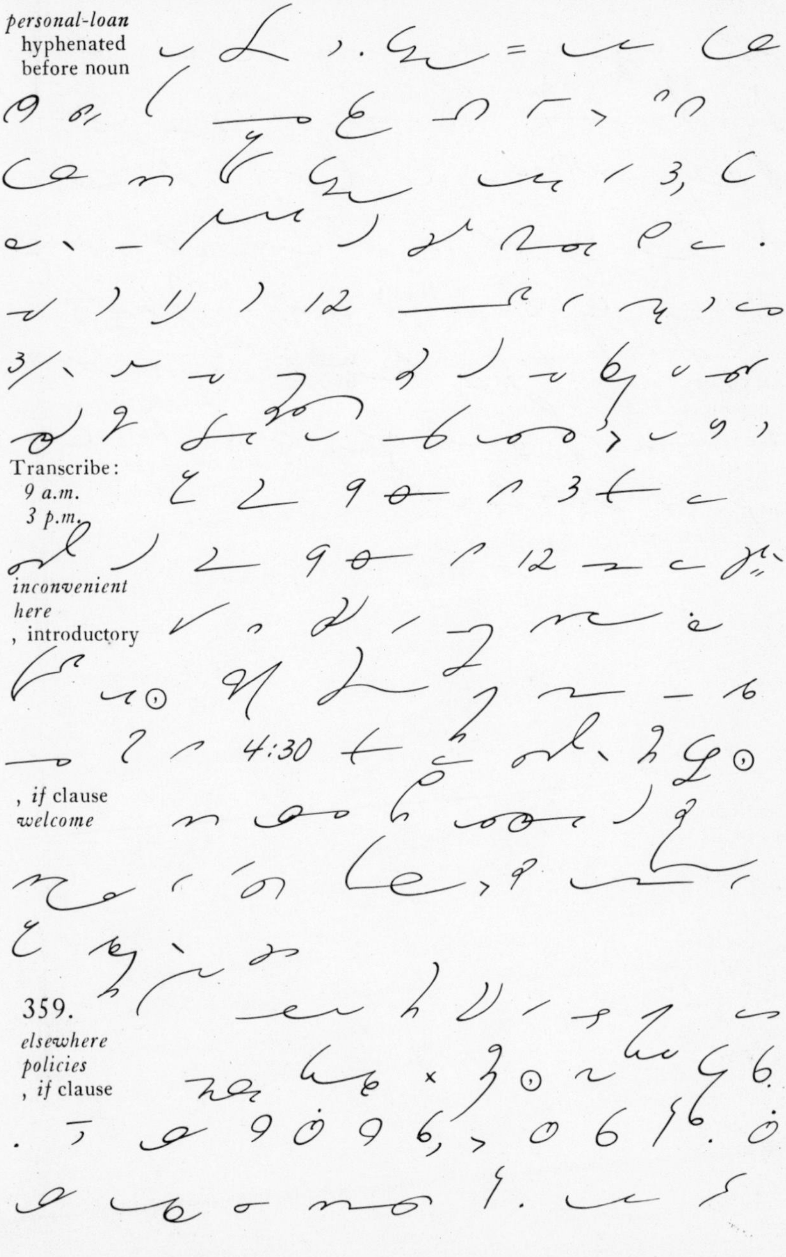

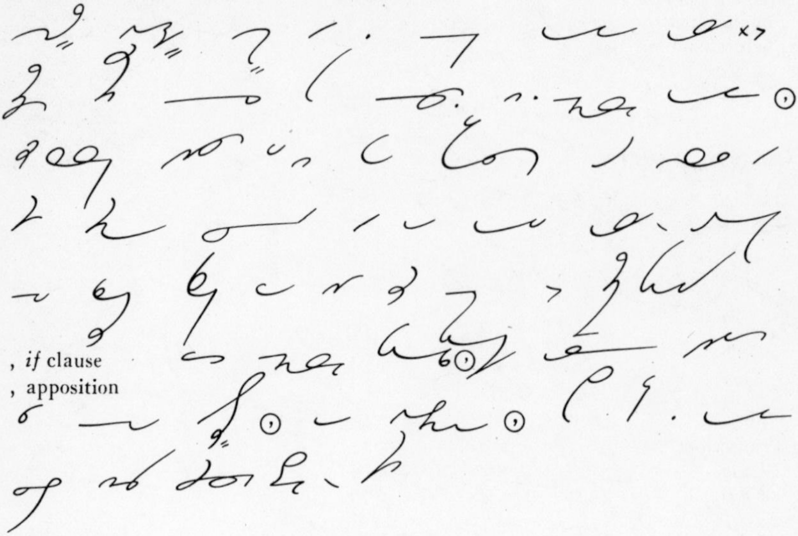

, *if* clause
, apposition

ASSIGNMENT 47

360. Word Families

RE- FOLLOWED BY A VOWEL

DIA-

-IANCE

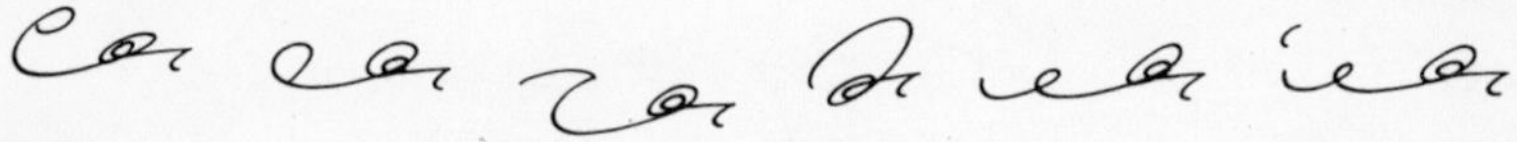

SER

SEL

Reading and Writing Practice

361.

, series
territory
past

, parenthetical

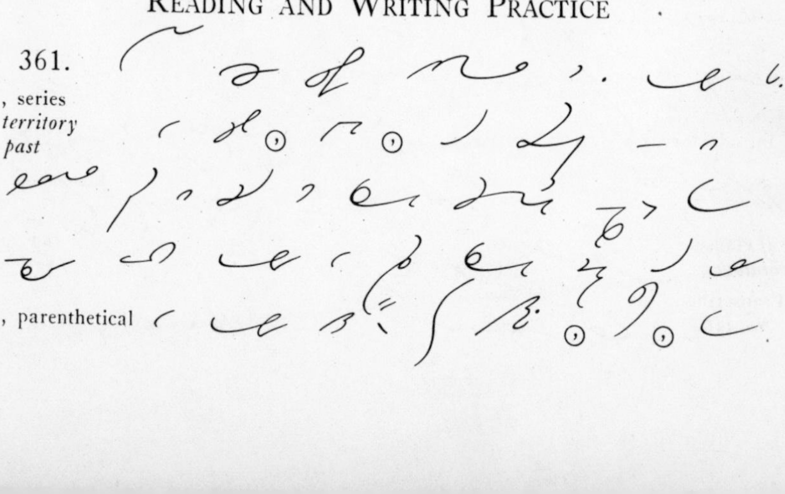

whether
weeks'
362.
patient's
, introductory
executive
, conjunction
, introductory
, if clause
catalogue
Transcribe:
No. 116.
116

363.

knowledge
their

capabilities
performance
forty-six

yours
up-to-the-minute
hyphenated before noun

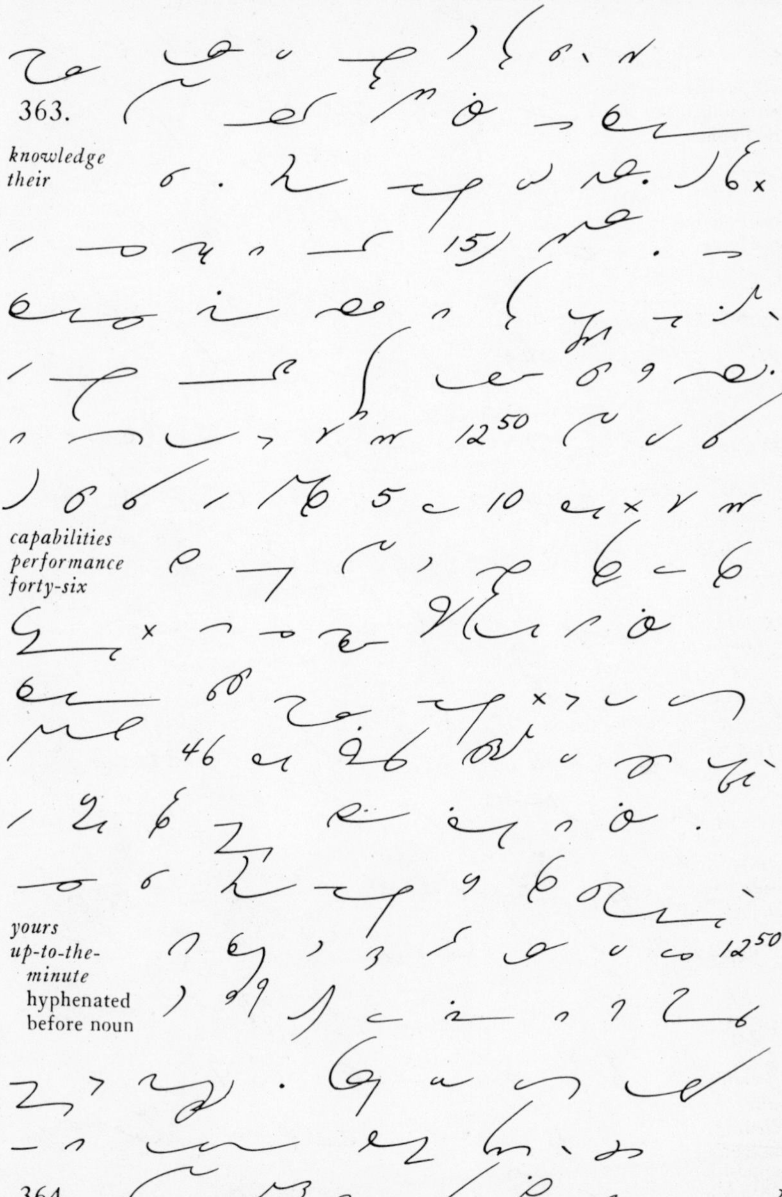

364.

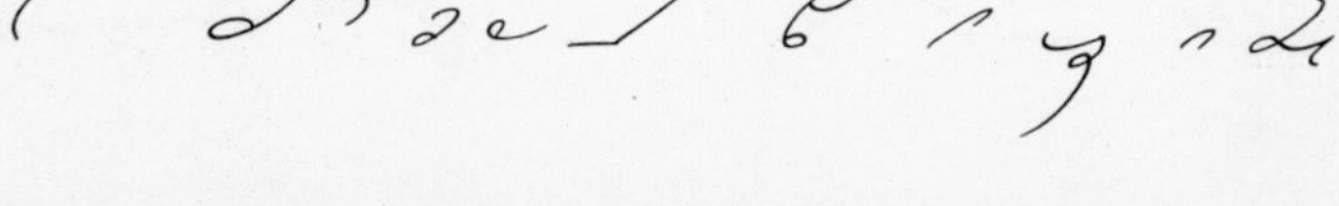

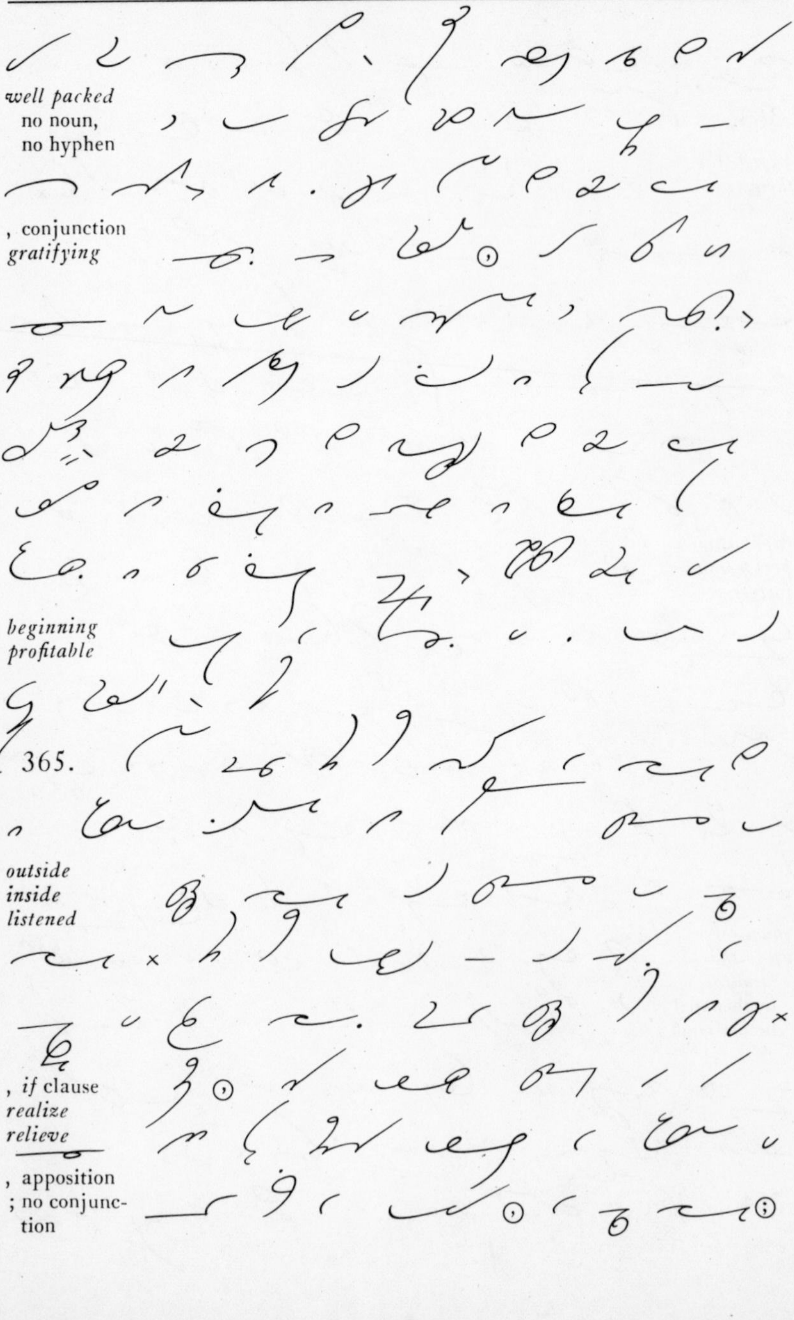

well packed
no noun,
no hyphen

, conjunction
gratifying

beginning
profitable

365.

outside
inside
listened

, *if* clause
realize
relieve

, apposition
; no conjunction

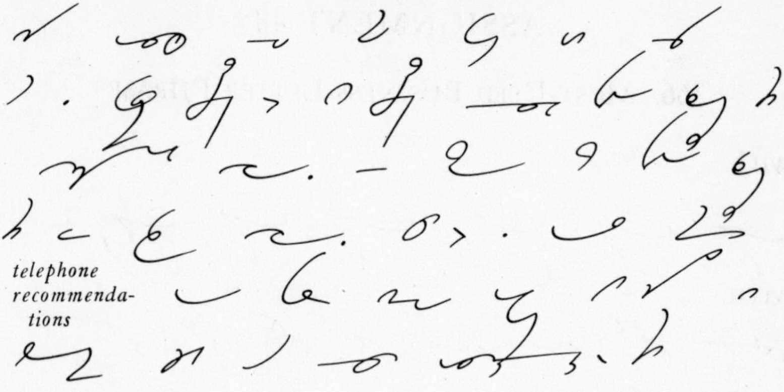
telephone
recommendations

ASSIGNMENT 48

366. Most-Used Business-Letter Phrases

WILL

WITH

YOU

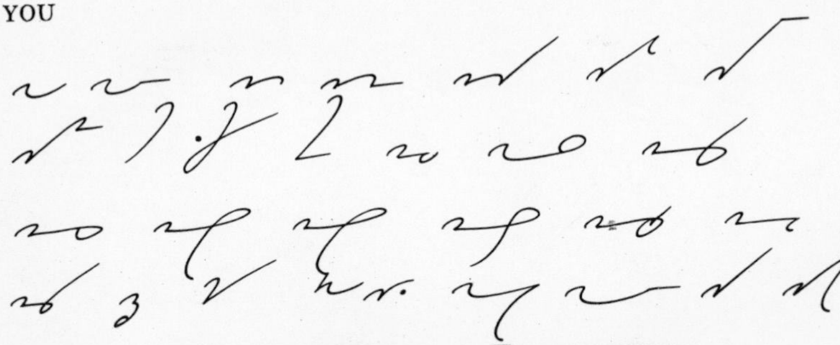

367. Geographical Expressions

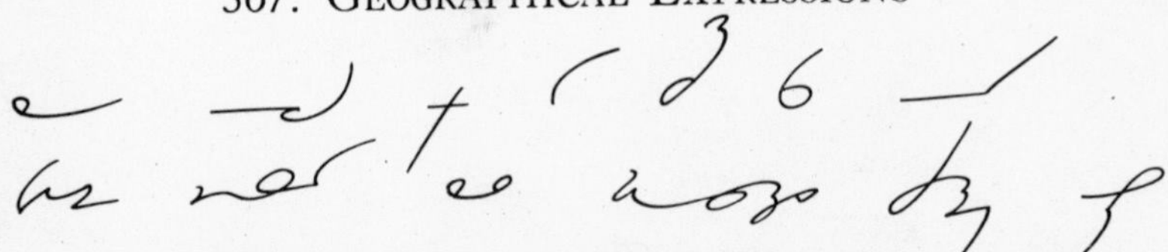

Reading and Writing Practice

368.
, apposition
steel
, series

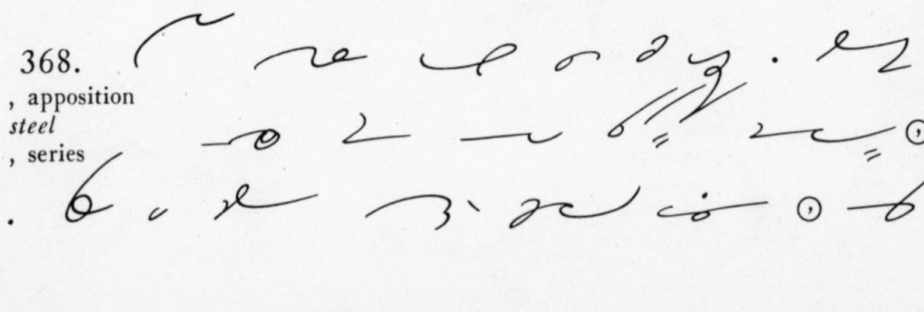

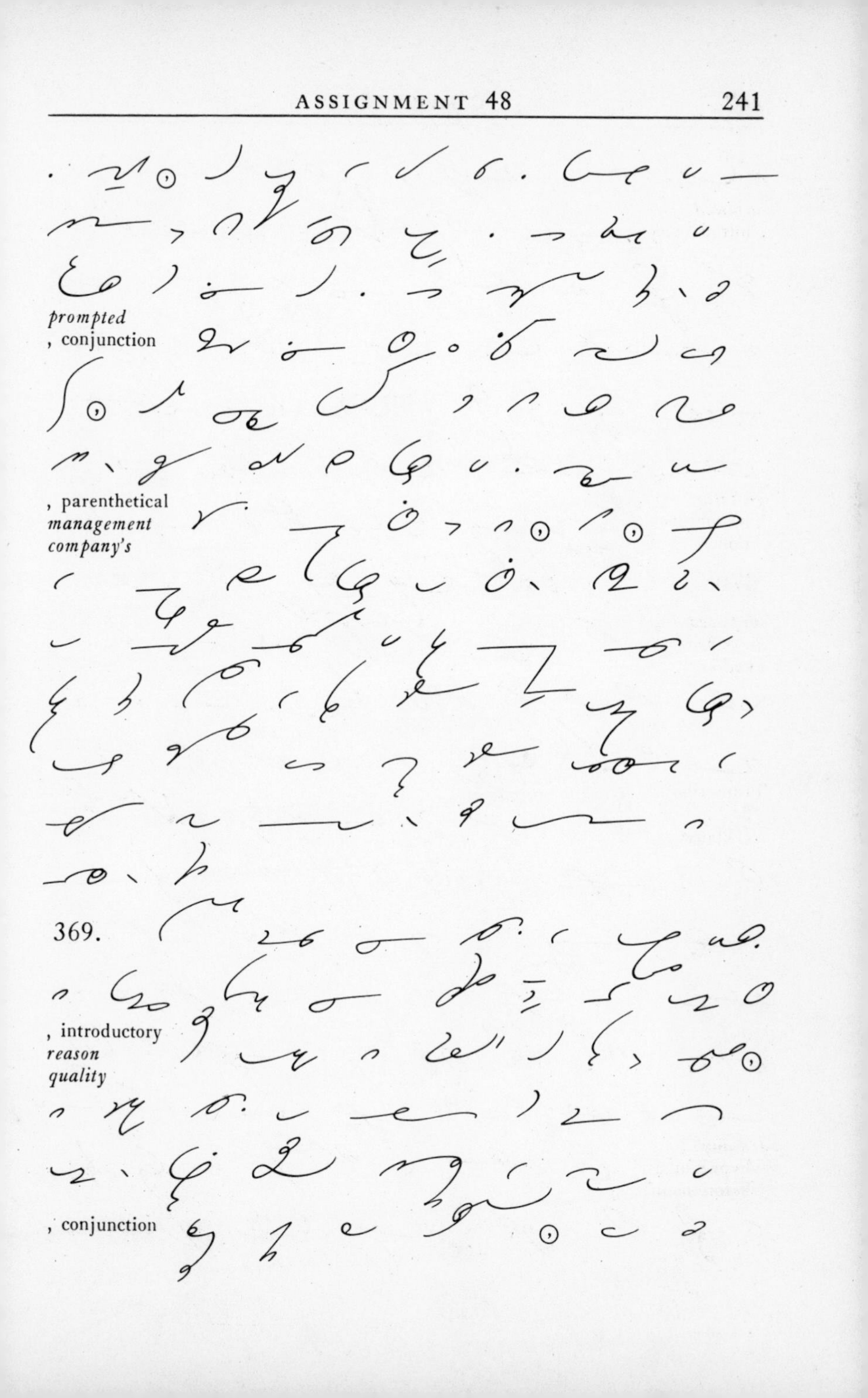

prompted
, conjunction

, parenthetical
management
company's

369.

, introductory
reason
quality

, conjunction

adjusted
, introductory

grateful
; no conjunction

370.

surprised
described
bundles

Transcribe:
$235.
, *if* clause

ten-day
hyphenated before noun

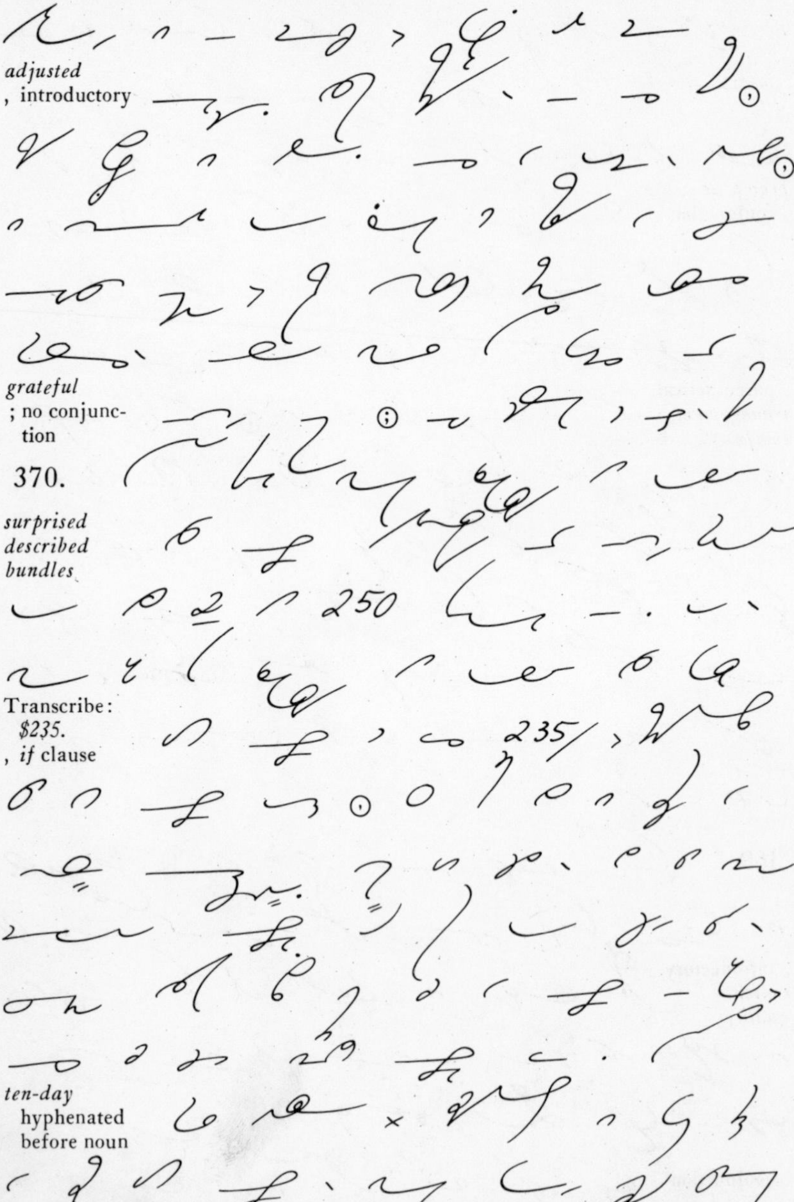

371.

impressions
, *if* clause

, introductory
secretary

decision
research
manufacture

today
. courteous
request

372.

; because of
comma
, *when* clause

recently
eager
, parenthetical

past
firm's
, conjunction

ASSIGNMENT 49

373. VOCABULARY BUILDER—OMISSION OF VOWELS

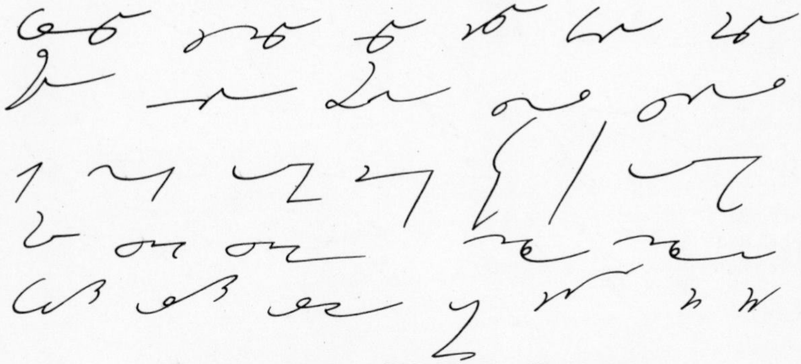

READING AND WRITING PRACTICE

374.

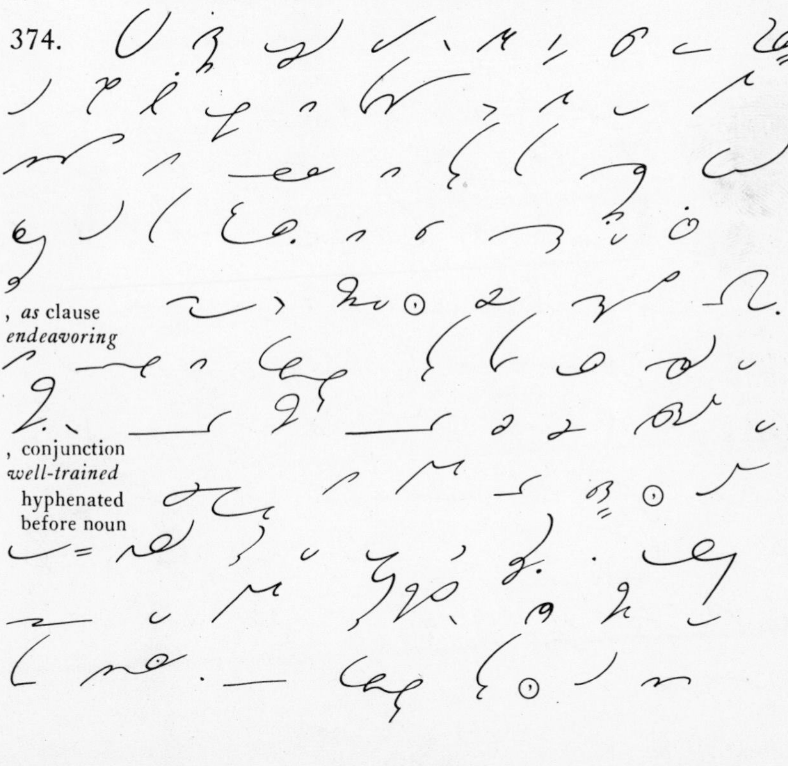

, *as* clause
endeavoring

, conjunction
well-trained
hyphenated
before noun

catalogue
, introductory

375.

well-known
hyphenated
before noun

, series
accuracy
supplies

, *if* clause
effective
efficiency

376.

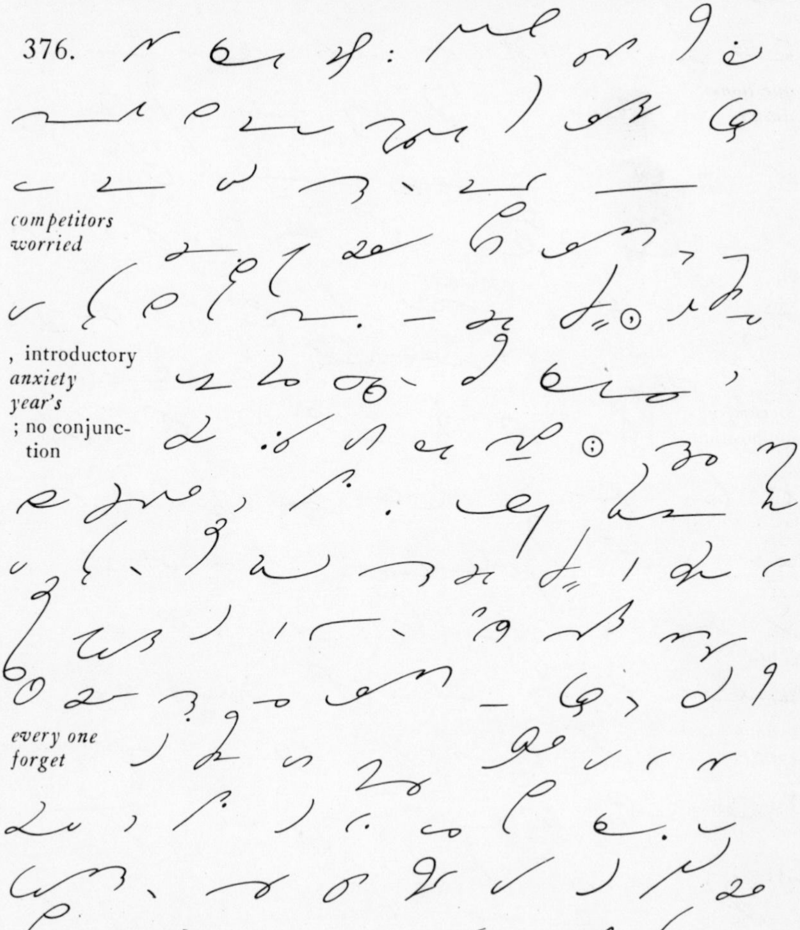

competitors
worried

, introductory
anxiety
year's
; no conjunction

every one
forget

377.

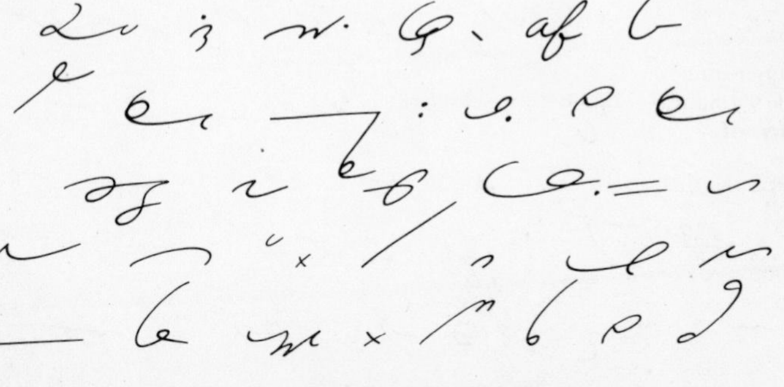

campaign
believe

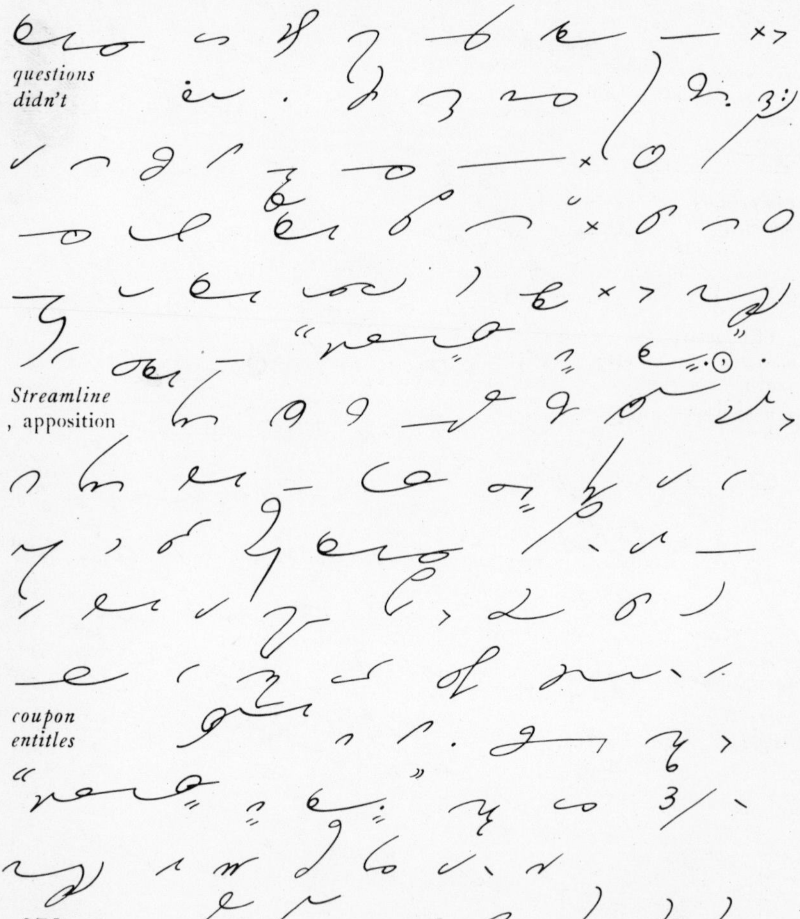

questions
didn't

Streamline
, apposition

coupon
entitles

378.

, apposition
, parenthetical
referred

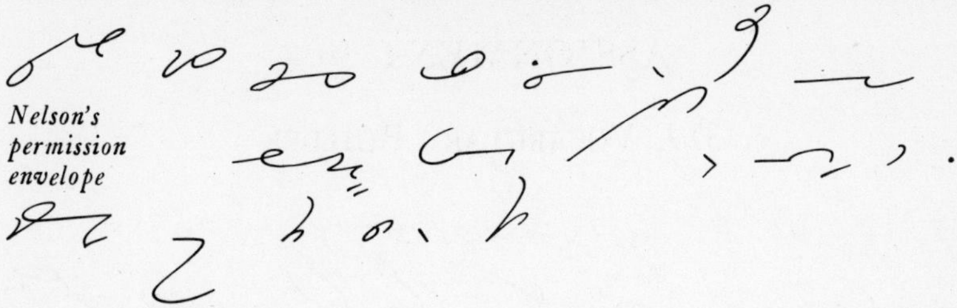

Nelson's permission envelope

ASSIGNMENT 50

379. Vocabulary Builder

SES

-RD

-LD

TED

MEM

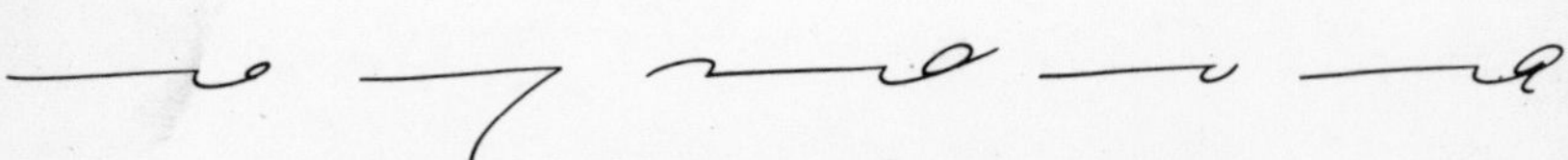

Reading and Writing Practice

380.

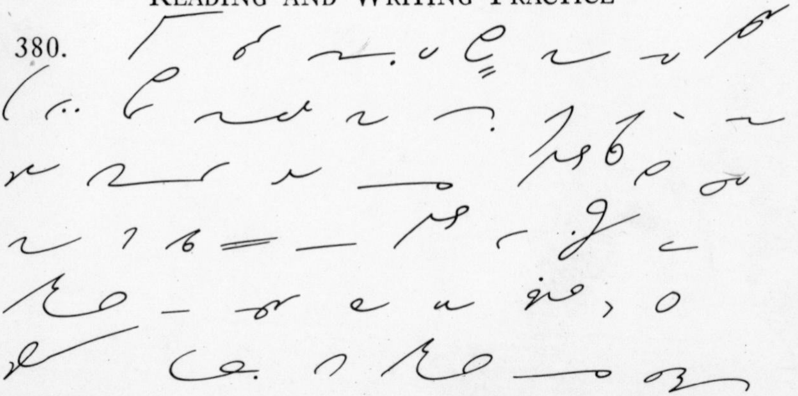

381.

, apposition
; no conjunction
, parenthetical

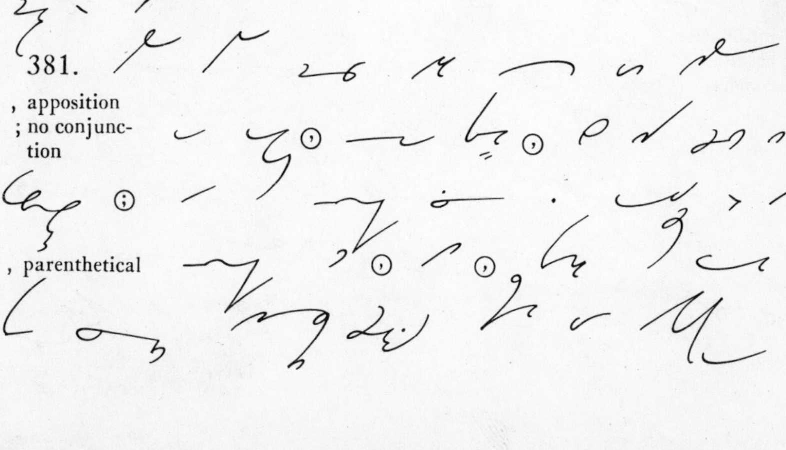

382.

forward
, parenthetical

383.

prescriptions
heart

, introductory
; because of comma

. courteous request
Jones's
Smith's

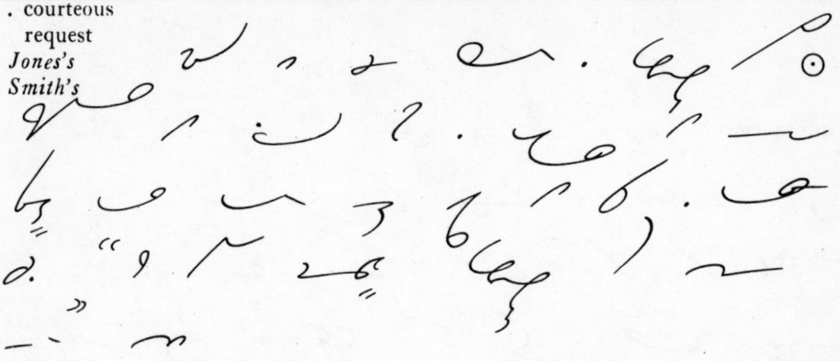

384.

, parenthetical
confident
simply
, introductory
privilege

385.

Transcribe:
August 16
, conjunction
whether
, introductory

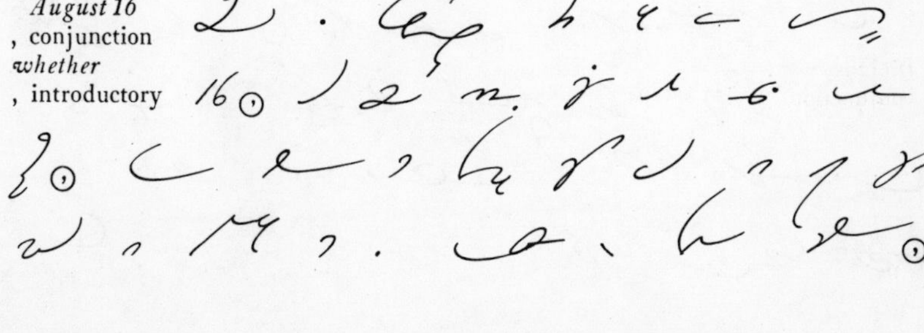

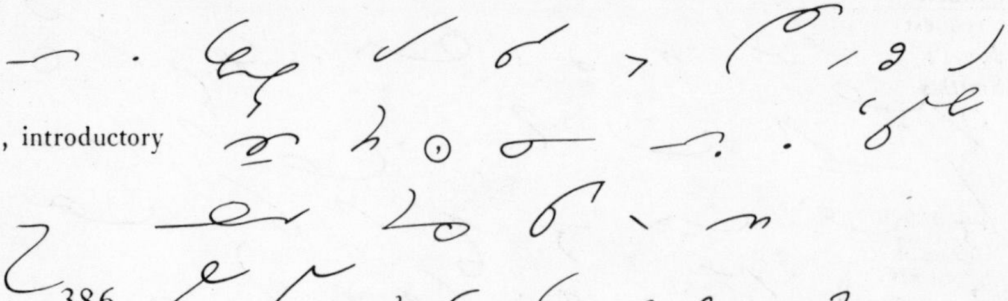

, introductory

386.

, introductory
carbon

387.

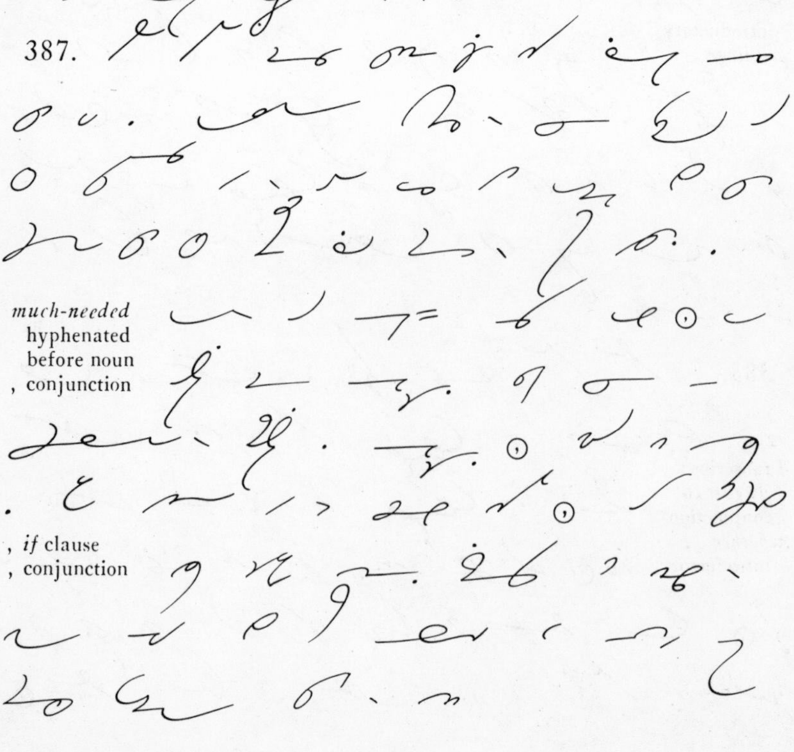

much-needed
hyphenated
before noun
, conjunction

, *if* clause
, conjunction

388.

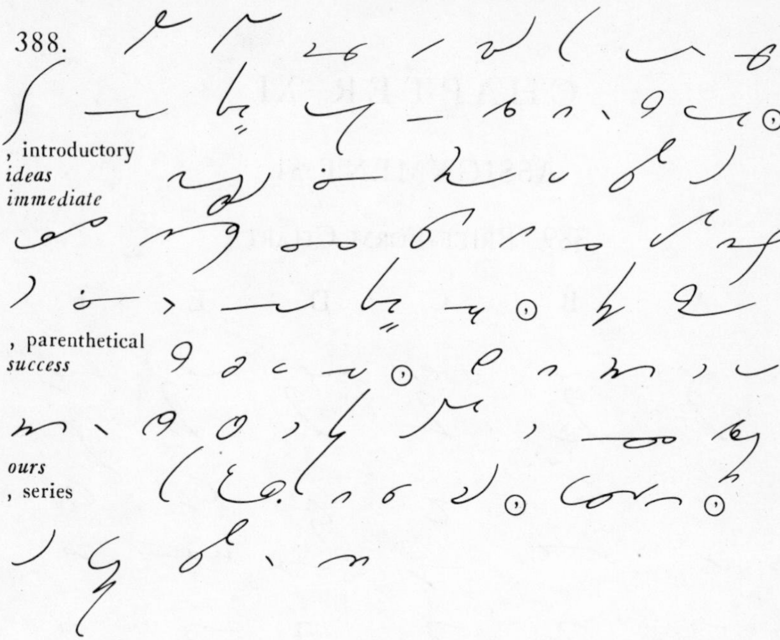

, introductory
ideas
immediate

, parenthetical
success

ours
, series

CHAPTER XI

ASSIGNMENT 51

389. Brief-Form Chart

A B C D E F

1.
2.
3.
4.
5.
6.
7.
8.
9.

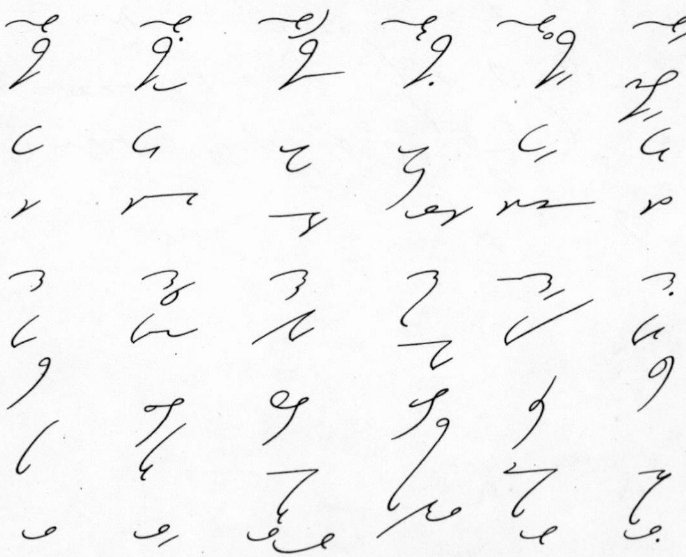

Reading and Writing Practice

390.

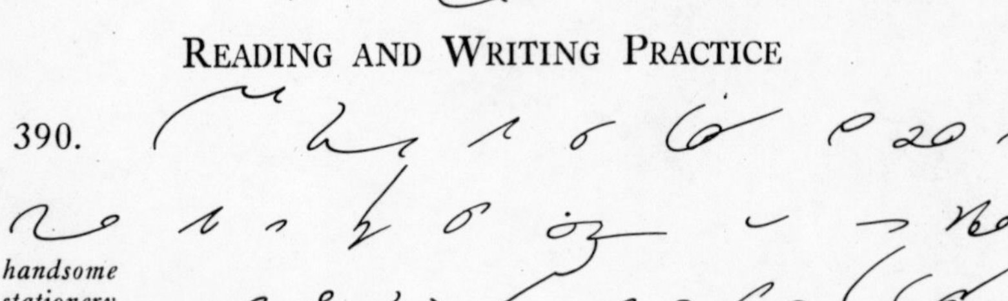

handsome
stationery
, parenthetical

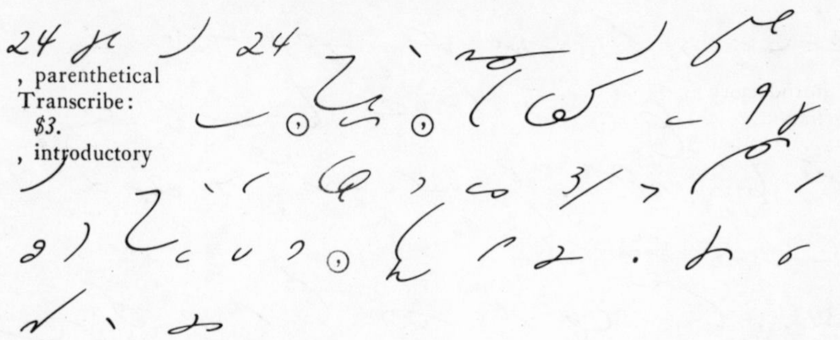

, parenthetical
Transcribe:
$3.
, introductory

391.

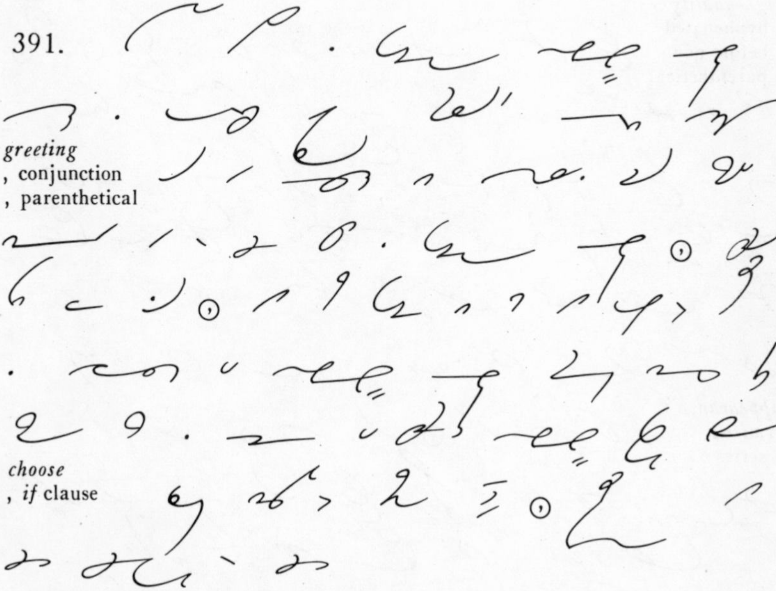

greeting
, conjunction
, parenthetical

choose
, *if* clause

392.

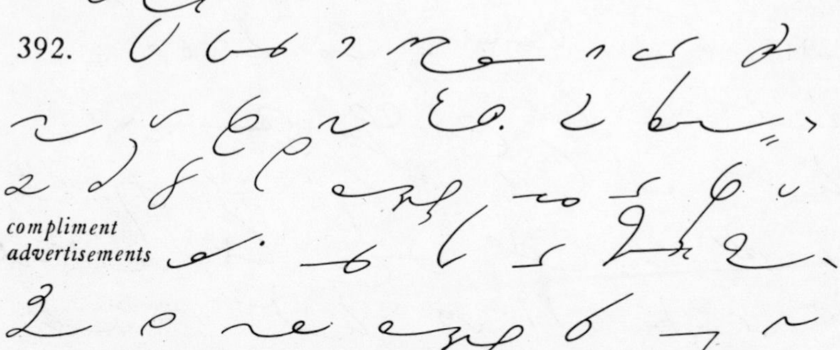

compliment
advertisements

, introductory
believe

393.
high-quality
hyphenated
before noun
, parenthetical

appearance
reader's
, series

394.

; because of
comma
, introductory

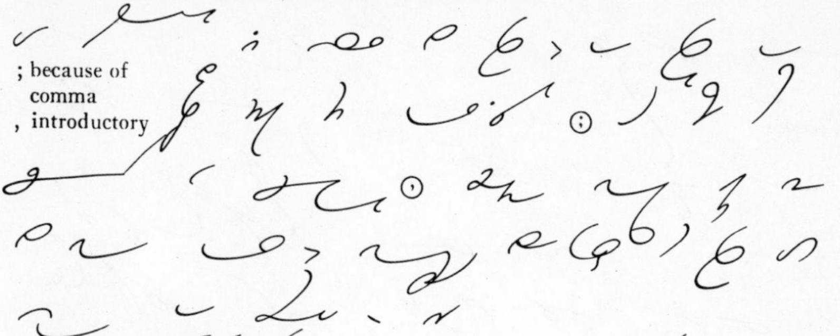

395.
, apposition
Performance
supplies
, introductory
; no conjunction
, *when* clause

396.
, introductory
, apposition
thoroughly

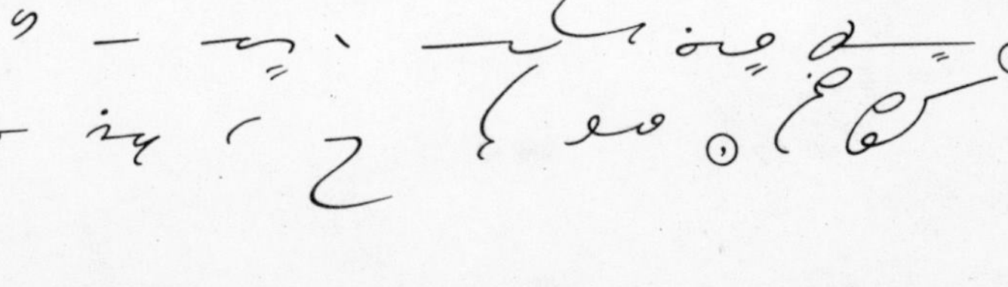

Simon's

ASSIGNMENT 52

397. Vocabulary Builder—Omission of T and D

-CT

-IST, -EST

ST FOLLOWING AN ABBREVIATED FORM OR VOWEL

Omission of D

Reading and Writing Practice

398.

letterhead
probably
respect

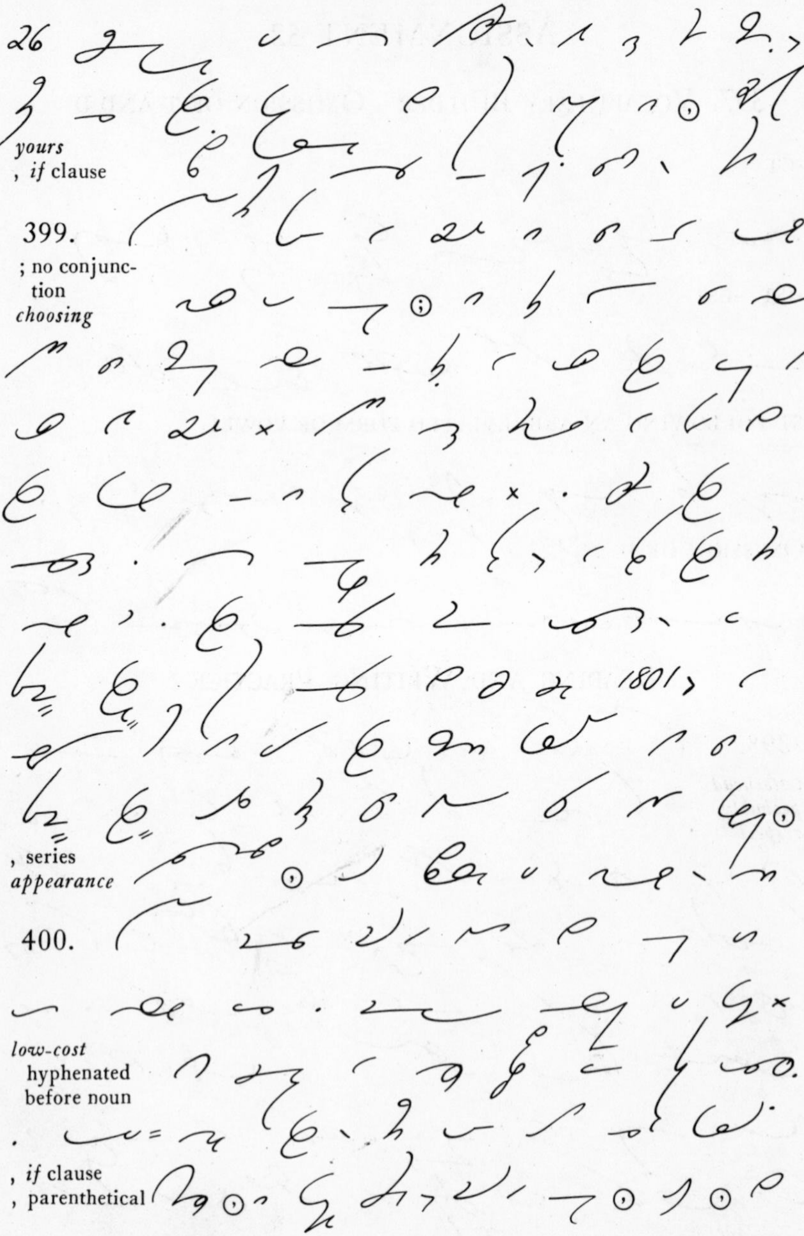

26

yours
, *if* clause

399.
; no conjunction
choosing

, series
appearance

400.

low-cost hyphenated before noun

, *if* clause
, parenthetical

tempted
measured
performance
, parenthetical

, *when* clause
preference

; no conjunction

401.

popular
; no conjunction

reader's

brilliant
colors

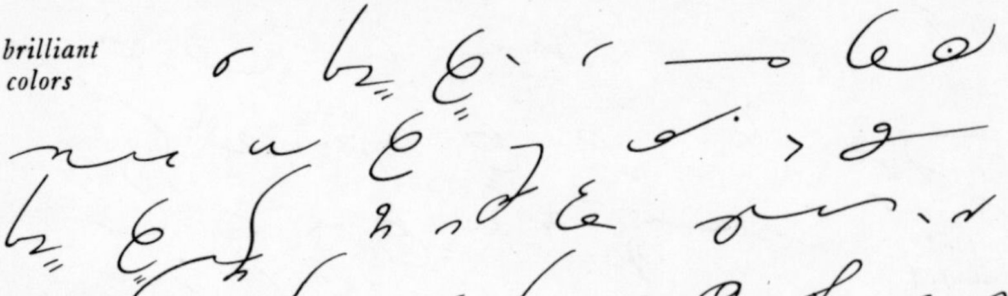

402.

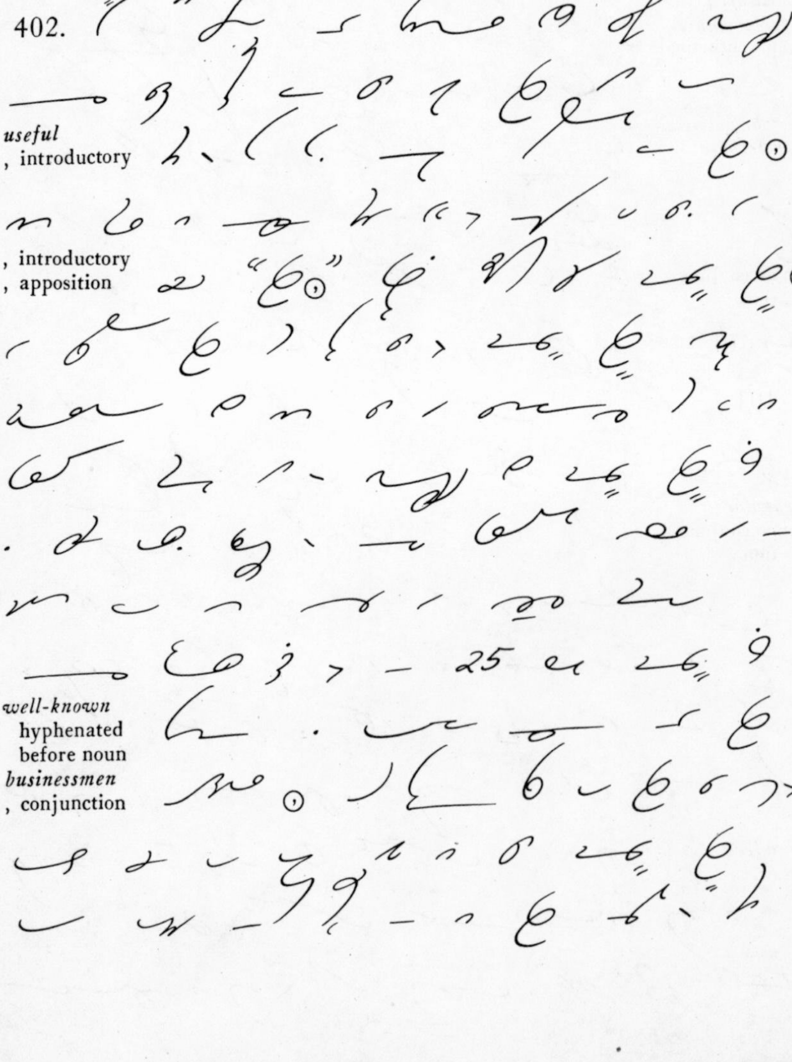

useful
, introductory

, introductory
, apposition

well-known
hyphenated
before noun
businessmen
, conjunction

ASSIGNMENT 53

403. Most-Used Business-Letter Phrases

T FOR TO

B FOR BEEN

A FOR ABLE

404. Geographical Expressions

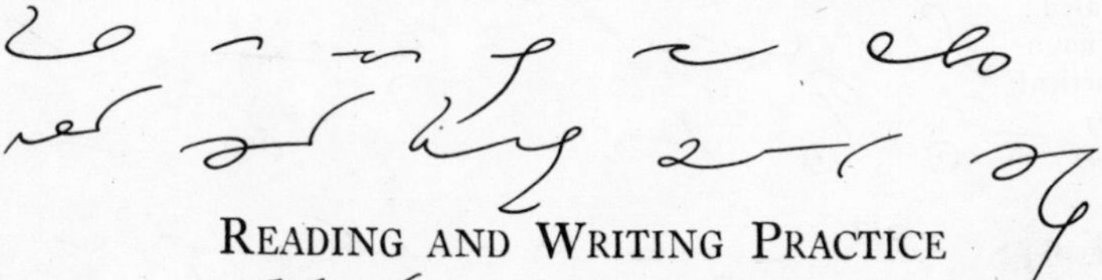

Reading and Writing Practice

405.

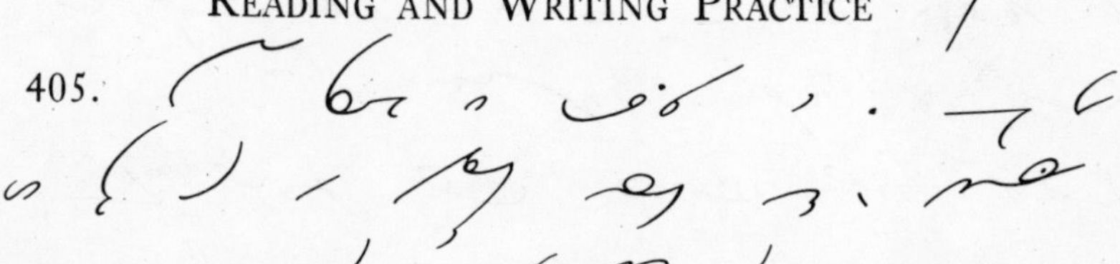

everyone

, introductory

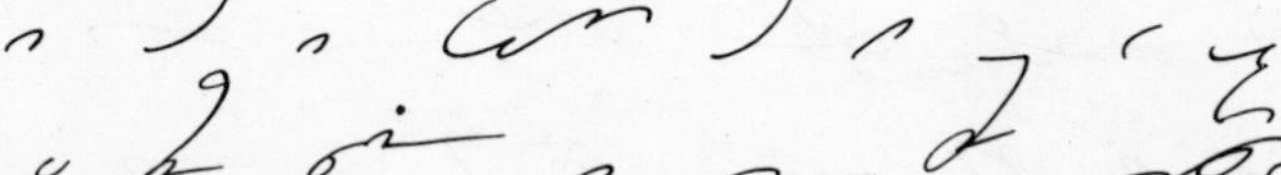

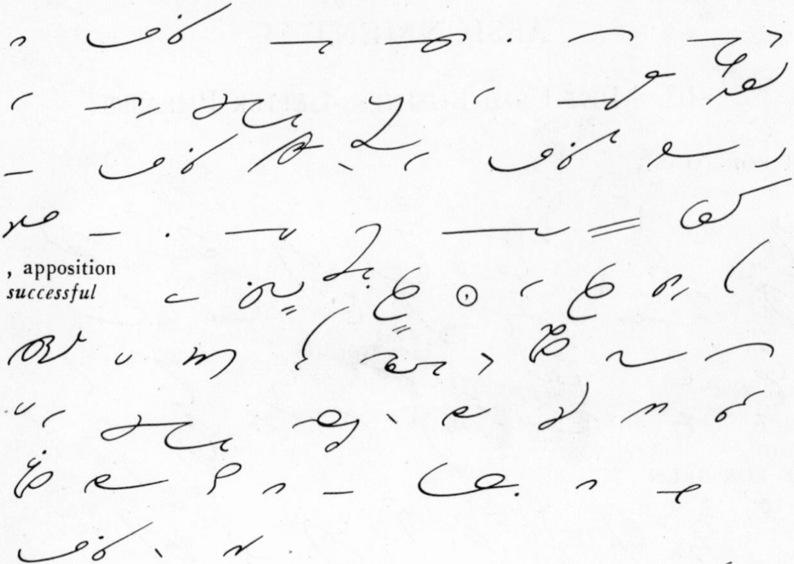

, apposition
successful

406.

, conjunction
well-dressed
hyphenated
before noun
, parenthetical
customer's

additional
, *when* clause
, *if* clause
. courteous request
, conjunction

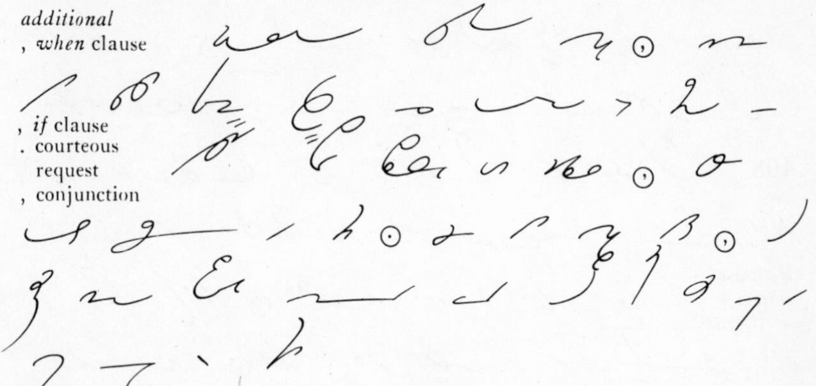

407.

wrapping
, conjunction
, *if* clause
break
immediate
. courteous request

, *if* clause

408.

, *if* clause
, series

409.

, apposition
sometime
questions

year's
patterns
favorably

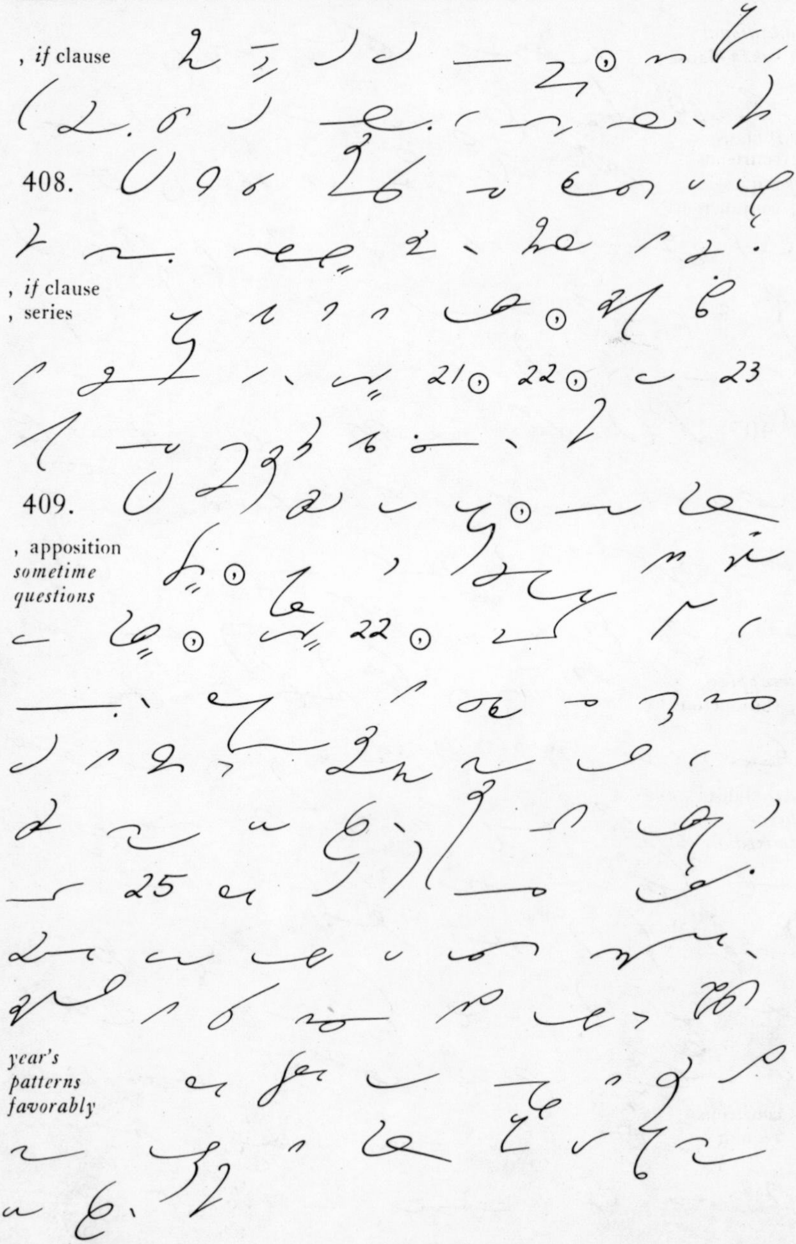

410.

, apposition

, series

attractive

411.

Transcribe:

No. 420

; no conjunction

, apposition

, introductory

, parenthetical

profitable

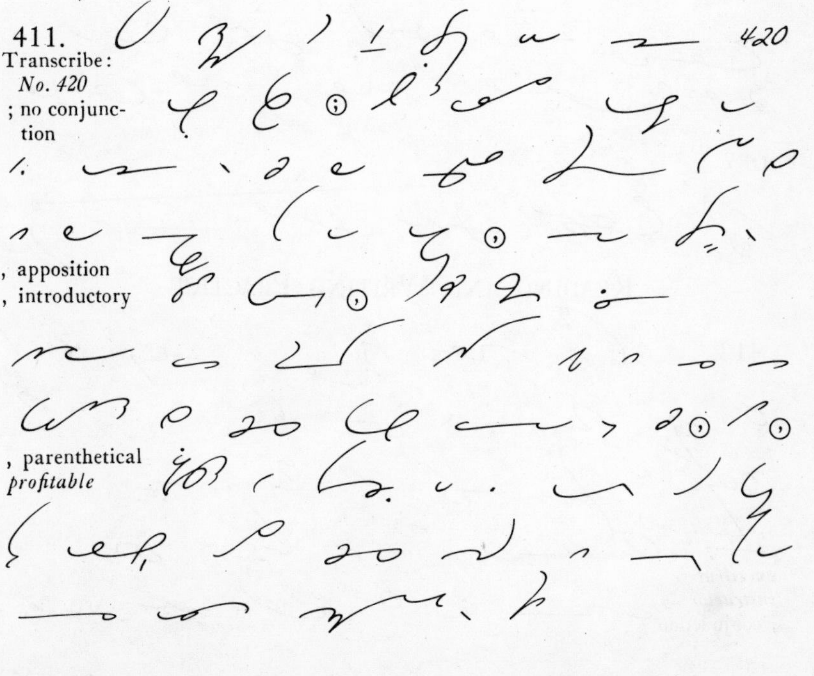

ASSIGNMENT 54

412. Word Families

-ER

-OR

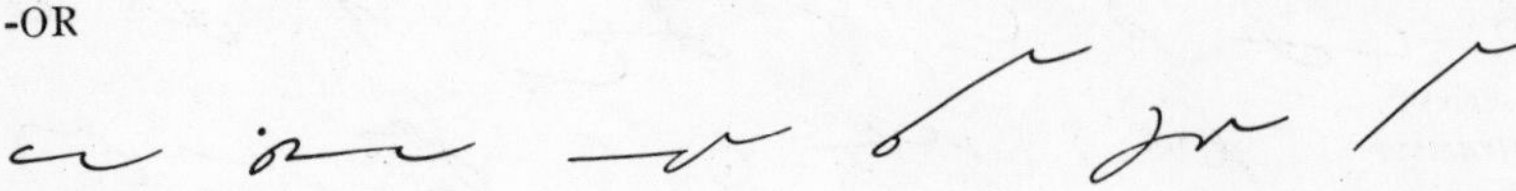

-ERY

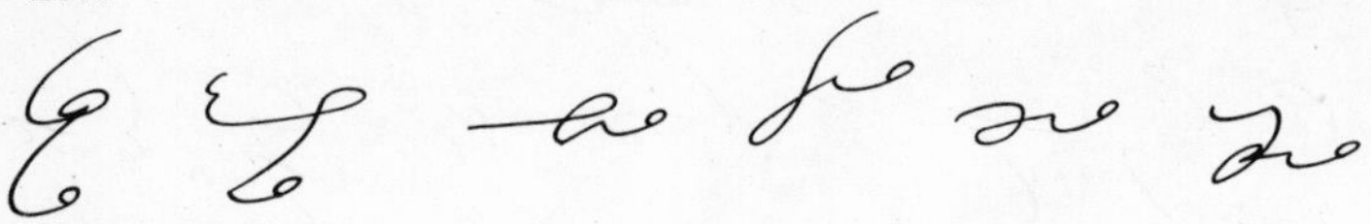

-ARY

-ORY

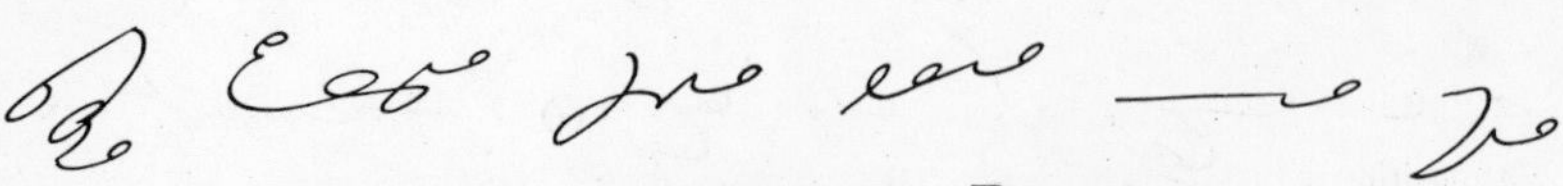

Reading and Writing Practice

413.

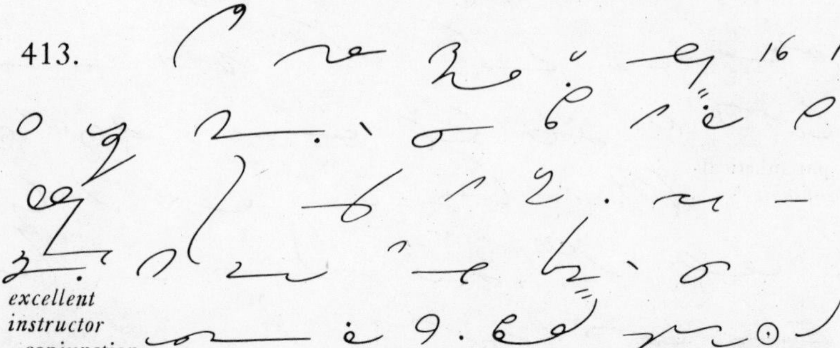

excellent
instructor
, conjunction

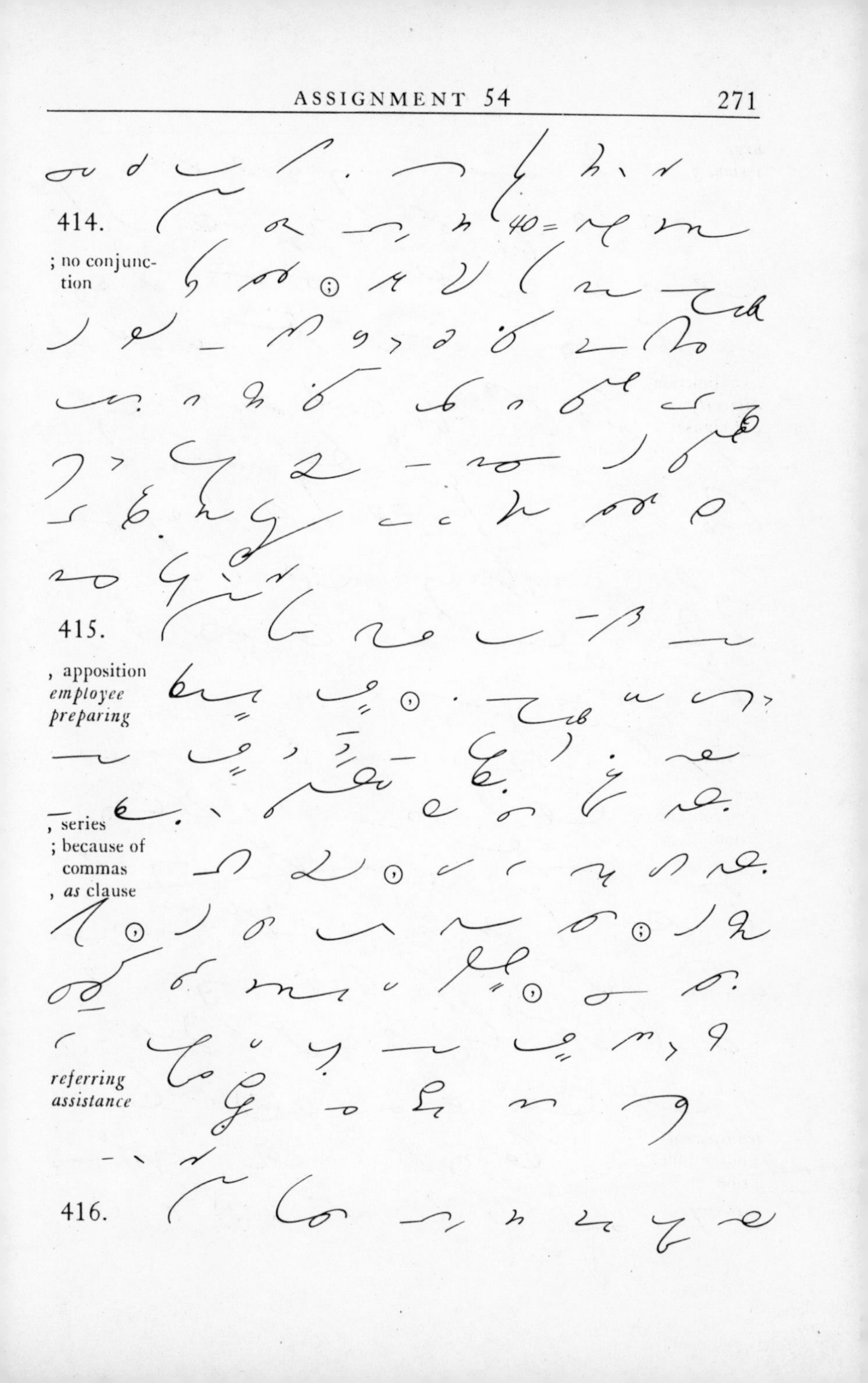

414.

; no conjunction

415.

, apposition
employee
preparing

, series
; because of commas
, *as* clause

referring
assistance

416.

urge
seriously

, conjunction
difficulty
, *if* clause

417.

son's
; no conjunction

transparent
; no conjunction

418.

, introductory

, parenthetical

director

Smith's

419.

, introductory
parents

fill

ASSIGNMENT 55

420. Chart of Word Beginnings and Word Endings

A B C D E F

1.
2.
3.
4.
5.
6.
7.
8.
9.

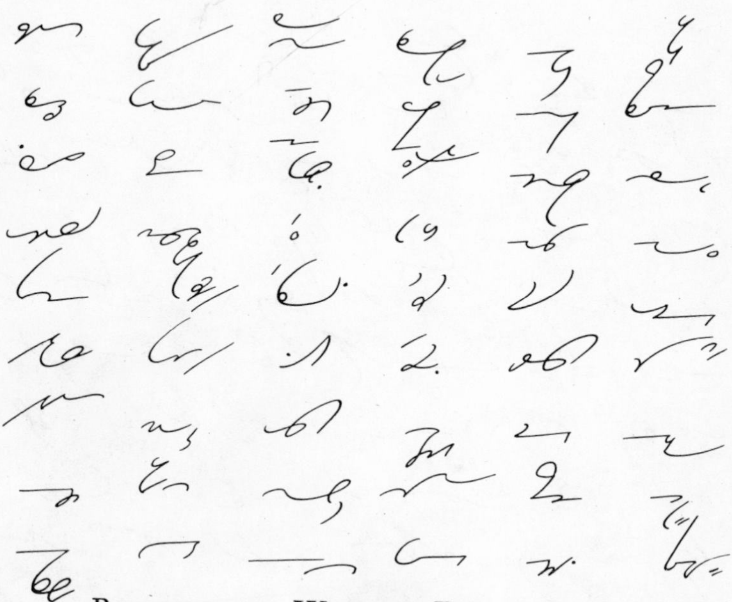

Reading and Writing Practice

421.

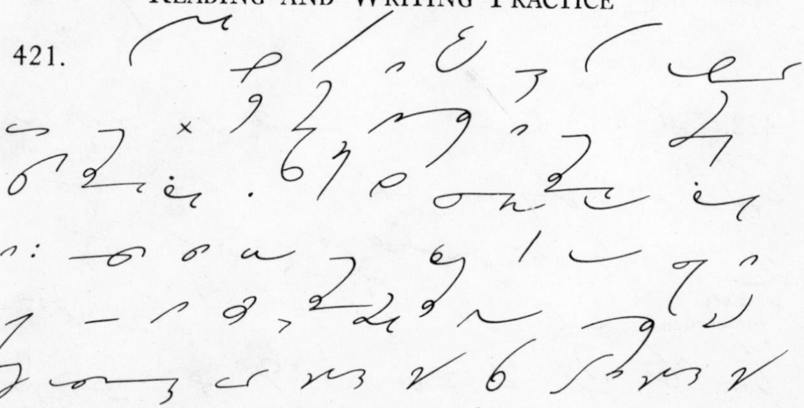

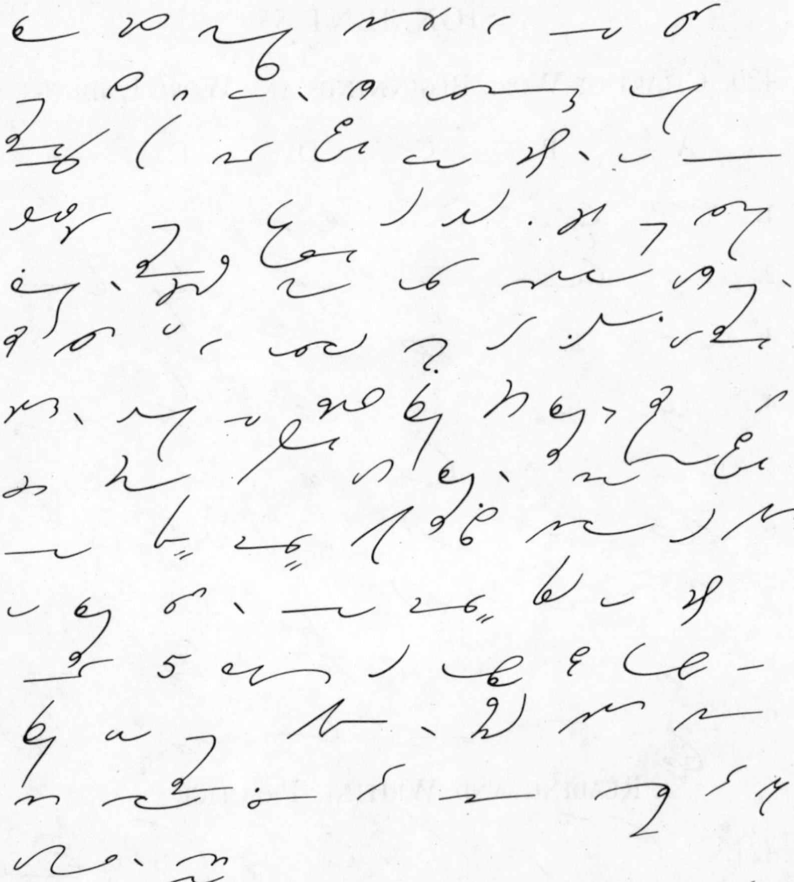

422.

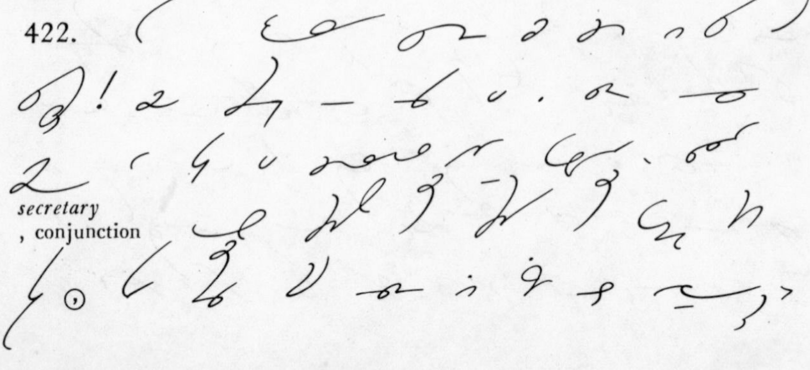

secretary

, conjunction

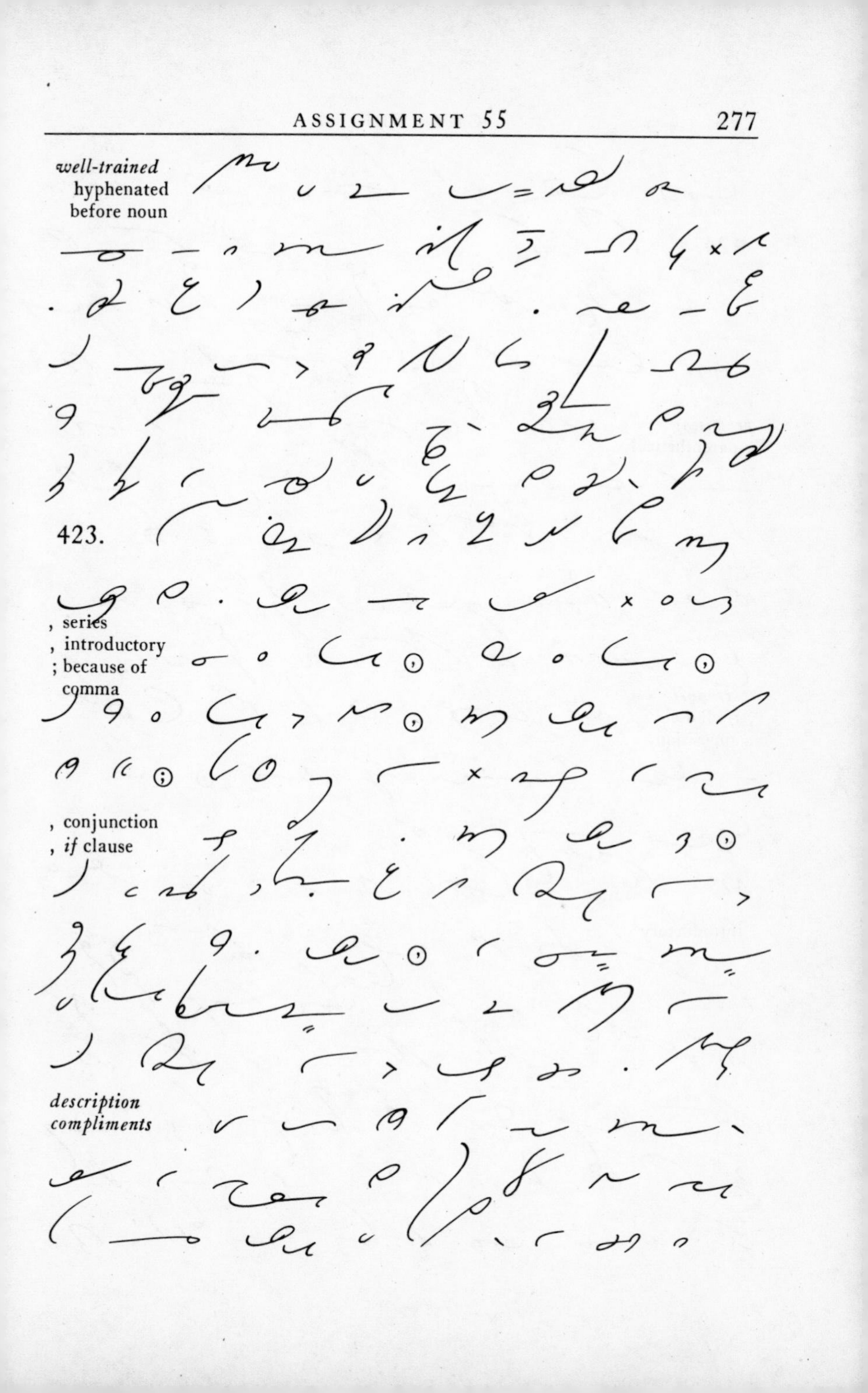

well-trained
hyphenated
before noun

423.

, series
, introductory
; because of
comma

, conjunction
, *if* clause

description
compliments

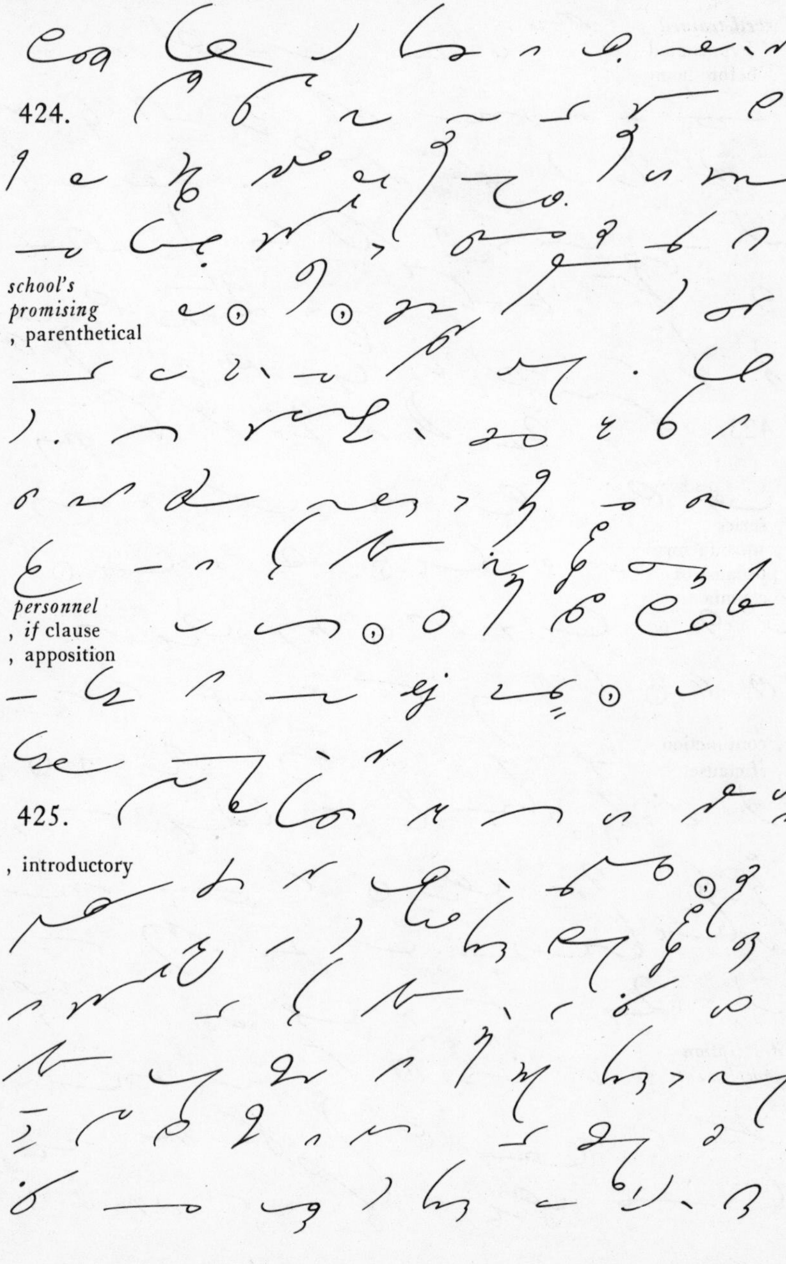
424.
school's
promising
, parenthetical
personnel
, if clause
, apposition
425.
, introductory

received
, parenthetical

426.

Transcribe:
8 a.m.

, *if* clause
superintendent
, introductory

427.

greeting
occurred
, introductory

, parenthetical

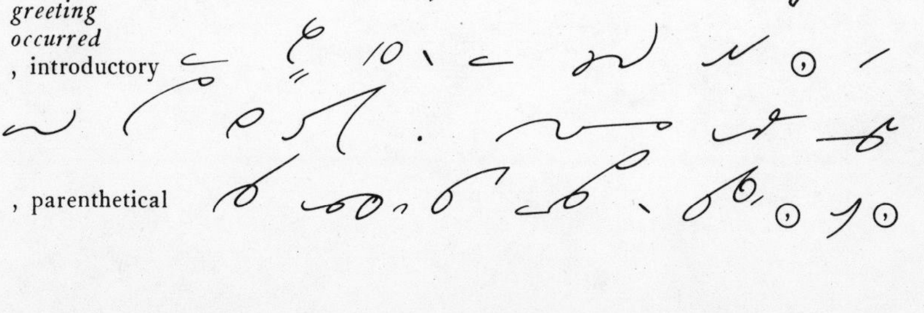

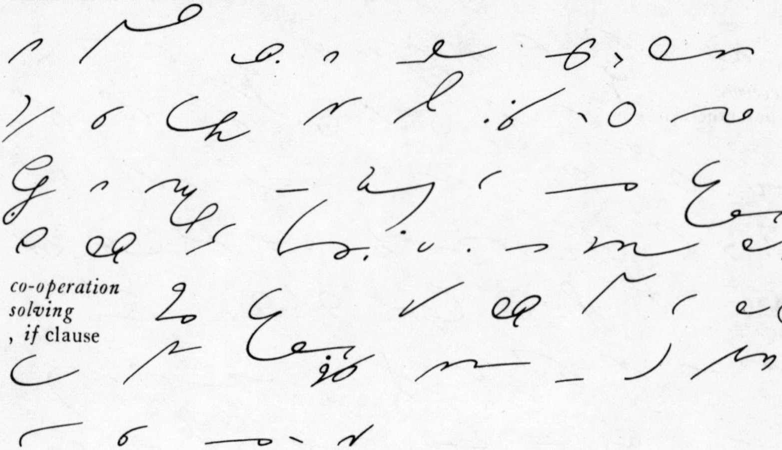

co-operation
solving
, *if* clause

CHAPTER XII

ASSIGNMENT 56

428. Accuracy Practice

429. Vocabulary Builder

-THER

W

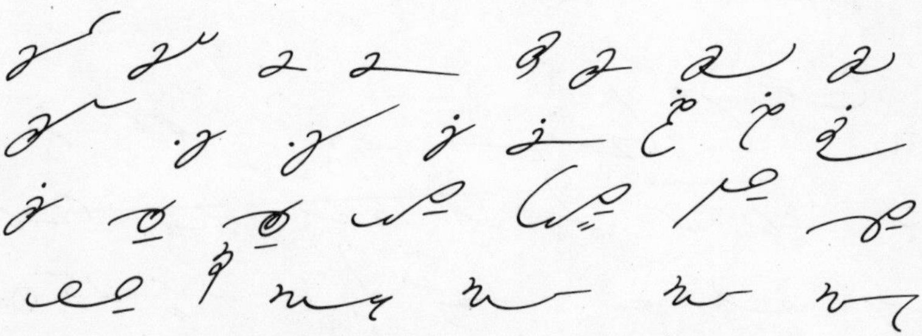

Reading and Writing Practice

430.

up-to-the-minute hyphenated before noun

, *when* clause

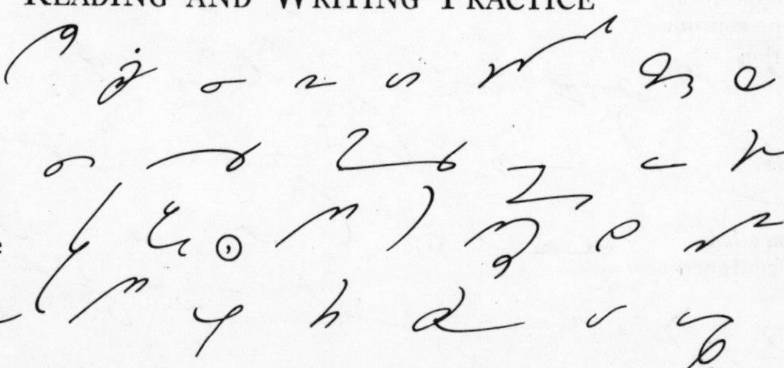

references
student's

, introductory
, conjunction

431.

, apposition
; no conjunction

enrolled
, conjunction

, *if* clause

, parenthetical

, apposition

secretary

, *as* clause

sincerely

432.

aiding

English

language

, series

, *if* clause

; because of comma

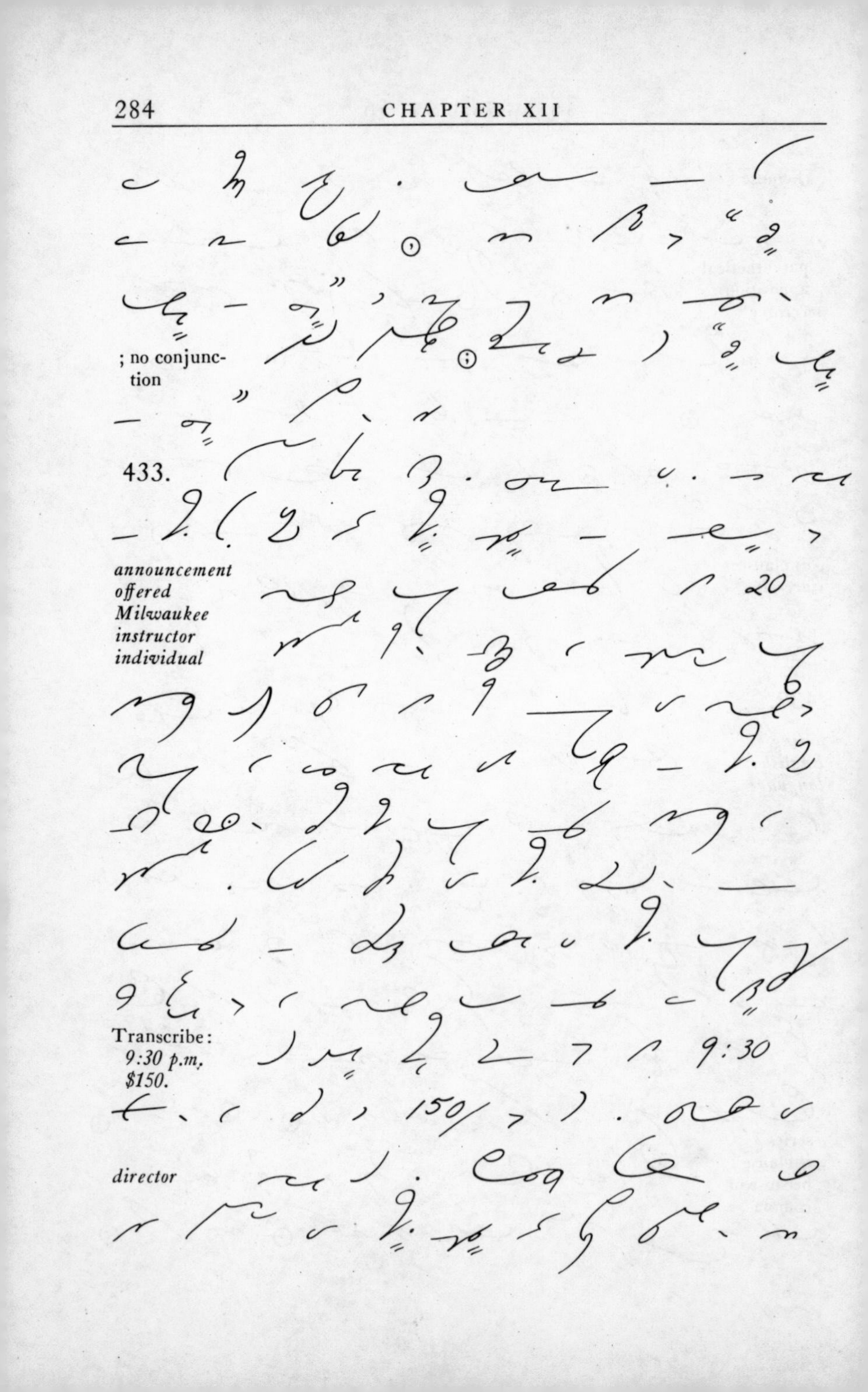

; no conjunction

433.

announcement
offered
Milwaukee
instructor
individual

Transcribe:
9:30 p.m.
$150.

director

434.

, conjunction

, *as* clause

, introductory

whether

year's

ASSIGNMENT 57

435. Vocabulary Builder

-TATION, ETC.

TERN, TERM

-ORT

NUMBERS, ETC.

Reading and Writing Practice

436.

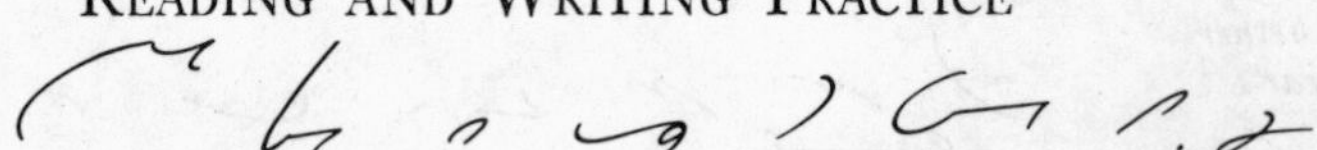

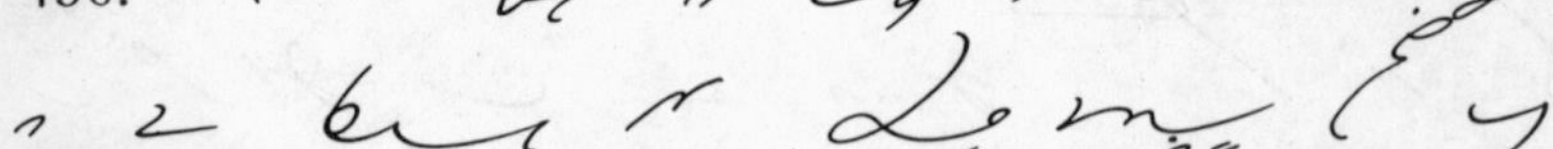

referred
husband
, *as* clause

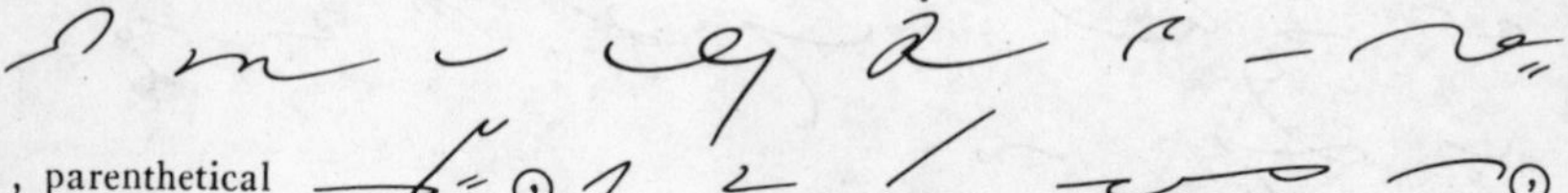

, parenthetical
normally

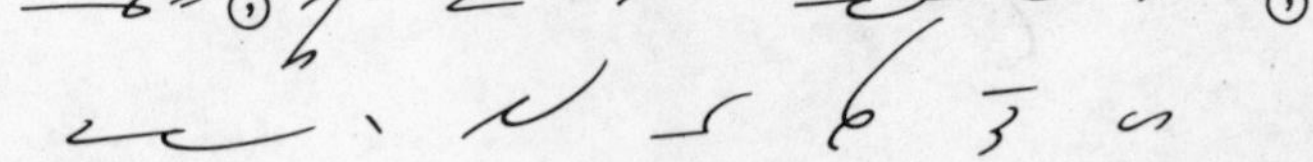

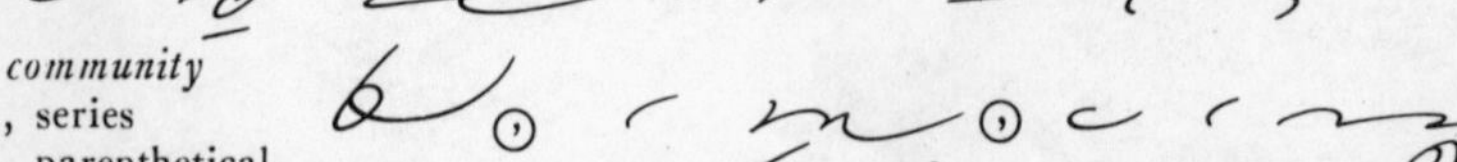

community
, series
, parenthetical

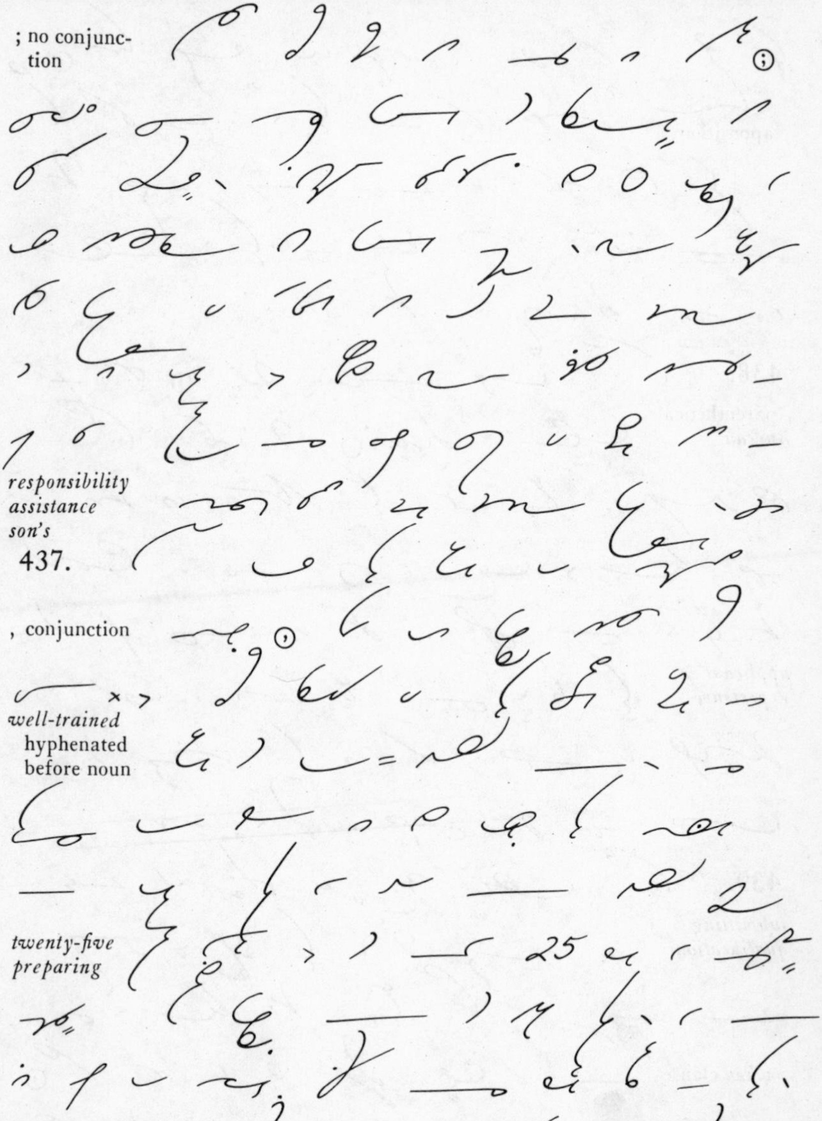

; no conjunction

responsibility
assistance
son's

437.

, conjunction

well-trained hyphenated before noun

twenty-five
preparing

, apposition

438.

, parenthetical
Bureau

applicant
experience

439.

submitting
qualifications

, *when* clause

substitute
, parenthetical

vacancy
permission
convenience

440.

Easter
opportunity
, *if* clause

441.

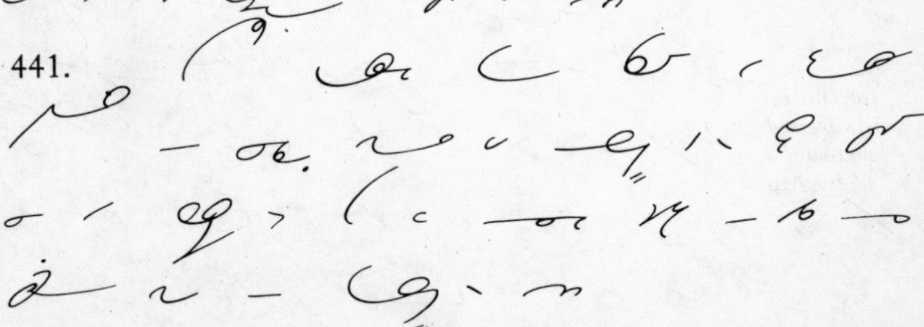

ASSIGNMENT 58

442. Most-Used Business-Letter Phrases

IS NOT, WAS NOT

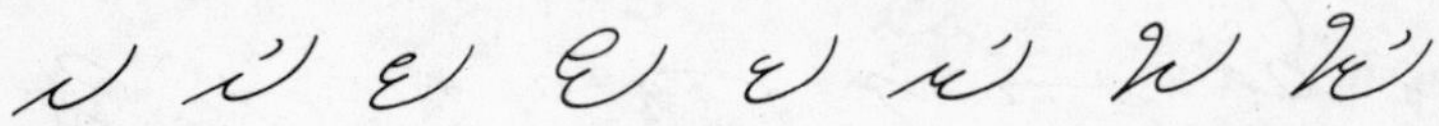

WANT

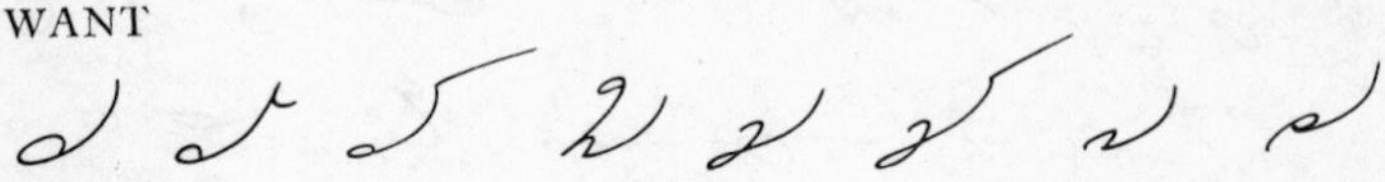

AGO

443. Geographical Expressions

Reading and Writing Practice

444.

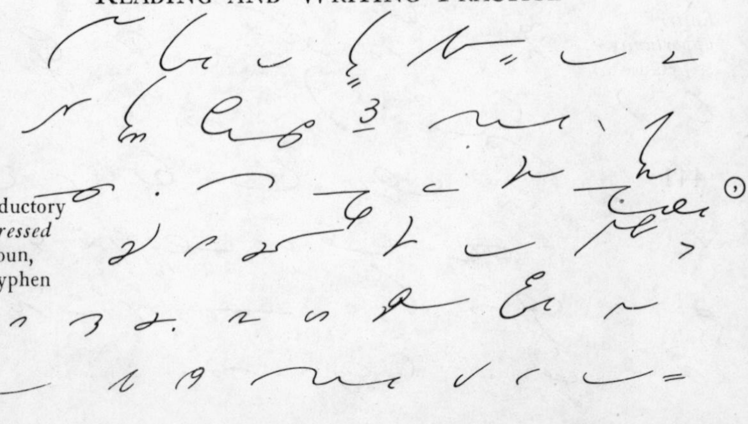

, introductory
well dressed
no noun,
no hyphen

well-dressed
hyphenated
before noun
grooming
city's
, conjunction
budget
, introductory

445.
well-dressed
hyphenated
before noun
wear
; because of
comma
, apposition
, introductory

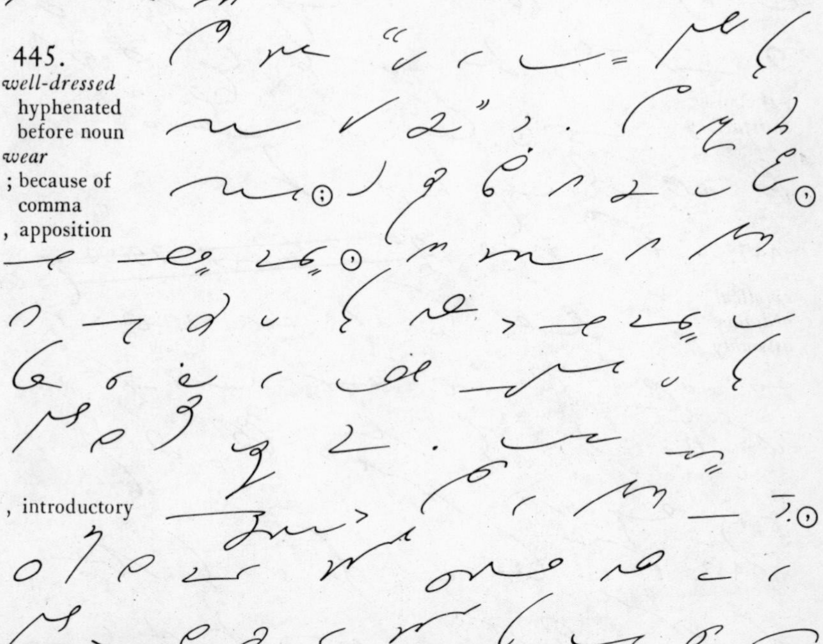

dignified
businesswoman
Smith's
schedule
, *if* clause

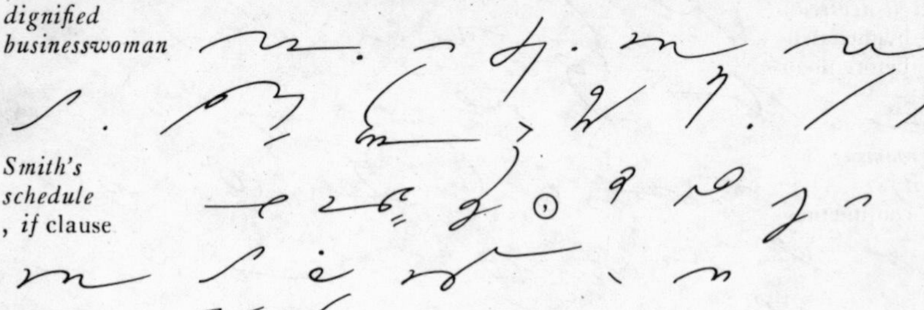

446.

, introductory
, series
, *if* clause
satisfactory

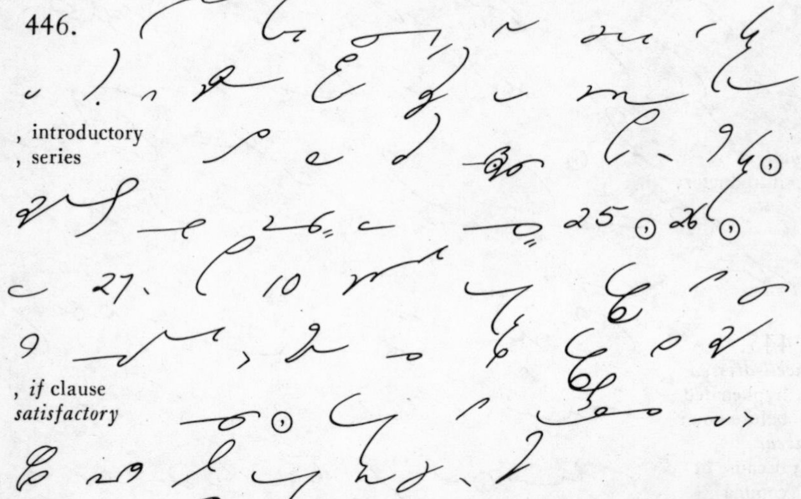

447.

excellent
ordinary
assembly

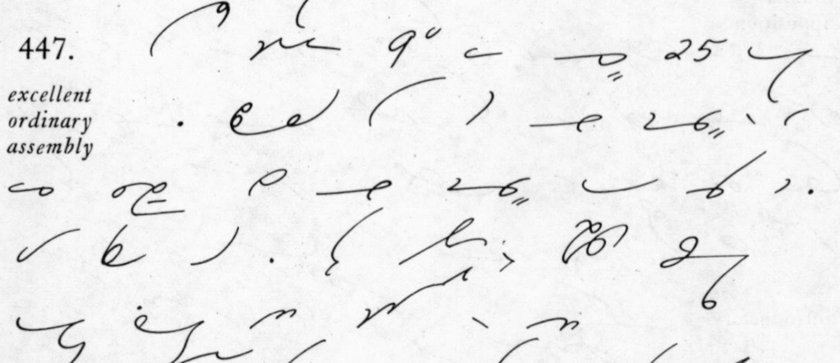

448.

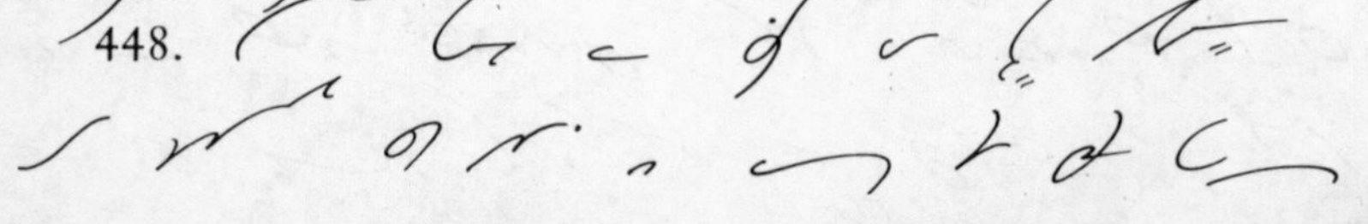

guiding
clothing
sometime

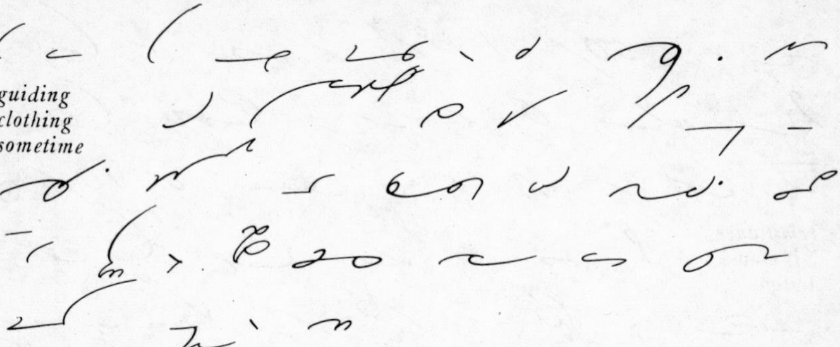

449.

correspondence
course
, introductory
, parenthetical
advice

450.

pamphlets
everything

remittance
, *if* clause
lesson
, *if* clause

ASSIGNMENT 59

451. Word Families

-UATE

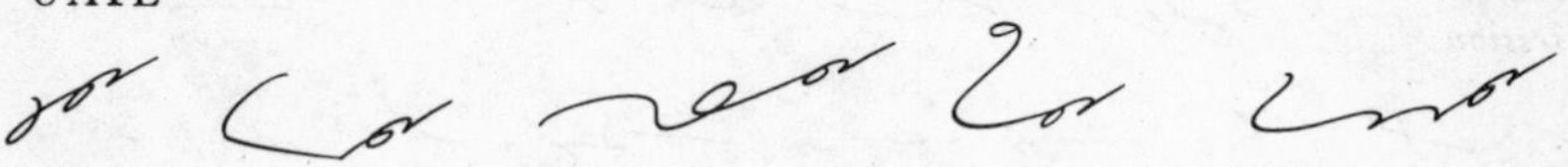

-IOUS

-PUTE, -PUTATION

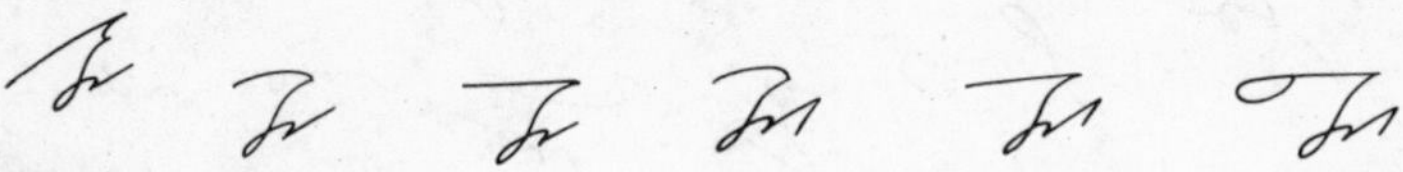

-IC

-KEN

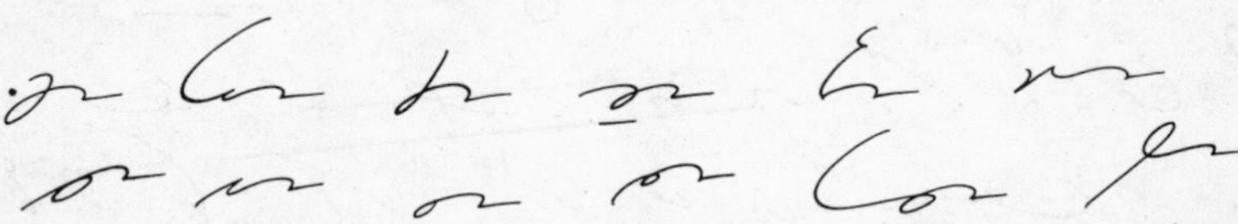

Reading and Writing Practice

452.

, *as* clause

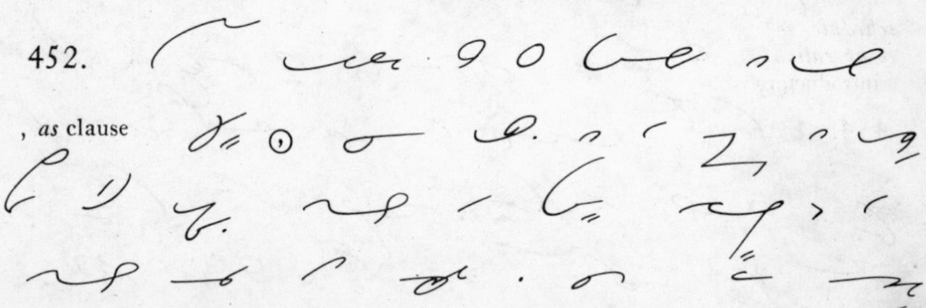

advanced
course
session

453.

received
promptness
discussed

, conjunction

schedule
co-operation
, introductory

454.

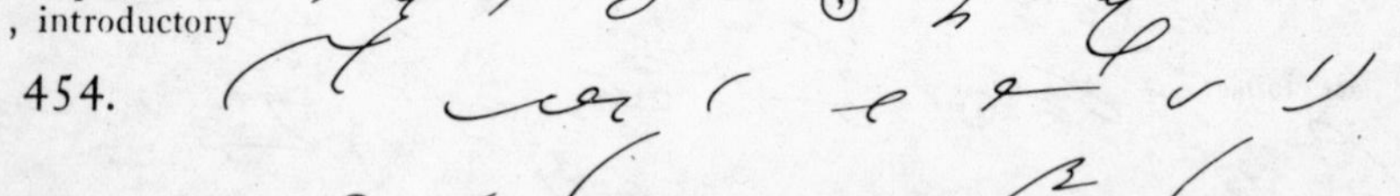

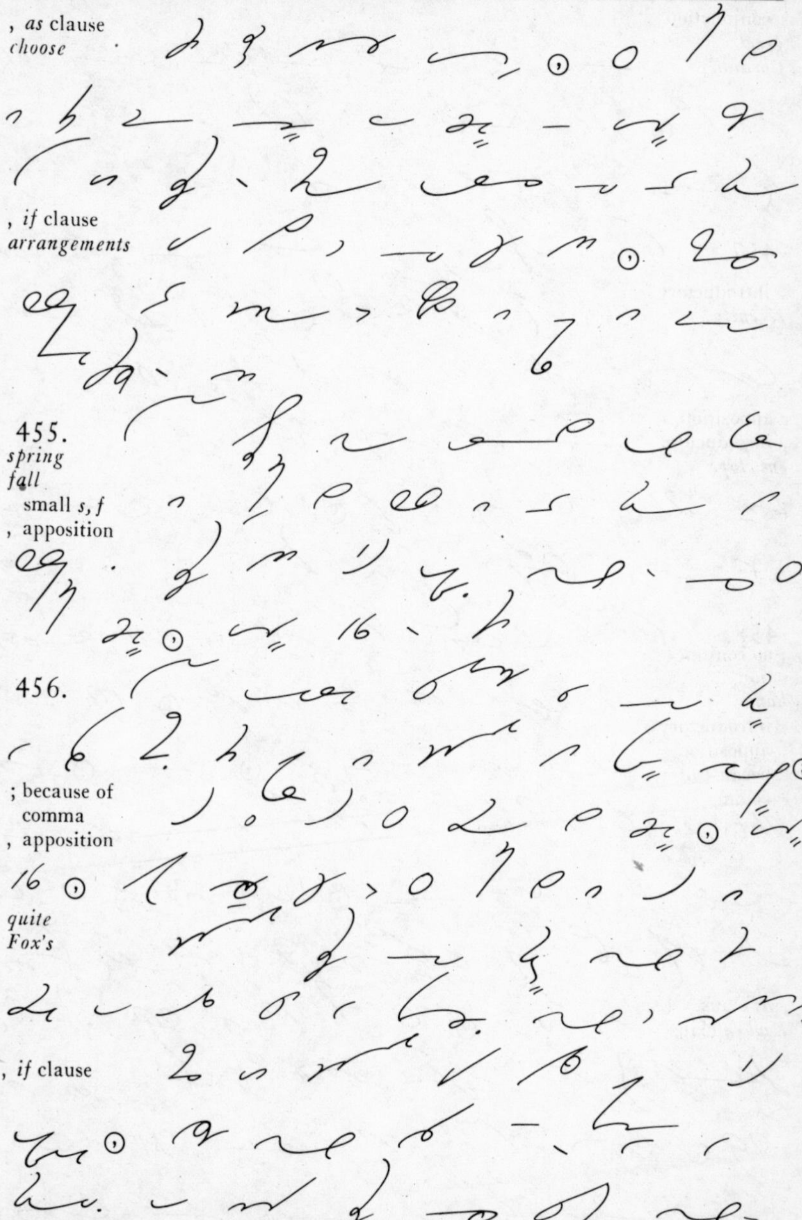

, *as* clause
choose

, *if* clause
arrangements

455.
spring
fall
small *s, f*
, apposition

456.

; because of
comma
, apposition

quite
Fox's

, *if* clause

, conjunction
greet
Cordially

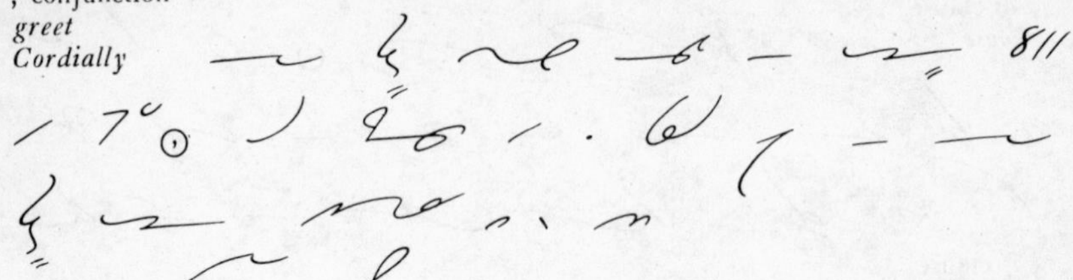

457.

, introductory
recently
, apposition
, introductory
envelope

458.

; no conjunction
honor
, introductory
, apposition
; because of comma
, *as* clause
, *when* clause

459.

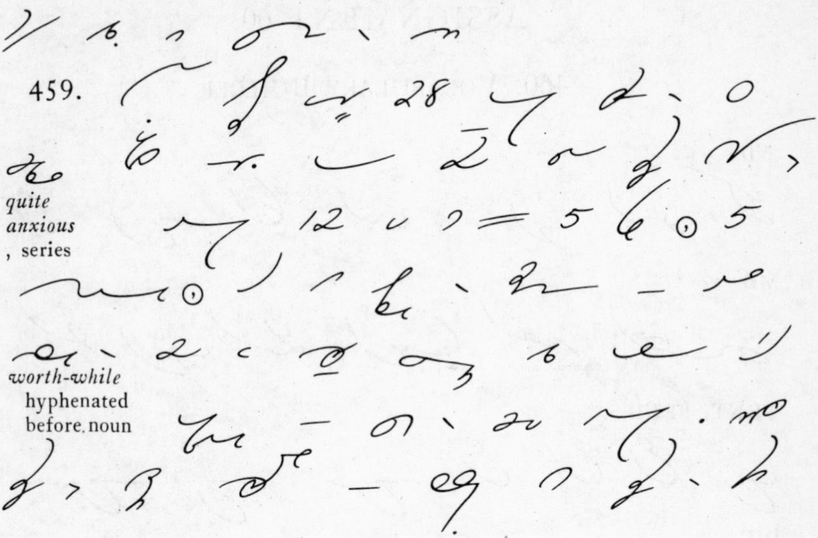

quite
anxious
, series

worth-while
hyphenated
before noun

ASSIGNMENT 60

460. Vocabulary Builder

ND

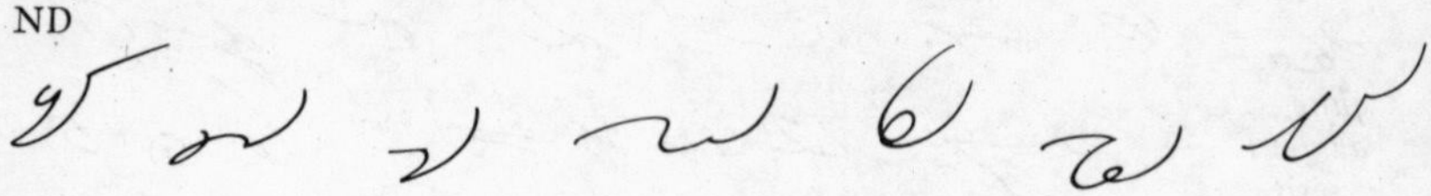

MD

PENT, PEND

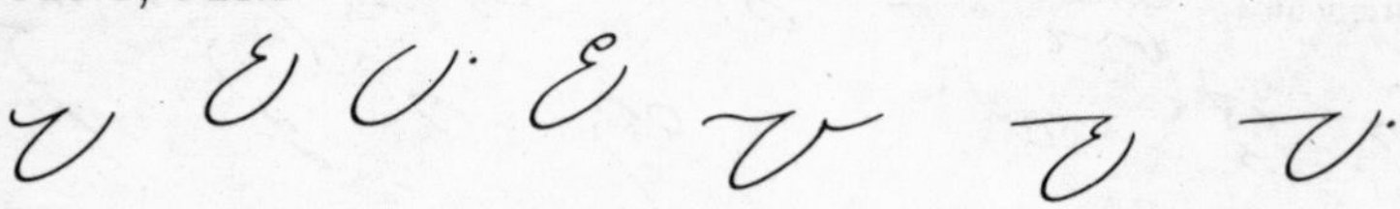

DIF

Reading and Writing Practice

461.

462.

colleges
graduated
, *as* clause

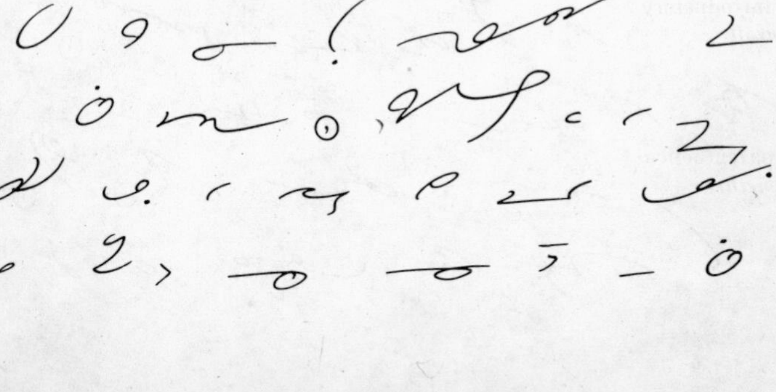

, introductory
, *as* clause
part-time
hyphenated
before noun
, series

463.
written
accounting
school's

; no conjunction
, introductory

464.
, introductory
enroll

, parenthetical
whether

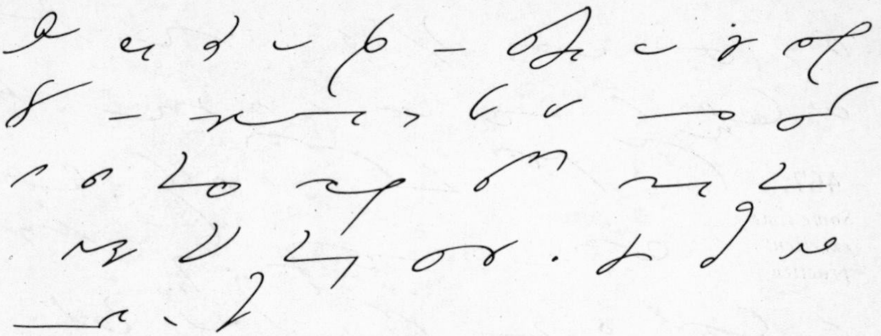

465.

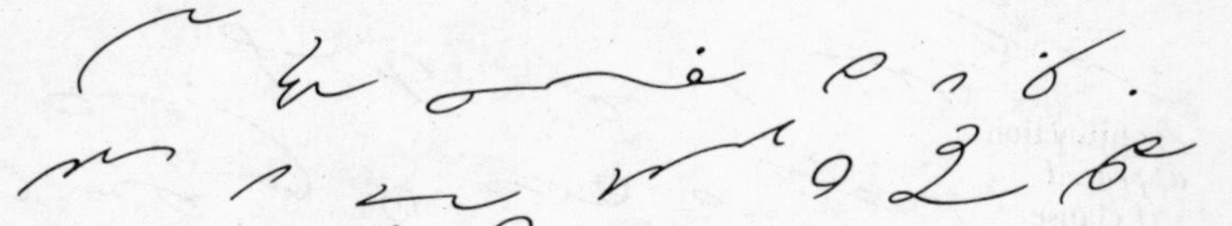

advertisements
satisfactory

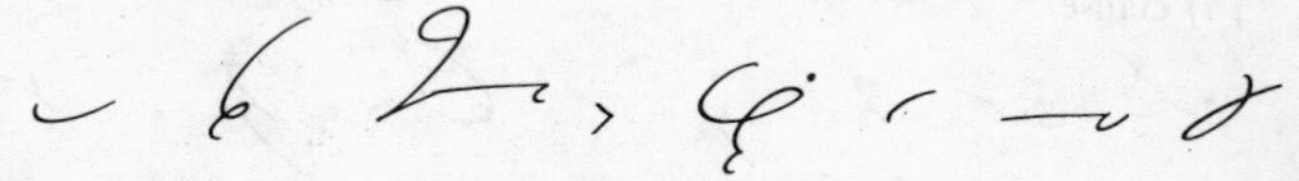

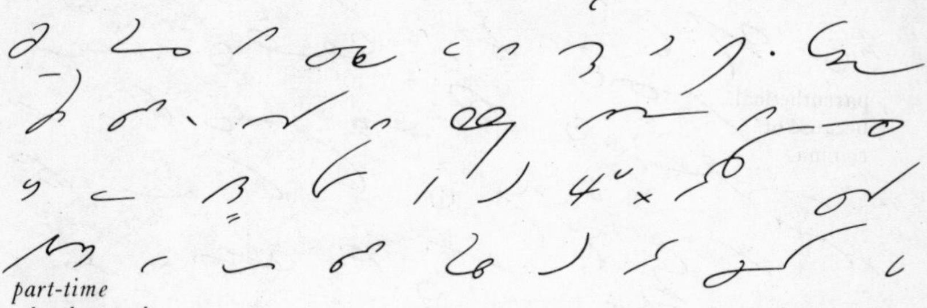

part-time
hyphenated
before noun
, apposition

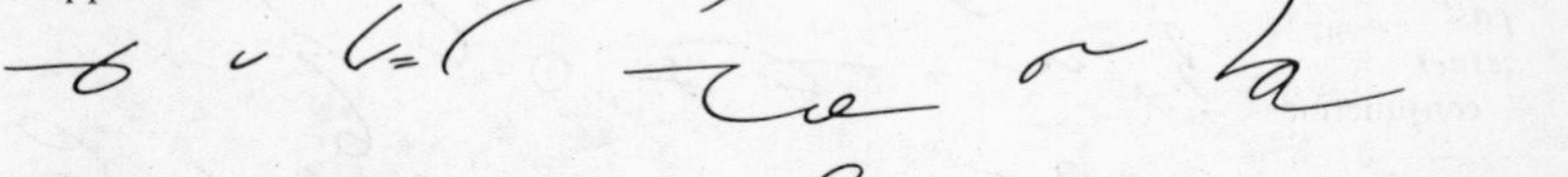

466.

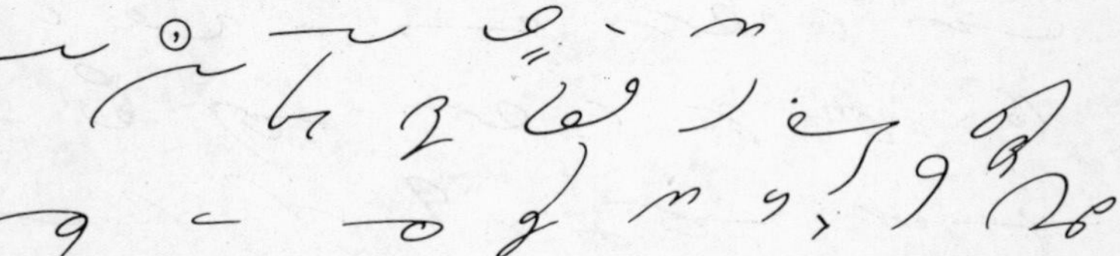

, conjunction

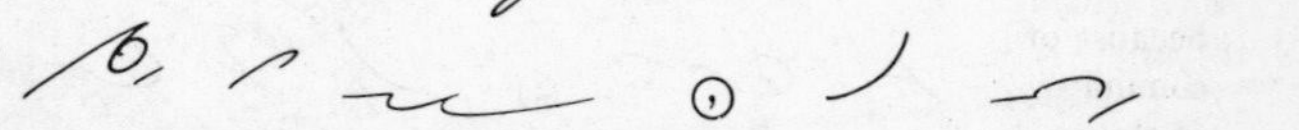

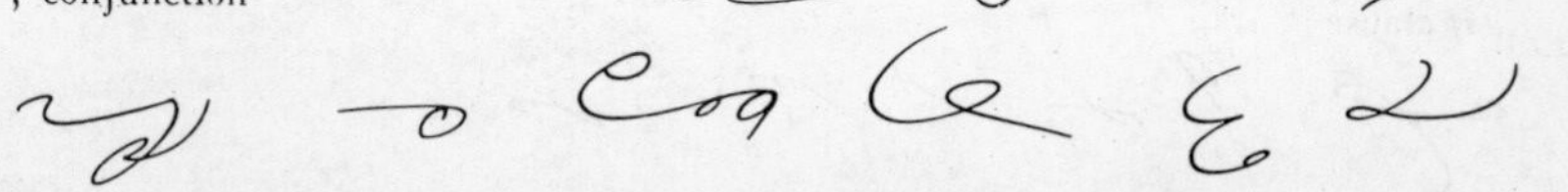

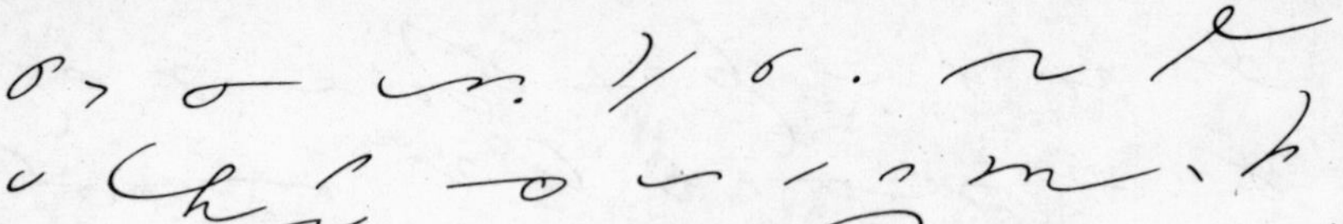

467.

Some time
excellent
practice
, conjunction
appeared
, *if* clause
, parenthetical
; because of
comma

468.

past
issues
, conjunction
; because of
comma
, *if* clause

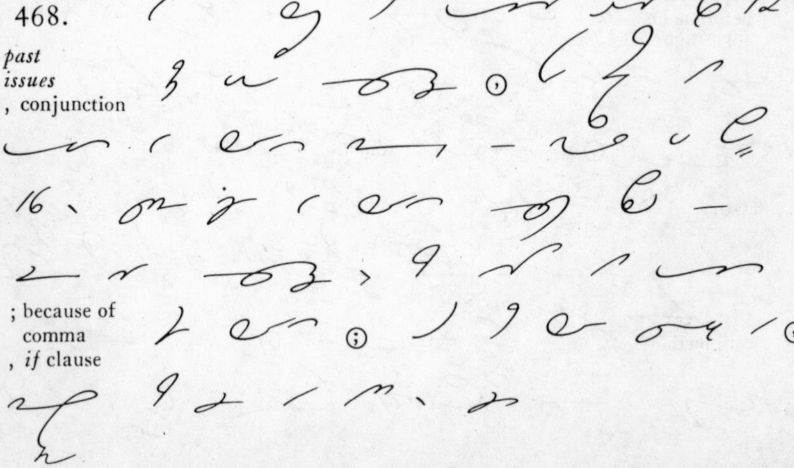

CHAPTER XIII

ASSIGNMENT 61

469. Brief-Form Chart

A B C D E F

1. 2. 3. 4. 5. 6. 7. 8. 9.

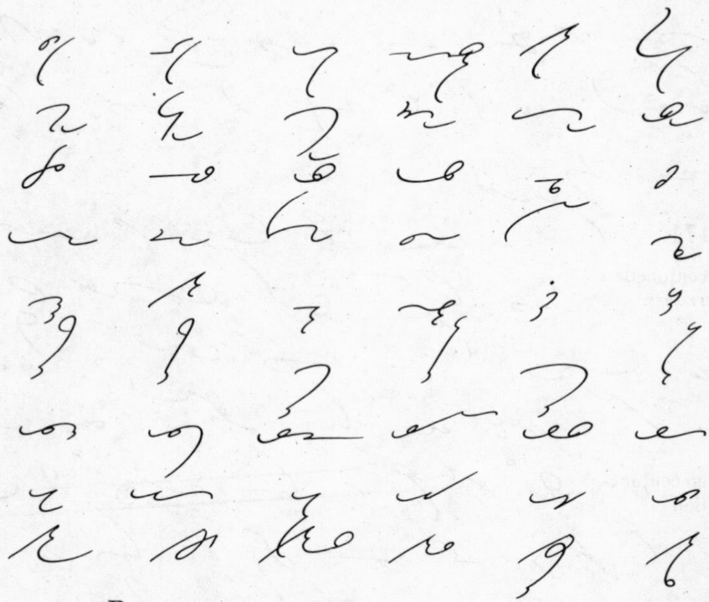

Reading and Writing Practice

470.

, parenthetical

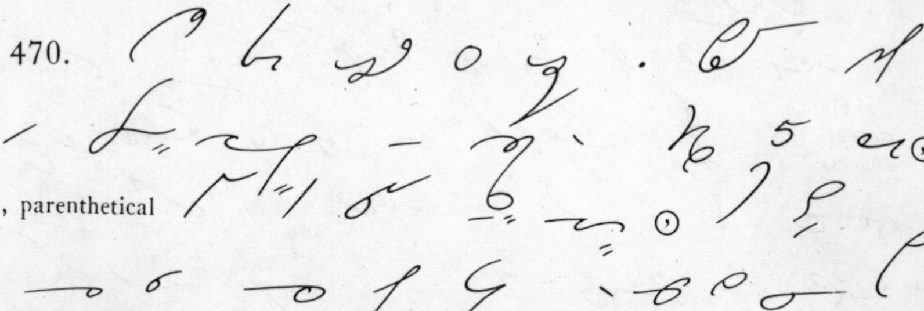

, introductory
, series

worth-while
hyphenated
before noun

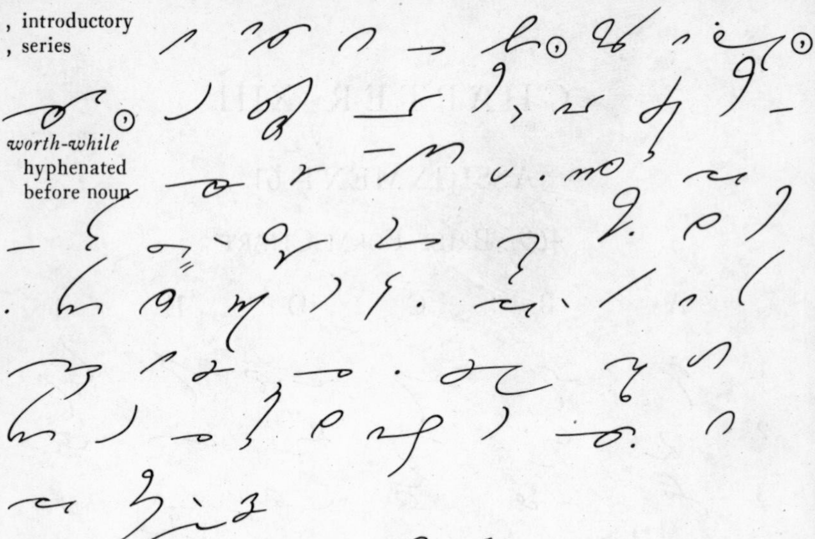

471.

, conjunction
territory

; no conjunction

, *if* clause
accept
success

, introductory
assistance

472.
, apposition
pamphlet
already

business
, conjunction

, *when* clause

, introductory
difficulty

473.
confident
whether
familiar

titles
, *if* clause

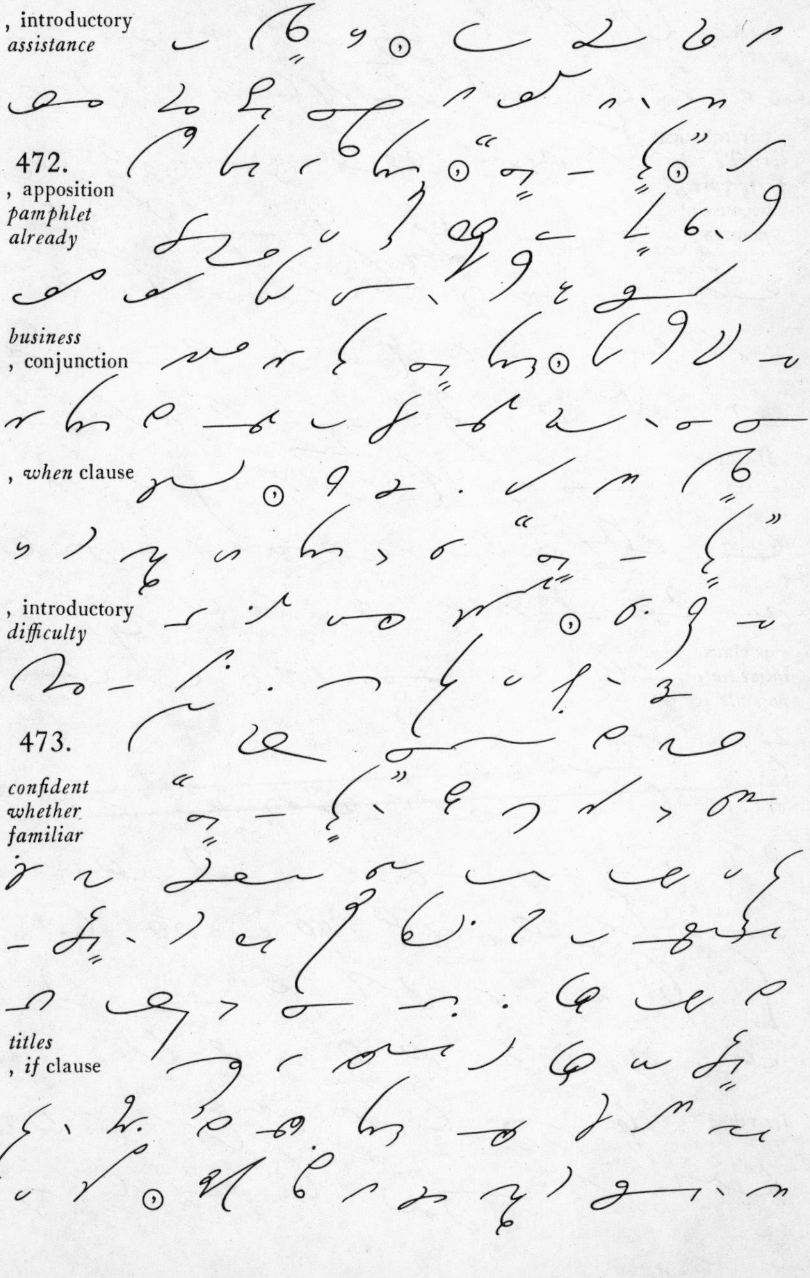

474.

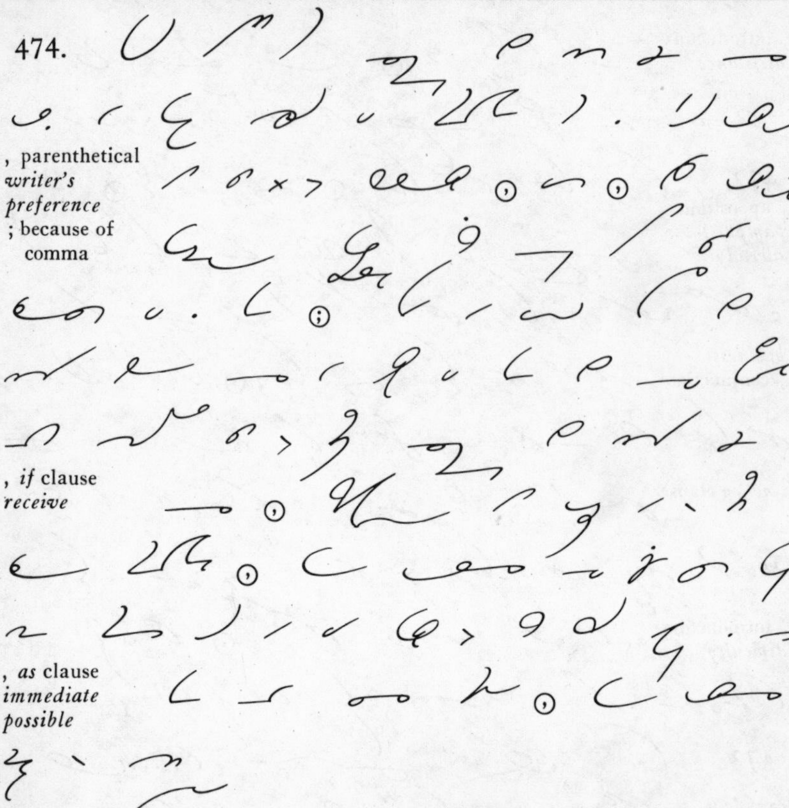

, parenthetical
writer's
preference
; because of comma
, *if* clause
receive
, *as* clause
immediate
possible

475.

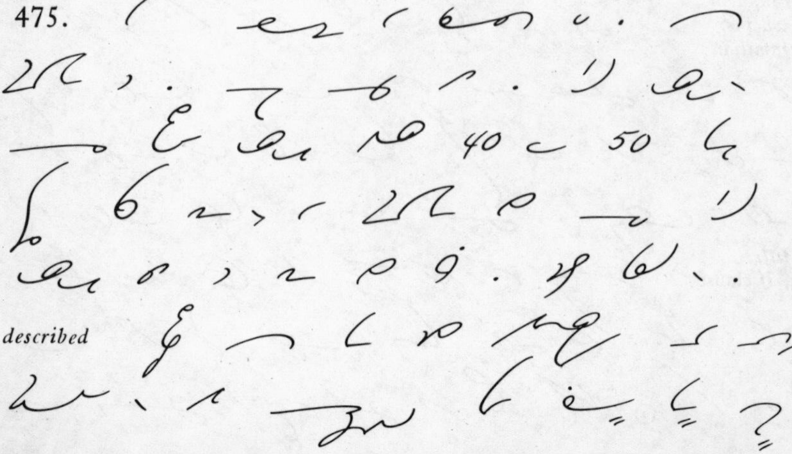

described

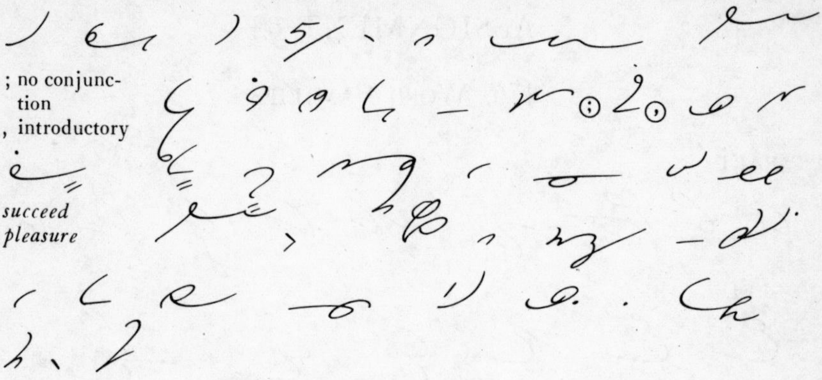
; no conjunction
, introductory
succeed
pleasure

ASSIGNMENT 62

476. Word Families

PART

-PEL

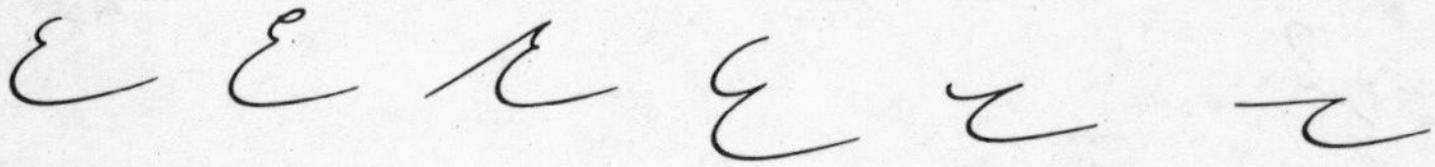

-TITUDE

-QUIRE

TEN, DEN

TEM, DEM

Reading and Writing Practice

477.

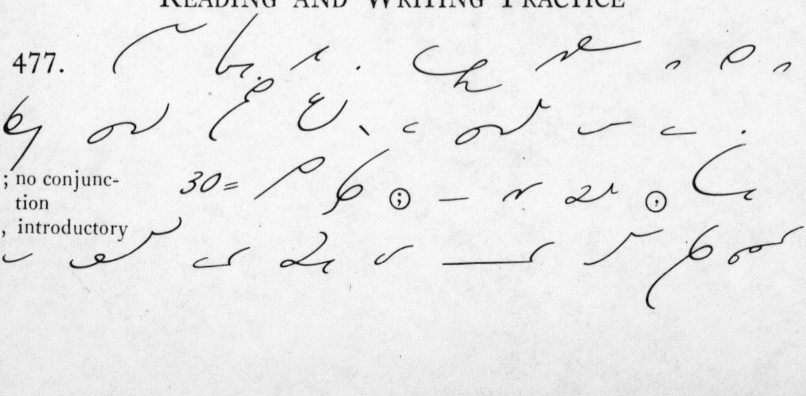

; no conjunction

, introductory

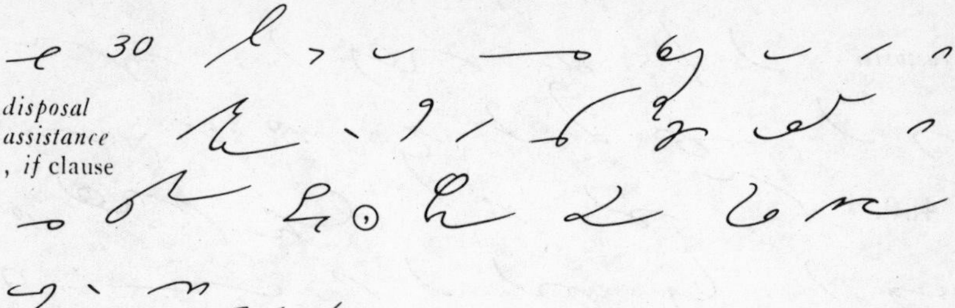

disposal
assistance
, *if* clause

478.

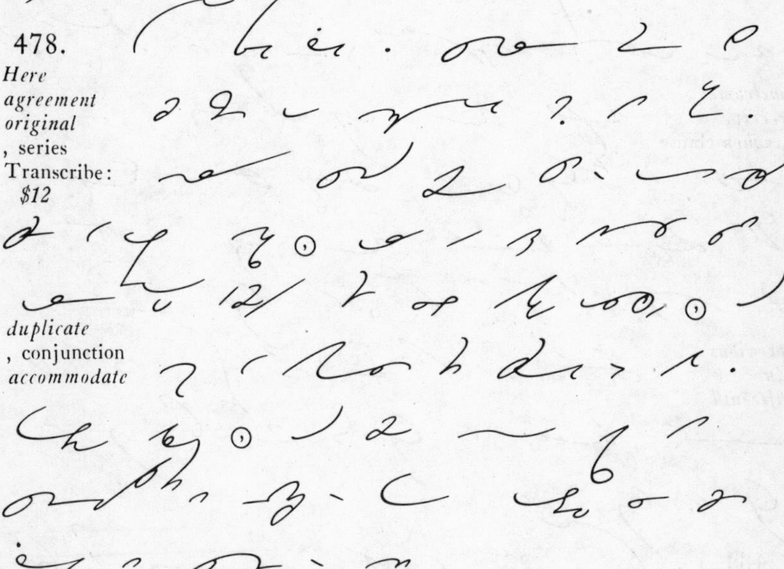

Here
agreement
original
, series
Transcribe:
$12

duplicate
, conjunction
accommodate

479.

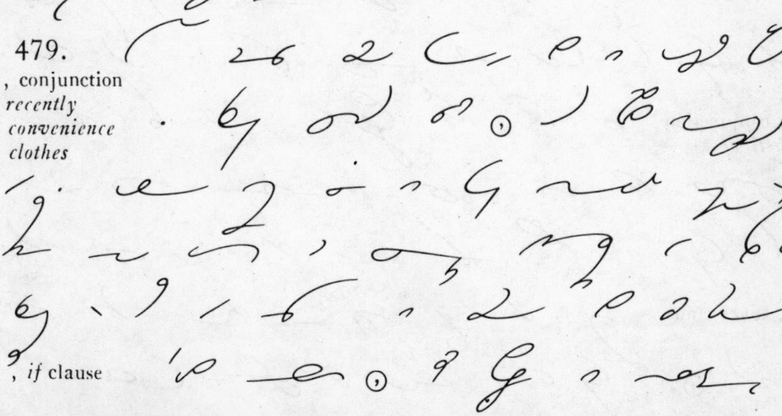

, conjunction
recently
convenience
clothes

, *if* clause

customer's

480.

welcome
receive
, *when* clause

previous
due
fifteenth

481.

, conjunction
believe

, *when* clause

forward
, parenthetical

482.
immediate
adopting
enclosed

companies
customers'

483.

charge-account
hyphenated
before noun

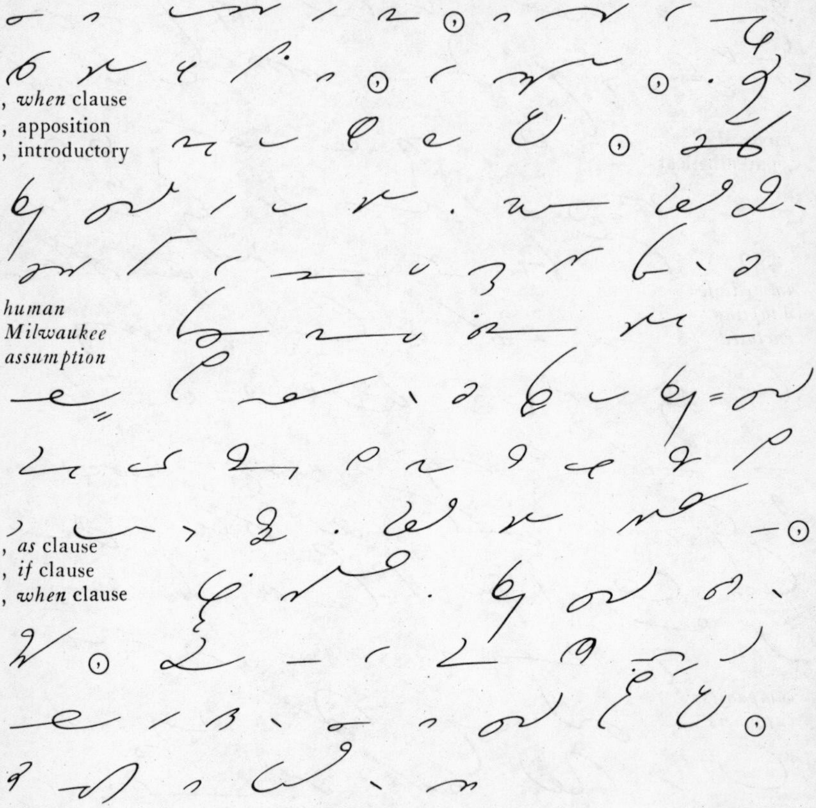

, *when* clause
, apposition
, introductory

human
Milwaukee
assumption

, *as* clause
, *if* clause
, *when* clause

ASSIGNMENT 63

484. Most-Used Business-Letter Phrases

(Omission of Words)

A OMITTED

AND OMITTED

OF OMITTED

OR OMITTED

485. Geographical Expressions

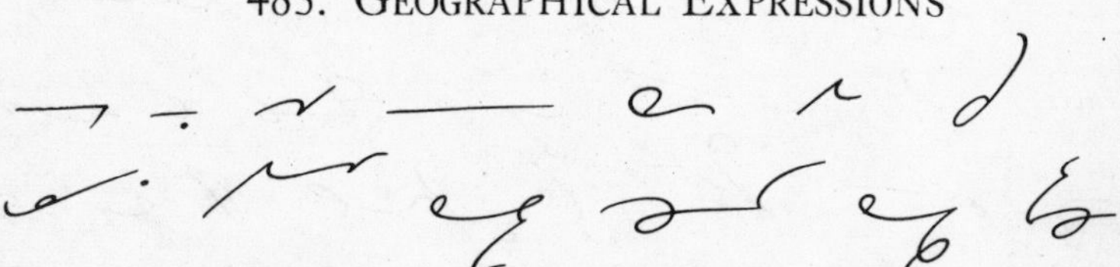

Reading and Writing Practice

486.

deferred-payment
hyphenated
before noun

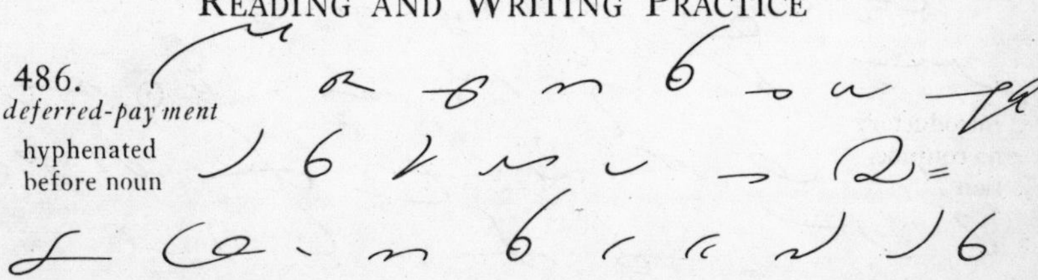

customer's
steady

, series
remaining

487.

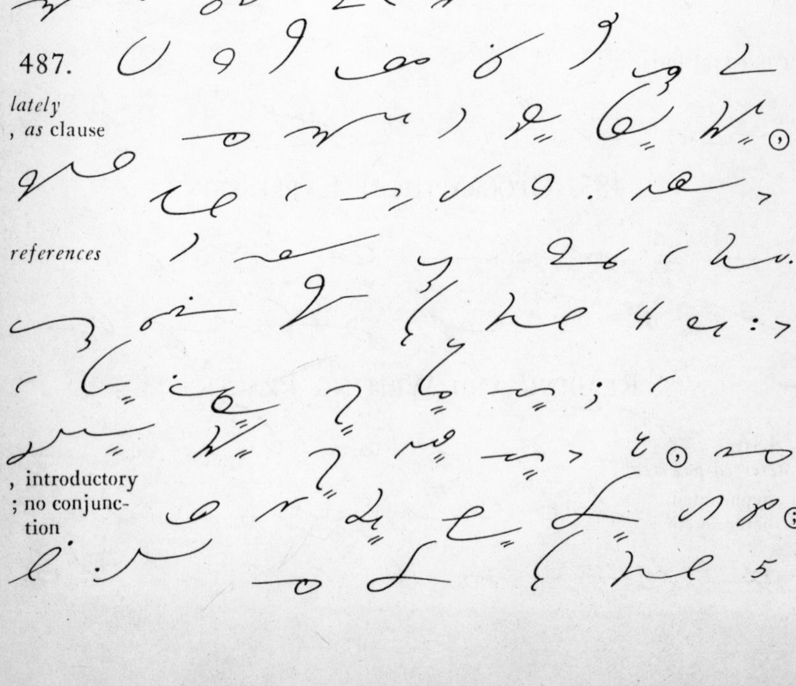

lately
, *as* clause

references

, introductory
; no conjunction

, *if* clause

488.

, apposition
reference

, series
volume
confidence

489.
experience
pleasant
averaging

remittance
, conjunction

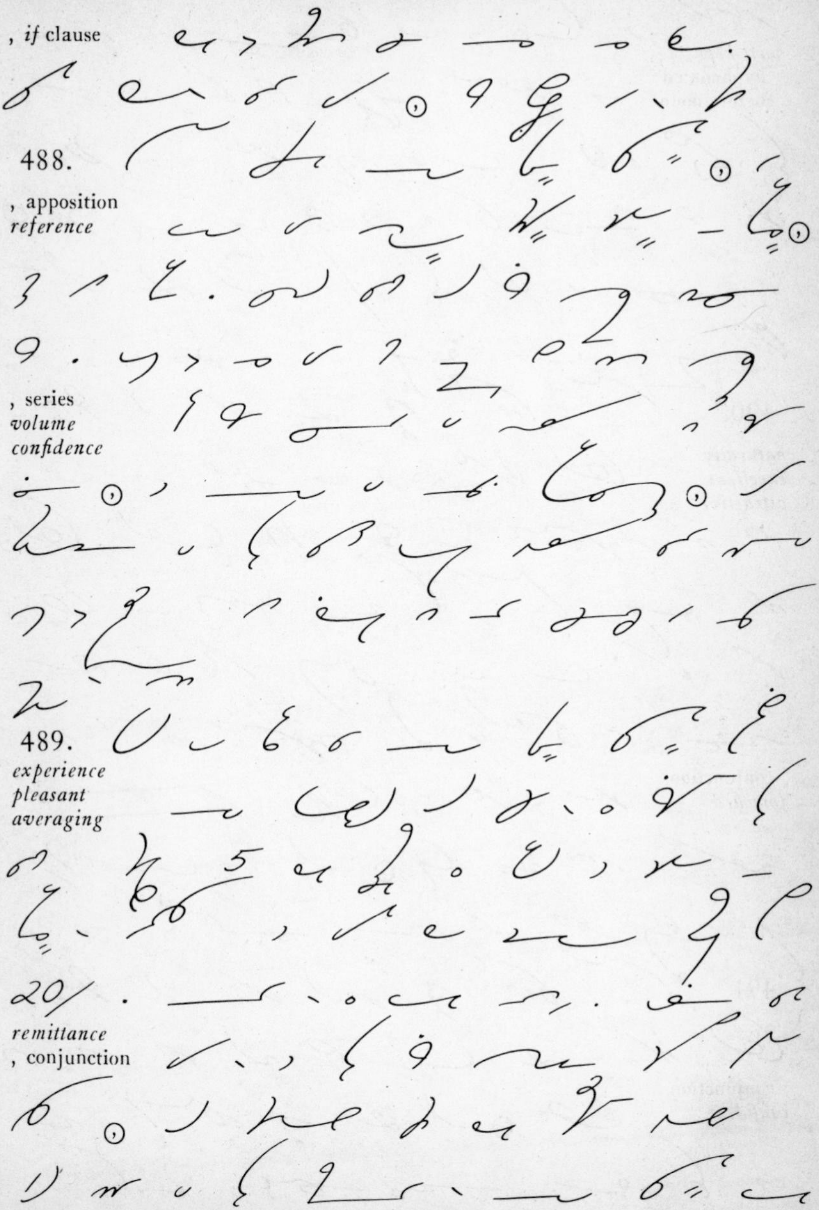

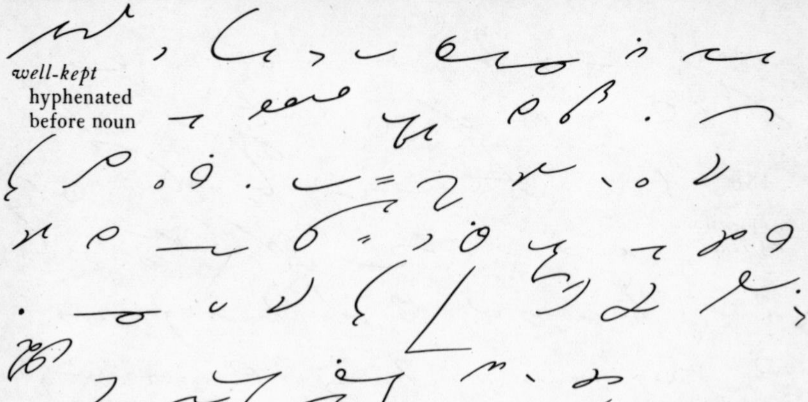

well-kept hyphenated before noun

490.

naturally
excellent
attractive

, conjunction
forward

491.

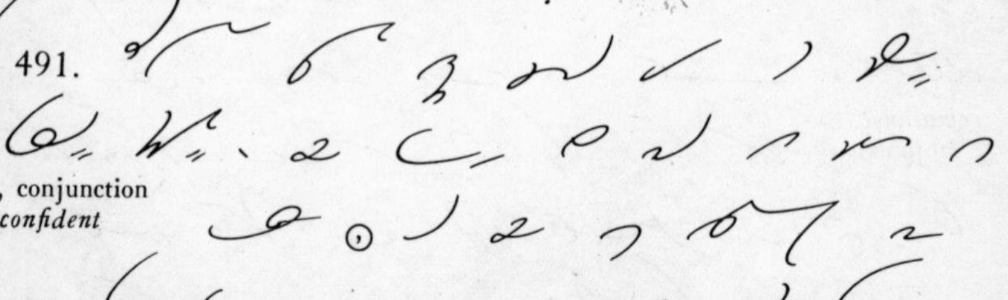

, conjunction
confident

country's

, parenthetical

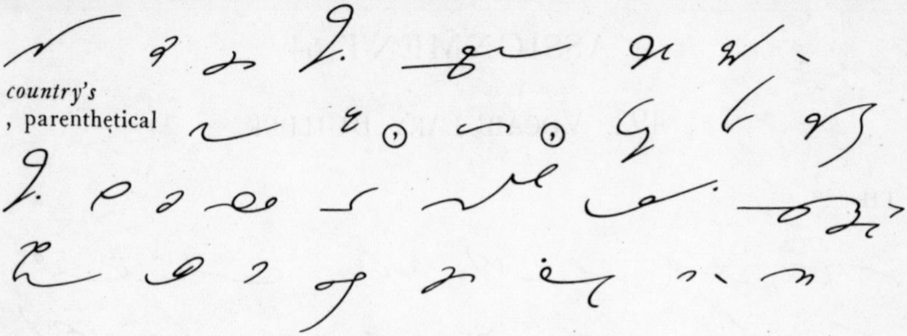

ASSIGNMENT 64

492. Vocabulary Builder

TH

-TION, -TIAL

OI

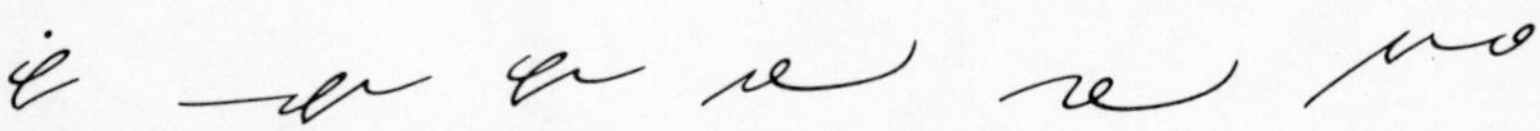

I

OW

U

Reading and Writing Practice

493.

, series

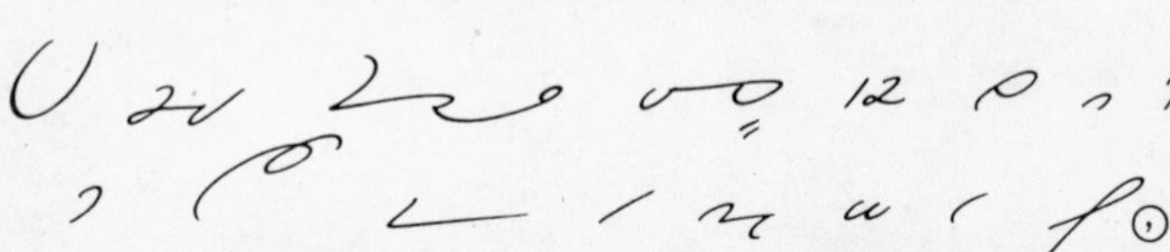

, apposition
instructions

494.

unable
, apposition

495.

planning
economical
filing

, conjunction

discuss
circular
describes

496.

, parenthetical
employees
specializes

skilled
excellent

, conjunction
requirements
reasonable

497.

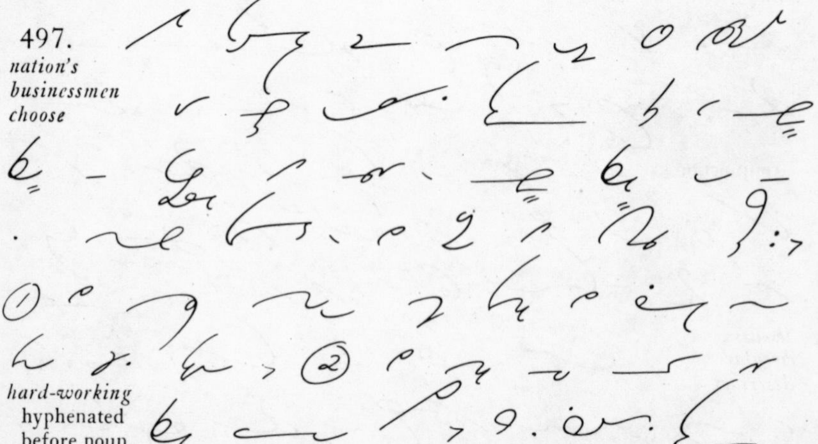

nation's
businessmen
choose

hard-working
hyphenated
before noun

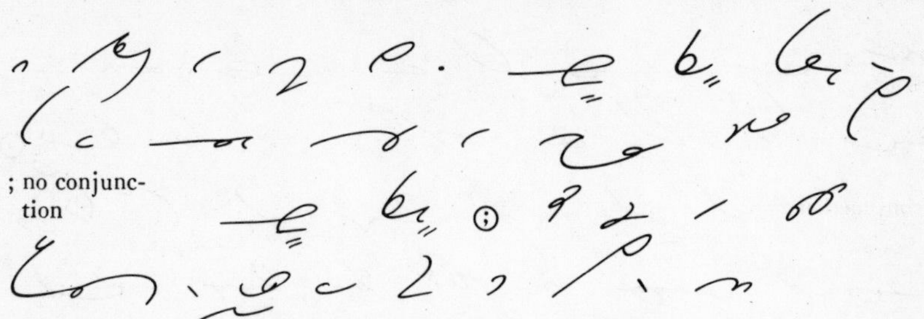

; no conjunction

498.

past
attendance
, conjunction
, *when* clause
initial
offered
, introductory

499.

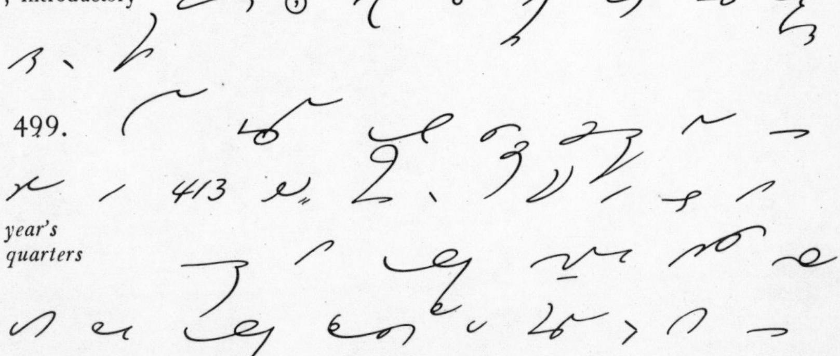

year's
quarters

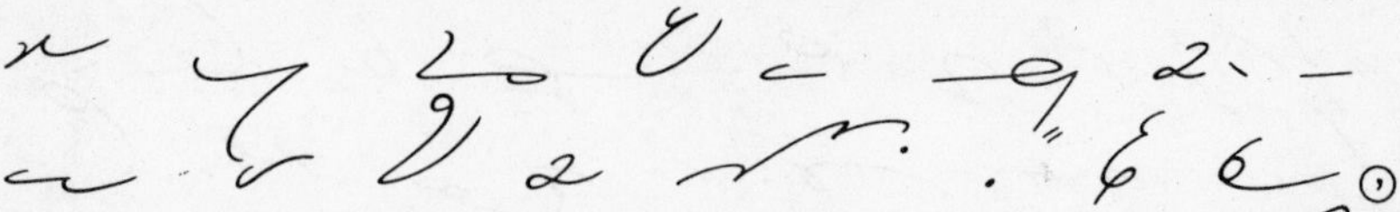

, conjunction

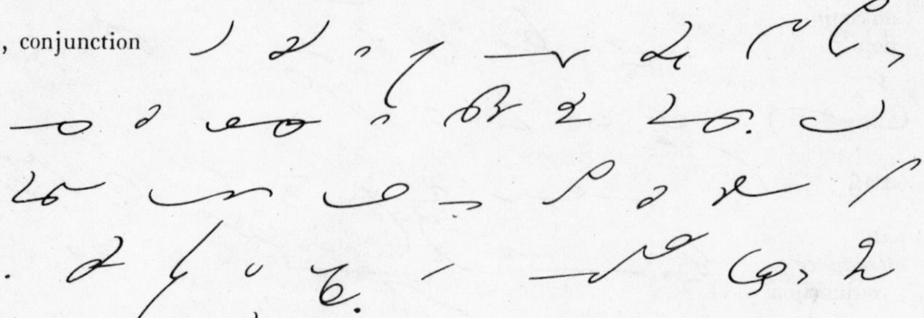

, *if* clause

ASSIGNMENT 65

500. Chart of Word Beginnings and Word Endings

A B C D E F

1.
2.
3.
4.
5.
6.
7.
8.
9.

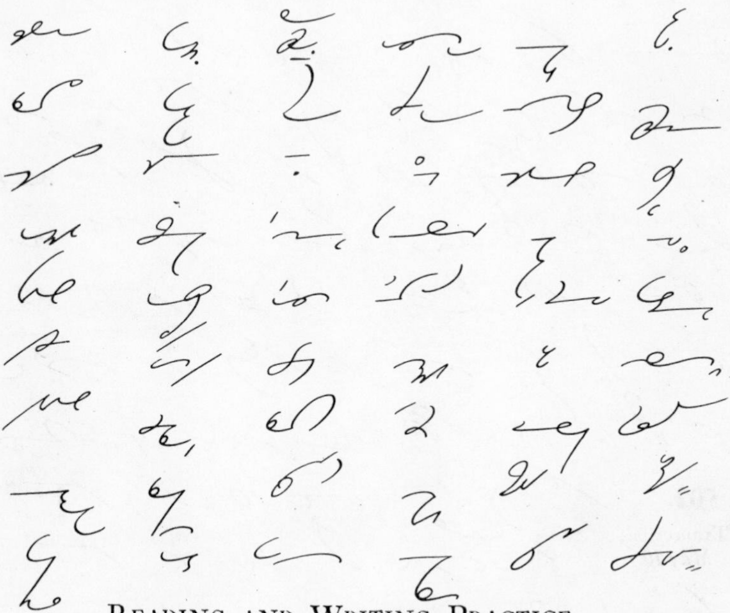

Reading and Writing Practice

501.

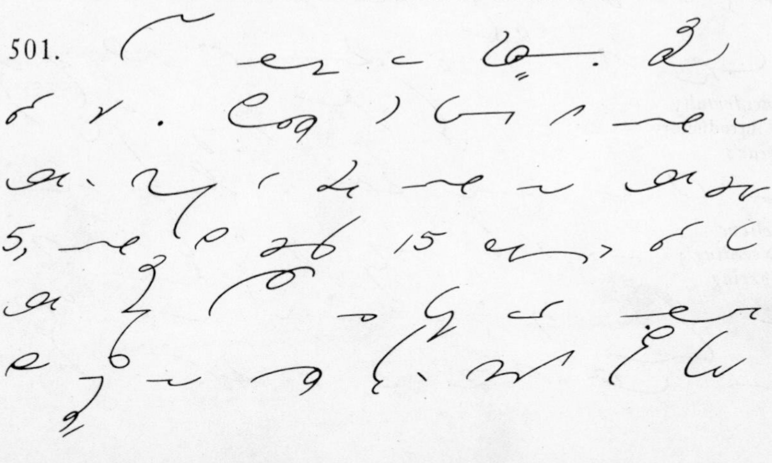

502. Transcribe:
May 10

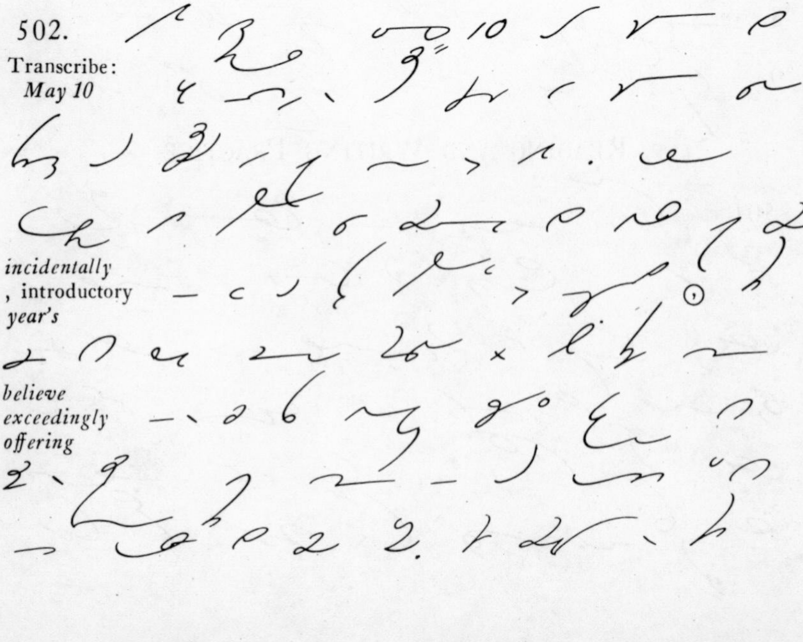

incidentally
, introductory
year's

believe
exceedingly
offering

503.

aware
respect
efficiently

spacious
, series
.

company's
discuss
, apposition

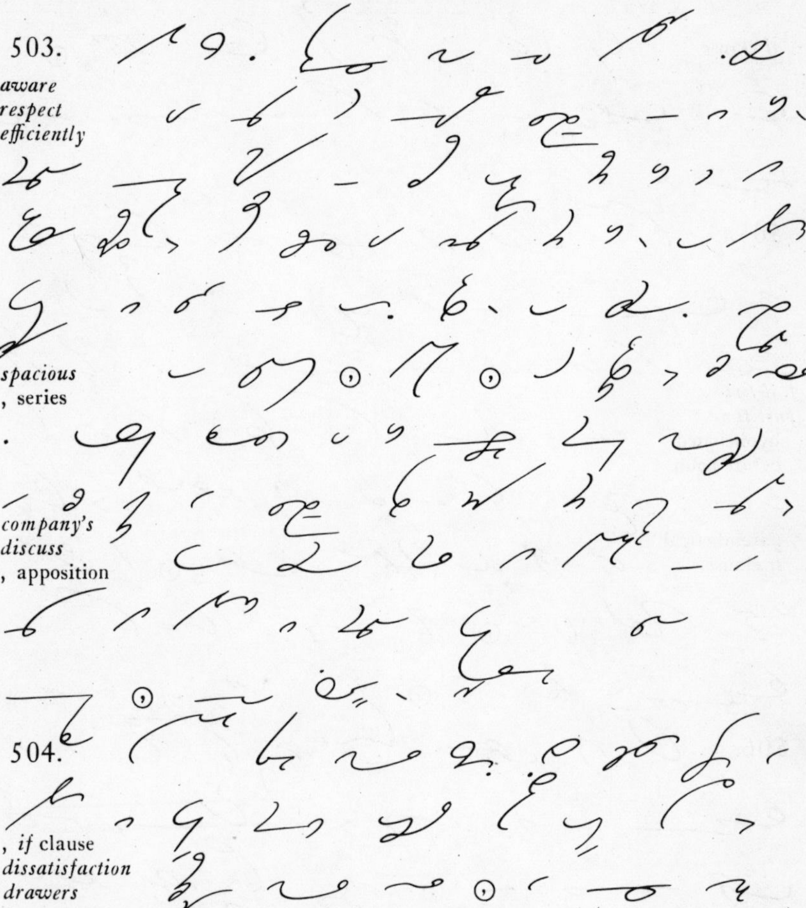

504.

, *if* clause
dissatisfaction
drawers

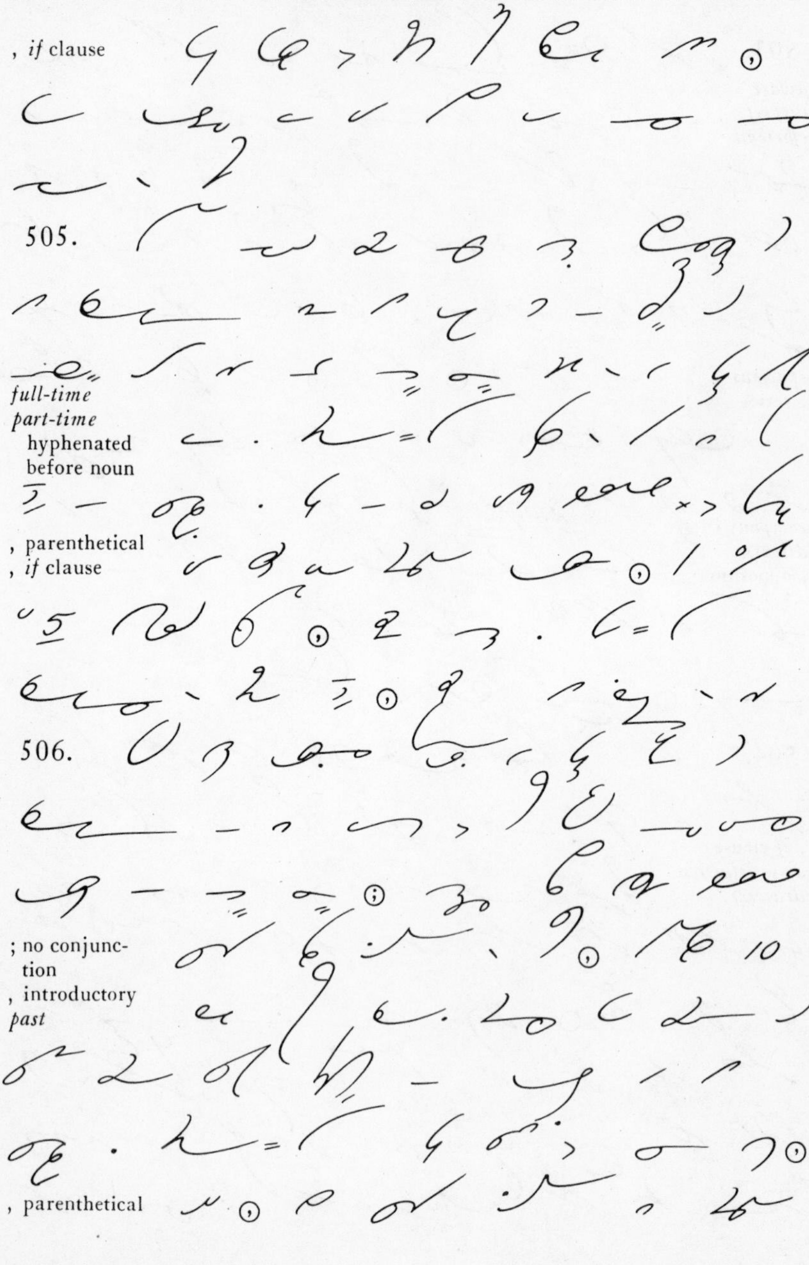
, *if* clause
505.
full-time
part-time
hyphenated
before noun
, parenthetical
, *if* clause
506.
; no conjunction
, introductory
past
, parenthetical

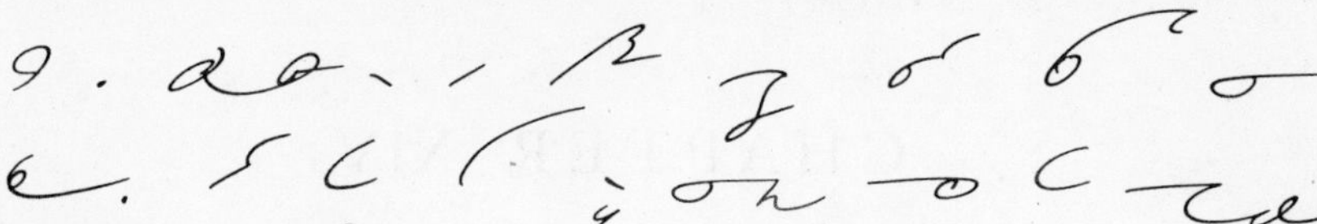

agreeable
, *if* clause

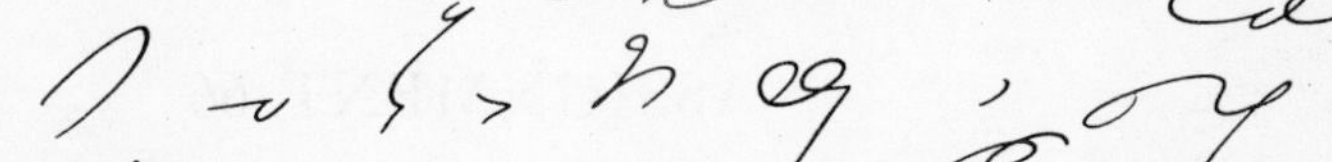

507.
devote
, introductory

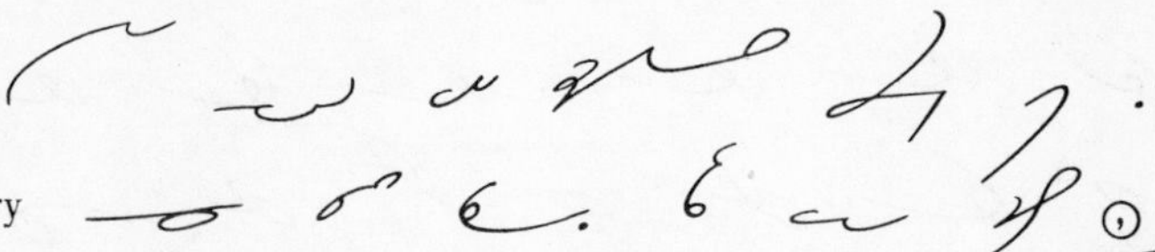

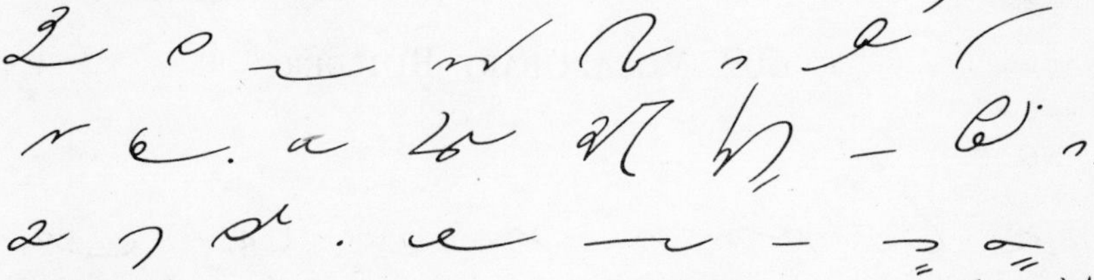

, conjunction
profitable

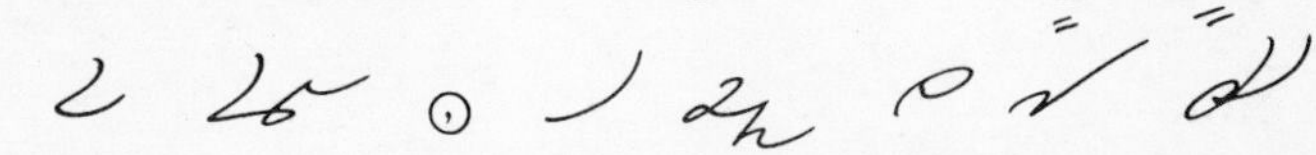

full-time
hyphenated
before noun
, introductory

CHAPTER XIV

ASSIGNMENT 66

508. Accuracy Practice

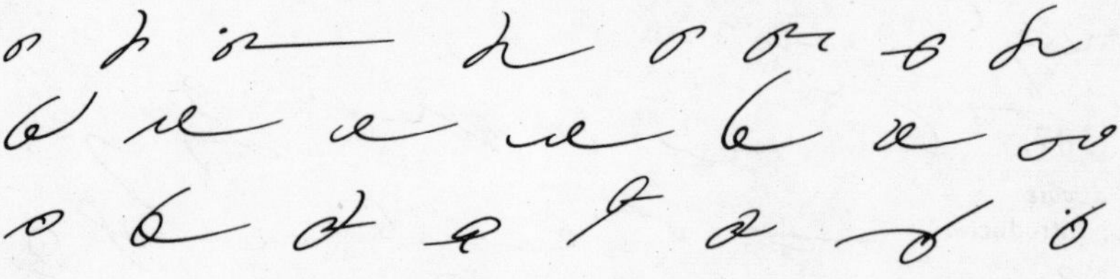

509. Vocabulary Builder

NG

NGK

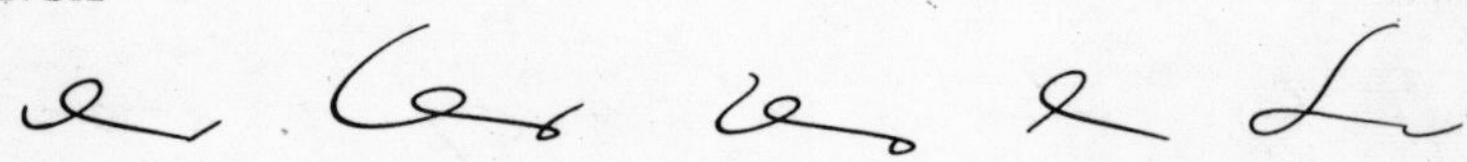

Months and Days

Reading and Writing Practice

510.

modern visitors

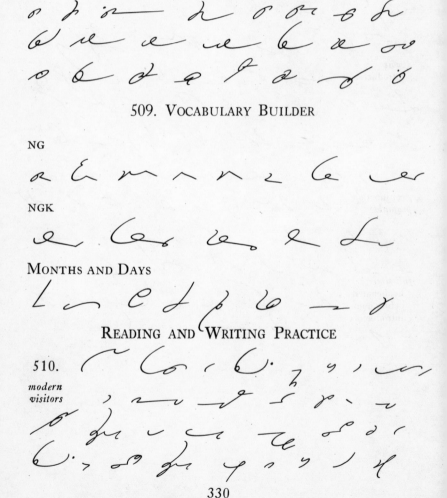

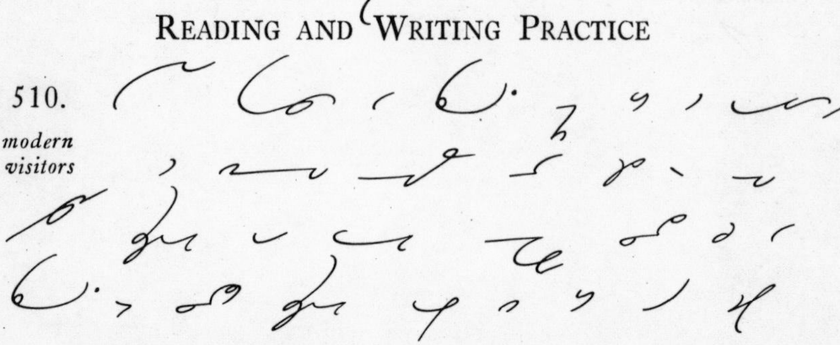

, *when* clause
equally

, introductory

received
their

511.
Transcribe:
No. 136
, parenthetical

warehouse
, *if* clause

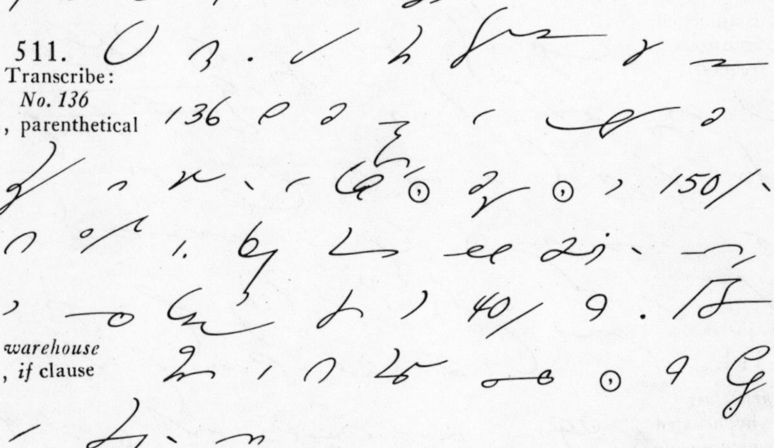

512.

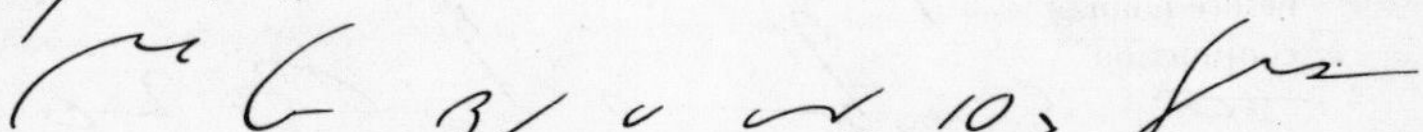

, apposition

years'
circular
offering
per cent

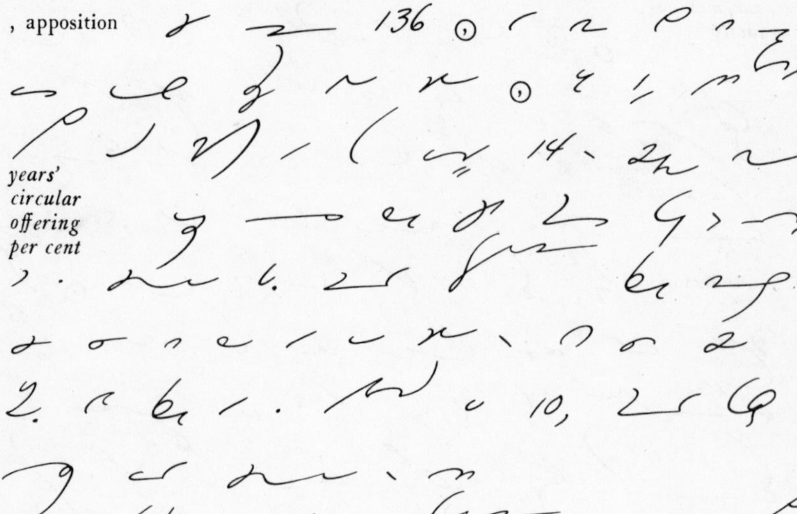

513.

pieces
today
except

, conjunction
. courteous request

514.

first-class
hyphenated before noun
, conjunction

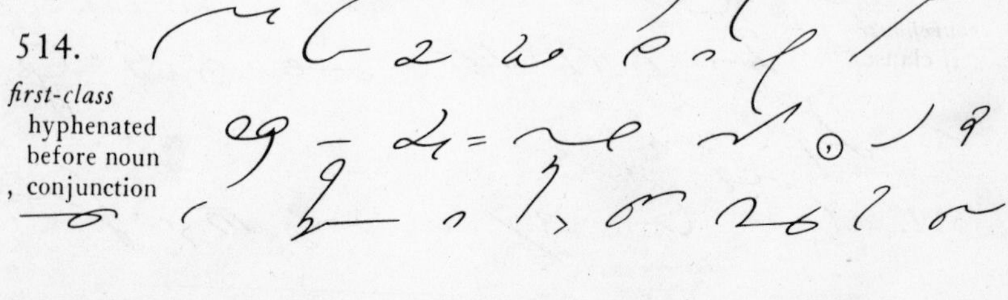

, introductory
occurred
company's

, *as* clause
similar
Cordially

515.

, *when* clause
adjust

, series
; no conjunction

516.

, introductory
disappoint

ASSIGNMENT 67

517. Word Families

-ISM

-VENT

-NTED, -NDED

-SIVE

-ISH

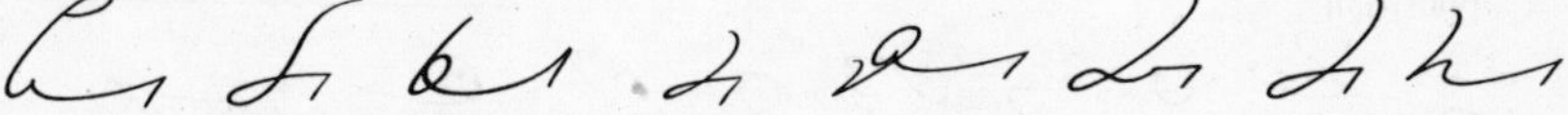

Reading and Writing Practice

518.

, apposition
sketches

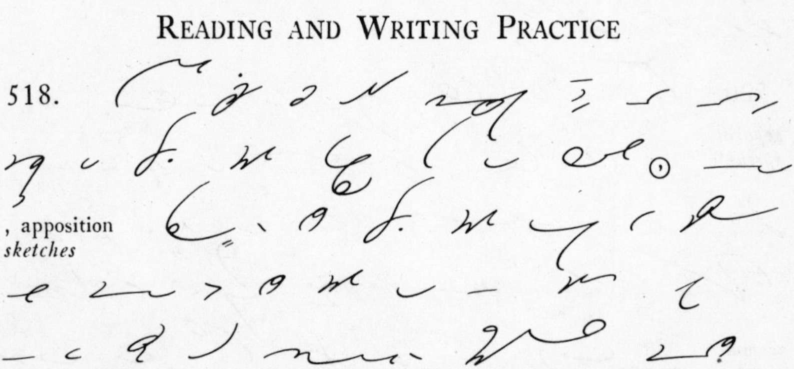

, *if* clause

derive
past

519.

, apposition

sale

cordially
Sincerely
, apposition

520.

separate
spring's

woman

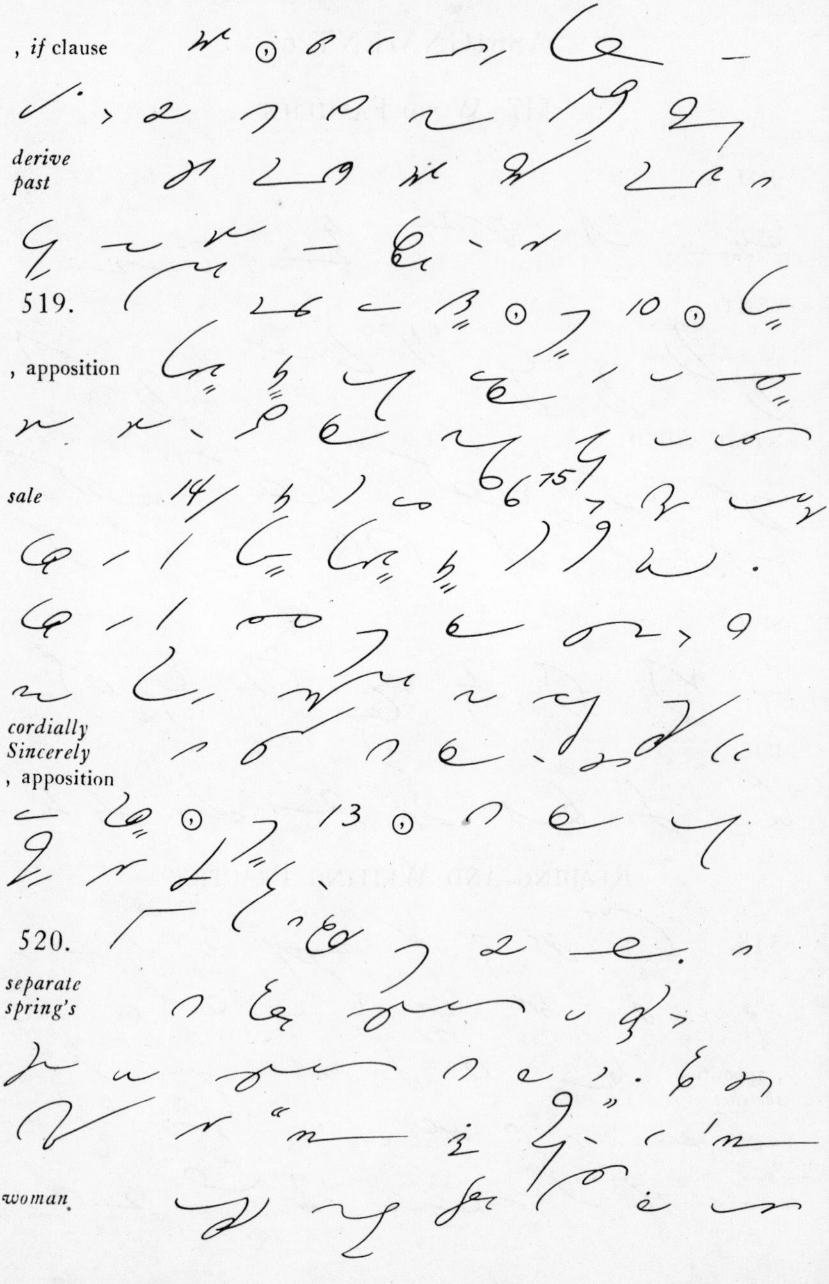

; no conjunction
, series

, *if* clause
promptly

521.

realize
weather
moths

, *if* clause
easy-payment
hyphenated before noun

522.

, introductory
catalogue

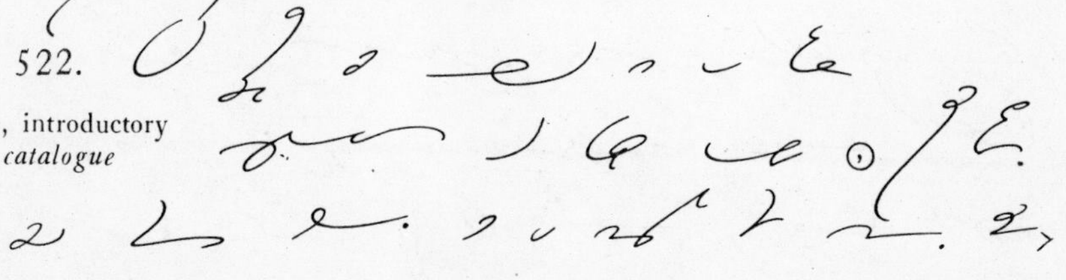

season's
, conjunction
good-looking
hyphenated before noun
customary
busy

523.

clothes
wearing
, introductory

524.

, *as* clause
, parenthetical
scarce

, introductory
; because of
comma

Easter
. courteous
request

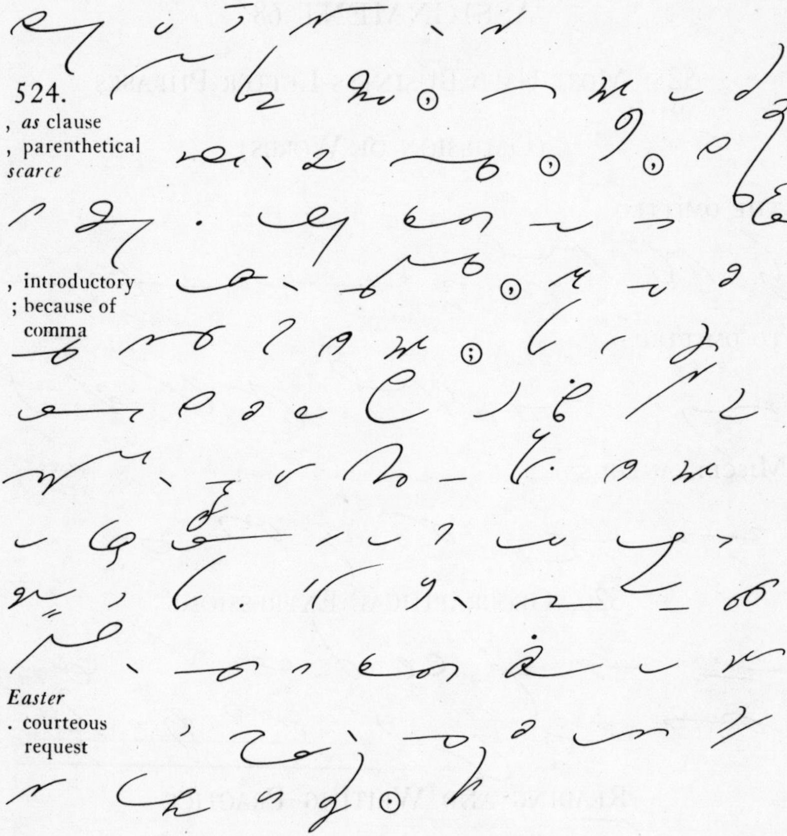

ASSIGNMENT 68

525. Most-Used Business-Letter Phrases

(Omission of Words)

THE OMITTED

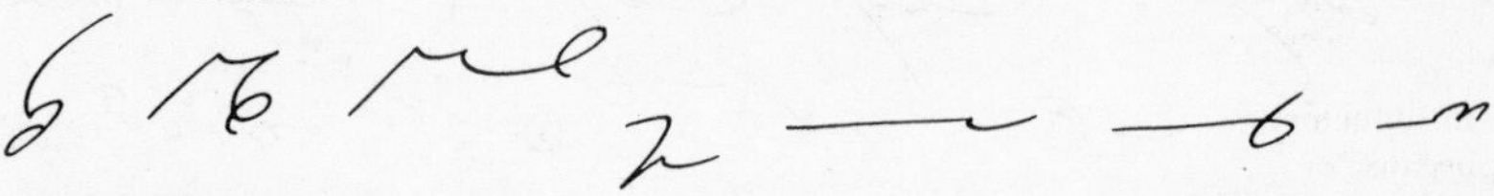

TO OMITTED

Miscellaneous

526. Geographical Expressions

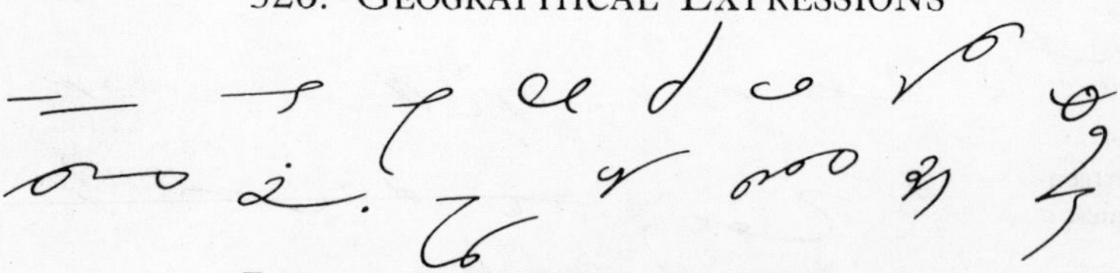

Reading and Writing Practice

527.

wholesale

, *as* clause

, conjunction

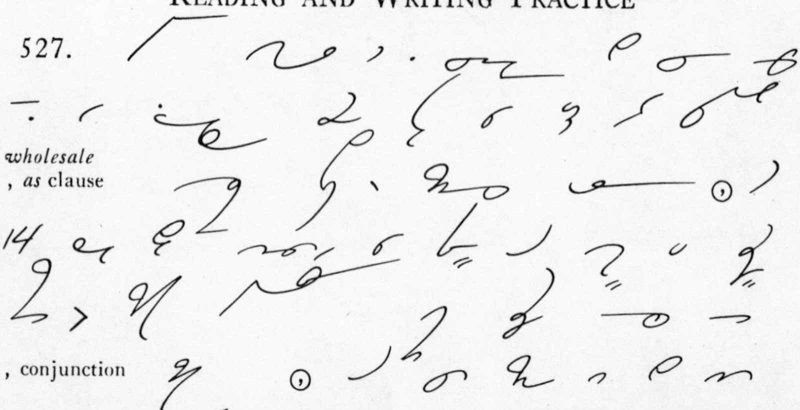

up-to-the-minute
hyphenated before noun
, conjunction

528.

, apposition
women's

, introductory
; no conjunction

quantities
margin

529.

variety

, parenthetical
tailors
, series
unless

choose
individual

530.

advantageous
, introductory

dollars'
today's
per cent

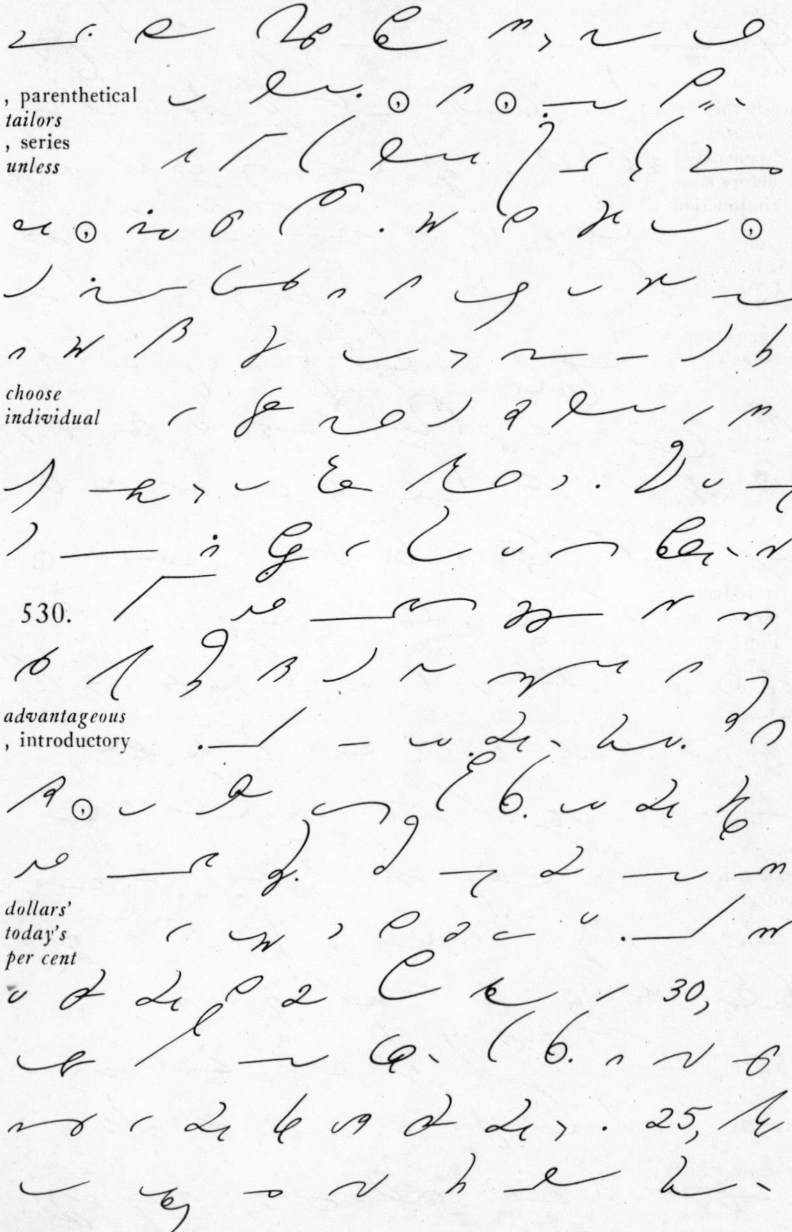

, *if* clause
easy-payment hyphenated before noun

531.

storage
, introductory

entrusted
thoroughly

, series

532.

completion

, *if* clause

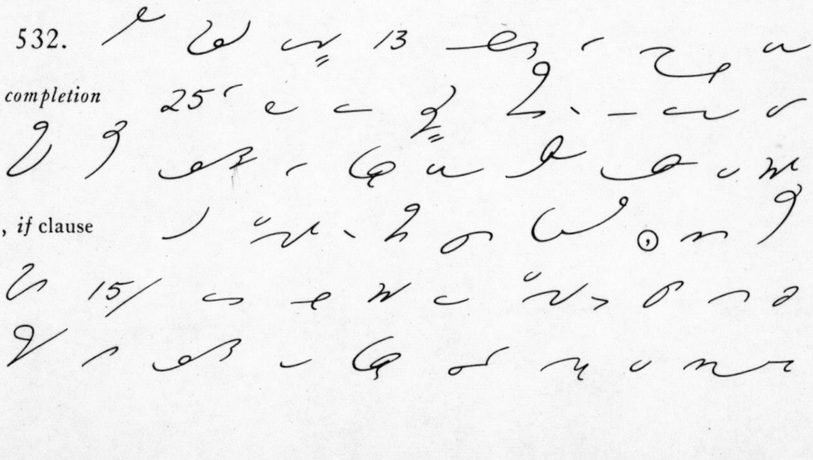

, introductory
; because of comma

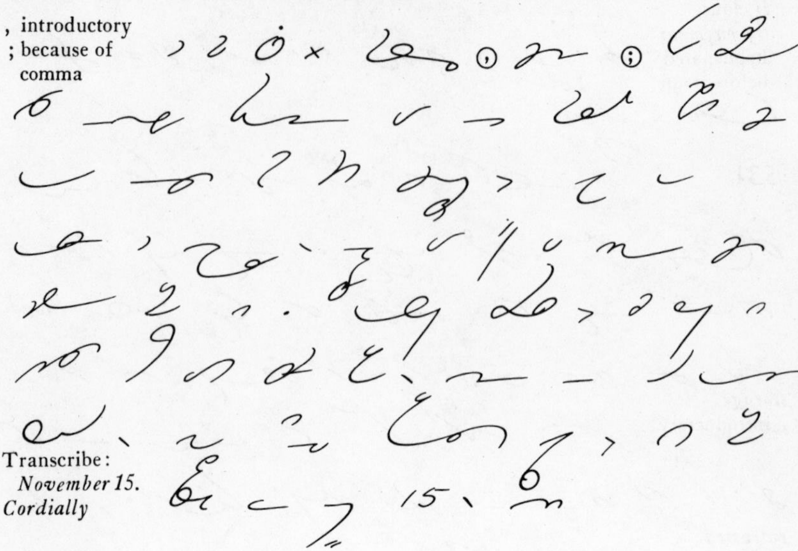

Transcribe:
November 15.
Cordially

ASSIGNMENT 69

533. Vocabulary Builder—Omission of Vowels

Reading and Writing Practice

534.

, parenthetical
wear

, series
, *if* clause

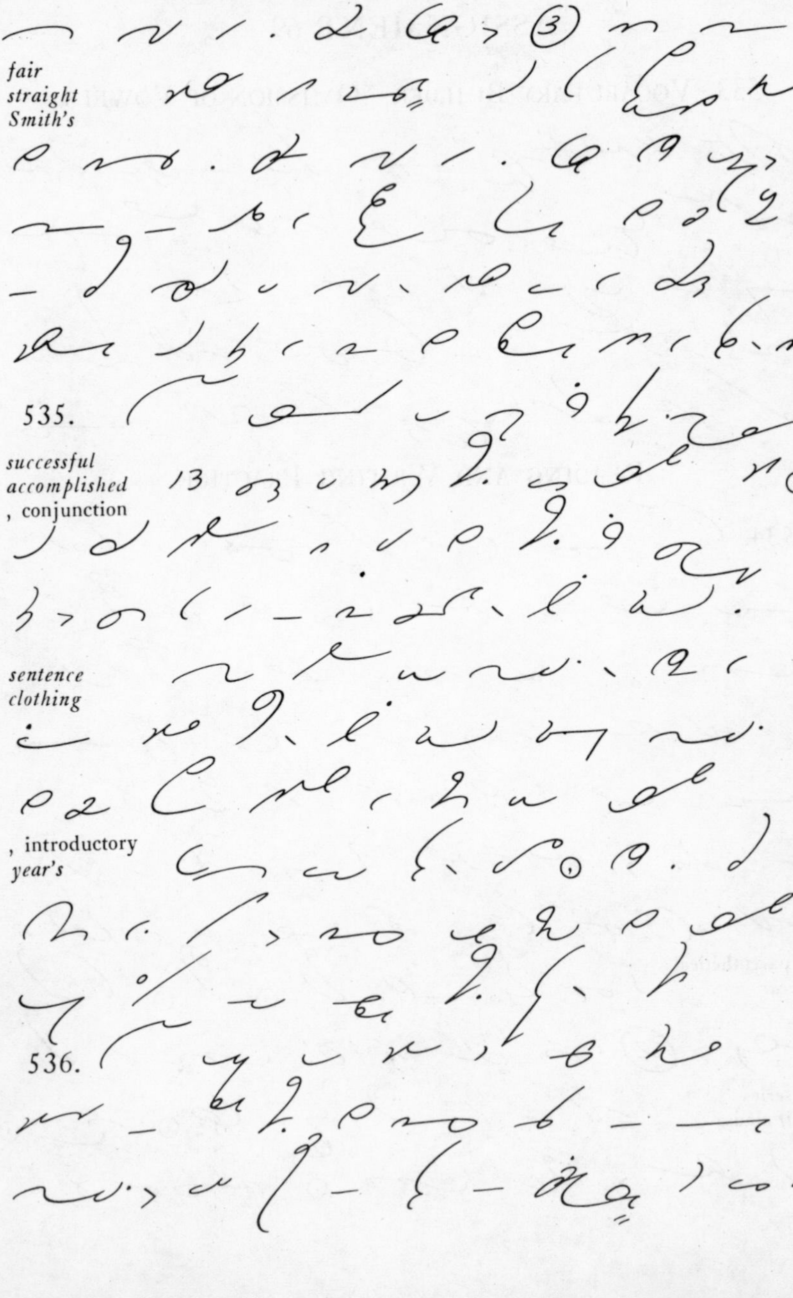

fair
straight
Smith's

535.

successful
accomplished
, conjunction

sentence
clothing

, introductory
year's

536.

men's
, introductory
well-tailored
hyphenated before noun

537.

healer
often
, *if* clause

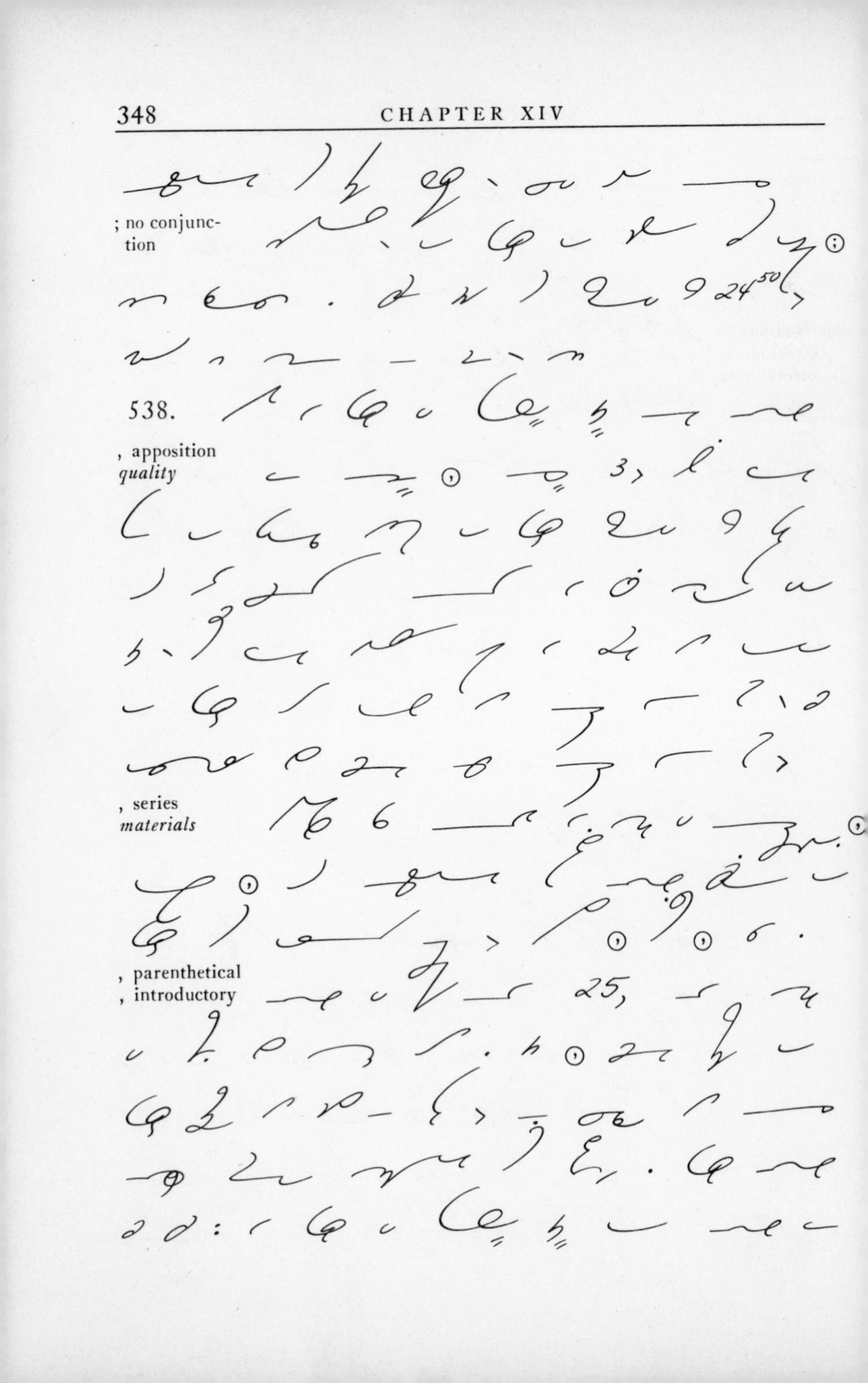

; no conjunction

538.

, apposition
quality

, series
materials

, parenthetical
, introductory

, apposition

539.

, *as* clause
recent
, parenthetical

custom-made
ready-made
hyphenated
before noun

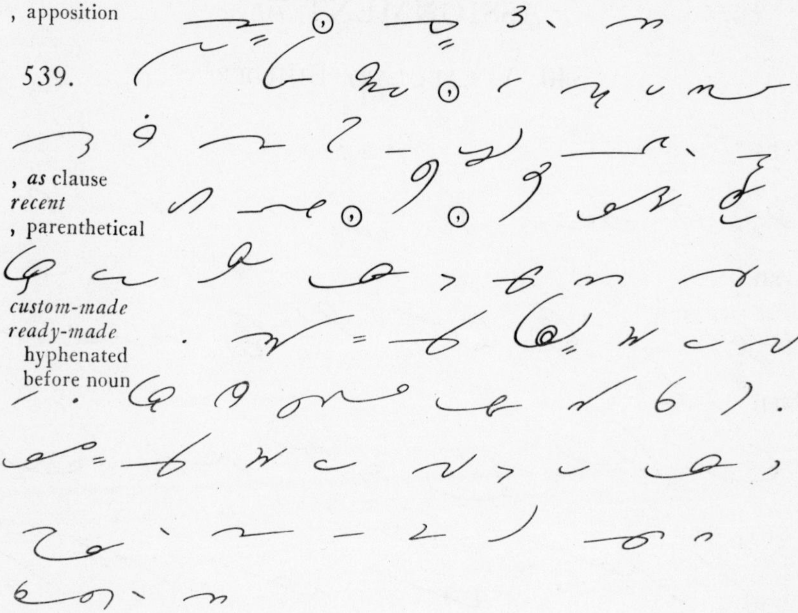

ASSIGNMENT 70

540. Vocabulary Builder

SES

-RD

-LD

DET, -TED

MEN

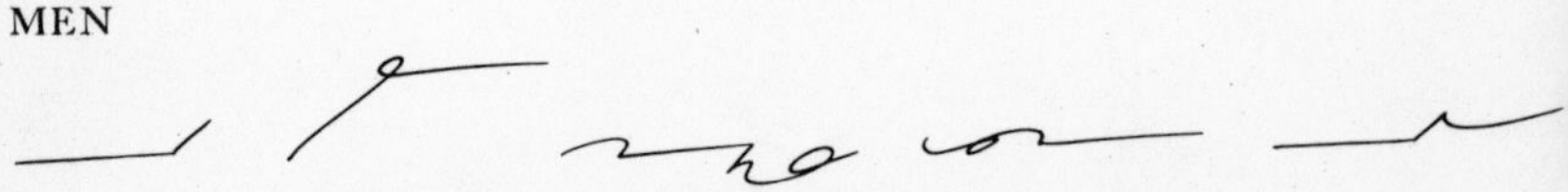

Reading and Writing Practice

541.

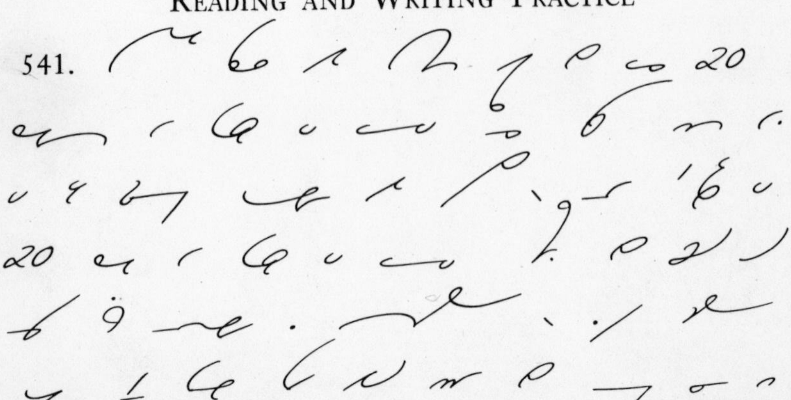

542.

, *as* clause
pleasure
, conjunction

, series
Won't

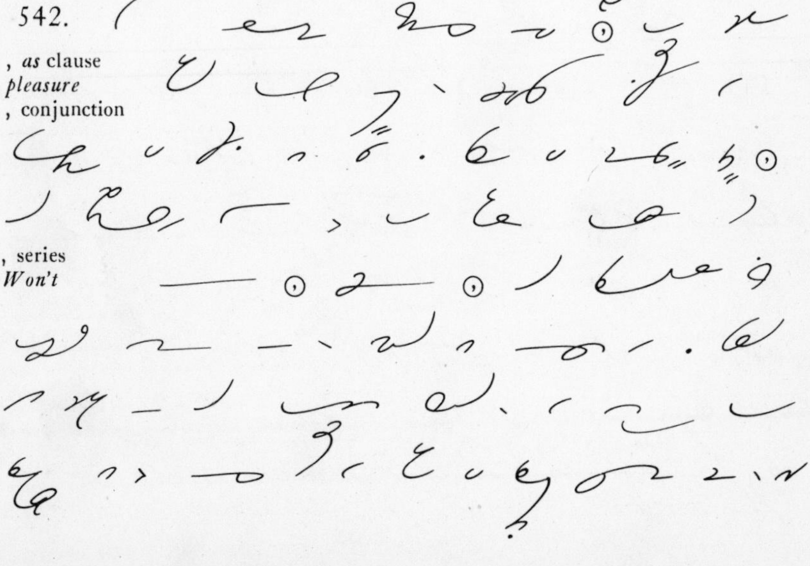

543.

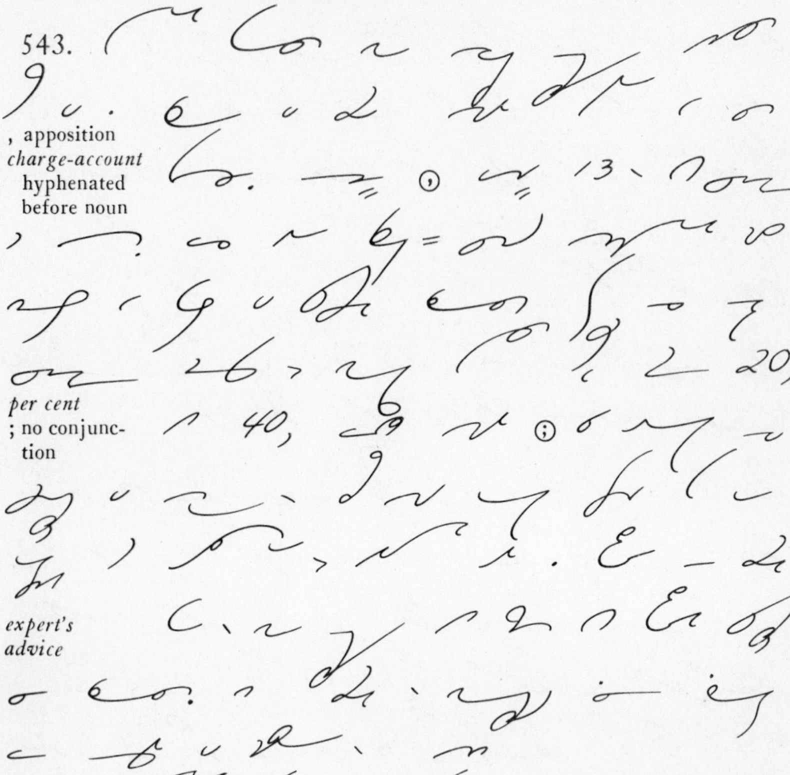

, apposition

charge-account hyphenated before noun

per cent

; no conjunction

expert's advice

544.

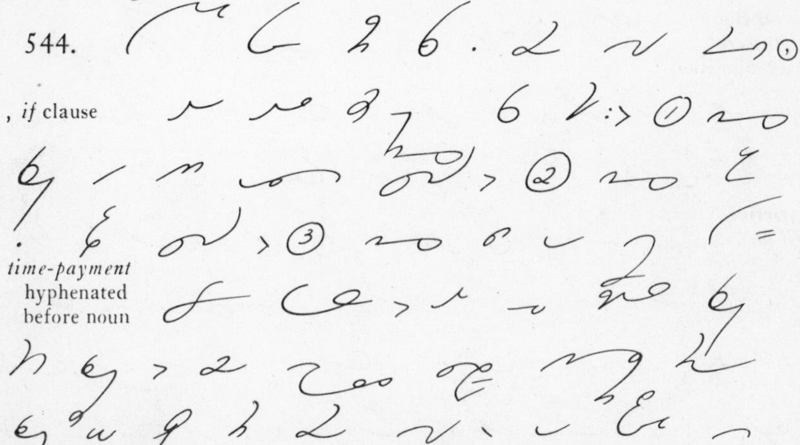

, *if* clause

time-payment hyphenated before noun

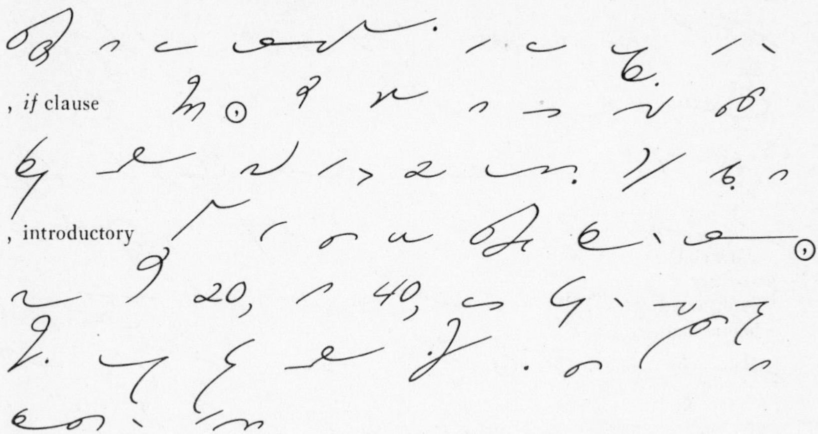
, *if* clause
, introductory

545.

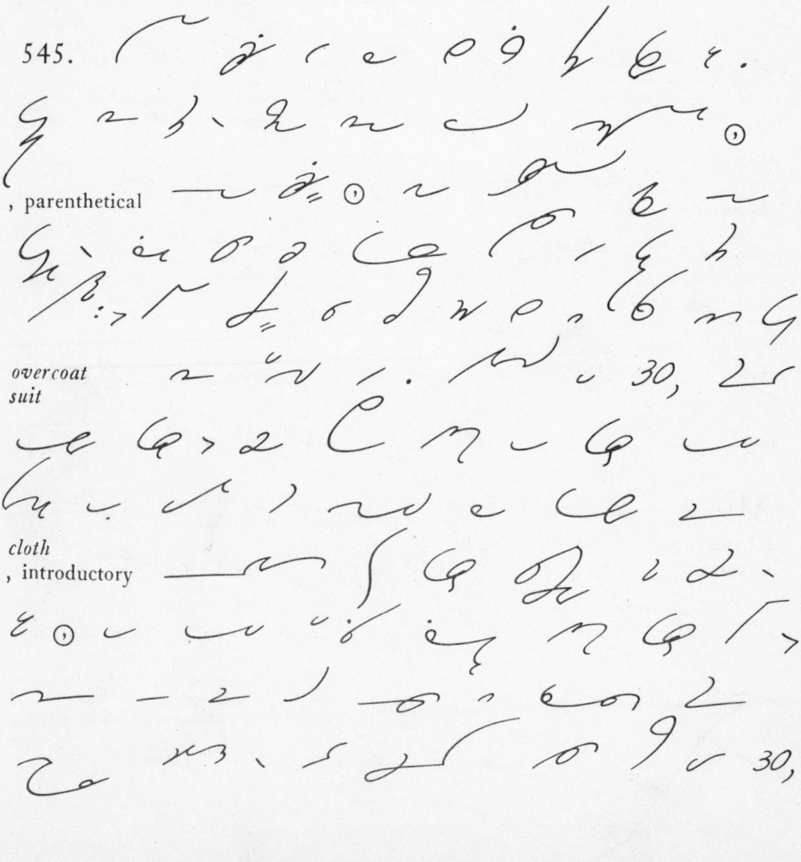
, parenthetical
overcoat
suit
cloth
, introductory

546.

, *when* clause
first-class hyphenated before noun
proceed
year's
reasonable

547.

acknowledge
authorized

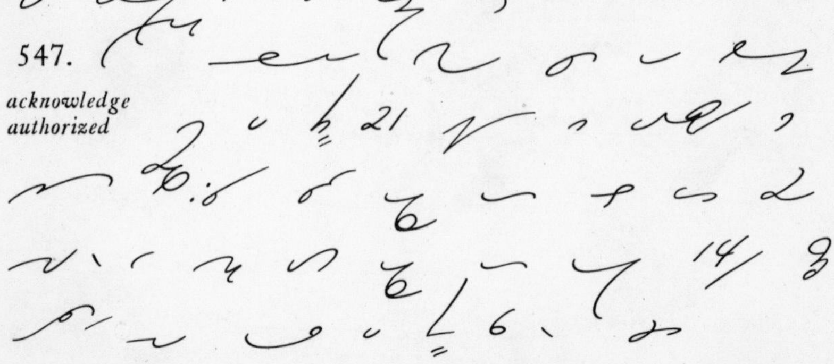

CHAPTER XV

ASSIGNMENT 71

548. Brief-Form Chart

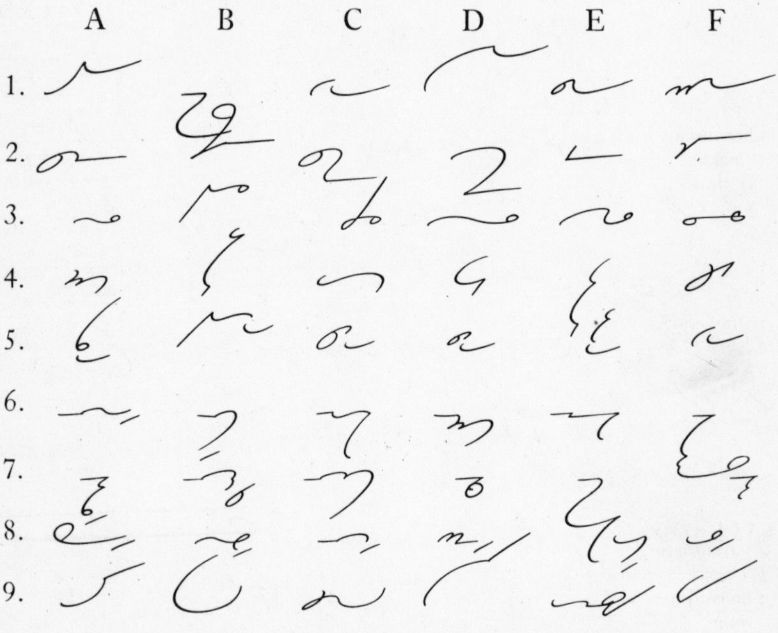

Reading and Writing Practice

549.

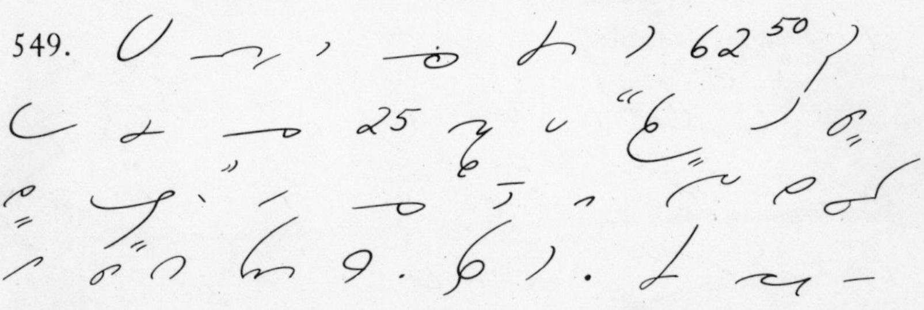

valuable
everyday

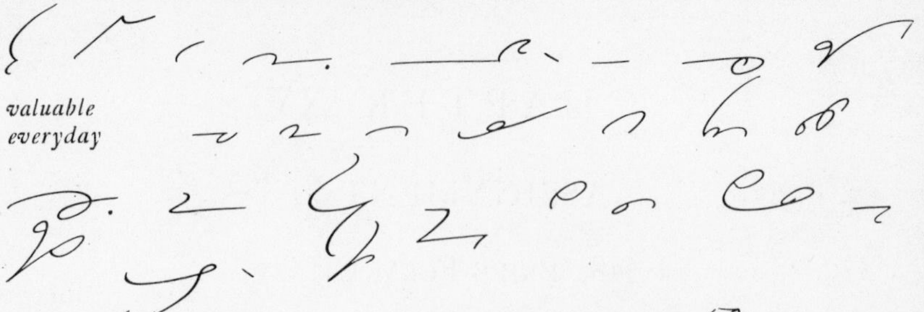

550.

; because of comma
, *if* clause

senior
advice

551.

, parenthetical
previous
; no conjunction
, introductory

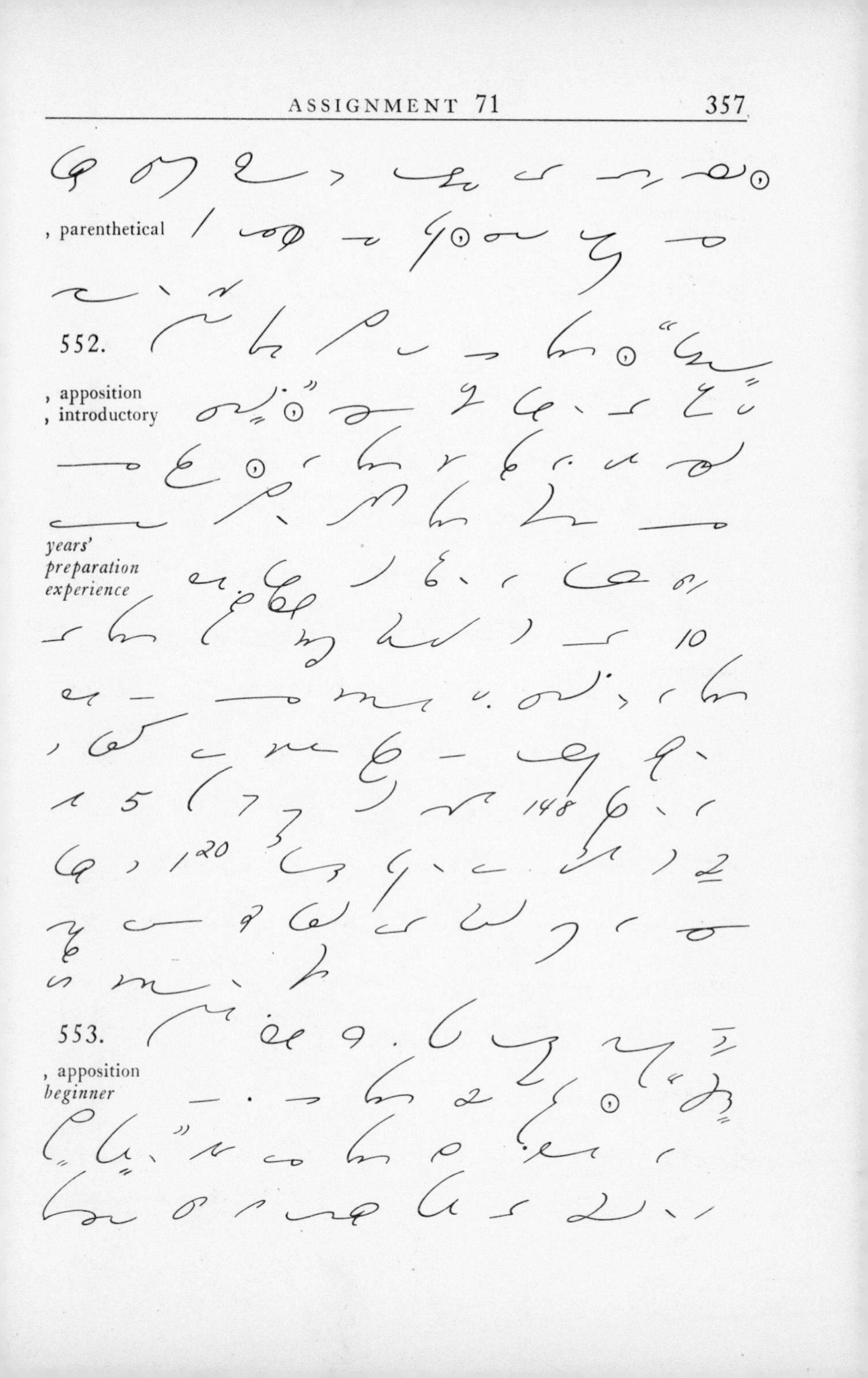

, parenthetical

552.

, apposition
, introductory

years'
preparation
experience

553.

, apposition
beginner

, parenthetical
author's

, conjunction

554.

; no conjunction

, series

five-day
hyphenated before noun
, *if* clause
; no conjunction

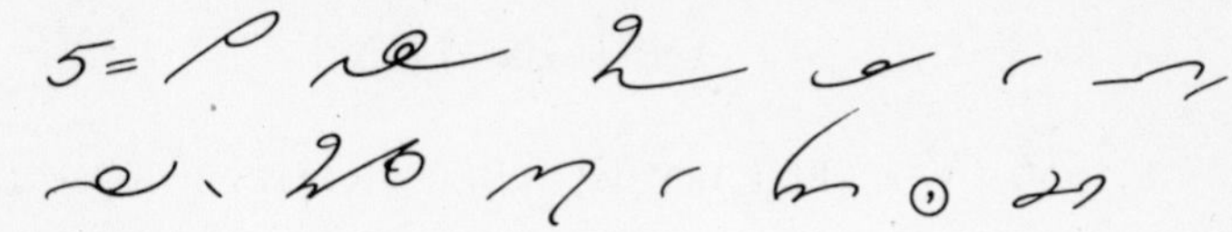

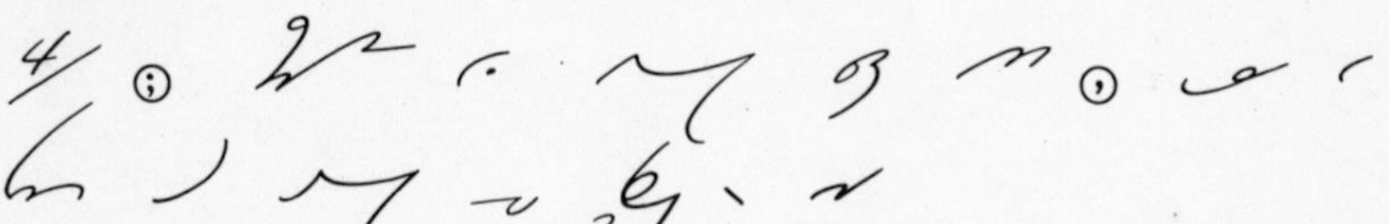

555.

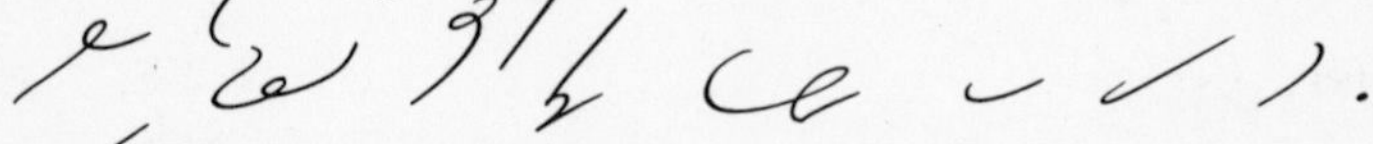

describing
remarkable
, apposition

Transcribe:
1,000
400,000

, *if* clause

ASSIGNMENT 72

556. Vocabulary Builder—Omission of T and D

-CT

-IST, -EST

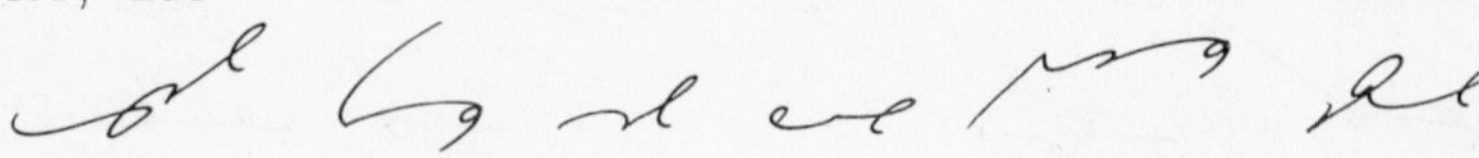

ST FOLLOWING AN ABBREVIATED FORM OR VOWEL

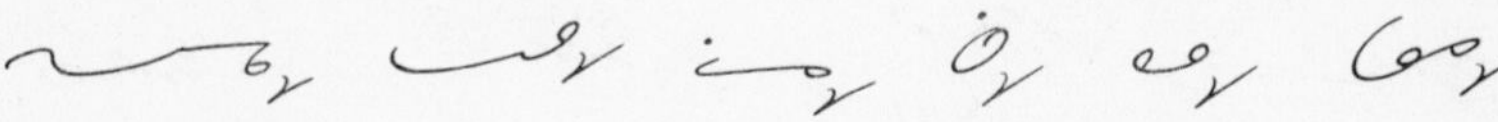

Omission of D

Reading and Writing Practice

557.

received
practical
, series

businessmen
adapt

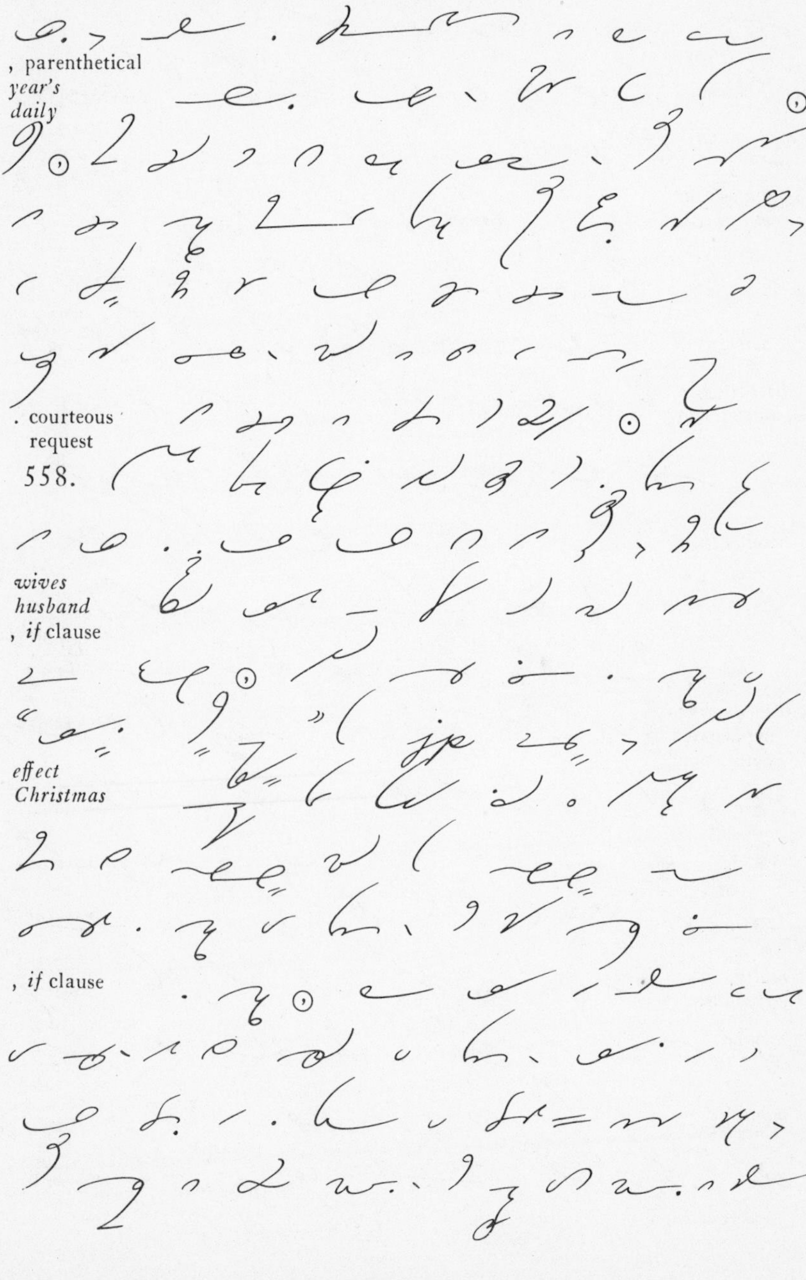

, parenthetical
year's
daily

. courteous
request

558.

wives
husband
, *if* clause

effect
Christmas

, *if* clause

, *if* clause

, apposition

remittance

559.

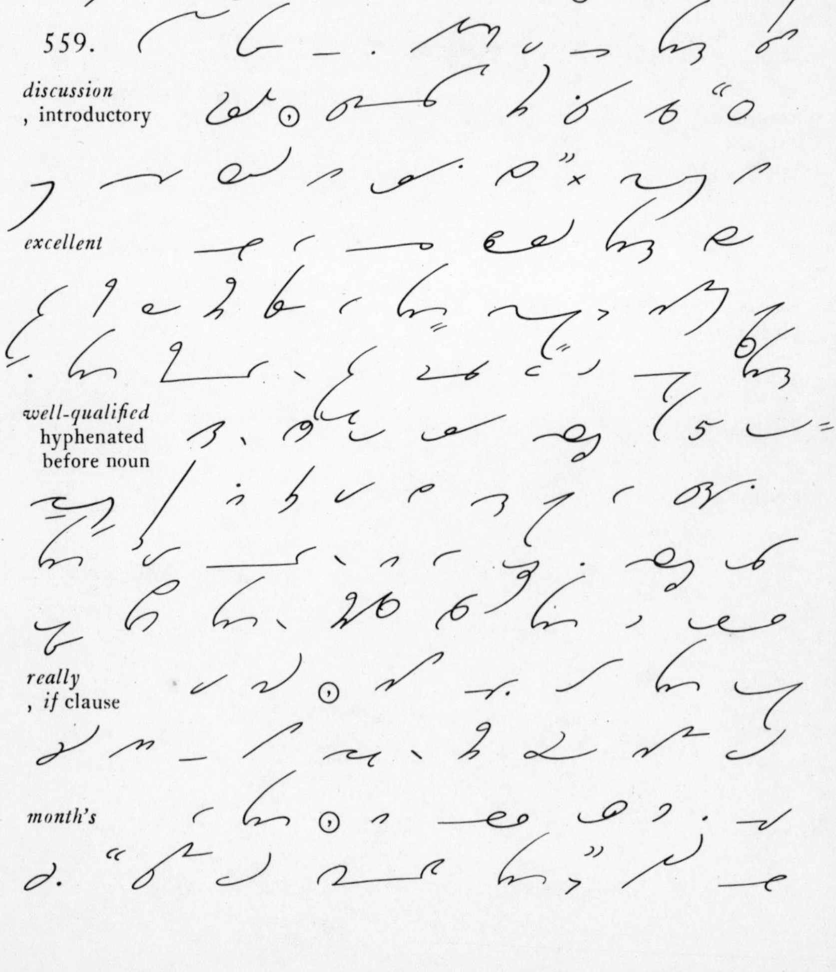

discussion

, introductory

excellent

well-qualified hyphenated before noun

really

, *if* clause

month's

560.

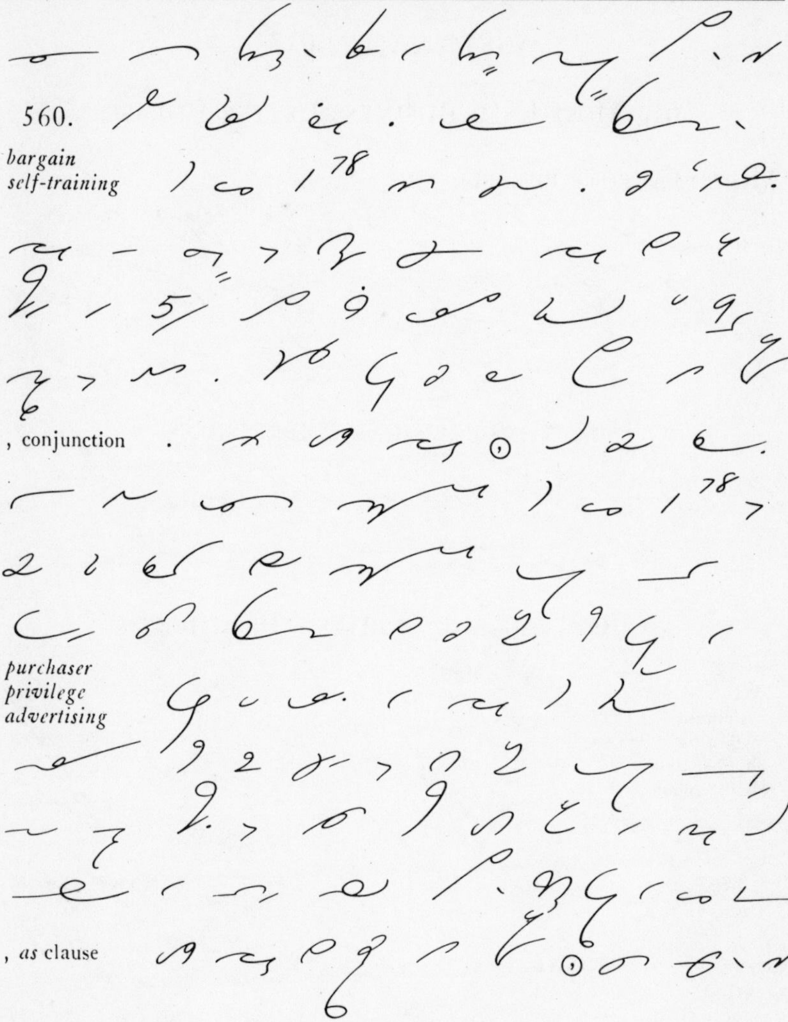

bargain
self-training

, conjunction

purchaser
privilege
advertising

, *as* clause

ASSIGNMENT 73

561. Most-Used Business-Letter Phrases

Miscellaneous phrases

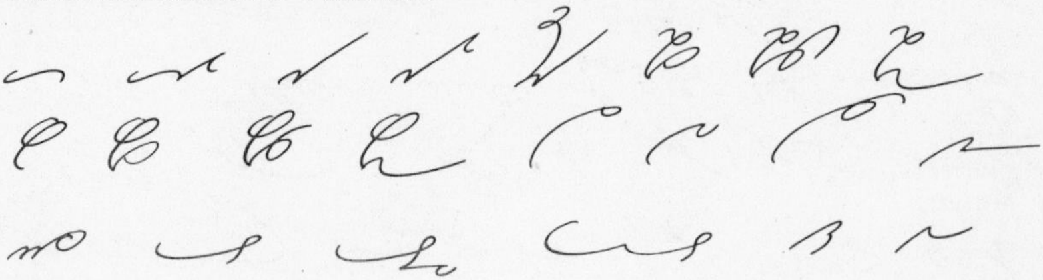

562. Geographical Expressions

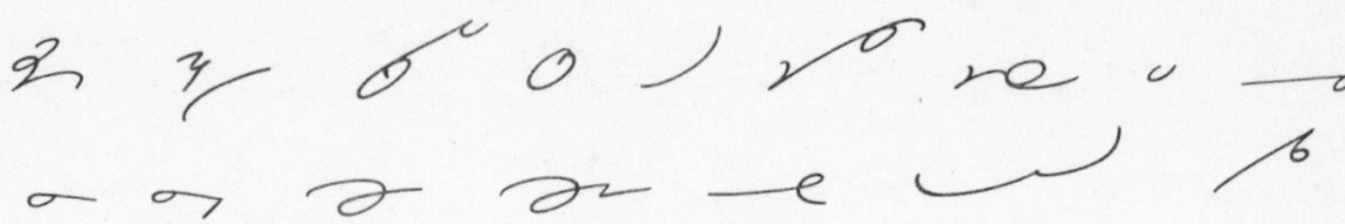

Reading and Writing Practice

563.

, *as* clause
up-to-date hyphenated before noun

revising
, conjunction

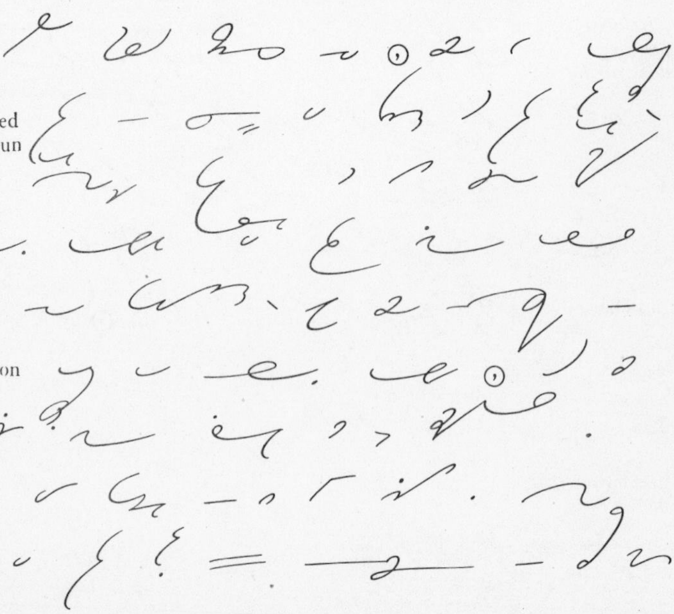

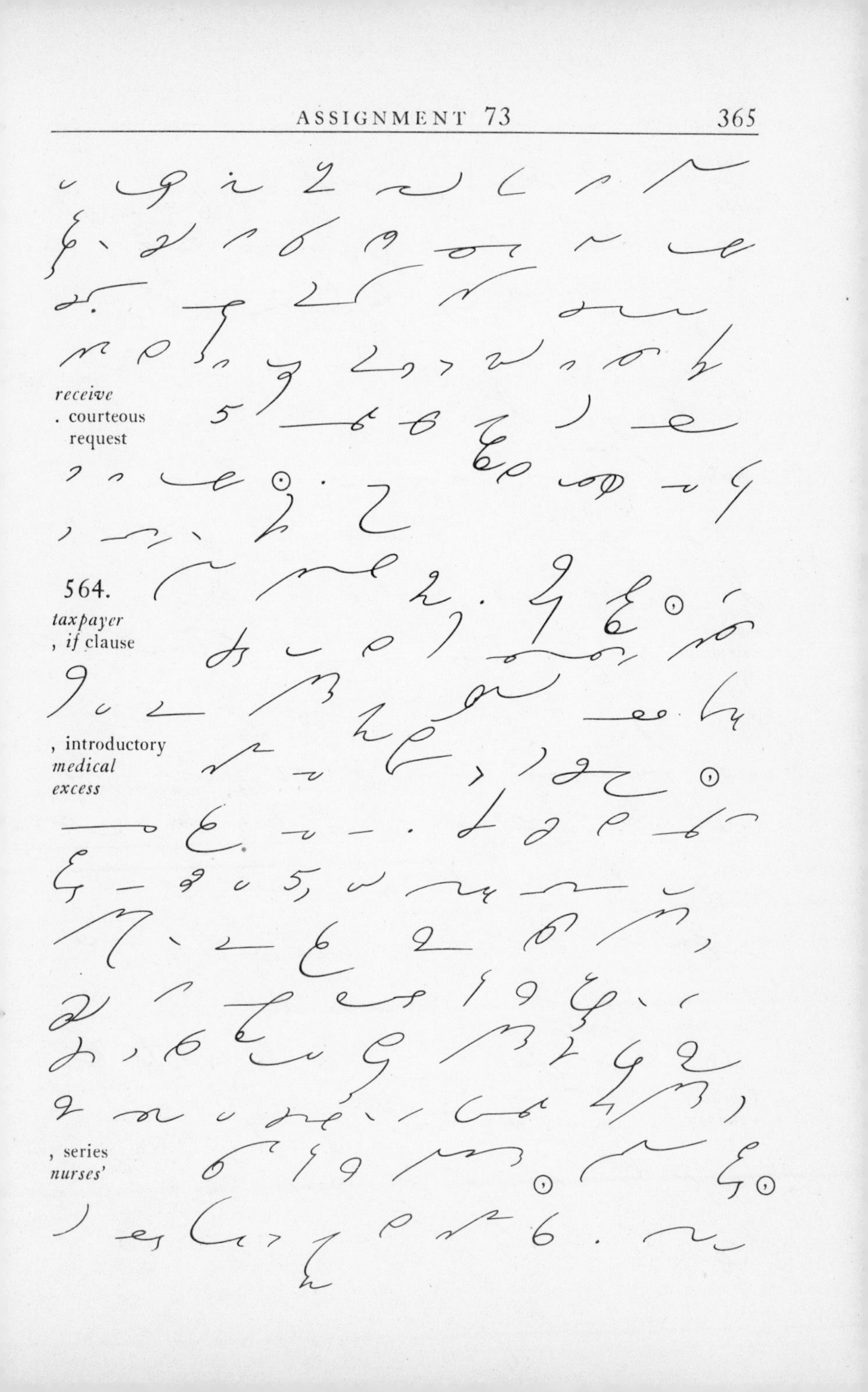

receive
. courteous request

564.
taxpayer
, *if* clause

, introductory
medical
excess

, series
nurses'

, introductory
year's
ideas

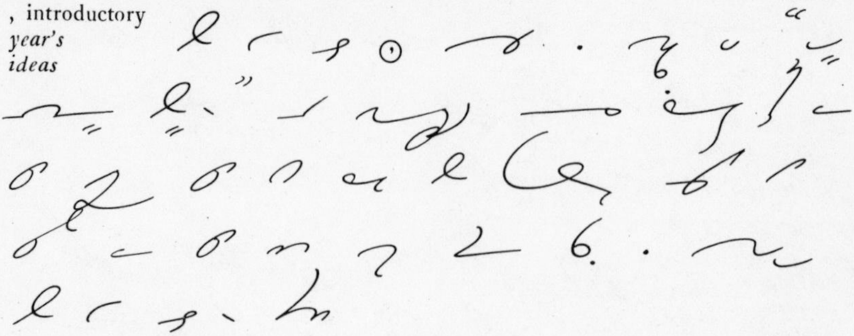

565.

teachers'
complaint
dye

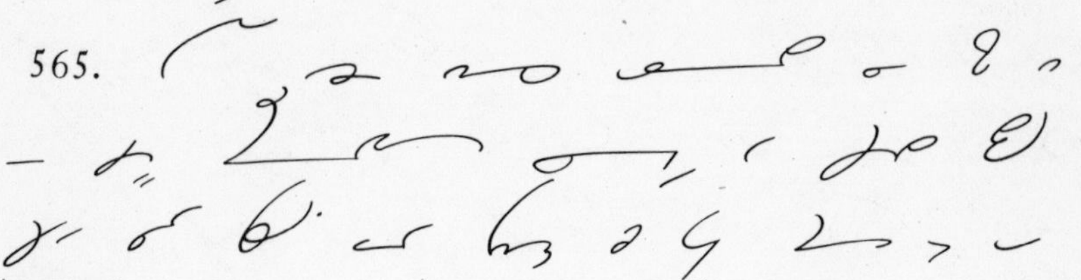

566.

February
unhappy

cloth
, apposition
, *when* clause
plain
occurs
, parenthetical
color
, *if* clause

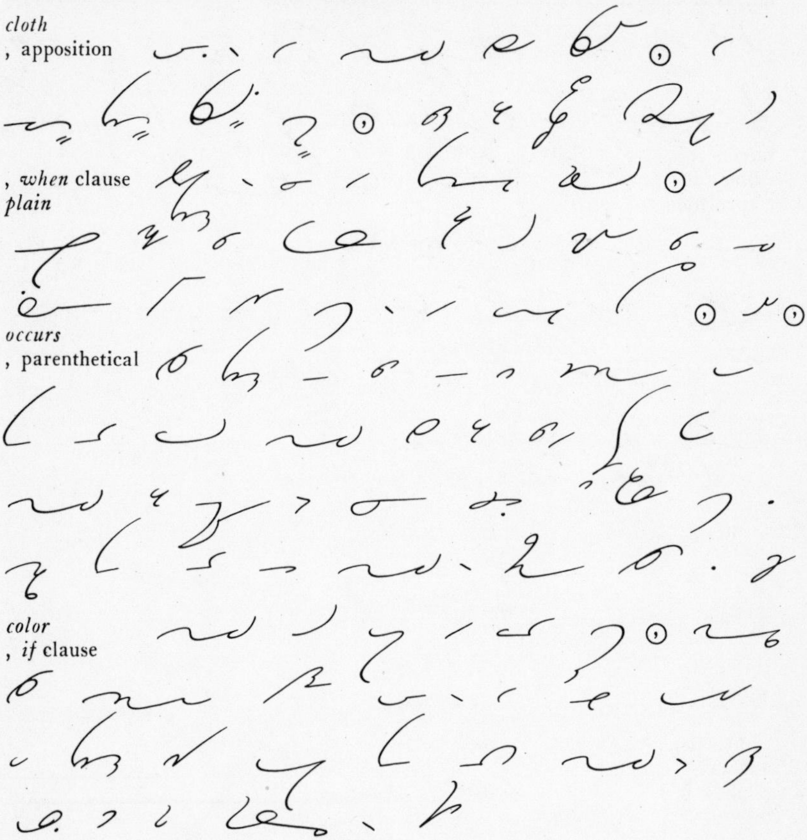

567.
editors
; no conjunction

568.
committee
accept

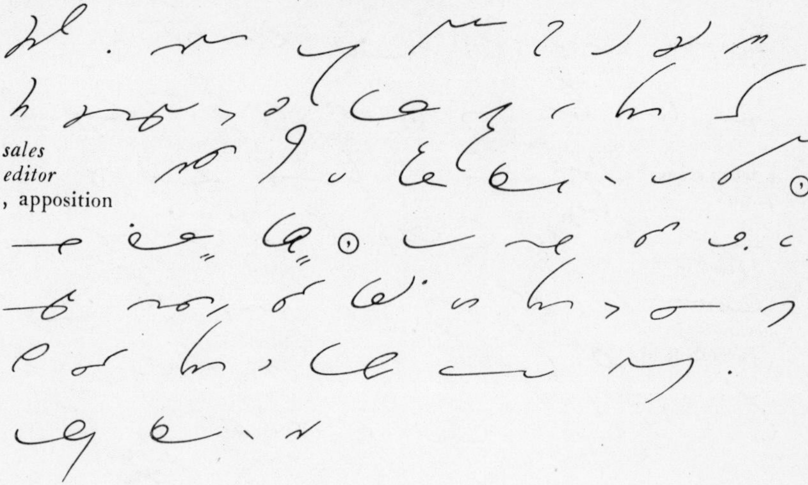

sales
editor
, apposition

ASSIGNMENT 74

569. Word Families

-CATE

-CATION

-LET

-GATE

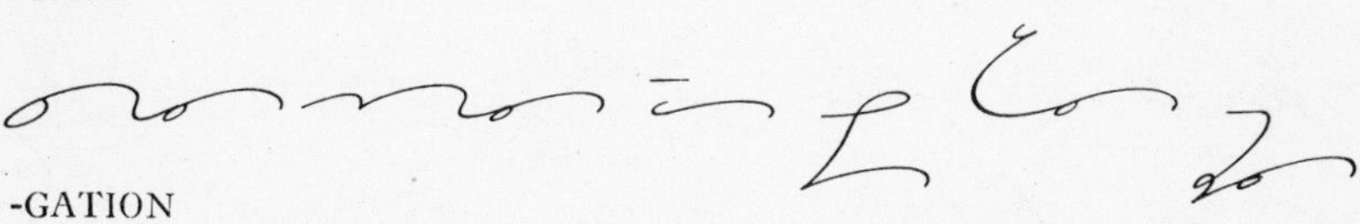

-GATION

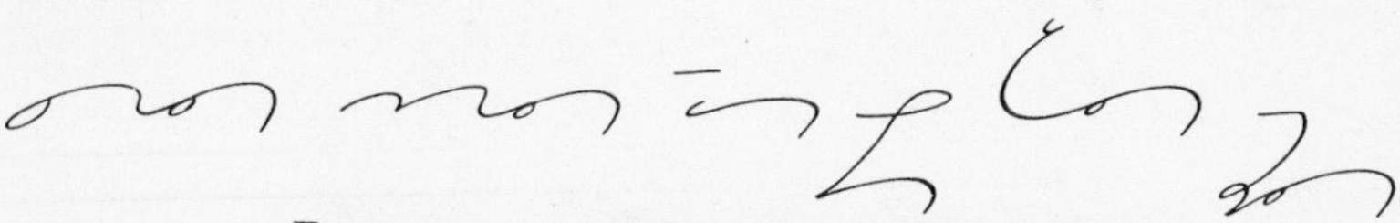

Reading and Writing Practice

570.

postmaster
forwarded
magazine

, series

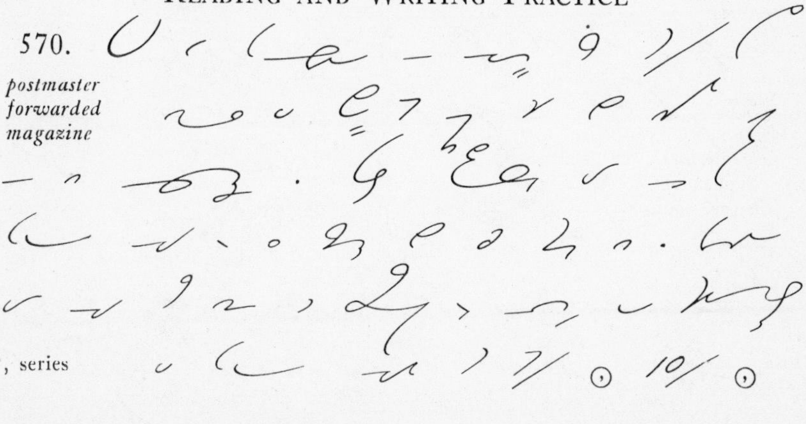

circular
material

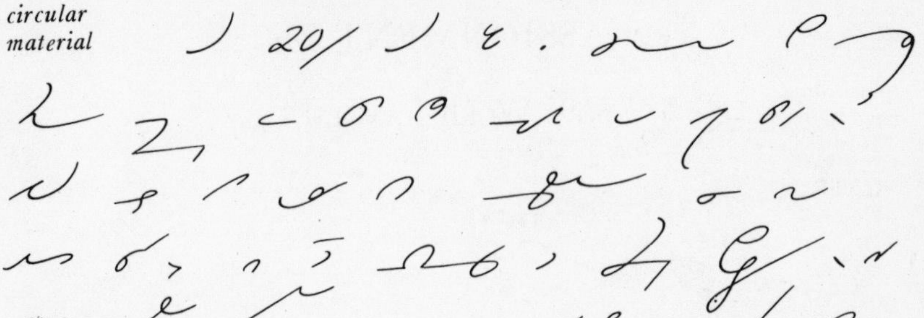

571.

women
editors
stories

enough
whether
receive

572.

country's
worth-while
hyphenated
before noun

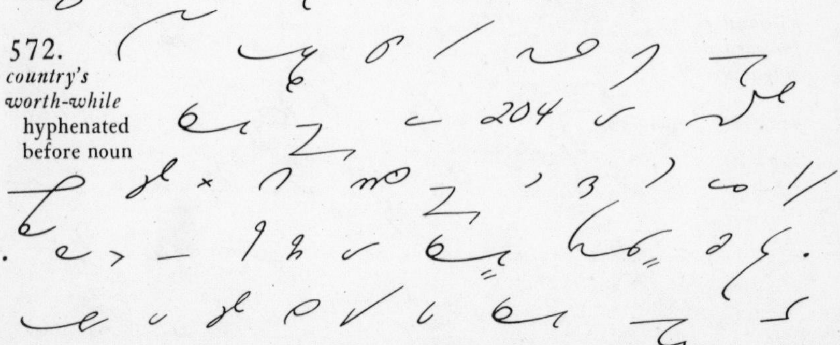

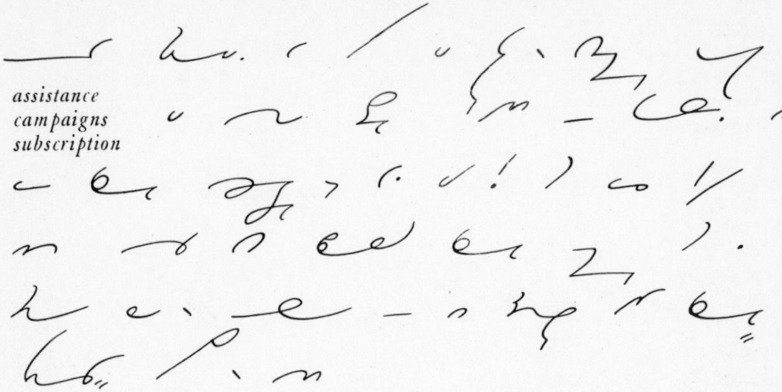

assistance
campaigns
subscription

573.

copies
Christmas

, parenthetical
Transcribe:
December 15.

574.

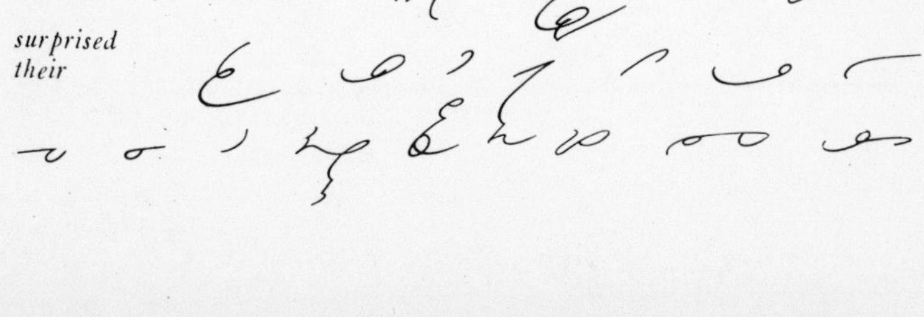

surprised
their

; because of comma

, introductory

month's

Transcribe: *100,000*

, conjunction

self-addressed envelope

575.

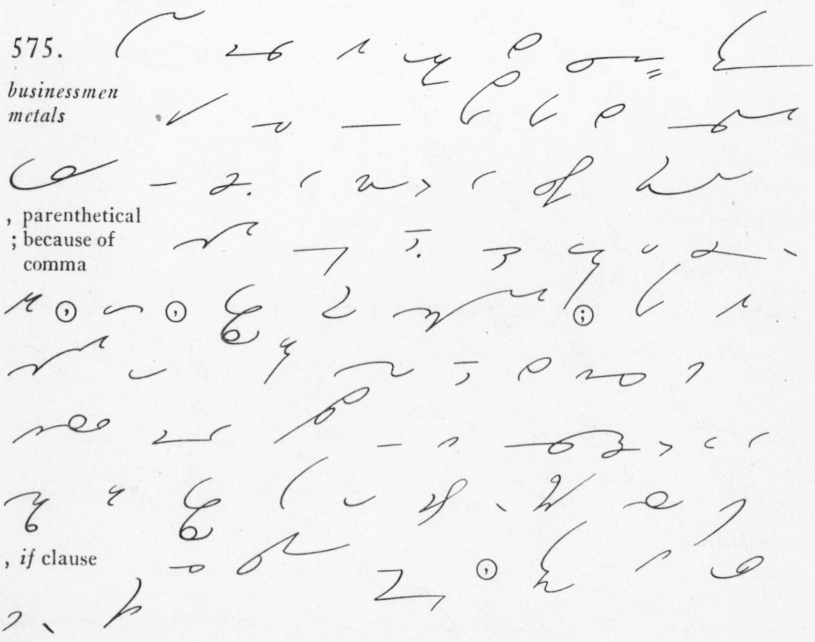

businessmen

metals

, parenthetical

; because of comma

, *if* clause

576.

, apposition
venture
explain

, introductory
unusual
peace

known
, *as* clause

ASSIGNMENT 75

577. Chart of Word Beginnings and Word Endings

A B C D E F

1.
2.
3.
4.
5.
6.
7.
8.
9.

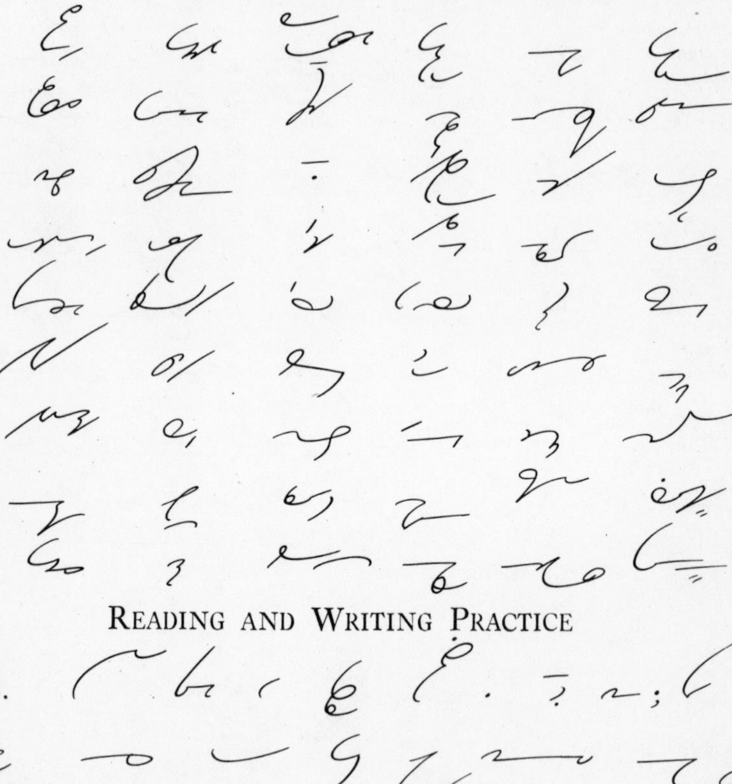

Reading and Writing Practice

578.

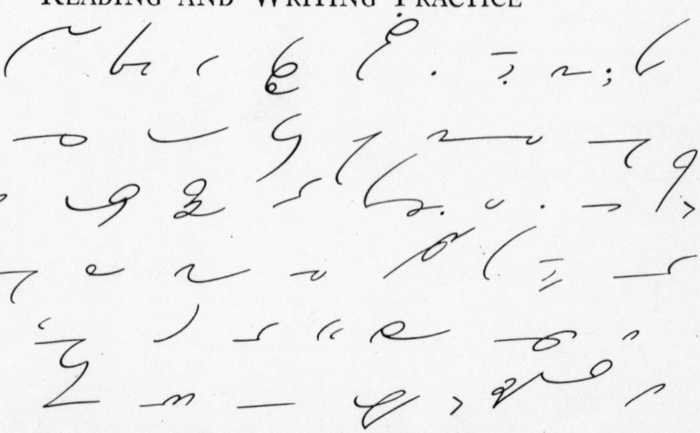

579.

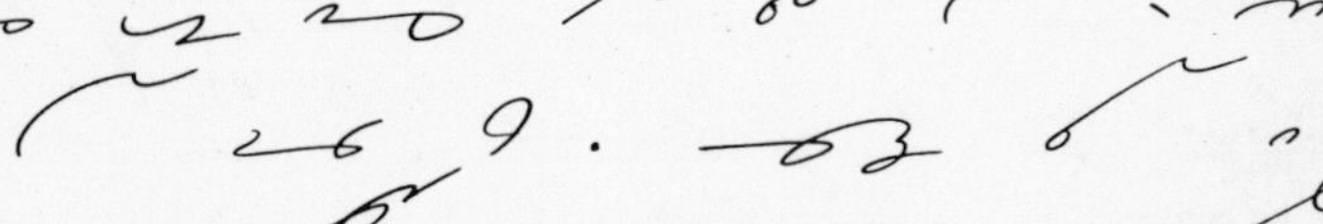

magazine editor

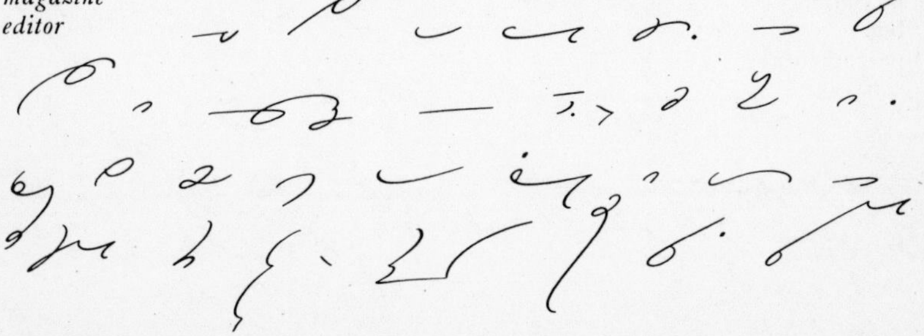

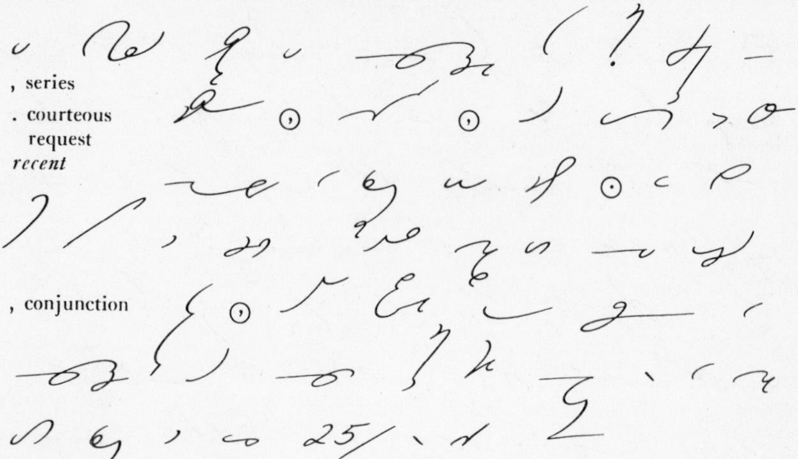

, series
. courteous request
recent

, conjunction

580.

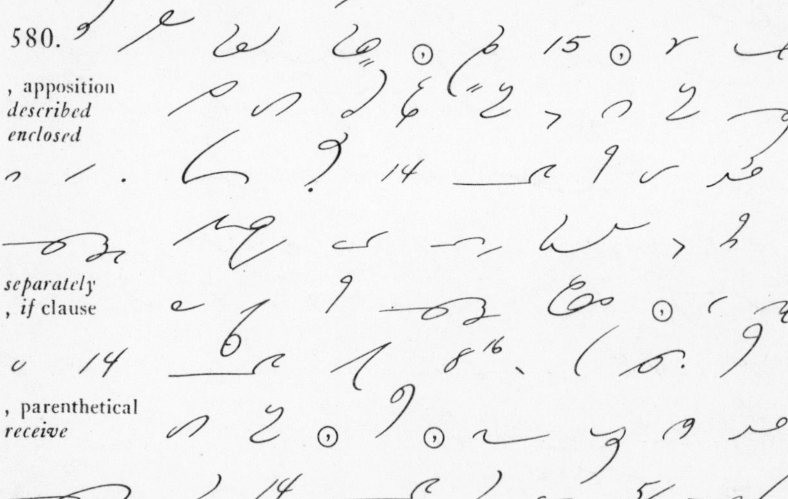

, apposition
described
enclosed

separately
, *if* clause

, parenthetical
receive

; no conjunction
, parenthetical

581.

, *as* clause
ever-increasing hyphenated before noun
various
experiences
carrying
, *if* clause

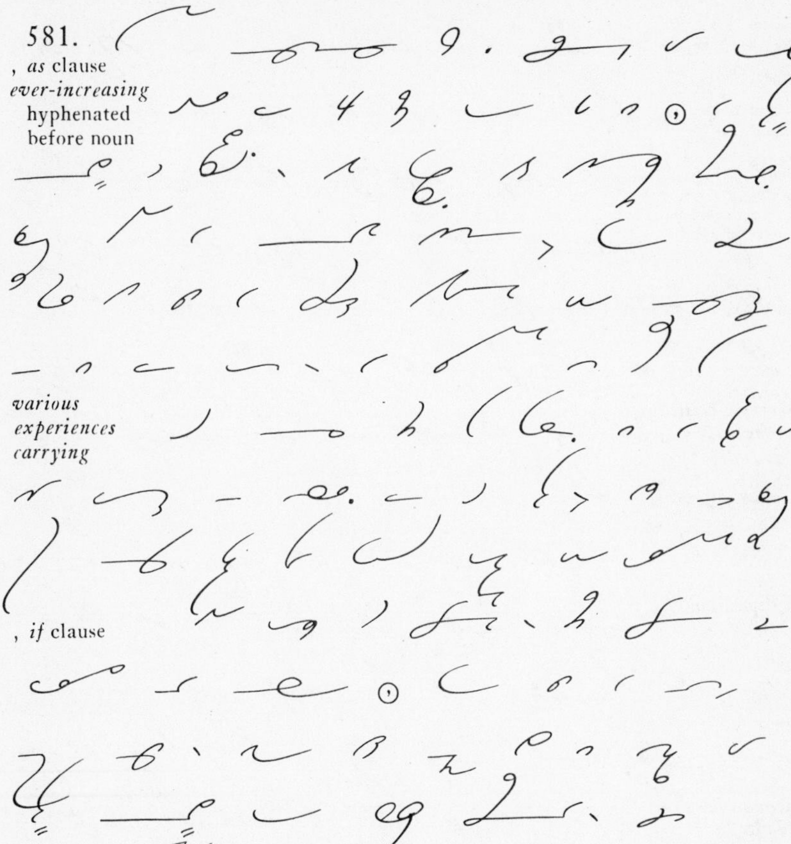

582.

instructions
announcing

Merry Christmas
cordially

583.

, apposition
America's

acquainted
country's

article
, *if* clause

CHAPTER XVI

ASSIGNMENT 76

584. Accuracy Practice

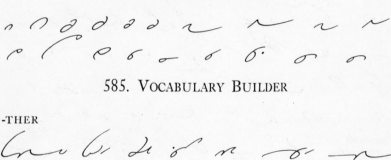

585. Vocabulary Builder

-THER

W

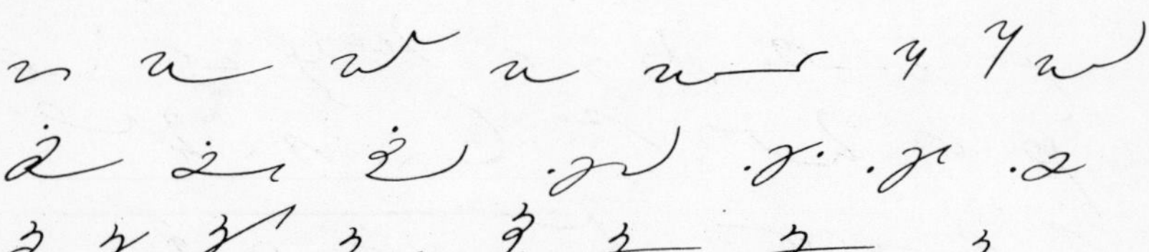

Reading and Writing Practice

586.

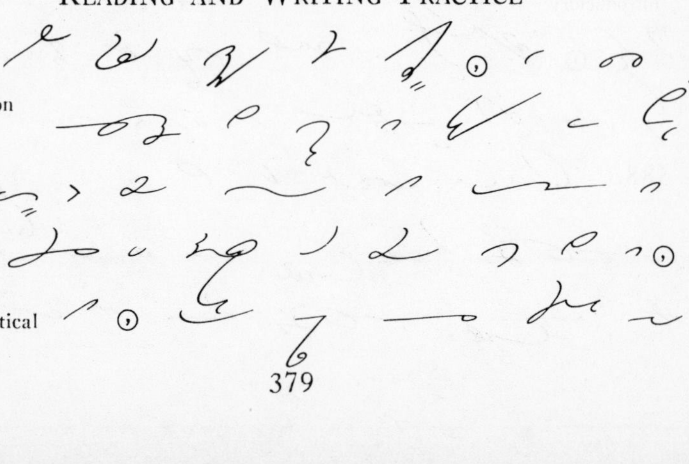

, apposition
weekly

welcome
features
, parenthetical

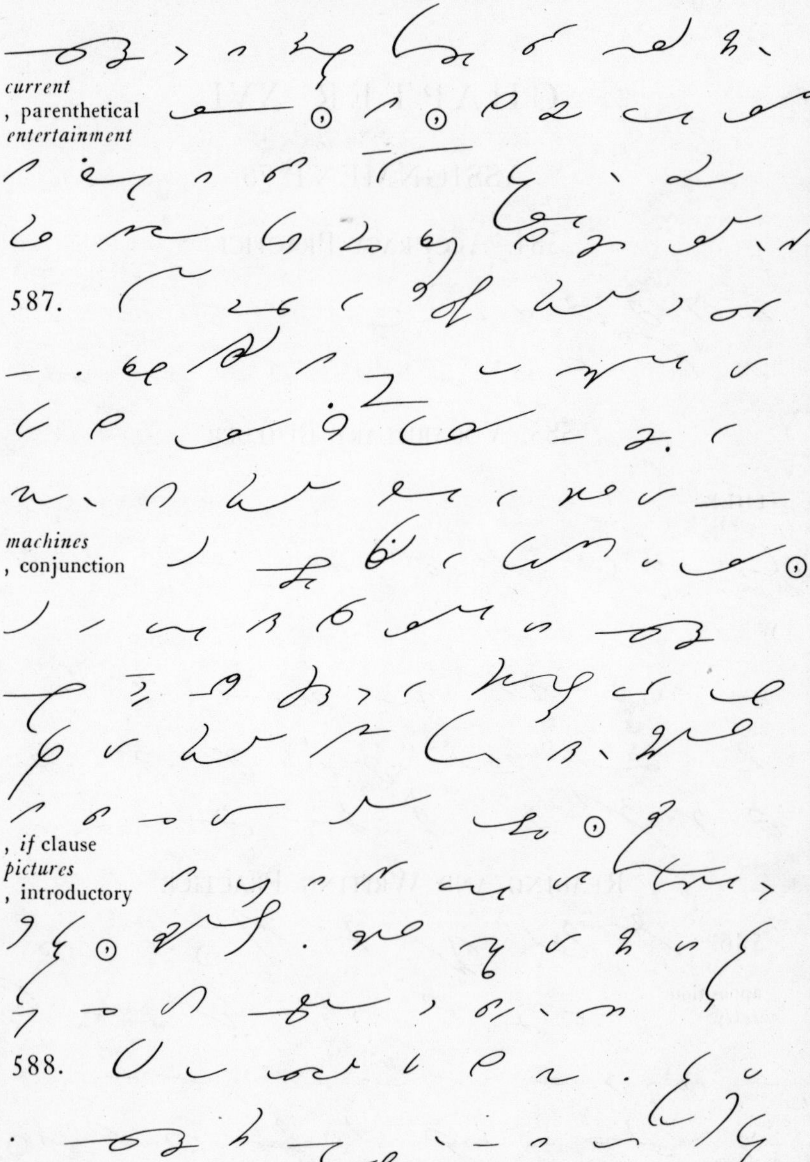

current
, parenthetical
entertainment

587.

machines
, conjunction

, *if* clause
pictures
, introductory

588.

, *as* clause

; no conjunction

, *if* clause

589.

usually
acquaintance
receiving

, introductory

, introductory
month's
believing

worth-while
hyphenated
before noun
, *if* clause

590.

response
, apposition
, *as* clause

already
familiar
choose

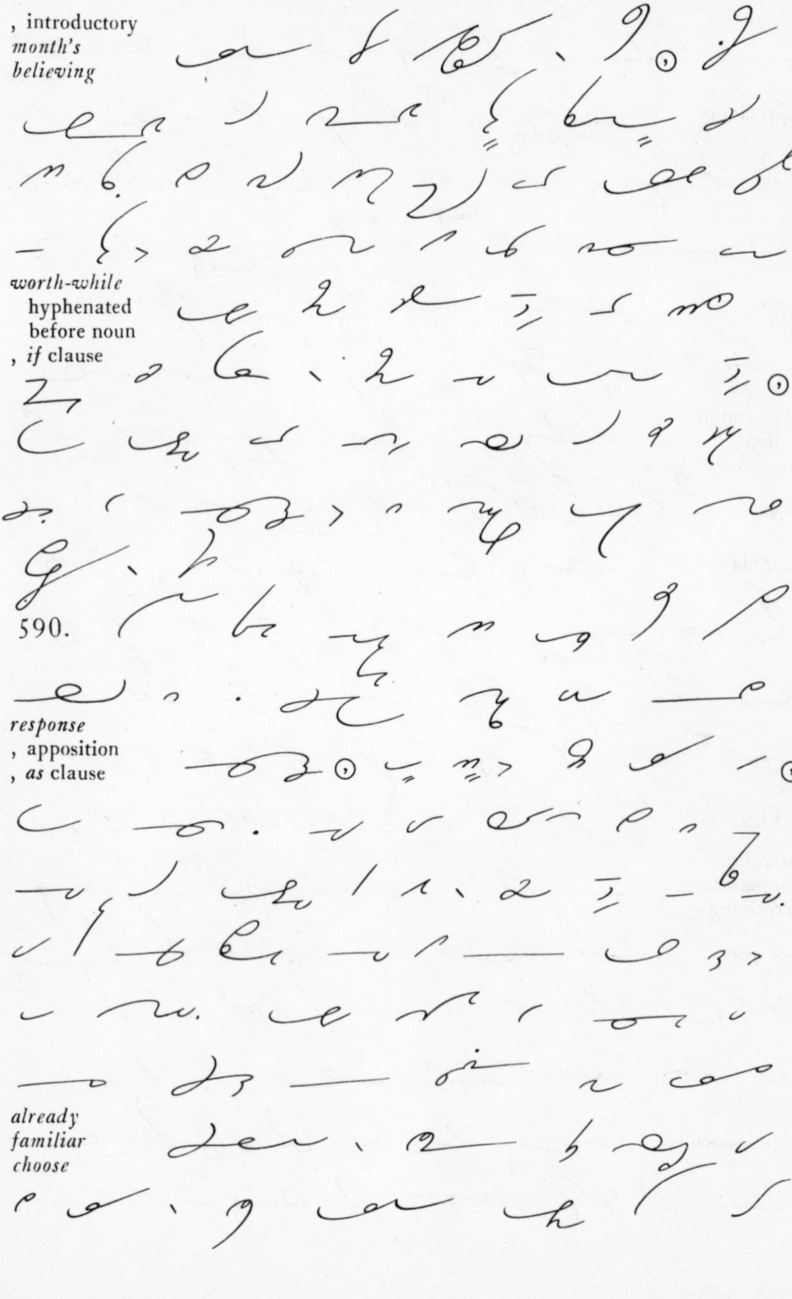

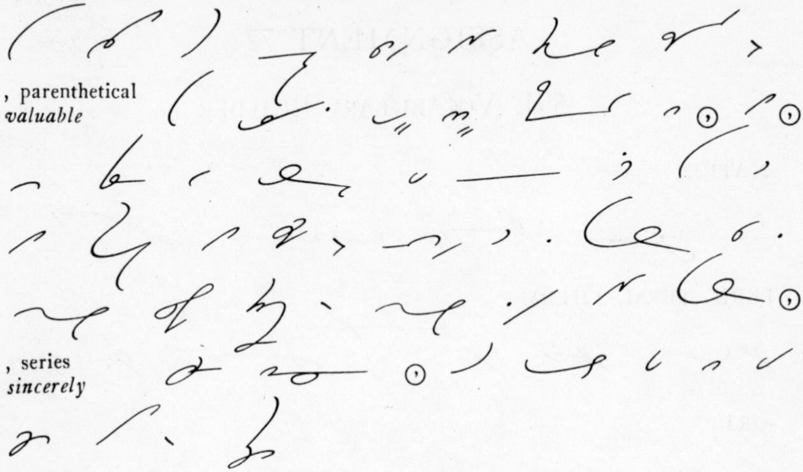

, parenthetical
valuable

, series
sincerely

ASSIGNMENT 77

591. Vocabulary Builder

-NATION

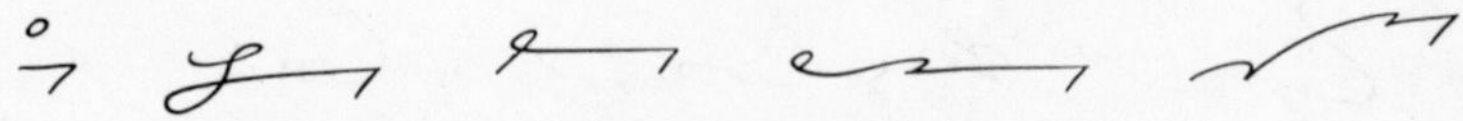

TERN, TERM, THERM

-ORT

Numbers, etc.

Compounds

Reading and Writing Practice

592.

, apposition
, conjunction
, introductory

money-saving
single-copy
hyphenated before noun

period
month's

593.

businessmen
accountant
, series

sometimes
important
hears

, introductory
government

, *if* clause

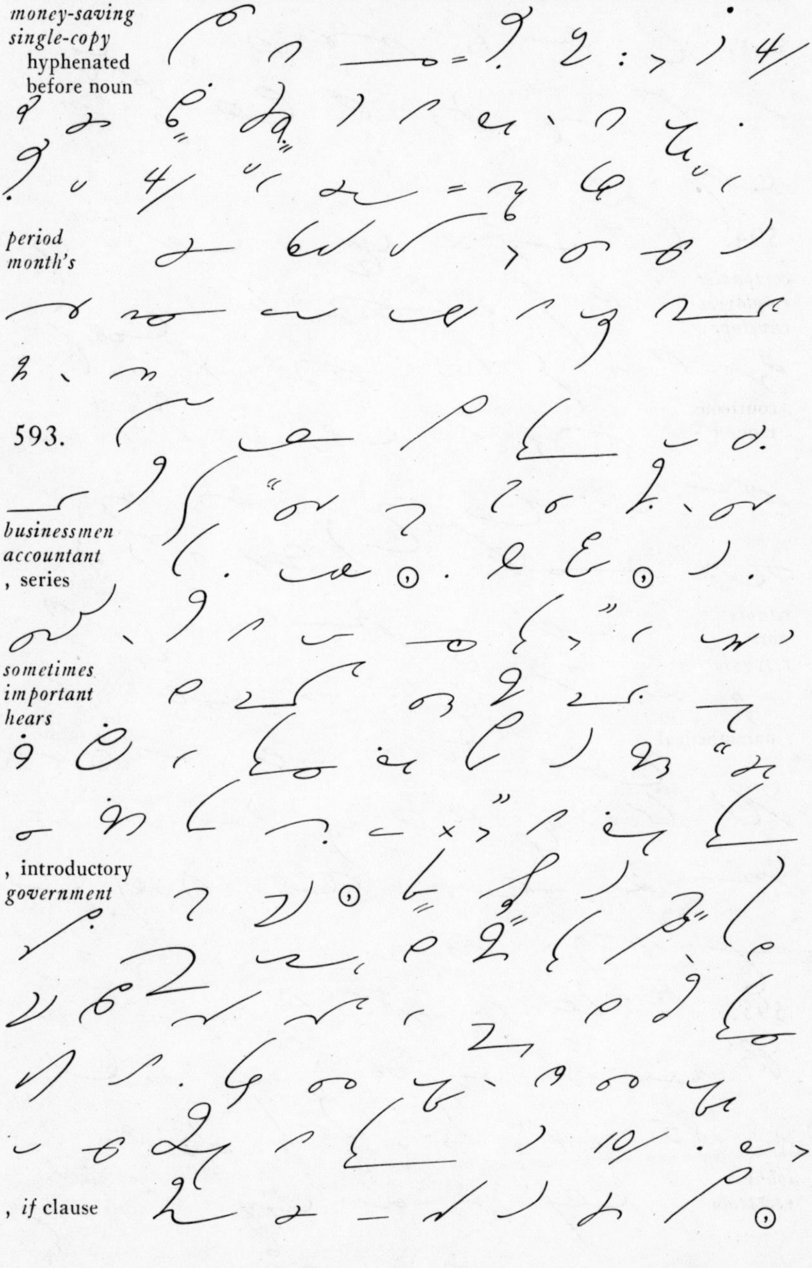

week's

594.

companies
employees
envelope

. courteous
request

editors
past
response

, parenthetical

595.

185

lobby
reception

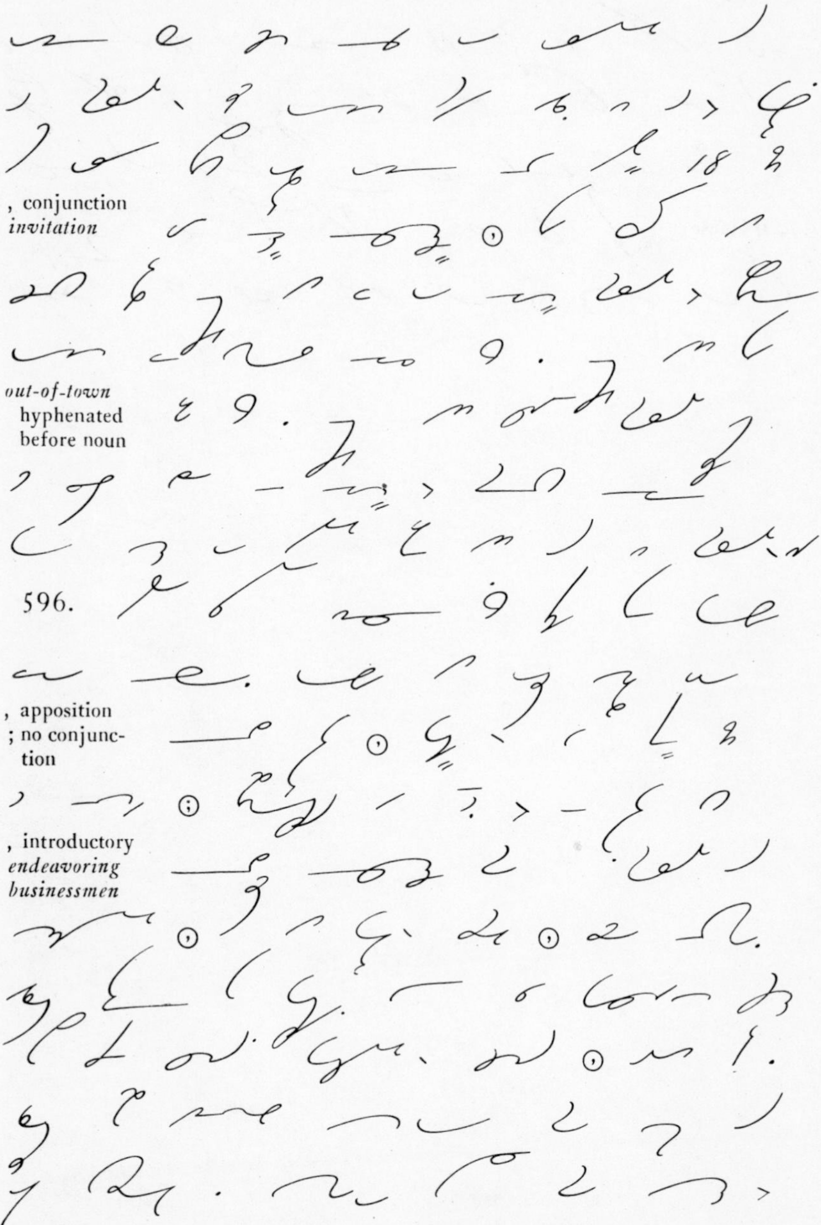

, conjunction
invitation

out-of-town
hyphenated
before noun

596.

, apposition
; no conjunction

, introductory
endeavoring
businessmen

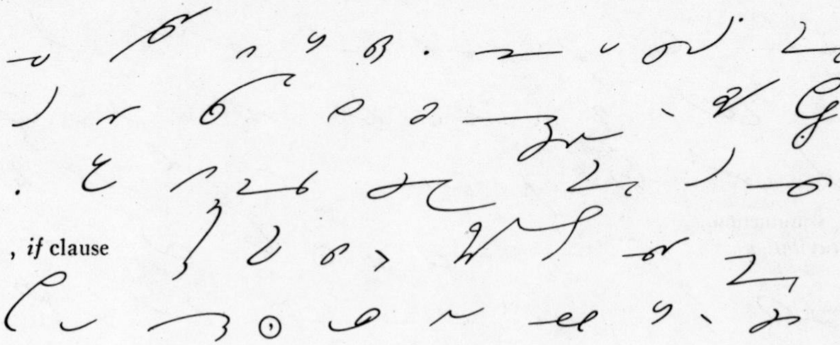

, *if* clause

ASSIGNMENT 78

597. Most-Used Business-Letter Phrases

UNDERSTAND, UNDERSTOOD

INTERSECTION

598. Geographical Expressions

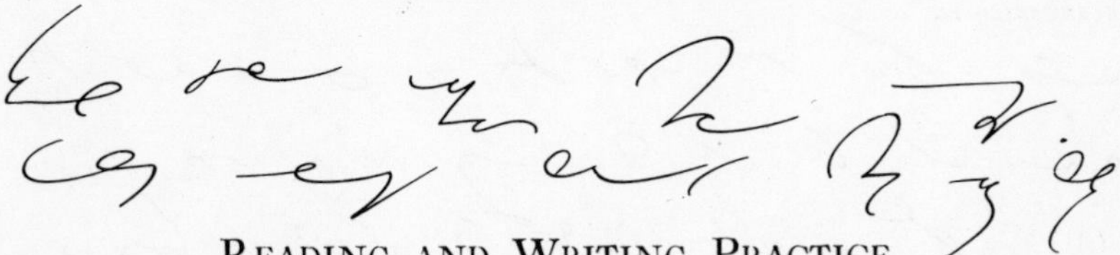

Reading and Writing Practice

599.

receipt
client
assistance

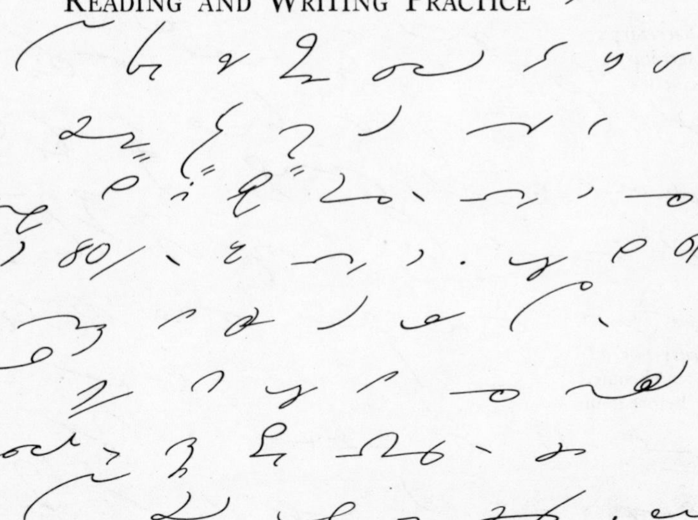

600.

commission
Transcribe: *$5,000 worth*

remainder
Bell's
, introductory

, conjunction
error
inconvenienced

601.

Secretary's
secretaries
, series

easy-to-read
hyphenated before noun

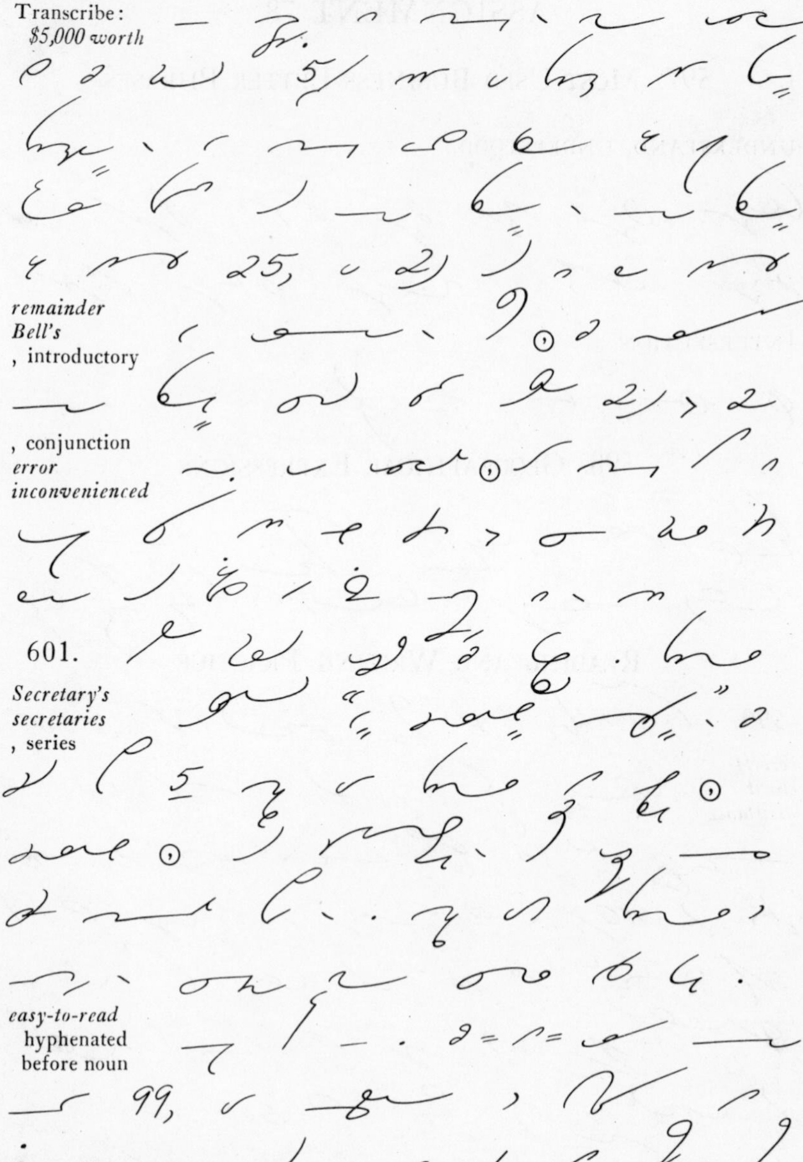

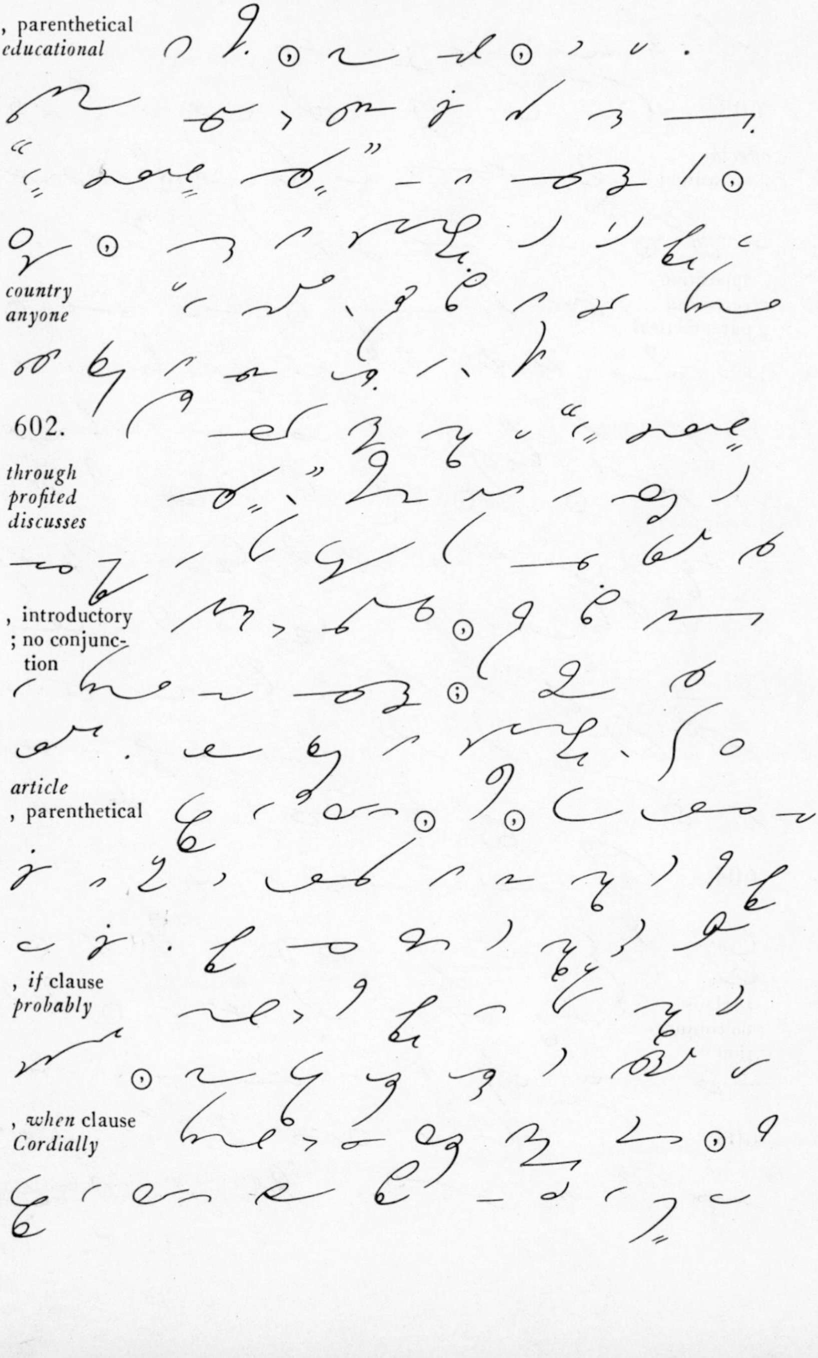

, parenthetical
educational

country
anyone

602.

through
profited
discusses

, introductory
; no conjunction

article
, parenthetical

, *if* clause
probably

, *when* clause
Cordially

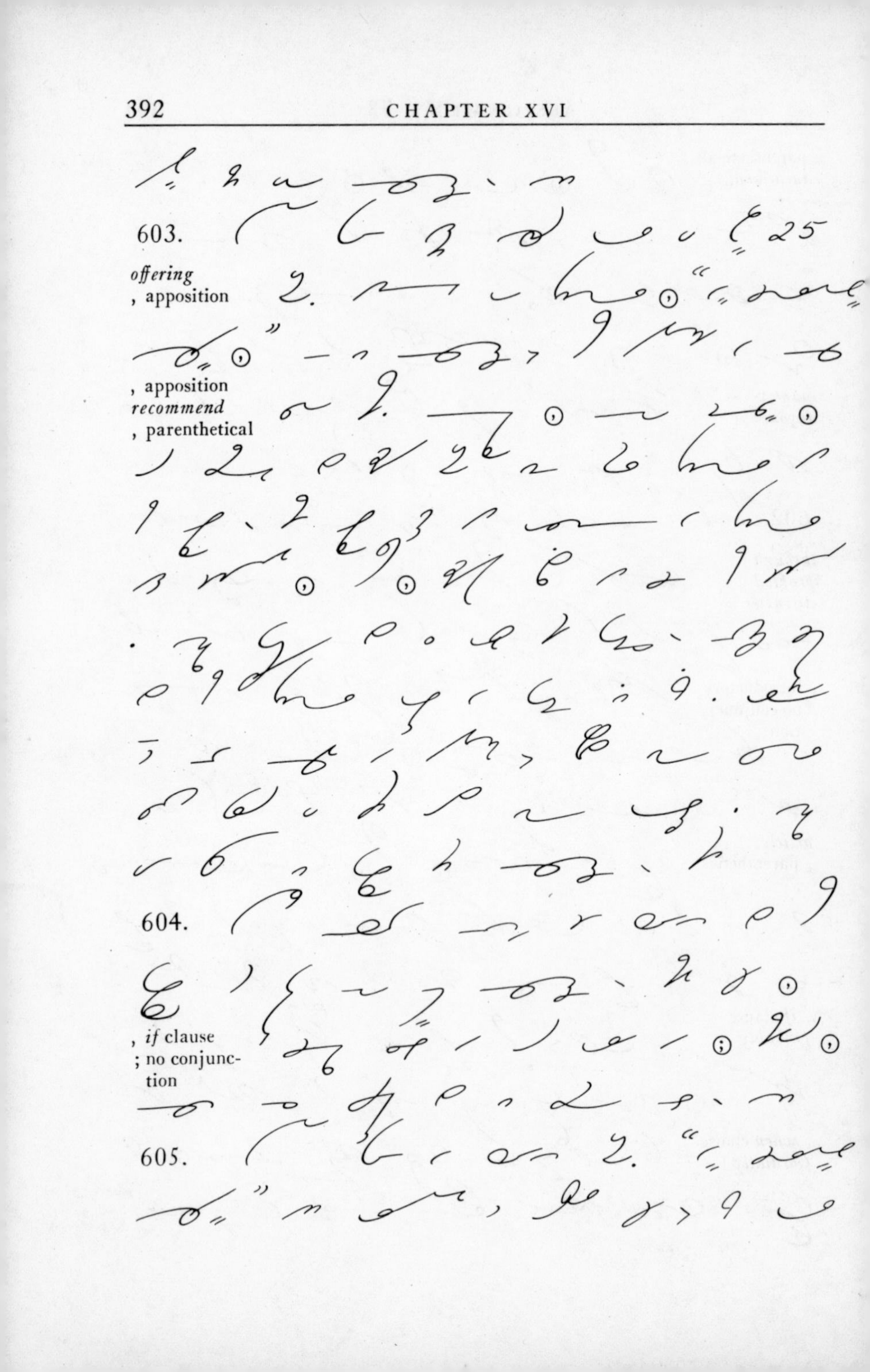

603. 25

offering
, apposition

, apposition
recommend
, parenthetical

604.

, *if* clause
; no conjunction

605.

requests
received

606.

, conjunction
tribute
source

, introductory
co-operation

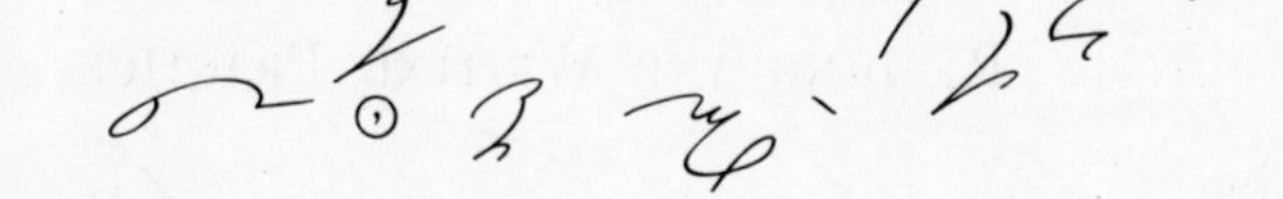

ASSIGNMENT 79

607. Word Families

IMM-

UNN-

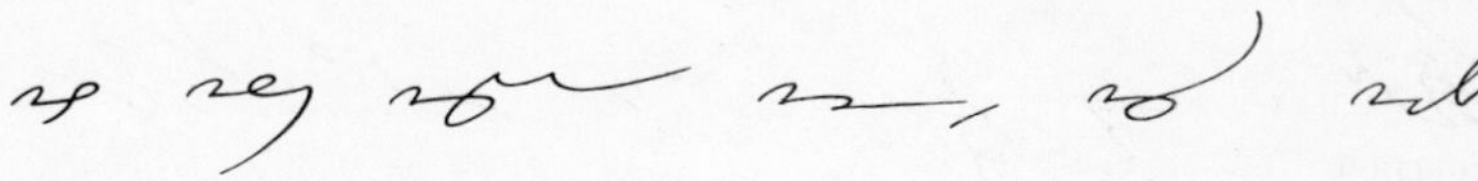

-AGE

-THING

Reading and Writing Practice

608.

, *as* clause
; because of comma

, *if* clause
guest

additional
pleasure

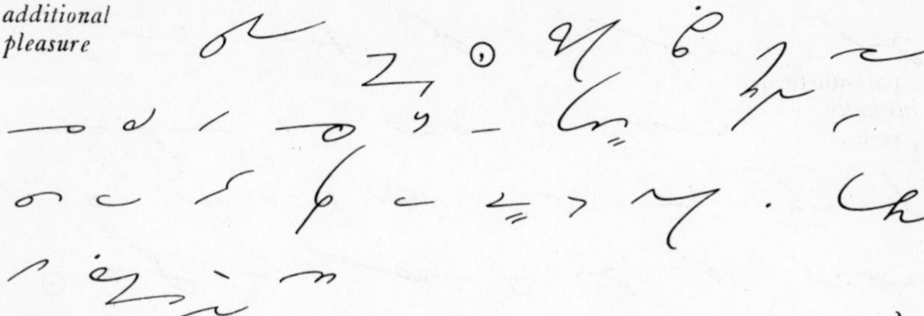

609.
, *as* clause
Government
, introductory

everyone's
ceilings
, conjunction

610.

overlooked
, introductory

, parenthetical
instantly
, series

occasion
co-operation

611.

eager
seriously

, introductory
approaching

, apposition

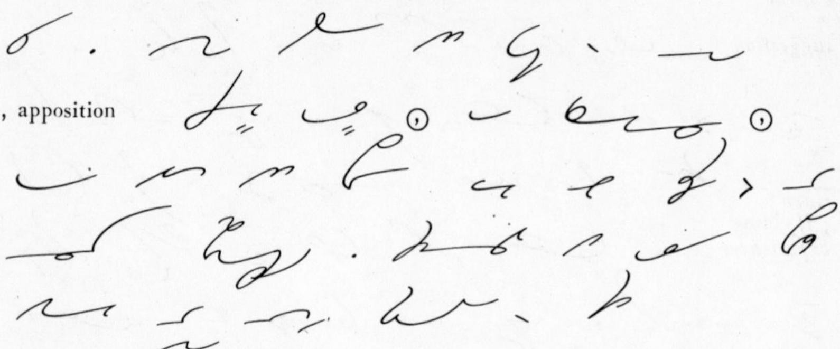

612.

, introductory

; no conjunction

time-saving

labor-saving

hyphenated before noun

, *if* clause

investment

Transcribe: *$320.*

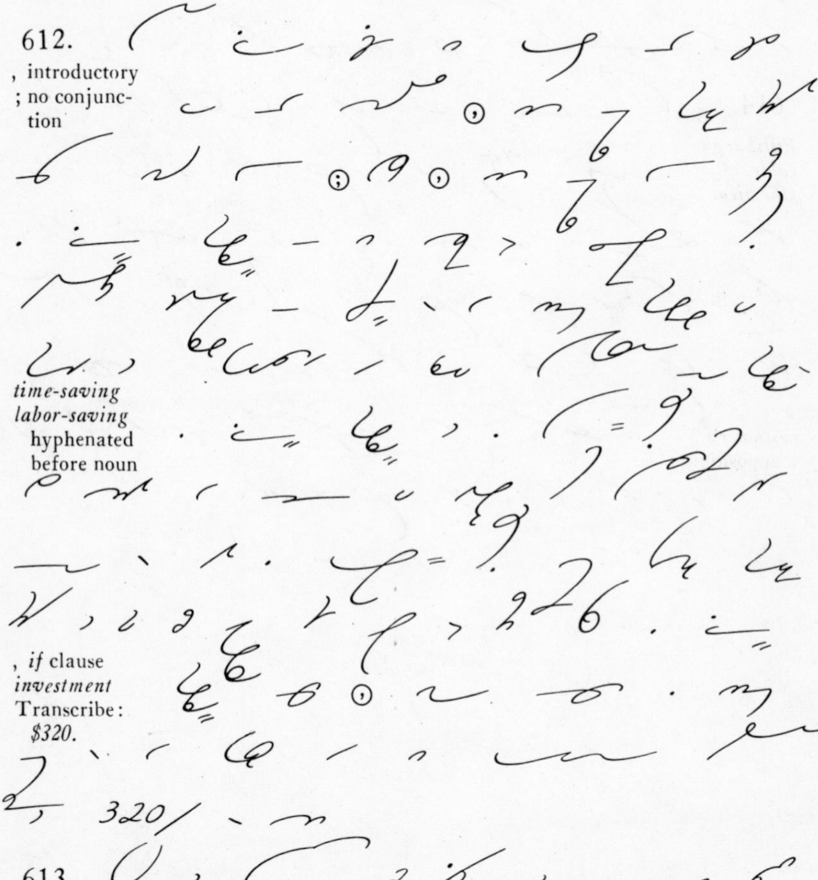

613.

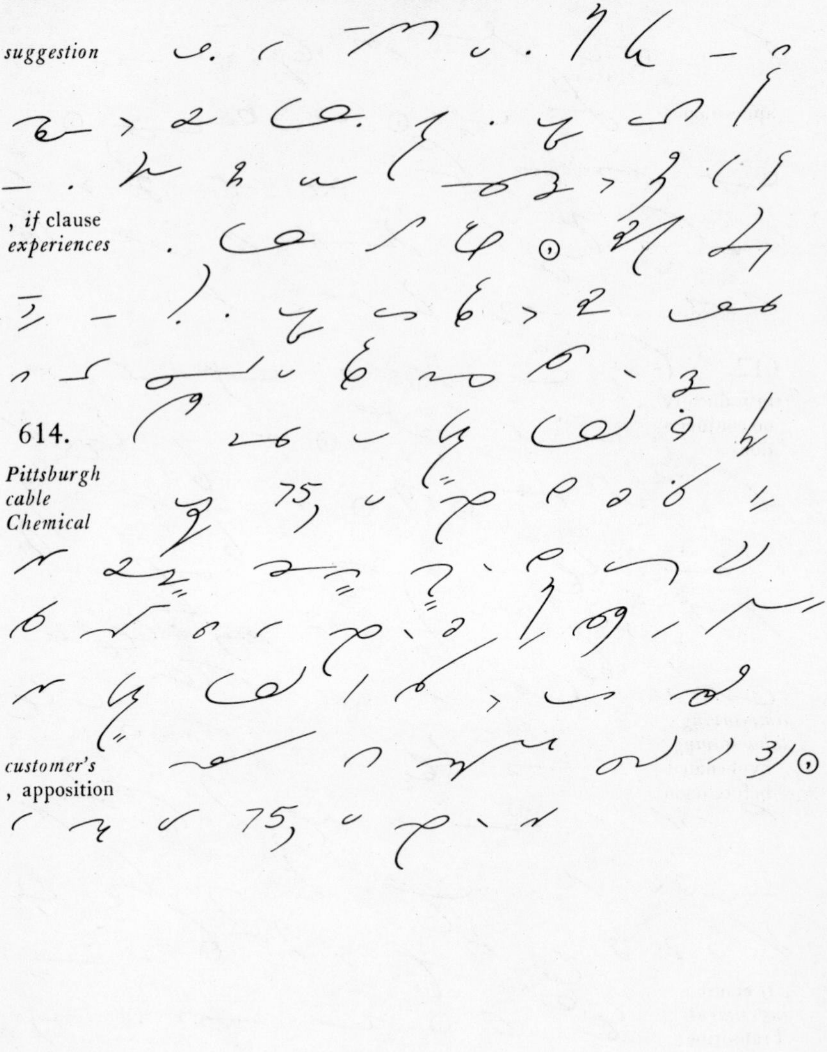

suggestion

, *if* clause

experiences

614.

Pittsburgh

cable

Chemical

customer's

, apposition

ASSIGNMENT 80

615. VOCABULARY BUILDER

NT

MT, MD

GENT

TIVE

TEN

TEM, DEM

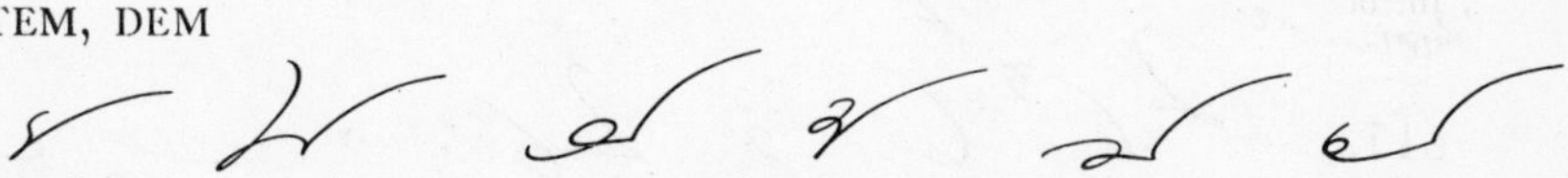

READING AND WRITING PRACTICE

616.

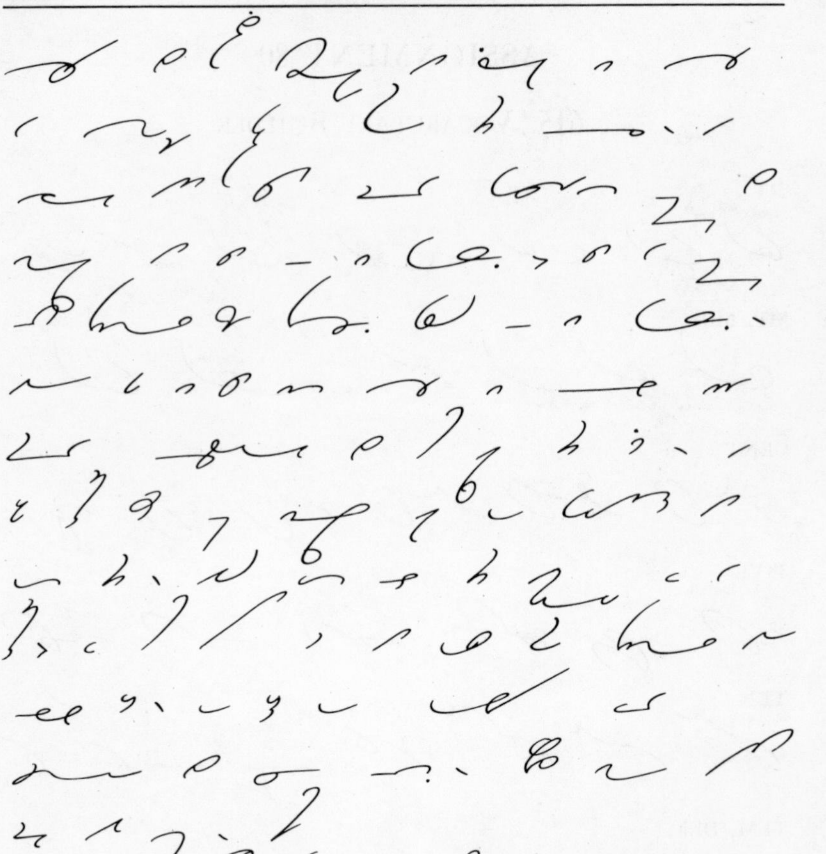

617.

, introductory
entitled

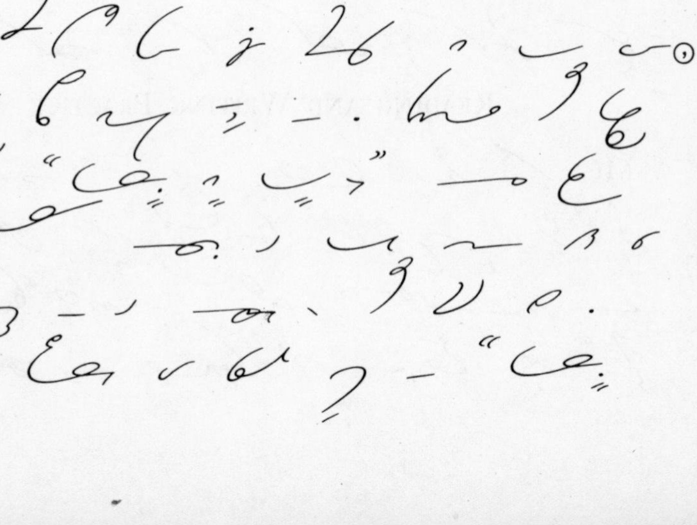

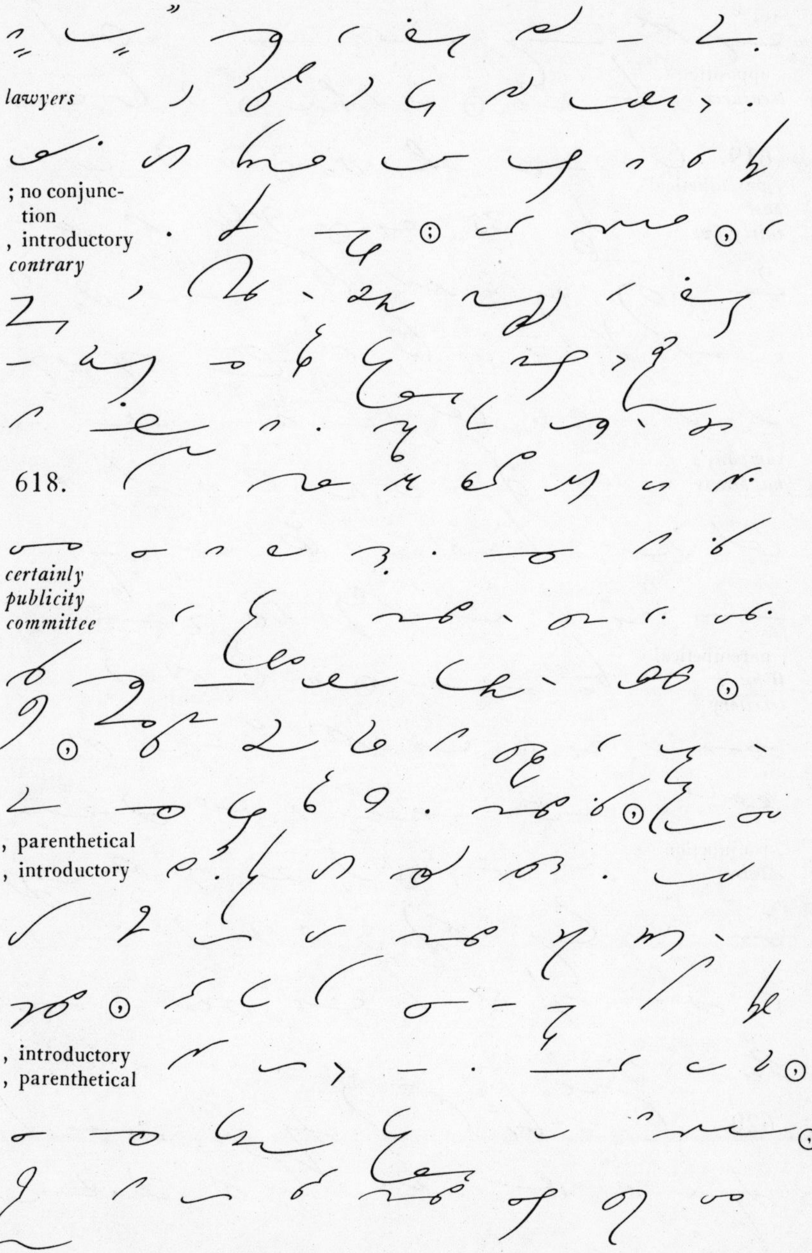

lawyers

; no conjunction

, introductory

contrary

618.

certainly

publicity

committee

, parenthetical

, introductory

, introductory

, parenthetical

, apposition
treasurer

619.

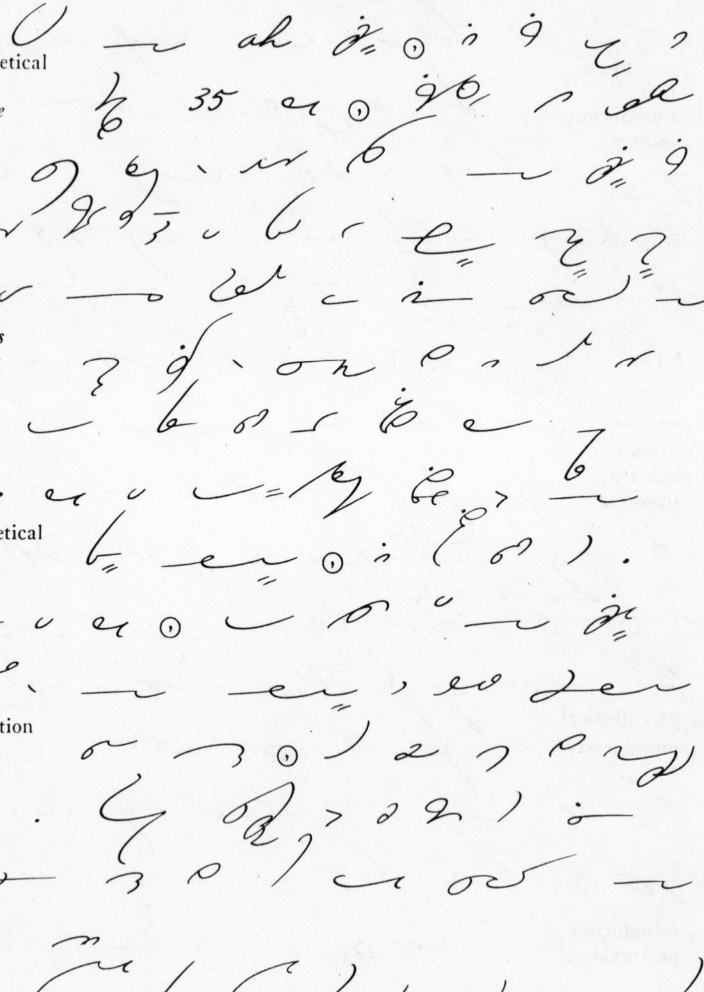

, parenthetical
past
thirty-five

35

company's
happiness

, parenthetical
White's
territory

, conjunction
adviser

620.

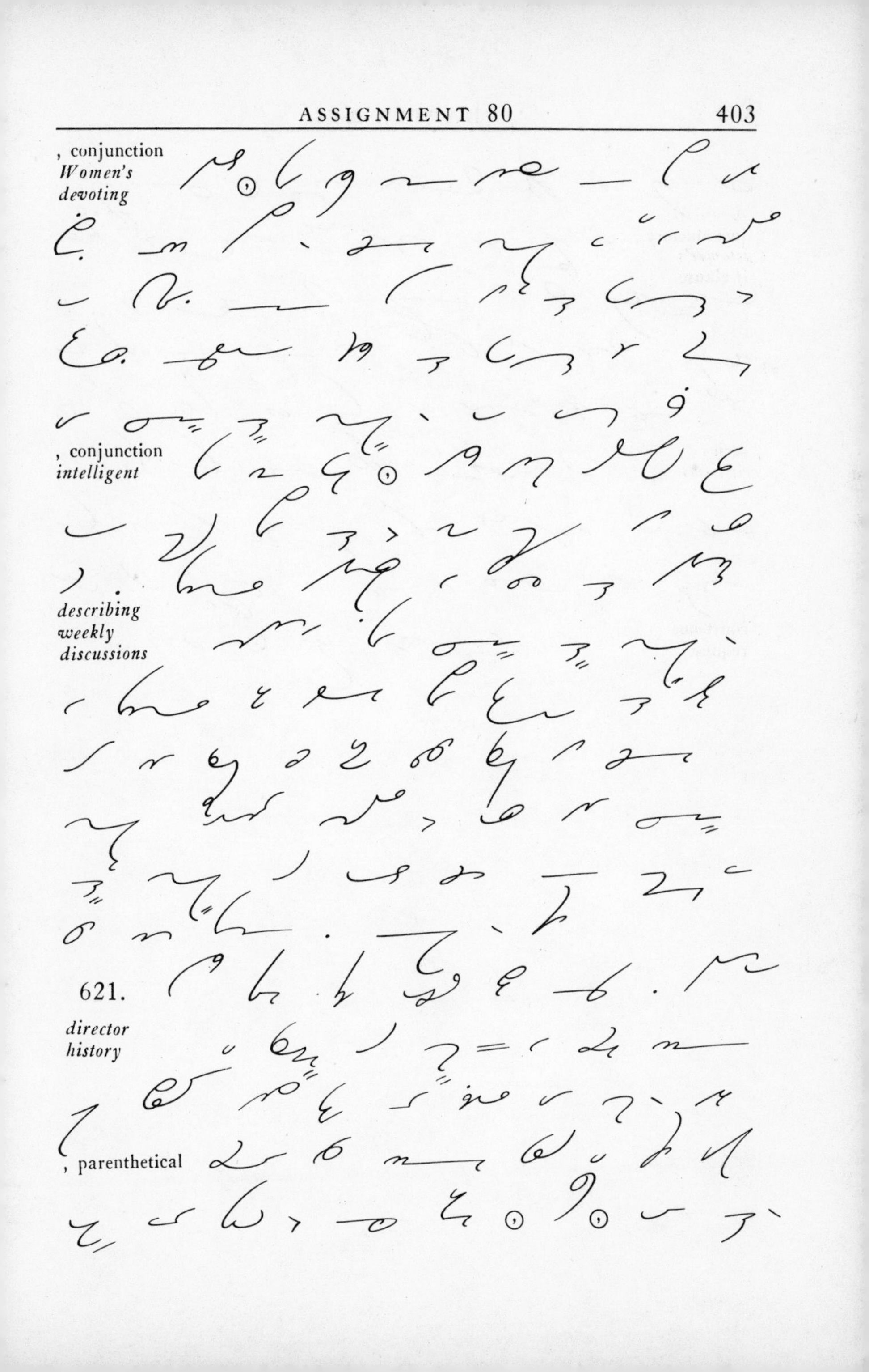

, conjunction
Women's
devoting

, conjunction
intelligent

describing
weekly
discussions

621.

director
history

, parenthetical

, introductory
Customer's
, *if* clause

, series
criticisms

. courteous
request

APPENDIX

SHORTHAND SPEED

Martin J. Dupraw
World's Champion Shorthand Writer

Why read so much shorthand?

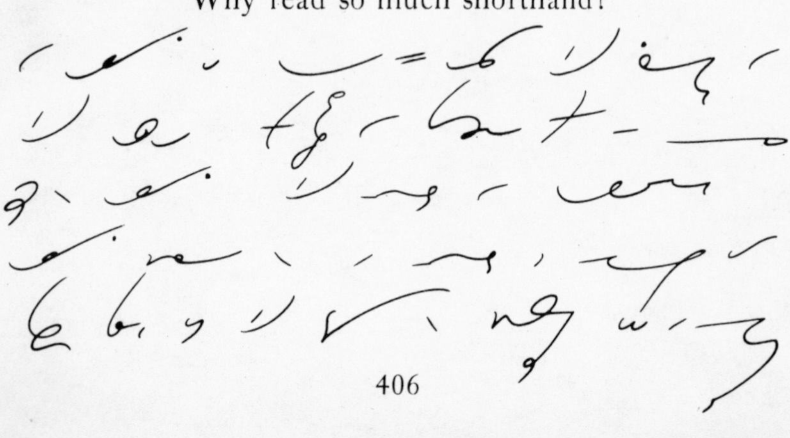

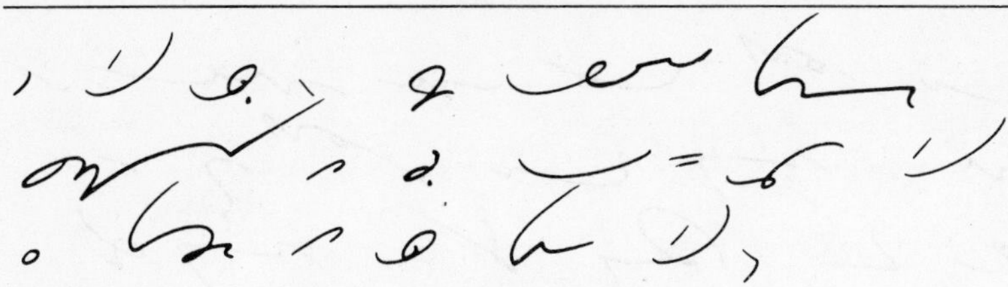

What kind of dictation?

Why is my hand so slow?

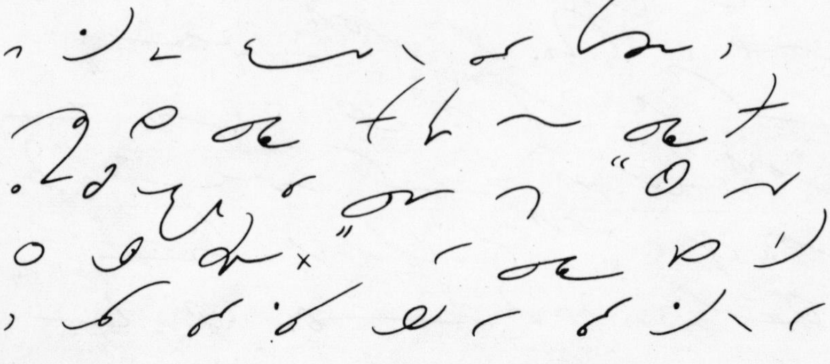

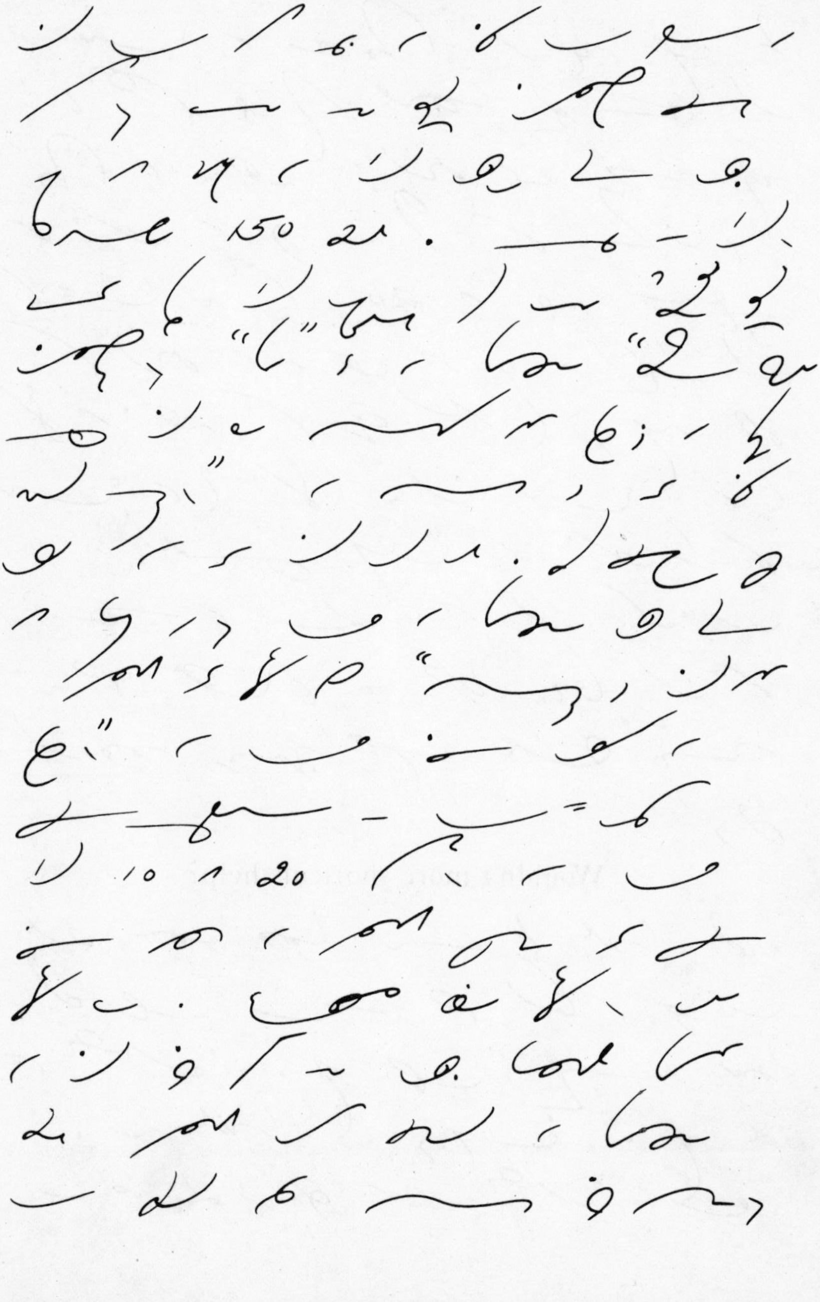

Wouldn't more shortcuts help?

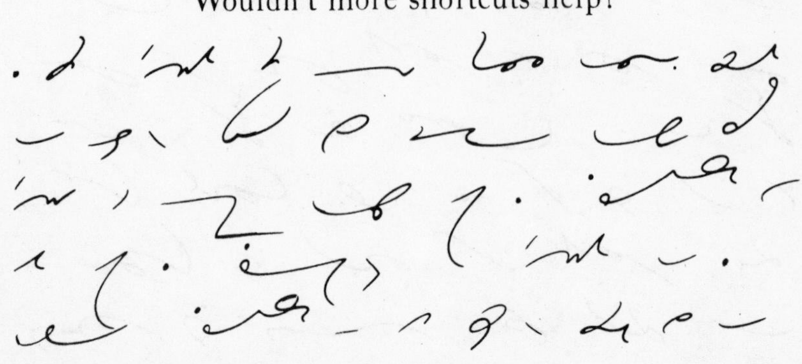

Isn't phrasing the key to speed?

50,
250,
3, 536
33, 202
46

How big should my shorthand be?

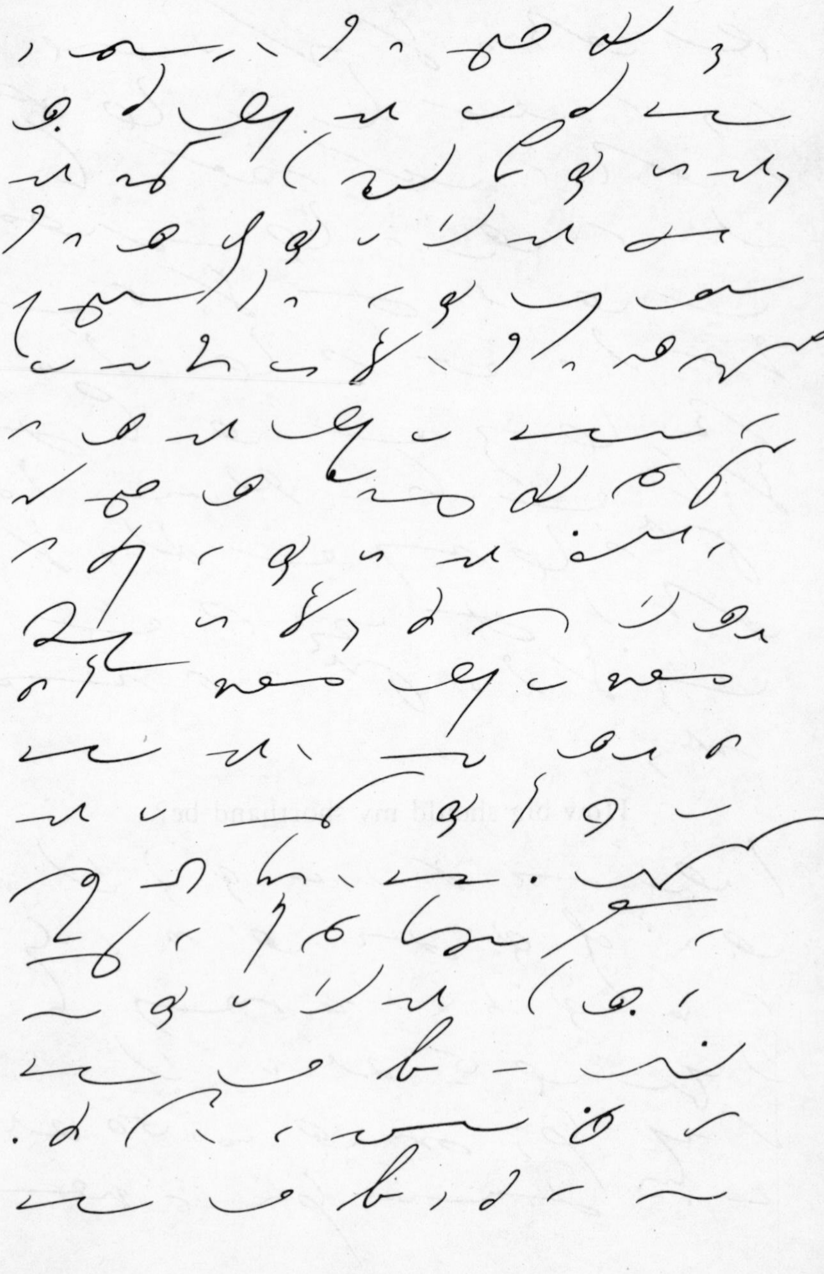

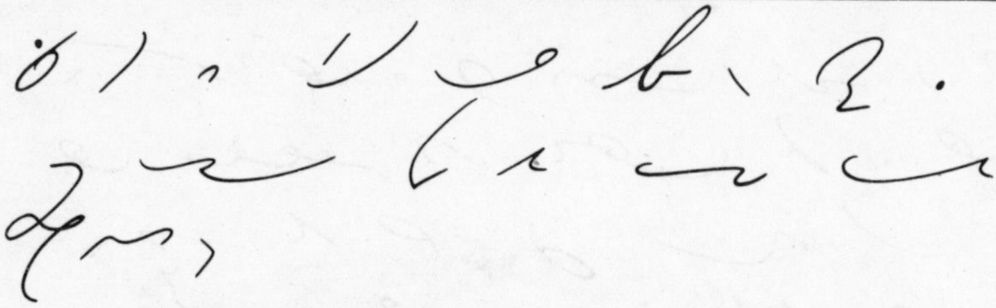

Can the left-hander write shorthand well?

How should I hold the pen?

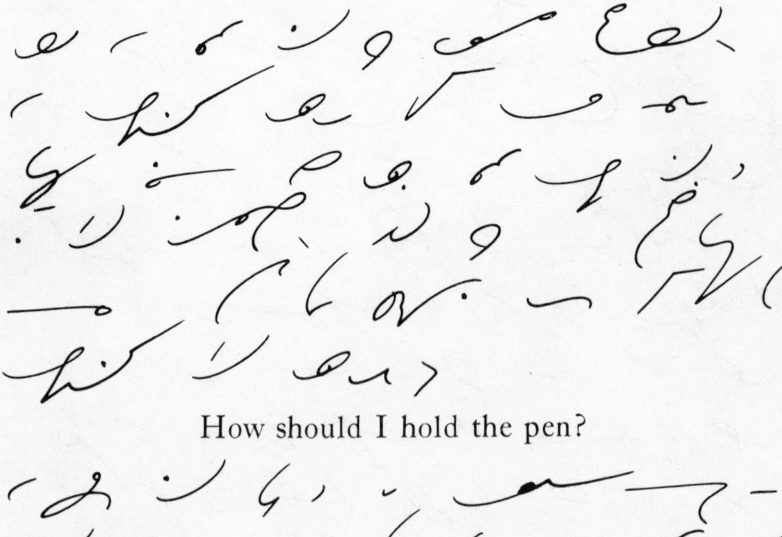

How can I stop pinching the pen?

Should I use pen or pencil?

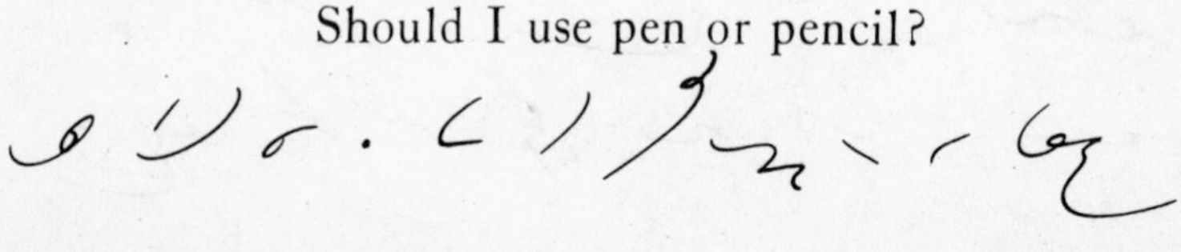

21
150

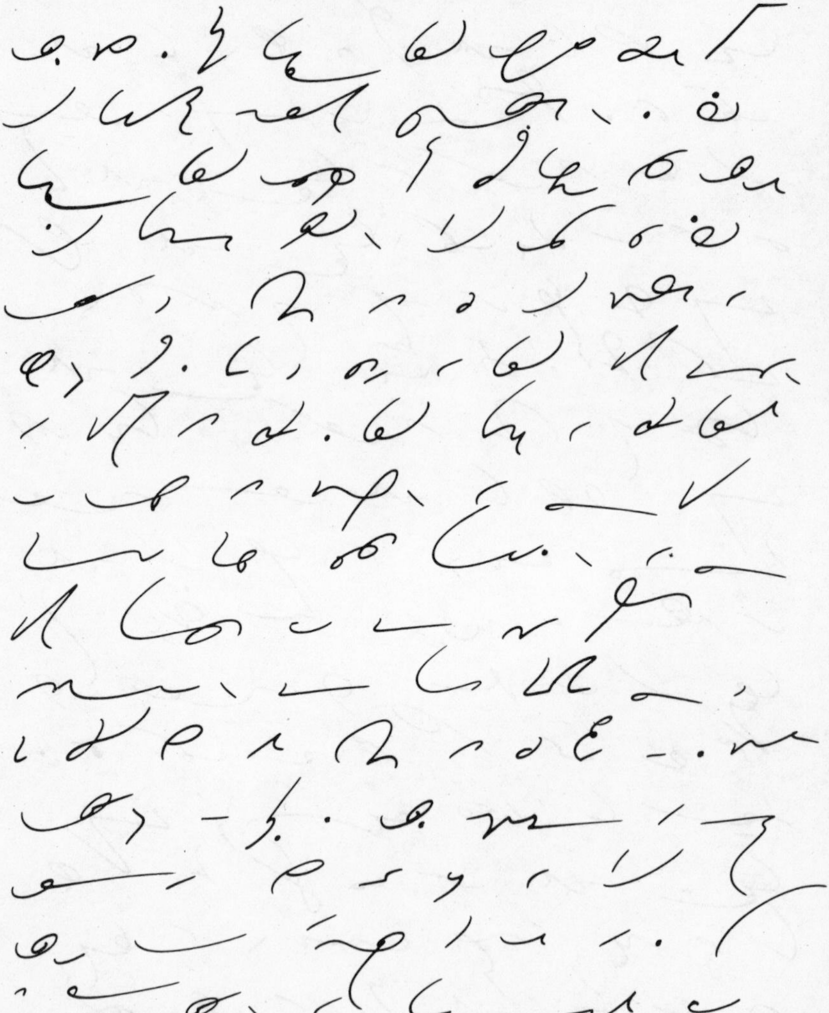

Can everybody learn shorthand?

Marginal Reminders Explained

In the following pages will be found more complete statements of the principles of punctuation and other pretranscription aids briefly indicated in the marginal reminders of this book. It is not intended that the pupil should attempt to learn these principles; they are presented here as an aid to the understanding of the marginal reminders. The ability to apply the principles will come from the constant repetition of the reminders in the margin.

The main purpose of the pretranscription punctuation reminders given in the margins of this text is to help the learner to get the "knack" of punctuating the constructions most frequently used in ordinary business correspondence. For that reason (and because of the obvious necessity for extreme brevity) the reminders have been made so short and so simple that the grammarian might well quarrel with the wording of some of them. In this section each of the very brief reminders is discussed more fully and with a careful explanation of the grammatical relationships involved. It is more important, however, that the learner form the habit of correctly punctuating these simple business constructions than that he be able to give the complete and accurate grammatical explanation.

The headings given below are the same as those used in the marginal reminders. The number in parentheses is the number of the letter in this text from which the example is taken.

, parenthetical

In order to make his meaning clearer, a writer sometimes inserts a comment or explanation that could be omitted without changing the meaning of the sentence. These added comments and explanations are called parenthetical and are separated from the rest of the sentence by parentheses, dashes, or commas. Every assignment in this text gives at least one example of a parenthetical expression set off by commas.

> (8) You owe us the $25, however, and you have not paid .
> (13) . . . you should remember us, too, with a payment?

A special type of parenthetical expression is called appositive and is explained below.

, apposition

Sometimes a writer mentions a certain person or thing and then, in order to make his meaning perfectly clear to the reader, says the same thing in different words. There is at least one example of such a construction in each assignment of this text.

> (11) . . . call our assistant manager, Miss Johnson, at Main 6000.
> (17) Here it is Friday, May 23, and we have not . . .

In many cases these constructions in apposition resemble the constructions in which the commas are used to set off parenthetical expressions. It is really immaterial whether the transcriber thinks he is using the commas to set off an apposition or to set off a parenthetical expression. They are substantially the same thing and the result is identical.

An apposition may occur at the end of a sentence, in which case only one comma is needed.

> (43) . . . send us your check for $18.20 by Friday, January 12.

, series

When three or more similar expressions (words, phrases, or clauses) occur in a series with a conjunction before the last expression, a comma should be placed before the conjunction. Every assignment in this text gives at least one example of the comma in series.

> (10) . . . provide you with the envelopes, letterheads, and cards that . . .
> (18) . . . goods shipped on March 10, April 7, and May 4.
> (119) The Mutual Insurance Company found the plan she wanted, set it up for her, and made her happy.

, introductory
, if clause
, when clause
, as clause

One of the most frequent errors made by the beginning transcriber is the failure to make a complete sentence. In most cases the incomplete sentence is a dependent or subordinate clause introduced by *if, when,* or *as*. The dependent or subordinate clause deceives the transcriber because it seems to be a complete sentence, when actually it is introduced by a word such as *if* or *as* and therefore requires a main (independent) clause to complete the thought. If . . . *what?* When . . . *what?*

The dependent or subordinate clause signals the coming of another clause with a relative pronoun or a subordinate conjunction. The relative pronouns are *that, who, what, which, whoever, whatever, whichever*. The commonest subordinating conjunctions are *if, though, although, whether, unless, as, because, when, since, while, where, after, wherever, until, before, how, however*.

In this text each *if* clause, *when* clause, and *as* clause has been marked as such in the margin because these are by far the three commonest subordinating conjunctions found in business correspondence.

(6) If there is any error, please let us know . . .
(16) . . . when many customers owe us small balances, the total amounts to a surprising sum.
(69) As I am leaving for a two months' vacation abroad, I should like to rent my apartment . . .

The other and less frequent dependent clauses have been grouped under the general marginal reminder ", introductory."

The rule covering the group of introductory dependent clauses is that a comma is used to separate a subordinate clause from a *following* main clause. If the main clause comes first, no comma is required. A comma was placed in the preceding sentence after the subordinate clause (*if the main clause comes first*) because that clause came before the main clause. No comma would be required if the position of the two clauses were reversed so that that sentence would read: *No comma is required if the main clause comes first.*

Thus the comma is required when the subordinate clause introduces the main clause. Similarly a comma is required after other introductory or explanatory expressions, such as *on the contrary, in brief, for instance.*

(140) Supplementing the annual report, I have occasionally written to the members of our company. . .
(109) For your convenience in returning this letter, we are enclosing a prepaid envelope.

The example from letter 109 shows the use of the comma after the introductory or explanatory expression *For your convenience in returning this letter*. The preceding letter contains a similar sentence with the explanatory expression at the end of the sentence in which, therefore, no comma is required.

(108) A self-addressed envelope is enclosed for your convenience in returning the form.

The learner will find it safe to use a comma after any introductory or explanatory expression or after any element of a sentence that is used at the beginning of the sentence out of its natural word order. The writer whose judgment has been formed by constant practice will often prefer to omit the comma after a short introductory expression that seems to flow into the rest of the sentence without a break.

The constant observation of good models is the best and surest way to become proficient in the art of punctuation. In this text the learner will have called to his attention by the marginal reminders 544 examples of the correct punctuation of introductory or explanatory elements at the beginning of the sentence under the four headings discussed in this section. Each assignment gives a number of examples of one or another of the four headings; most assignments give an illustration of each of the four.

, conjunction
; no conjunction

Each assignment in this textbook gives at least one example of the first of these two headings; seventy-four assignments give at least one example of the second. In some assignments there are as many as four or five marginal reminders of one or the other of these headings. Although in some ways this is one of the easiest punctuation problems, and certainly one of the most frequent, few beginning transcribers seem to be able to solve it rapidly and accurately.

The first heading above represents a brief reminder that a comma is used to separate two independent clauses that are joined by one of the conjunctions *and, but, or, for, neither, nor.* If the two independent clauses are not joined by one of those conjunctions, they are separated by a semicolon.

An independent clause (sometimes called a *main* or *principal* clause) is one that has a subject and predicate and could stand alone as a separate sentence.

> (29) We have to meet all our bills, but we cannot do so until we collect what is due from our customers.

The first independent or principal or main clause is

> We have to meet all our bills . . .

because that could stand as a separate sentence. The second independent clause, which could also stand as a separate sentence, is

> . . . we cannot do so until we collect what is due from our customers.

These could be written as two separate sentences with a period after each. Because the thought of the two sentences is closely related, it seemed better to the writer of the letter to put them into one sentence. Because the two independent clauses are connected by the co-ordinating conjunction *but,* a comma is used between them. The writer could have said:

> We have to meet all our bills; we cannot do so until we collect what is due from our customers.

In this case the semicolon would be used to separate the two independent clauses because there is no conjunction.

In the marginal reminders there is no room for all this explanation. Therefore, when you see in the margin

, conjunction

it is a reminder that the comma is used between the two independent clauses because they are separated by one of the co-ordinating conjunctions *and, but, or, for, neither, nor.* When you see in the margin

; no conjunction

it is a reminder that the semicolon is used between the two independent clauses because they are not separated by one of the six conjunctions just listed. In such sentences the transcriber may remember that he should not use a semicolon unless he could just as correctly use a period and divide the one sentence into two.

The source of most of the confusion and difficulty is the use of the semicolon that is explained in the next section.

; because of comma

If the comma were always used between independent clauses connected by a conjunction and if the semicolon were always used between independent clauses not connected by a conjunction, the learner would have little trouble becoming accustomed to the correct punctuation. The one exception referred to by the above heading serves to confuse the learner. The exception is that the semicolon is used instead of the comma if a comma is found within either of the independent clauses joined by a conjunction.

The reason for this change from comma to semicolon seems simple enough. If there are other commas in the sentence, something stronger than a comma is required to separate the two parts of the sentence.

For example, the sentence from letter 29 used a comma to separate the two independent clauses joined by the conjunction *but*:

> (29) **We have to meet all our bills, but we cannot do so until we collect what is due from our customers.**

When the sentence is changed by the addition of one word and a comma, as shown below, the comma after *bills* must be changed to a semicolon.

> **Moreover, we have to meet all our bills; but we cannot do so until we collect what is due from our customers.**

It is clear that the punctuation between the two independent clauses, the two main parts of the sentence, must be of greater strength than the punctuation within the first clause. Therefore, the semicolon is used instead of the comma.

Such a sentence should present no problem to the transcriber because the comma occurs in the first clause. The good transcriber, however, must keep his eyes several words ahead of his fingers, because often the commas will occur in the second clause. Here is the same sentence with a parenthetical phrase added in the second clause, necessitating the change from a comma to a semicolon before the *but*.

> We have to meet all our bills; but we cannot do so, as a practical matter, until we collect what is due from our customers.

The transcriber might put a comma after *bills* unless he had already read far enough to notice the parenthetical expression in the second clause.

Sometimes the marginal reminder

; no conjunction

is used for a sentence in which the semicolon is used primarily because no conjunction joins the two independent clauses but in which it would have been used in any event because of the presence of commas within one or both the independent clauses.

Comparative Review of Uses of Comma and Semicolon

1. Comma between preceding dependent (subordinate) clause and following independent (main) clause:

> If we are to meet our bills, we must collect what is due from our customers.

2. No punctuation at all if the dependent (subordinate) clause comes after the main clause:

We must collect what is due from our customers if we are to meet our bills.

3. Comma between two independent (main) clauses joined by the conjunctions *and, but, or, for, neither, nor:*

(29) We have to meet our bills, but we cannot do so until we collect what is due from our customers.

4. Semicolon between two independent (main) clauses joined by the conjunctions *and, but, for, or, neither, nor* if there is a comma in either clause:

A. Moreover, we have to meet our bills; but we cannot do so until we collect what is due from our customers.
B. We have to meet our bills; but we cannot do so, as a practical matter, until we collect what is due from our customers.
C. Moreover, we have to meet our bills; but we cannot do so, as a practical matter, until we collect what is due from our customers.

5. Semicolon between two independent (main) clauses that are not joined by the conjunctions *and, but, or, for, neither, nor:*

We have to meet our bills; we cannot do so until we collect what is due from our customers.

The Apostrophe

No attempt has been made to explain the reason for each apostrophe noted in the marginal reminders. Each assignment gives at least one word in which the apostrophe is used, usually two or more. The transcriber nearly always knows the reason but simply doesn't remember to use the apostrophe. This book provides the learner with 153 reminders of the correct use of the apostrophe.

Hyphenated before noun
No noun, no hyphen

The presence or absence of the hyphen in expressions like *worth while* and *up to date* causes transcription errors largely because of the infrequency of the problem. The principle is extremely simple. If a noun follows the expression, the hyphens are inserted—no following noun, no hyphen.

The book is up to date. (No noun after the expression.)
The up-to-date book ... (Noun follows the expression.)

Each assignment gives at least one expression hyphenated before a noun; about half the assignments give expressions without the hyphen, using the marginal reminder: *No noun, no hyphen.*

Dates

The learner will not be transcribing, as a rule, when using this text. The emphasis in the marginal reminders, therefore, has been on spelling and punctuation rather than on typing style. Although there are a large number of dates in the letters, only a few of them have been put in the margins as reminders that the correct form is *March 20,* without the *th* after the figure. An occasional reminder in the margin seems sufficient to keep the learner aware of the correct form.

Amounts

The correct form for transcribing even amounts of dollars is *$83* with no decimal point and no ciphers.

(21) ... remittance of $25 or return the merchandise.
(21) ... your overdue account of $25.
(42) The amount, as you know, is $166; and ...

As may be seen in the examples above, sometimes the figures representing the amount will be followed by a period, a semicolon, or another mark of punctuation required by the context of the sentence.

Some of the amounts are noted in the margin as reminders; many of them are not, as their mere presence in the letter serves as a reminder.

. courteous request

The marginal reminder shown above appears forty-eight times in the book. This usage is seldom found except in business correspondence. The businessman is always trying to persuade the customer or prospective customer to take some action desired by the businessman. The customer might take offense if the businessman were to say directly, *I want to hear from you by return mail.* Therefore, the businessman says

(5) May we hear from you by return mail.

Attention is called to these in the margin to give the learner many reminders of the difference between a question and a courteous request. The question must be followed by a question mark, the courteous request by a period.

The learner may remember that the courteous request always calls for an answer in the form of an action; the question calls for an answer in the form of words.

The businessman who said *May we hear from you by return mail* did not expect the answer to be *yes.* He expected the answer to be a letter by return mail.

(16) The small things are the ones that we overlook, aren't they?

The question mark is used in the above sentence because the only possible answer would be the word *yes.*

Street address

The correct form for the street address in the transcript is

(11) . . . 138 East 38 Street, . . .

The use of the *th* after the street number wastes the time of the transcriber and the post office employee who must read the address.

Spelling and capitalization

Words that present any difficulty in spelling or capitalization are correctly printed in the margin. Certain of them occur many times in the course of the text. This constant repetition in the natural context is more successful in teaching material of this sort than the most intensive study of any one form at a time.

Self-addressed is given repeatedly. It is unusually common in business correspondence because of the custom of sending self-addressed envelopes to facilitate a reply. Like all *self-* compounds, it is written with a hyphen.

Per cent is given repeatedly. It is written in two words, without capitals, with the amount given in figures. The correct form is

. . . and 20 per cent of the . . .

Brief Forms

A B C D E F

1.
2.
3.
4.
5.
6.
7.
8.
9.
10.
11.
12.
13.
14.
15.
16.
17.

A
B
C
D
E
F
18.
19.
20.
21.
22.
23.
24.
25.
26.
27.
28.
29.
30.
31.

Recall Chart

This word list contains an example of every shorthand character, every abbreviating and phrasing device, and every principle of joining.

A B C D E F

1. 2. 3. 4. 5. 6. 7. 8. 9. 10. 11. 12. 13. 14. 15. 16.

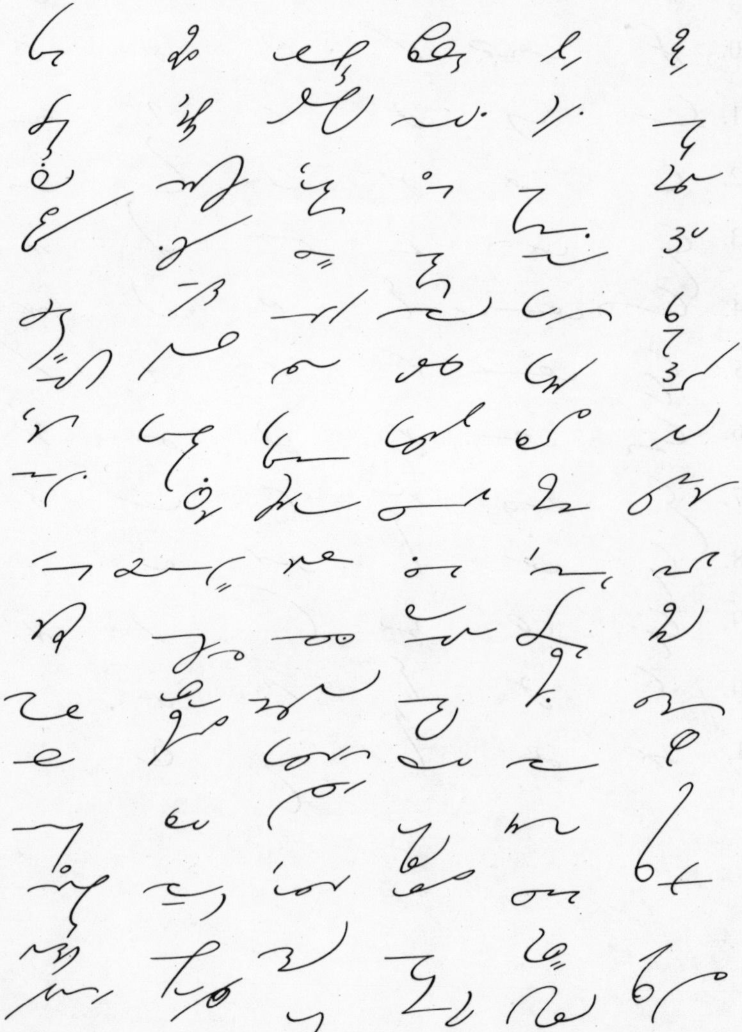